Chemical and Biological Controls in Forestry

ACS SYMPOSIUM SERIES **238**

Chemical and Biological Controls in Forestry

Willa Y. Garner, EDITOR
Environmental Protection Agency

John Harvey, Jr., EDITOR
E. I. du Pont de Nemours & Co.

Based on a symposium sponsored by
the Division of Pesticide Chemistry
at the 185th Meeting
of the American Chemical Society,
Seattle, Washington,
March 20–25, 1983

American Chemical Society, Washington, D.C. 1984

Library of Congress Cataloging in Publication Data
Chemical and biological controls in forestry.

(ACS symposium series, ISSN 0097-6156; 238)

Includes bibliographies and index.

1. Forest insects—Control—Congresses. 2. Forest
insects—Biological control—Congresses. 3. Forest
protection—Congresses. 4. Pesticides—Congresses.
5. Pesticides—Environmental aspects—Congresses.
6. Pesticides—Toxicology—Congresses.
  I. Garner, Willa Y., 1936-   . II. Harvey, John,
1925-   . III. American Chemical Society. Division of
Pesticide Chemistry. IV. Series.

SB761.C43   1983   634.9′69   83-22440
ISBN 0-8412-0818-2

ACS Symposium Series

M. Joan Comstock, *Series Editor*

Advisory Board

FOREWORD

The ACS Symposium Series was founded in 1974 to provide a medium for publishing symposia quickly in book form. The format of the Series parallels that of the continuing Advances in Chemistry Series except that in order to save time the papers are not typeset but are reproduced as they are submitted by the authors in camera-ready form. Papers are reviewed under the supervision of the Editors with the assistance of the Series Advisory Board and are selected to maintain the integrity of the symposia; however, verbatim reproductions of previously published papers are not accepted. Both reviews and reports of research are acceptable since symposia may embrace both types of presentation.

CONTENTS

vii

PREFACE

O̶UR FORESTS ARE LIMITED RESOURCES, valuable for recreation, soil and water management, and timber. Thus, control of various forest pests is receiving increased attention.

The chapters in this volume examine the state of the art of the development of effective chemical and biological agents, as well as the unique application problems not encountered in conventional agricultural situations. The effectiveness of pesticides or pheromone technology in combating forest pests is not the only determinant. Factors peculiar to the forest situation, including the delicate balance of the ecosystem, must be considered in both the development and application stages of all control tactics.

We have attempted to highlight the major components involved in forestry pest management: Control Agents; Spray Deposition; Target and Nontarget Residue Distribution; and Ecotoxicology and Hazard Assessment. We believe we have covered most aspects.

We wish to thank all the authors for their participation in the symposium and their contributions to this volume. Our special thanks go to Illo Gauditz for her never-failing interest, advice, and cooperation in putting the symposium together.

WILLA Y. GARNER
Hazard Evaluation Division
Office of Pesticide Programs
Environmental Protection Agency
Washington, DC 20460

JOHN HARVEY, JR.
Experimental Station
E. I. du Pont de Nemours & Co.
Wilmington, DE 19898

August 1983

Chemical and Biological Agents in Forest Pest Management

Historical Overview

VIRGIL H. FREED

Department of Chemistry, Oregon State University, Corvallis, OR 97331

To early settlers, the North American forests appeared limitless. They were often considered a barrier to travel, commerce and agriculture. As a result, the forests were cut and burned with little thought to conservation and reforestation.

Within the past half century, and more so in the last two decades, we have realized that our forests are limited resources. Their value not only for timber, but for recreation and soil and water management has been recognized. With this came the realization of the need to manage the resource for the benefit of man and the environment.

Various pests – insects, diseases, undesirable plant species – have long been recognized as threats to the standing timber and a barrier to reforestation. Many management techniques have been tried to abate these pests, but among the most effective have been found to be the chemical and biological agents.

Interest in use of chemicals in forestry started many years ago by perceptive foresters. But early chemicals were limited in number and effectiveness. Now an array of chemicals is available for pest management.

The use of chemical and biological agents in forestry, while important, is not so extensive as in agriculture. Treatment is usually required only once or twice in growth cycle and that on scattered parcels of land.

The utilization of forests by the public for recreation and as watersheds has lead to questioning the use of chemicals. Some groups vigorously protest the practice despite assurances of need and relative safety. On the resolution of this and certain other forest management issues hangs the future of our forests.

0097-6156/84/0238-0001$06.00/0
© 1984 American Chemical Society

To the early immigrants to the North American continent, the
hundreds of millions of acres of forest must have appeared almost
endless. In their eyes, it could have appeared as a limitless
resource extending into perpetuity. For their numbers this may
indeed have been the case, but little could they have reckoned
with the population growth, and with it the demand for forest
products some 300 years later.

While the forest was a supply of timber for homes, fuel, and
often times, food, they were also sometimes regarded as a barrier.
The labor to cut and burn the forest, to eke out crop land and
impediments to vehicular travel, were not regarded as a benefit.
Thus, for years the migrants cut and burned their way until they
crossed the Appalachians and began the process again at the
Rockies after having crossed the Great Plains.

In later years as demand for timber products boomed with the
population, the economic value of the virgin stands of deciduous
and coniferous forests became the foundation of substantial
fortunes. Commercial lumbering moved westward with the population
until reaching the Pacific Coast with its tremendous stands of
Douglas Fir, Redwood, and Pine.

In some regions of the country, notably the Northwest and now
in the Southeast, lumbering is a major factor in the economy. The
Northwest is a classic illustration of the economic importance of
lumbering. The decline in demand for timber products, due to the
economy, resulted in a loss of thousands of jobs in the Pacific
Northwest. The fifteen to twenty billion dollar a year industry
has been almost at a standstill.

Until into this century, little thought was given to the need
for conservation of the timber resource, or reforestation. The
large tracts of virgin timber invited exploitation, and when
depleted, the lumbering moved on. A few with sufficient foresight
began to appreciate the need for conservation and management of
this resource. The practice began early in Federal forests and
soon was picked up by the more progressive, large lumbering
interests.

Following World War II, greater attention was given to
management of the lumber resources. Large firms began holding
tracts of land for reforestation and talked of sustained yield.
In passing, I'd like to mention a former staff member of Oregon
State University who was one of the pioneers in conservation and
reforestation. He contributed much to the science of forestry
and demonstrated that with the Douglas Fir a 50 year growth cycle
was quite adequate.

Management of our forests is now well appreciated by almost
everyone. The need to maintain growing stands of timber for
water management, erosion control, timber yield, recreation, as
well as for timber products and grazing, is well recognized.

Some still debate the multiuse concept of forests, but most
acknowledge it as a viable management practice.

Pests of the Forest

To the casual observer, it would mostly appear that our forests
grow with little attention and have few problems. This is not
exactly the case. Very few plants are without their biological
competitors, and our forests are no exception (10). A long list
of insect pests that attack both coniferous and deciduous trees,
are known. Some are introduced from other areas of the world,
and some are indigenous to the North American continent. Among
the more familiar of the insect pests include the tussock moth,
spruce budworm, the looper, bark beetle, the pine sawfly, woolly
balsam aphid, shoot moth, gypsy moth, and many others. Some
attack the young trees resulting in death or at the very least,
much reduced growth; in the older stands, the insects causing
defoliation or attacking the cambium, may kill or seriously
weaken the stand with significant losses of timber yield (10,11).
Many of the insects have a cyclical population pattern.
That is, in a given year under certain circumstances, the population will explode causing extensive damage followed by a
collapse of the population. Those opposed to the use of control
agents in the forest argue that the best management is simply to
wait for the population collapse. However, in the meantime,
thousands of acres may be damaged or killed, and the dead or
dying trees become a distinct forest fire hazard.
Insects are not the only problem pests in forest management.
Other plants, i.e., grass, shrubs, trees, afford a serious
problem in reforestation and in young stands (11). Indeed, as
young stands develop, even their own kind may serve as a compet-
itor and require thinning to develop a commercial forest.
After a fire or logging, a variety of plants will spring up
in the open area. Grasses and certain herbaceous plants may
first occupy a large portion of the bare area. These compete
with any young seedlings for moisture, nutrients, and often will
choke out the seedling in the first year or two. Also invading
the area will be the shrubs and certain competitive trees. In
the Pacific Northwest, plants such as salmonberry, ceanothus,
manzanita, blackberry, and occasionally, leguminous shrubs will
completely inhabit the land. This makes reforestation extremely
difficult, if not impossible, without effective control measures.
Later, stands of alder or other tree species, competitive with
the conifer, will overgrow the area causing damage and delayed
growth to the conifer.
Insects and competitive plants are not the only problems
facing the tree, particularly the young one. Vertebrates,
ranging from small rodents through the deer and other unglates,
do their share of damage. While the damage to larger trees is
insignificant, the browsing on young seedlings is much more
serious. Domestic livestock also may be troublesome.

Adding to the forest pest complex are a variety of diseases. This can include parasitic plants such as mistletoe, fungal diseases, and a variety of bacterial diseases (10).

Taken in total, the pest complex has been estimated to cause annual losses equivalent to 12 to 18 percent of the total annual cut. This runs into 15 or so billion board feet per year. The losses are significant enough to have interested forest managers in the use of pest management methods to abate the problems. To be sure, the problems are generally localized and the management practices for pest control are applied on a quite limited area. Pest management practices in forestry involve only a small percentage of the standing timber, in contrast to agriculture where a much larger percentage of the cropland is treated annually (10).

Chemical and Biological Agents of the Past

The idea of use of chemical and biological agents in forest management, is not new. As long ago as 1918, a water soluble mixture was used to ring girdles of trees of many species in India. The material, a proprietary wood preservative that has claimed to within a few weeks kill the roots as well as the aerial portions of the trees. The arboricidal properties of arsenicals were described in 1920. These arsenicals, usually based on trivalent arsenic, were used for girdling trees to kill them, and treatment of stumps to prevent regrowth.

Other chemicals tried in the two decades between 1920 and 1940 include sodium or calcium chlorate, mineral oils, rock salt, copper sulfate, creosote, and ammonium thiocyanate. These latter compounds while tried never showed enough promise to be widely used (1,2).

In the early 1940's, a new inorganic chemical, not having the toxicity of some of the others, was introduced. The compound, ammonium sulfamate, proved quite effective as an arboricide, applied either in frills or sprayed on the entire plant (3,4). During this era also, various borates were used to maintain firebreaks in forests through control of both herbaceous and shrubby plants (5).

The introduction of the phenoxy compounds - 2,4-D and 2,4,5-T - in the mid 40's, provided much more effective arboricides than had heretofore been available (2,6,8). Control of many brushy species for site preparation in reforestation was now available. Perhaps one of the early applications of this was made by Fred Furst in the Siuslaw National Forest where approximately 10,000 acres of conifer, overstoried by alder, were released by treatment with 2,4-D. Other chemicals used in this era included trichloroacetic acid (TCA), used in girdling treatment of trees, and for control of grass prior to reforestation. Aminotriazole, also introduced during this period, found some use for control of Rhus species and grass in forest nurseries.

However, the phenoxy acetic acids, 2,4-D and 2,4,5-T, were by far the most widely used, being employed for stand thinning, control of brushy species in reforestation, and control of brush and trees in rights of way (11).

The insecticides used in the early part of this century did not lend themselves well for control of insects in the forest. The heavy rates of application of such materials as lead or calcium arsenate, was ill suited to the type of application equipment then available. It must be remembered that aerial application of chemicals in forestry came with the improved planes after World War II. Rotenone and pyrethrum, two insecticides used in agriculture in that era, had but limited applicability in forestry because of their properties (10).

DDT, discovered by Dr. Mueller in Switzerland, and used for insect vector control during World War II, quickly found a place in forestry, as well as agriculture. The material proved highly effective in the control of such insects as the spruce budworm, tussock moth, hemlock looper, and many others. It was widely used in the Northeast for control of the introduced Gypsy moth during these early years. The low toxicity of DDT to mammals made it to appear to be an excellent insecticide for forestry use. It was only after subsequent studies revealed the impact on other species that reservations about its use was raised.

Though parasitic plants such as mistletoe, fungal disease, and bacterial diseases were indigenous to the forest, then as they are now, control in the standing timber was largely achieved by management practices. However, after cutting, chemical treatment, such as with pentachlorophenol, would be employed.

Chemical and Biological Agents - Present

Through the years since 1945, more and more biologically active chemicals have been developed, first for agriculture and subsequently many adopted in forestry. By now, some 25 to 30 different chemicals are used as herbicides in forestry (11). They are employed for weed and grass control in the forest nurseries, preparing sites for reforestation, control of invading species in young stands, and for thinning and control of weeds and trees (9) in the more mature stands. Equally, a number of new agents have been introduced for insect control. Following the chlorinated hydrocarbons came various organophosphate esters, among them such things as malathion, fenthion, and fenitrothion, carbamate insecticides such as the nmethyl naphthyol carbamate, and synthetic pyrethroids.

The herbicides commonly used as arboricides include members of the triazines, ureas, and uracils, for grass and weed control in nursery and Christmas tree plantings. Other compounds include phosphonate and phosphate derivatives, pyridine-based organic acids of high activity, and organic arsenicals. Such a wide array of active compounds allows selection of an agent to control most of the troublesome plant and woody species.

The choice of an insecticide is somewhat narrower because of the criteria that must be met in forest use. Nonetheless, a number of the organophosphate and carbamate insecticides have been found to meet the necessary standards. For example, the insecticide carbaryl has been employed for control of gypsy moth and some of the related lepidopterous insects of the forest.

Biological agents such as Bacillus thuringensis, BT, has been coming to the fore as a forest insecticide, as more has been learned about its use. Attention is now being given also to the viruses such as the polyhedrosis virus of the tussock moth.

The synthetic pyrothroids, as would be expected, engaged the interest of those concerned with control of forest insects. These highly active compounds, whose chemistry is based on a natural product, may offer considerable potential. In their early use, or even yet in the developmental stage, are such things as the pheremones, juvenile hormone, and exoskeleton inhibitors, as potential agents in forest pest management (12).

Chemical and Biological Agents - Future

It would appear that we are coming on a time where much more effective and safer chemical and biological agents for forest pest management will be developed. But even beyond these new agents that will be coming on is a keener insight and more clever ways in which to use these agents to the benefit of forest management.

As to agents for control of plants and undesirable trees, it would appear that in the foreseeable future we will rely on synthetic chemicals. There are, under development and in use, some chemicals that are applied at ounces rather than pounds per acre for control of particularly, grasses. I think we can expect to see as a following development, equally active compounds developed for control of the broad leaf and woody species. In the more distant future, we may be able to find ways of using allelopathy for managment of undesirable species, but much is to be learned about this yet. In terms of biological agents, we can only hope that some of the experiments now going on investigating specific fungi for control of certain species.

It is the field of forest insect control that the most exciting developments now appear. The new techniques of using pheremones and pheremones combined with selective insecticide treatment is a significant advance. One looks also for great advances in the use of agents such as BT, and viruses for insect control. These agents, modified by genetic engineering, are likely to be far more potent and selective than those materials currently available. It would seem reasonable also, to see the number of different biological agents available increased in the near future.

In the space of 40 years, tremendous advances have been made, not only in forest pest management, but in the way we view and manage this valuable resource. It would seem unquestionable that the chemical and biological agents will play an ever increasing role to maintain our forests for all their varied purposes. The papers that we will hear in this symposium can only confirm the great advances that have been made in the use of these agents, and indicate the even greater advances that can reasonably be expected in the future.

Acknowledgments

This manuscript was issued as technical paper no. 6905 from the Oregon Agricultural Experiment Station.

Literature Cited

1. Cope, J. A.; Spaeth, J. N. J. For. 1931, 29, 775.
2. Fryer, J. D., J. Sci. 1955, 6, 73.
3. Afanasieu, M., Oklahoma Agricultural Experiment Station, Misc. Pub., NP-8.
4. Ahlgren, J. H.; Klingman, G. C.; Wolf, D. E. "Principles of Weed Control"; John Wiley and Sons: New York, 1951.
5. Robbins, W. W.; Crafts, A. S.; Raynor, R. N. "Weed Control"; McGraw Hill: New York, 1952.
6. "Research Paper Number 13," Dahms, W. G.; James, G. A., The U.S. Department of Agriculture Forest Service, Pacific N.W. Forest and Range Experiment Station, 1955.
7. "Effects of Certain Common Brush Control Techniques and Materials on Game Foods and Cover on a Power Line Right of Way," Bramble, W. C.; Byrnes, W. R., Pennsylvania State University Agricultural Experiment Station, 1955.
8. Chemical and Brush Control Techniques in California Rangelands," Leonard, O. A.; Carlson, C. E., 1955.
9. Peevy, F. A.; Campbell, R. S. J. For. 1949, 47, 443.
10. "Pest Control: An Assessment of Present and Alternative Technologies, Forest Pest Control," 4, National Academy of Science, 1975.
11. Newton, M.; Knight, F. B. "Handbook of Weed and Insect Control Chemicals for Forest Resource Managers"; Timber Press: Beaverton, Oregon.
12. "_____ The Future of Insecticides: Needs and Prospects"; Metcalf, R. L.; McKelvey, J. J., Jr., Ed.; John Wiley and Sons: New York.

RECEIVED October 3, 1983

CONTROL AGENTS

Use of Herbicides
for Industrial Forest Vegetation Management
in the Southern United States

LARRY R. NELSON, DEAN H. GJERSTAD, and PATRICK J. MINOGUE

Department of Forestry, Auburn University Agricultural Experiment Station, Auburn, AL 36849

Projections by the U.S.D.A. Forest Service indicate that the Southeastern United States is likely to lead the nation in wood production by the beginning of the next century. The forestry capacity of the South in terms of productive forest acreage is greater than other forested regions such as the Pacific Coast, the Rocky Mountains and the Northeast. Of the 482 million acres of commercial forests in the country, only thirty percent is capable of producing greater than 85 cubic ft. of wood per acre per year. Sixty million acres, or 41 percent of this land occurs in the South while 38, 25, and 13 percent occur in the North, Pacific Coast and Rocky Mountain regions respectively. Approximately half of the remaining acres capable of producing 50 to 85 cubic ft. per acre per year also occurs in the South (Anonymous 1982).

In 1976 the Pacific Coast supplied 50 percent of the nations softwood products while the South provided 36 percent. These figures are expected to reverse by 2030 after old growth timber on the Pacific coast has been cut (Anonymous 1982). However, the total forestry land base over this period is expected to remain fairly constant. A major increase in forest management activity will be necessary if the South is to increase production to the predicted levels.

Greater exploitation of privately owned forest lands (70% of the total in the South) and more intensive forest management on all sectors of forest ownership offer possibilities for increasing the wood supply. Significant increases in production from the private sector can be induced over time through incentives programs or from increased stumpage prices. Meanwhile, current attempts at increasing production per acre are being conducted by forest industry. Genetic improvement, fertilization, and tree spacing control are being utilized to increase the growth of southern pines. Another area receiving a

0097–6156/84/0238–0011$06.00/0

great deal of recent interest is that of controlling competition from non crop vegetation. Competition from herbaceous weeds and low quality hardwoods is one of the major factors reducing productivity of pine forests in the South. (Fitzgerald et al. 1973, Kozlowski 1969, and Schneider and Stranskey 1966).

The southern pine species, loblolly (Pinus taeda L.), shortleaf (Pinus echinata Mill.), slash (Pinus elliottii Engelm), and longleaf (Pinus palustris Mill.) comprise the greatest economic component of the southern forests. Because pines grow more rapidly than hardwoods, are currently easier to regenerate, and have superior wood properties for a variety of uses, they are the desired commercial species. But, these species are a subclimax component of the forest. Without interference by man or fire, the majority of pine forests in the the South would eventually revert to oak-hickory or southern mixed hardwoods in the various regions (Monk 1965, Hebb and Clewell 1976, and Kuchler 1964). In order to grow pine in successive rotations on a given acreage, foresters implement cultural techniques that favor pine over low quality hardwoods and other non-pine vegetation, i.e. plant succession is delayed.

Such techniques are generally categorized under the term forest vegetation management and involve the use of machinery, fire, and or chemicals during silvicultural practices such as site preparation, weed control for plantation establishment, pine release from overtopping brush, timber stand improvement, etc.

Recently, the use of chemical herbicides in forest vegetation management has gained interest over the use of fire or machinery alone. A southwide effort by industry is in progress through the Auburn University Silvicultural Herbicide Cooperative to investigate the benefits of herbicide usage and to develop and register effective herbicides for various purposes. The following is a description of the use of herbicides by the southern forest industry. Reasons for using herbicides information on benefits, and the available chemistry are categorized by silvicultural practice.

Site Preparation

Until 1979, the primary herbicide used by foresters for brush control in the South was 2,4,5-T. This chemical could be applied inexpensively ($15 -30/acre) at rates of 4 to 6 pounds per acre for site preparation. Most applications were conducted with aircraft. Surveys (1977) of herbicide usage on industrial forest lands in the South showed that of the 1,175,350 acres site prepared for planting, 118,100 acres (10%) were treated with 2,4,5-T, 48,700 (4%) were treated with other herbicides, and 909,000 acres (77%) were treated mechanically (anonymous 1978). Obviously, the majority of the forest acreage was site prepared with machinery. Nevertheless herbicides filled an important capacity. Chemicals were generally used on marginally productive sites because of costs relative to mechanical methods and on lands with steep slopes on which machinery could not operate efficiently.

In 1979 an injunction against the use of 2,4,5-T on forest lands, rights-of-ways, and pasturelands was imposed by the Environmental Protection Agency. The use of herbicides declined sharply from the previous period of 2,4,5-T availability. Alternative chemicals were generally more expensive than 2,4,5-T, foresters were not familiar with them, and pressures from environmental groups favored a move away from the use of herbicides.

After four years without 2,4,5-T foresters are expressing increased interest in the use of herbicides for forest site preparation. Reasons include higher costs of mechanical methods and the fact that recently used herbicide treatments have been very effective.

Mechanical site preparation methods are used to: (1) control brush, (2) remove slash and debris, (3) enhance aesthetics, and (4) occasionally rehabilitate damaged soils. Methods include shearing cull hardwoods and brush with a "KG" or "V" blade mounted on a bulldozer, chopping with large drum choppers mounted behind a bulldozer, and crushing trees and brush with 40-60 ton devices such as the LeTourneau brush crusher. These and other mechanical methods are all highly energy consumptive and require large investments in mechanical equipment. Costs for mechanical site preparation range from $50 to more than $150 per acre. Examples are shown in Table I.

Table I. Approximate costs of four mechanical site preparation methods commonly used by forest industry in the South.

Method of Site Preparation	Cost per Acre ($)
Single pass drum chopper	50 - 70
Double pass drum chopper	90 - 120
Shear and pile	90 - 140
Root rake	100 - 150

Herbicide usage in conjunction with burning offers a viable alternative to machinery on many sites. Products registered for site preparation are listed in Table II. A variety of products are registered although several contain the same active ingredient under a different trade name. Four of the five ingredients, triclopyr, hexazinone, fosamine, and glyphosate are relatively new having been registered for only three to four years.

Table II. Herbicides registered for forest site preparation
in the Southeastern United States.

Herbicide		
Common Name	Trade Name	Manufacturer
Picloram + 2,4-D	Tordon 101	Dow Chemical USA
Picloram	Tordon 10K	Dow Chemical USA
Triclopyr (amine)	Garlon 3A	Dow Chemical USA
Triclopyr (ester)	Garlon 4	Dow Chemical USA
2,4-D	Esteron 99	Dow Chemical USA
2,4-D	Verton 2D	Dow Chemical USA
2,4-D + Dicamba	Banvel 520	Velsicol Chemical Corp.
2,4-D + Dicamba	Banvel 720	Velsicol Chemical Corp.
Dicamba	Banvel 4WS	Velsicol Chemical Corp.
2,4-D + 2,4-DP	Weedone 170	Union Carbide
2,4-DP	Weedone 2,4-DP	Union Carbide
MSMA	Transvert	Union Carbide
Hexazinone	Velpar Gridball	E.I. DuPont de Nemours & Co.
Fosamine	Krenite	E.I. DuPont de Nemours & Co.
Glyphosate	Roundup	Monsanto Ag. Products Co.
2,4-D + Dicamba	Trimec 450-E	PBI Gordon

Some of the more commonly used treatments approach the
lower range of costs ($50-$100) expected for mechanical site
preparation methods (Table III). Approximately $10 - $15 should
be added to the table values for application costs (generally for
contract aerial applications).

Table III. Approximate Costs of Some Herbicides in Treatments
Commonly Used in the Southeastern United States.

Herbicides	Rate (Gal/Ac) or (lb/Ac)	Cost ($)
Tordon 101 + 2,4-DP	2 + 1	64
Tordon 101 + Garlon 4	2 + 1/2	77
Garlon 4	1	64
Velpar Gridball	40	154

One recent study indicates that herbicides can reduce
resprouting of hardwood species more effectively than drum
chopping brush (Table IV). Most southern hardwoods are capable

of resprouting from stumps and root systems after stem portions are mechanically removed (Grano 1961 and Johnson 1961). The underground portions can be killed by applications of translocatable herbicides. Future brush competition with newly planted pines can thus be reduced.

Table IV.   Numbers of stems per acre of major hardwood species that occurred prior to the application of various site preparation treatments and approximately one year after treatment.[1] The site including all test plots was control burned a few months after treatment.

Treatment Herbicide (Common name)	Rate (gal/ ac)	1st yr (initial)	2nd year	% reduction
Hexazinone	3	2275	225	89
Triclopyr	1	2112	255	88
Hexazinone + triclopyr	2 +1/2	3002	563	81
(Drum chopped)	---	1967	1493	24

[1] Major species include: white oak, black tupelo, sweetgum, red oaks, hickories, Prunus spp., dogwood, red maple, Ulmus spp.

A long term comparison of the relative benefits of chemical versus mechanical site preparation will require growth and yield research. Numerous studies are presently being initiated. However, these will not be completed for many years. Scientists at Auburn University are attempting to provide interim results by measuring older studies and comparisons. Meanwhile, foresters are likely to continue use of herbicides on steep slopes or sites with fragile and erodable soils on which machinery cannot be operated or would likely cause visible and long term damage.

Release

"Release" is conducted in young pine plantations on which brush has established a competitive growth advantage over pines. Hardwood sprouts from stumps and roots are capable of early rapid growth and occupation of a site. This was evidenced in Arkansas, where sprouts covered 58 and 92 percent of the site surface area three and six years, respectively, after complete top removal of the previous stand (Grano 1961). Similarly, in Mississippi, 7,500 stems per acre of ash (Fraxinus sp.) and bitter pecan [Carya aquatica (Michx. f) Nutt.] up to 15 feet in height dominated a site five years after bulldozing (Johnson 1961).

Pines generally do not demonstrate such rapid early growth, particularly when in competition with other vegetation. Dominant loblolly pines under old field conditions range from 8 to 12 feet in height after five years on site index$_{25}$ 40 to 60 lands. However, if suppressed, pines will respond to brush control at an early age (Malac 1961, Martin 1973).

Brush control in established pine stands is nearly always conducted with herbicides. As in site preparation, 2,4,5-T was the primary herbicide used until the injunction against its use in 1979. It was the only herbicide that controlled a variety of brush species without badly damaging pine when broadcast sprayed over plantations. Research has been conducted to establish other effective herbicides for this use.

Recently, three other herbicides have been registered for pine release (Table V). These products have been shown effective under certain conditions.

Registered formulations of hexazinone are soil active products. Selective brush control around pines occurs when lethal amounts of chemical is absorbed by brush species but not the pines. Pines are generally more resistant to the active ingredient than hardwoods. Thus a threshold level of chemical can be applied without damaging pines. However, selective rates of this herbicide vary by soil type and the applicator must carefully prescribe rates accordingly.

Table V. Herbicides registered for releasing pines from brush in the Southeastern United States.

Herbicide		
Common Name	Trade Name	Manufacturer
Hexazinone	Velpar Brush Killer (1/2cc)	E.I. DuPont de Nemours & Co.
Hexazinone	Velpar Gridball (2cc)	E.I. DuPont de Nemours & Co.
Glyphosate	Roundup	Monsanto Ag. Products Co.
2,4-DP	Weedone 2,4-DP	Union Carbide

[1]The 2,4-DP product is registered under state labels in AR, AL, MS, LA, GA, NC, and TN.

Glyphosate is used primarily in late summer to early fall applications. In certain regions of the South, i.e. Virginia, North Carolina, and Tennessee, the product has provided good, selective control of brush in loblolly pine plantations. Growth activity of pines in these areas declines during the summer to early fall resulting in resistance to glyphosate at 1 1/2 to 2 quarts of product per acre. At the same time, hardwood brush species are more susceptible to late versus early growing season applications. Selective brush control has not been demonstrated as widely in the deep South.

The 2,4-DP product is recommended for use in broadcast applications to be sprayed after pines have completed the first growth flush of the season. It is quite effective on oak species. At present another method of application involves directed sprays with knapsack sprayers.

All three of the above herbicides can cause pine damage if not applied under the conditions specified on the product label. Research is underway to improve release treatments with these herbicides, and to examine other products with potential for this use.

Tree Injection

Single tree injection is used to remove cull hardwoods from sites during site preparation, pine release, or for timber stand improvement. Tree injection is efficient on sites with a sparse distribution (100 stems per acre, or less) of hardwoods greater than 1 inch dbh. The method is useful for control of species resistant to foliar treatments or stems missed during foliar application.

Treatments consist of injecting herbicide through the bark and into the vascular system of target trees. The most commonly used herbicides are 2,4-D, and Tordon 101 (2,4-D + picloram). The total list of registered products is shown in Table VI.

Table VI.   Herbicides registered for tree injection in the Southeast.

Common Name	Trade Name	Manufacturer
2,4-D	DMA-4	Dow Chemical USA
2,4-D	Formula 40	Dow Chemical USA
2,4-D	Weed Rap	Vertac
2,4-D	2,4-D	Rhodia
2,4-D	Weedone 64	Union Carbide
Triclopyr	Garlon 3A	Dow Chemical USA
Picloram + 2,4-D	Tordon 101R	Dow Chemical USA
Hexazinone	Velpar L	E.I. DuPont de Nemours & Co.
Dicamba	Banvel	Velsicol
Dicamba	Banvel CST	Velsicol
Glyphosate	Roundup	Monsanto

Two types of injection devices are available. Long tubular models are used to place chemicals into the base of trees and the ax-like Hypo-hatchet for injection higher on the stem. Both tools are effective (Holt 1975).
Injection treatments are effective year-round. Various studies show that greater than 90 percent control of most species is possible (Table VII).

Table VII. Percent kill of hardwood species after hypo-hatchet injection with 2,4-D and Tordon 101[a]

	Herbicides		
Species	2,4-D	Tordon 101	References
Hickory	95	95	McNab and Moyer, 1969; Moyer 1967; Starr 1972; Sterrett 1969a; Sterrett 1969b.
Southern red oak	96	100	McNab and Moyer 1969; Moyer 1967; Peevy 1968b; Starr 1972.
White oak	89	100	Starr 1973; Sterrett 1969b.
Post oak	98	97	Starr 1972.
Elm	91	100	Peevy 1968a.
Sweetgum	100	100	McNab and Moyer 1969; Peevy 1968b.
Dogwood	79	83	McNab and Moyer 1969; Moyer 1967.
Red Maple	21	100-S[b]	Carvell 1968; Peevy 1972; Sterrett 1969a; Sterrett 1969b.

[a]Data and references from Holt 1975.
[b]Sprouting.

Control of Herbaceous Weeds

Under intense management systems foresters have become interested in controlling of herbaceous weeds around newly planted seedlings. Weed competition can be severe on good sites following mechanical site preparation. Grasses and forbs become abundantly established within months after soil disturbance. Recent studies show that control aids survival and growth of the pines (Fitzgerald 1976, Holt et al 1973, Holt et al 1975, Nelson et al 1981, Knowe 1982). Impressive pine growth response to weed control is shown in Table VIII. Trees receiving two years of weed control were twice as tall and had twice the ground line diameter as in nonweeded check plots after three growing seasons. Tree volumes had increased eight-fold over the check trees. The question of whether the above growth differences will remain throughout the rotation of the stand cannot be answered at this

point in time. However, after four growing seasons, differences
in height and diameter between the weeded and nonweeded trees in
the above study are still diverging (unpublished data).

Table VIII. Mean height, groundline diameter (GLD), and volume
             of loblolly pine trees at the end of three growing
             season following various levels of weed control.
             Treatments were initiated during the spring of
             the first growing season. Weeds were controlled
             on a broadcast basis (Total) and in a 5 ft.
             band over the row (band) for the first and
             second year.[1,2]

Level of Weed Control	Height (feet)	GLD (inches)	Volume (cubic inches)
Total - 2 years	7.61 a	2.64 a	185 a
Band - 2 years	6.26 b	2.09 b	108 b
Total - 1 year	5.30 c	1.65 c	67 c
Band - 1 year	5.35 c	1.61 c	62 c
Check	3.64 d	1.02 d	21 d

[1]The table is from Knowe, 1982.
[2]Means followed by the same letter are not significantly
different at the 5 percent level of Duncan's New Multiple Range
Test.

     The biological basis for the above growth response is not
completely resolved although relief from competition for
moisture, nutrients, and light is a likely factor. The effects
of weed competition on the moisture status of young pine is
indicated in figure 1 (Nelson et al. 1981).
     Pre-dawn water potential readings were conducted with a
pressure bomb on young seedlings growing under a stand of pure
ragweed and on weeded plots. Seedling moisture stress reached
approximately 15 and 4 bars on unweeded and weeded plots
respectively ten days after rainfall.
     Future biological research should provide more information
regarding effects of stress from competition on the establishment
and early growth of young pines.
     Herbicide treatments provide the only practical means of
controlling weeds in pine plantations. Applications can be made
with aircraft or with ground equipment such as that used in
agricultural row cropping systems. Registered herbicides are
shown in Table IX. Treatments of simazine and atrazine are
effective only when applied preemergence to weeds. Hexazinone
has both pre- and postemergence activity but can damage pines if
application rates are not carefully prescribed. The three

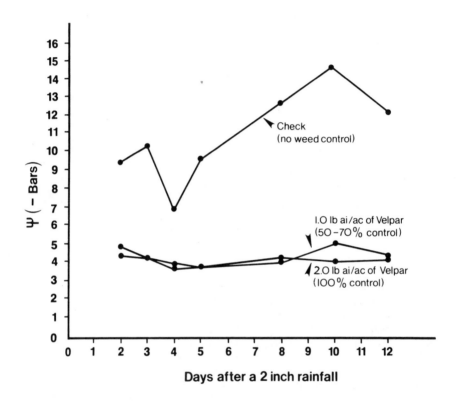

Figure 1. Effects of weed competition on the moisture status (●) of young pine.

registered herbicides generally control a variety of annual grasses and forbs although resistant weeds occur on many sites.

Table IX. Herbicides registered for controlling herbaceous weeds in young pine plantations in the southeastern United States.

Herbicide		
Common Name	Trade Name	Manufacturer
Simazine	Princep	Ciba-Geigy Corporation
Atrazine	Aatrex	Ciba-Geigy Corporation
Hexazinone	Velpar L	E.I. DuPont de Nemours & Co.

The concept of controlling herbaceous weeds in pine plantations is relatively new. In most cases it is not necessary in order to establish a pine stand although early growth studies recently indicate that weed control can be very beneficial. As a result, herbicide technology for this purpose is just beginning to develop. More effective herbicides and application methods are currently being assessed through various university and industrial research efforts.

Literature Cited

1. Anonymous. 1978. Current use of weed control on industrial forest lands. Pages 40-43. In Benefits of 2,4,5-T in forest management. American Paper Institute/National Forest Products Association. Washington, D.C.

2. Anonymous. 1982. Projected trends in domestic timber resources. Pages 147-199. In An analysis of the timber situation in the United States 1952-2030. Forest Resource Report No. 23. USDA Forest Service. Washington, D.C.

3. Carvell, K. L. 1968. "Tordon effective in red maple tree injection studies." Down to Earth 24:17-18.

4. Fitzgerald, C. H., F. A. Peevy and D. E. Fender. 1973. Rehabilitation of forest land -- the southern region. J. For. 71:148-153.

5. Fitzgerald, C. H. 1976. Postemergence effects of velpar in a piedmont pine plantation. South. Weed Sci. Soc., Proc 29:299.

6. Graco, C. X. 1961. Hardwood reoccupation of bulldozed sites. p. 7-8. In: Hardwood sprout development on cleared sites. USDA Forest Serv., South. Forest Exp. Sta. Occasional Pap. 186.

7. Hebb, E. A., and A. F. Clewell. 1976. A remnant stand of old-growth slash pine in the Florida Panhandle. Bull. of the Torrey Bot. Club 103:1-9.

8. Holt, H. A., J. E. Voeller, and J. F. Young. 1973. Vegetation control in newly established pine plantations. South. Weed Sci. Soc., Proc. 28:219.

9. Holt, H. A., J. E. Voeller, and J. F. Young. 1975a. herbaceous vegetation control as a forest management practice. South. Weed Sci. Soc. Proc. 28:219.

10. Holt, H. A., J. E. Voeller, and J. F. Young. 1975b. The hypo-hatchet injector and timber stand improvement. Purdue University, J. S. Wright Forestry Conf. Proc.: 93-197.

11. Johnson R. L. 1961. Hardwood sprouts dominate bottomland clearings. p. 9 In: Hardwood sprout development on cleared sites. USDA Forest Serv., South. Forest Exp. Sta. Occasional Pap. 186.

12. Knowe, S. A. 1982. Third year results for loblolly growth impact. 5 p. Auburn Univ. Silv. Herb. Coop. Res. Note No. 82-4.

13. Kozlowski, T. T. 1969. Soil water and tree growth. 17th Ann. LA. St. Univ. For. Symp., Proc.: 30-37.

14. Kuchler, A. W. 1964. Potential natural vegetation of the conterminous United States. Manual to accompany the map. Am. Geogr. Soc. Special Pub. No. 36 (With map, rev. ed., 1965, 1966).

15. Malac, B. F. 1961. Early indications of growth responses following foliar applications of herbicides. South. Weed Conf., Proc. 14:222-227.

16. Martin, J. W. 1973. Pickens County aerial spray release study. Four year Progress Rep., American Can Co., Butler, Ala. 4 p.

17. McNab, W. H. and E. L. Moyer, Jr. July 1969. Winter injection of 2,4-D and Tordon 101 for hardwood control, Research Note SE-115, USDA, USFS, 2 pp. Southeastern For. Expt. Sta., Ashville, NC.

18. Monk, C. D. 1965. Southern mixed hardwood forests of northcentral Florida. Ecol. Monogr. 35:335-354.

19. Moyer, E. L. Jr. 1967. Controlling off-site hardwoods with 2,4-D amine concentrate, Research Note SE-77, USDA, USFS, 2 pp.h, Southeastern For. exp. Sta., Ashville, NC.

20. Nelson, L. R., R. C. Pedersen, L. L. Autry, S. Dudley and J. D. Walstad. 1981. Impacts of herbaceous weeds in young loblolly pine plantations. South. J. Applied For. 5(3):153-158.

21. Nelson, L. R., P. J. Minogue, D. H. Gjerstad, and G. R. Glover. 1982. Second year results of a site preparation study using triclopyr and hexazinone. Auburn Univ. Silv. Herb. Coop. Res. Note No. 82-13. 6 p.

22. Peevy, F. A. 1968a. "Injection undiluted 2,4-D amine for control of bottomland hardwood." Proc. 21st Annual Meeting Southern Weed Conference: 223-227.

23. _____. 1968b. "Controlling upland southern hardwoods by injecting undiluted, 2,4-D amine." J. of For. 66(6):483-487.

24. _____. 1972. "Injection treatments for controlling resistant hardwood species." Proc. 25th Annual Meeting South. Weed Sci. Soc.: 252-256.

25. Schneider, G. and J. J. Stransky. 1966. Soil moisture and soil temperature under a post oak-shortleaf pine stand. Stephen F. Austin State College, School Forestry Bull. 8:24.

26. Starr, J. W. 1972a. The importance of long term research in forestry. Ind. Veg. Manage. 4(2):15-18.

27. Sterrett, J. P. 1969a. "Injection of red maple and hickory with picloram, 2,4-D and 2,4,5-T." Down to Earth 25(2):18-21.

28. _____. 1969b. "Injection of hardwoods with dicamba, picloram, and 2,4-D. J. of For. 67(11):820-821.

RECEIVED November 11, 1983

3

Management of Bark Beetle Populations
Impact of Manipulating Predator Cues and Other Control Tactics

T. EVAN NEBEKER, RUSSELL F. MIZELL III[1], and NORMAN J. BEDWELL

Department of Entomology, Mississippi State University, Mississippi State, MS 39762

Numerous predators of bark beetles utilize chemical
cues in locating host material as well as host
habitat. Control tactics that manipulate these
cues without consideration of the impact on
natural regulatory factors, such as predation,
is of serious concern. The role of chemical
communication, in relation to proposed control
tactics, of predators and bark beetles will be
discussed. Emphasis will be on Thanasimus dubius
(F.) (Coleoptera: Cleridae) and Medetera bistriata
Parent (Diptera: Dolichopodidae) which are primary
predators of the southern pine beetle, Dendroctonus
frontalis Zimmermann (Coleoptera: Scolytidae).
Impact of other management tactics such as salvage,
cut and leave, use of insecticides, etc. will also
be discussed as they relate to these predators in
forest pest management.

Management of bark beetles in the forest system requires a
knowledge of the elements which potentially regulate them.
The framework (Fig. 1) within which recent research has been
organized to arrive at ecologically sound pest management
decisions was first presented in 1974 (1) and modified slightly
in 1981 (2). This discussion will center around these treatment
strategies.
      Bark beetle populations fluctuate through time and
periodically pose a threat (decrease) to available forest
resources resulting in a subsequent loss of revenue. A number

[1] Current address: Agricultural Research Center, Rt. 4, Box 63, Monticello, FL 32344

0097–6156/84/0238–0025$06.00/0
© 1984 American Chemical Society

of management goals may be important in multiple-use forestry,
thus, many specific treatment tactics are required to aid in the
overall management of these fluctuating bark beetle populations.
The primary goals, in the management of bark beetles, are
presented conceptually in Fig. 2 and consist of: (1) reducing
the pest population or tree mortality to a level below some previously established threshold based on economic, socio-political
or esthetic criteria; (2) decreasing the amplitude of the fluctuation (outbreak); (3) increasing the time between outbreaks
(major fluctuations in population level and subsequent tree
mortality); (4) decreasing the duration of the outbreak; and
(5) maintaining the pest population or mortality at an
acceptable level identified in (1) above.

It is the intent of this paper to explore the various control
tactics that are being suggested in the management of bark beetles
in the forest system with specific attention given to the potential
impact on the predator population. Similar arguments could be
extended to other bark beetle mortality agents such as the
parasite community. Primary examples and control tactics
discussed will be drawn from our experience with the southern
pine beetle, D. frontalis, a major pest in the southeastern U.S.,
along with other bark beetles in North America.

Basically, bark beetle management tactics include: (1) doing
nothing; (2) direct control-salvage, cut and leave, insecticide
application, pile and burn, and trapping (trap-out or bait trees);
and (3) indirect control-"confusion" (pheromone disruption),
inhibition, stand modification (i.e. thinnings) and favoring
resistant host tree species. The positive effects of these
tactics will be addressed briefly while focusing primarily on
the negative effects of these tactics on the natural enemy
community. T. dubius and M. bristriata predators of the
southern pine beetle will be used as examples because both are
considered extremely helpful in the natural regulation of the
southern pine beetle, and with somewhat contrasting behaviors
subcortically. Discussions of the associated organisms and
natural enemies of the southern pine beetle can be found in
(3). In addition, a pictoral key of the most common natural
enemies of the southern pine beetle has been developed (4).

DOING NOTHING

In pest management decision-making, one tactic that is always
considered as an option in a benefit/cost analysis is that of
doing nothing. What are the implications of doing nothing?
From a historical point of view one can expect periodic outbreaks
as a result of population fluctuations. Hence, one can expect
that the amount of mortality taking place in our forests, will
be similar to the past and we would expect it to continue at

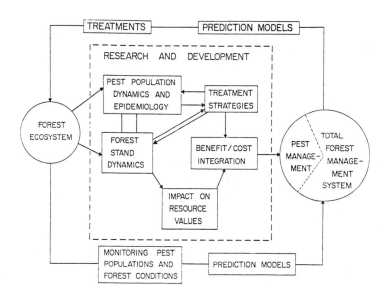

Figure 1. Conceptual framework organizing integrated forest pest management programs. (Reproduced with permission from Ref. 2. Copyright 1981, University of Georgia.)

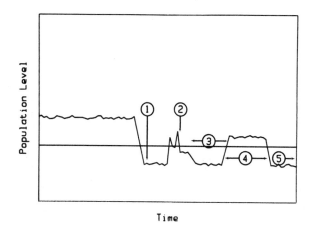

Figure 2. Goals in bark beetle management: (1) reduce the population to an acceptable level; (2) minimize the amplitude of the fluctuations; (3) increase the time between outbreaks; (4) decrease the duration of the outbreak and (5) maintain the population at a lower equilibrium level.

similar levels in the future. As additional resources become
available-increases in acreage of pine forest-increases in
pest population levels and subsequent tree mortality would be
expected. From the view of the predator population, letting
nature take its course would probably be the most desirable
tactic. This view is usually unacceptable, but has fewer
negative effects on the predator population.

DIRECT CONTROLS

Direct control tactics differ from indirect control tactics in
that immediate mortality to the target organism is expected from
direct treatments. An application of an insecticide is a good
example. Indirect control tactics, such as pheromone disruption
or confusion tactics, cause mortality indirectly to the population
by inhibiting or delaying tree colonization. Thus, the generation
time is increased and beetles die due to longer unprotected
exposure in the environment outside the bark. The following
are specific direct control tactics with varying degrees of
impact on the beneficial community.

Salvage. Land managers and owners usually prefer salvage removal
over other control options (tactics) because infested trees are
removed from the forest and used, giving the landowner some
financial return (5). Since salvage operations are directed
at the removal of bark beetle-infested trees, they also remove
a high percentage of the natural enemy complex to distant wood
yards and mills where survival is low. Surviving natural
enemies must rely on powers of dispersal to reenter the forest
and locate new host material from distant locations.
     During epidemic periods, greater than 80% of the southern
pine beetle spots consist of less than 10 trees and usually do
not spread. Hence setting priorities for salvage operations
would be beneficial in the following ways. First, infestations
which present the highest risk of spread should be salvaged first
reducing the risk of spread and subsequently reducing the
population buildup in that area. Second, the detection of the
smaller infestations, comprising the 80% and usually by aerial
surveys, often results in salvage of trees in which bark beetle
development is complete and dispersal has taken place.
Consequently, leaving only the natural enemies to
be destroyed because of their longer developmental time in the
trees. Concentration of salvage efforts on the actively growing
infestations (spots) would maximize both the detrimental
effects of the salvage on the bark beetles and conservation
of natural enemies verses salvaging these smaller spots.
     In the case of T. dubius, mortality could potentially be
reduced and survival enhanced by removing bark from the basal
portion of the tree prior to the movement of the material to the

mill or woodyard. This recommendation is based on a knowledge
of the distribution (6) of this predator during the pupal stage
as illustrated in Fig. 3. Similar consideration should be given
to the natural enemy complex as a whole, with the goal of
conserving natural enemies.

Cut and Leave. This method was first recommended by the Texas
Forest Service for controlling small southern pine beetle spots
(10-15 infested trees) that could not be salvaged (5). As the
treatment implies, trees are felled with the tops directed into
the infested area rather than random felling. Mortality to the
bark beetles is enhanced by the increased subcortical temperature
resulting from direct exposure of the bark to the sun's rays
and the inability of the immature stages to move to more
protected areas, i.e. the under-surface of the felled trees.
Many of the natural enemies, including M. bistriata, also
experience increased mortality due to their lack of mobility.
However, T. dubius being more mobile has the ability to move
either subcortically or over the surface to a more favorable
environment.

Cut and Spray. This tactic is a combination of cut and leave
and chemical control. It results in a great deal of mortality
to the natural enemy population (see below).

Chemical Control. Insecticides are available and registered for
treating bark beetle-infested trees and for preventing attacks
on green trees (7). However, recommendations extend primarily
toward high value trees occupying a limited space such as in
recreation areas, around homes, and other valuable settings.
It is interesting to note that in the registration process,
information concerning the impact on these non-target species,
such as the natural enemy community of bark beetles is not
required. In both the remedial and preventive modes, the
natural enemies are exposed to the insecticides. It has been
shown (8) that overall emergence of predators was reduced by
89% and the ratio of natural enemies to the western pine beetle
(D. brevicomis LeConte) emergence was reduced by 80% as a result
of remedial use of 2% lindane on D. brevicomis.

Cut, Pile and Burn. While some natural enemies do survive other
direct controls, most are killed as a result of this long-used
tactic. Much of the mortality to natural enemies incurred from
use of the aforementioned tactics could be eliminated by treating
only those trees that contain active beetle populations. T.
dubius and other predators have a longer developmental time than
their host. Since parasites arrive later in the colonization
process, they also remain in trees after pest emergence.

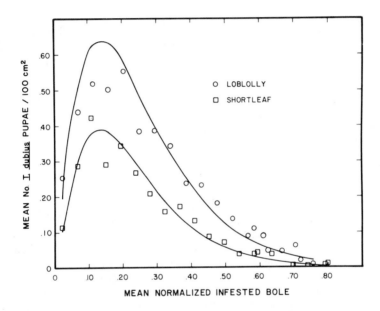

Figure 3.   Distribution of <u>Thanasimus dubius</u> pupae in loblolly and short leaf pine. (Reproduced with permission from
Ref. 6.   Copyright 1981, Entomological Society of Canada.)

Sampling of trees by removing bark or by condition of the tree and treating only those trees with active brood would conserve these valuable natural enemies.

Bait Trees and Trap Out. In these treatments, behavioral chemicals (i.e. aggregation pheromones) are combined with a direct control method to produce beetle mortality. Baited trees have been evaluated using frontalure in a trap-tree application with the herbicide cacodylic acid (9, 10). This treatment was only partially effective. However, this technique does not affect the adult natural enemy population, but rather the F1 generation of the natural enemy population which is killed.

The trap-out treatment generally utilizes the aggregation pheromone of the target bark beetle species in association with a trap that kills the adults, i.e. sticky traps or containers that prevent the escape of species coming in contact with them. These techniques are not species specific per se because of the attraction of the natural enemies to the aggregation pheromones, i.e. kairomonal activity. Hence, the natural enemies are also trapped resulting in mortality to the adults.

INDIRECT CONTROLS

Indirect controls, as stated earlier, are not designed to cause immediate pest mortality. Indirect treatments are preventive in nature while direct treatments are remedial. The goal of indirect treatments are aimed primarily at maintaining the bark beetle population or tree mortality below an acceptable level (Fig. 2). Indirect tactics rely on the manipulation of the bark beetle populations by: (1) interfering with the normal mating or tree colonization processes, i.e. pheromone disruption and inhibition; (2) decreasing the quantity and quality of the resource, i.e. thinning and/or selective harvest of damaged or dying trees; (3) selection of resistant tree species for reforestation; and (4) conservation and augmentation of natural enemies (see section on Salvage).

Pheromone Disruption and Inhibitors. Pheromones play an important role in the landing and attack behavior of bark beetles (9, 11, 12). Attractants orient flying beetles to a common host tree in high numbers over a relatively short time period. Two techniques have been recently developed to take advantage of the southern pine beetle response to pheromones. The first technique using pheromones to manipulate the southern pine beetle population relies on inhibition. Field bioassays have shown that aggregation of the southern pine beetle on attractant-baited traps can be significantly reduced by the

addition of an inhibitor endo- and/or exo-brevicomin (13).
Landing trap catches of the southern pine beetle on host
trees was reduced by 80% using verbenone plus brevicomin (14).
However, attacks by Ips avulsus (Eichhoff) increased.
Nevertheless, the total number of trees attacked and brood
production from attacked trees was reduced.

The second technique utilized frontalure which was placed
as a bait on dead- or non-host trees in an attempt to suppress
southern pine beetle spot growth (15). Since the technique
employs chemical cues that the natural enemies utilize, i.e.
kairomones in host location, it probably has little detrimental
affect on the adult predators. However, the use of inhibitors
and their impact on natural enemies is not known. The data base
is lacking and we can only express concern.

Silvicultural Treatments. Preventive silviculture should be
practiced (16) to promote individual tree resistance to bark
beetle attack by: (1) favoring the most resistant species;
(2) removing high-hazard trees; (3) regulating stocking;
(4) mixing stands of oak and pine; (5) minimizing logging
damage; and (6) regenerating overmature stands. As with the
previous pheromone disruption and inhibitor techniques, data
is lacking on the impact of silvicultural treatments on the
natural enemy community associated with bark beetles. Most
pest management programs focus on the target species with
little attention to the impact of treatment on natural enemies.

Conclusion

Control or management of insect populations in the forest
ecosystem has been of primary concern for decades. Efforts
have been directed at control tactics that satisfy cost/benefit
analysis, with minimum environmental disturbance. The major
objective of this paper was to stress the overriding concern of
many that a lack of attention is being given to the impact of
these tactics on the "beneficial populations".

Literature Cited

1. Waters, W. E. and B. Ewing. in "Modeling for pest management
    concepts, techniques, and applications" Tummala, R.L.;
    D. L. Haynes; B. H. Croft, Eds. Michigan State Univ.,
    East Lansing, 1974.
2. Coulson, R. N. J. Georgia Entomol. Soc. 1981, 16, 301-316.
3. Berisford, C. W. in "The Southern Pine Beetle" Thatcher,
    R. C.; J. L. Searcy; J. E. Coster; G. D. Hertel, Eds.
    USDA-FS-SEA Tech. Bull 1631, 1980; 31-52.

4. Goyer, R. A.; G. J. Lenhart; T. E. Nebeker; L. D. Jarrard. USDA-FS Agric. Handbook #563, 1980.
5. Swain, K. M.; M. C. Remion. USDA Agr. Handbook No. 575, 1980.
6. Mizell, R. F. III, and T. E. Nebeker. Can. Entomol. 1981, 113, 387-94.
7. Hastings, F. L.; J. E. Coster, Eds. USDA Gen. Tech. Rep. SE-21, 1981.
8. Swezey, S. L.; D. L. Dahlsten. Environ. Entomol. 1983, 12, 210-14.
9. Vité, J. P. Contrib. Boyce Thompson Inst. 1970, 24, 343-50.
10. Coulson, R. N.; J. L. Foltz; A. M. Mayyasi; F. P. Hain. J. Econ. Entomol. 1975, 68, 671-78.
11. Vité, J. P.; W. Franke. Naturwis. 1976, 63, 550-55.
12. Payne, T. L.; J. V. Richerson; L. J. Edson; E. R. Hart. Envir. Entomol. 1978, 7, 578-82.
13. Vité, J. P.; J. A. A. Renwick. Naturwis. 1971, 8, 418-19.
14. Richerson, J. V.; T. L. Payne. Environ. Entomol. 1979, 8, 360-64.
15. Richerson, J. V.; F. A. McCarty; T. L. Payne. Envir. Entomol. 1980, 9, 90-93.
16. Belanger, R. P.; B. F. Malc. USDA Agr. Handbook No. 576, 1980.

RECEIVED September 9, 1983

Sex Pheromones and Their Potential as Control Agents for Forest Lepidoptera in Eastern Canada

P. J. SILK and L. P. S. KUENEN

Pheromone Research Group, New Brunswick Research and Productivity Council, Fredericton, New Brunswick, E3B 5H1, Canada

The chemical and behavioral aspects of the sex pheromones of several forest defoliating insects of economic importance in eastern Canada are presented, with emphasis on the spruce budworm, Choristoneura fumiferana. Studies conducted over several years in New Brunswick on the use of pheromones as potential control agents, using in particular the air permeation technique to effect mating disruption, are discussed. The identification and the behavioral effects of minor components of the spruce budworm pheromone system are presented and the potential exploitation of their behavioral roles in the mating sequence in terms of control strategies are addressed.

Current strategies for managing high density populations (outbreaks) of forest Lepidoptera, which defoliate and in some cases destroy large areas of hardwood and softwood trees, depend almost entirely on chemical insecticide applications for the duration of the outbreaks. Although there have been technological refinements for insecticide application, the basic strategy of tree protection has changed little. Often, severe damage over large areas has occurred and insect populations have reached epidemic proportions before protection operations were initiated. Applications of insecticides are designed to prevent tree mortality; any long term effects on the population dynamics of the target insect are incidental. However, environmental and human health considerations have recently lead to a re-assessment of current insecticide usage and also to serious examination of potential new strategies for managing insect-susceptible and insect-damaged forests.

Behavior modifying chemicals, pheromones in particular, offer one of the potential alternatives for future control and management of forest Lepidoptera. These semiochemicals are generally non-toxic and highly specific for target insects, but their use in forest ecosystems is not without problems and possible limitations.

0097-6156/84/0238-0035$06.00/0
© 1984 American Chemical Society

Ecological and behavioral considerations, especially with regard to dispersal and mating characteristics, may ultimately determine whether or not the use of pheromones is feasible and practical for a given insect species.

Among the insects being studied in our laboratory, a number of tortricids, the spruce budworm, Choristoneura fumiferana (Clemens); the jack pine budworm, Choristoneura pinus Freeman; the western spruce budworm, Choristoneura occidentalis Freeman; the oak leaf shredder, Croesia semipurpurana (Kearfott); and a geometrid, the hemlock looper, Lambdina fiscellaria fiscellaria (Guenée) are important defoliators. We are examining the pheromone chemistry and pheromone-mediated behaviors of these insects to support potential monitoring and control programs in eastern Canada. The components of the female tortricid sex pheromones are a group of congeneric C_{14} aldehydes, alcohols, and acetates with blends, geometrical isomer ratios, and release rates specific to each species (Table 1). The hemlock looper on the other hand, appears to have a purely hydrocarbon pheromone (Silk, unpublished data).

This paper will review the uses of pheromones for detection, monitoring and possible control of eastern forest Lepidoptera. As an illustrative example, particular reference will be made to the control of the spruce budworm, the techniques used and the problems involved including limitations due to economics and lack of biological information on this species.

The coniferophagous spruce budworms, native to North America, comprise a group of closely related congeneric (Choristoneura) species with at least six recognizable species in the west, and two distinct allopatric species in the east (12). Among the western species, the western spruce budworm is the most widespread and economically the most important. The two eastern species, jack pine budworm (a pine feeder) and spruce budworm (which feeds primarily on balsam fir and white spruce), are both economically important forest defoliators. Spruce budworm, whose range extends into the U.S. and has the largest range of all the budworms, has been the target of annual tree protection operations since the early 1950's.

Population levels of spruce budworm are typically at low levels interspersed with intervals of very high densities (epidemic infestations). In the eastern part of its range, intervals between epidemic populations historically have been ca. 30 years. Further west, the intervals have been longer. Unchecked, the duration of epidemics is ca. 10 years and tree mortality may be extensive (e.g., Cape Breton Highlands of Nova Scotia). The rapid rise in populations to epidemic levels is generally attributed to a sequence of warm, dry springs coinciding with the maturing of even-aged stands of spruce-fir forest. The development of epidemic populations, however, is exacerbated by man's activities (e.g. current harvesting methods tend to favor balsam fir, which may result in a shortening of the population cycling and more extensive epidemics due to larger areas of even-aged trees).

TABLE I

Sex Pheromones Isolated and Identified from Tortricid Females

| Insert | Pheromone Components* | | |
	Primary	Secondary	Reference
Choristoneura fumiferana	E11-14:Ald	----	(1)
	96/4 E/Z11-14:Ald	----	(2)
	95/5 E/Z11-14:Ald	14:Ald	(3)
C. occidentalis	92/8 E/Z11-14:Ald	----	(4)
	92/8 E/Z11-14:Ald	89/11 E/Z11-14:Ac 85/15 E/Z-11-14:Ac	(5, 6)
C. pinus	85/15 E/Z11-14:OH 85/15 E/Z11-14:Ac	----	(7, 8)
Croesia semipurpurana	85/15 E/Z11-14:Ald	85/15 E/Z11-14:Ac	(9-11)

*   E/Z11-14:Ald ≡ E/Z-11-tetradecenal;
    E/Z11-14:Ac ≡ E/Z-11-tetradecen-1-ol acetate;
    E/Z11-14:OH ≡ E/Z-11-tetradecen-1-ol;
    14:Ald ≡ tetradecanal.

Eastern North America is now experiencing perhaps the most extensive epidemic yet recorded; susceptible stands have been defoliated for several years throughout more than 40 million hectares. This has prompted the large scale use of insecticides over millions of hectares annually in an attempt to protect the trees and to keep them alive until they can be harvested. Research is being conducted in Canada and the U.S. to find alternative strategies and techniques for controlling the budworm.

One of these methods, mating disruption by area-wide dissemination of synthetic sex pheromone, has been shown to be effective for a number of moth species. The method is used commercially to control pink bollworm (Pectinophora gossypiella (Saunders)) in southwestern U.S. cotton fields, and commercial systems are being developed for moths infesting a number of other high-value field crops. Although there have been demonstrated successes in disrupting mating in some western North American forest Lepidopterans (13), the commercial development and application of mating disruption systems for these insects has generally lagged behind for at least two reasons: (1) present commercial technologies for pheromone application are generally not compatible with forest protection needs, and (2) it is difficult to quantitatively assess the damage to trees or the savings derived from pest control measures.

The fact that mating disruption can be commercially feasible is encouraging but the actual mechanism(s) of disruption is still unclear. The possible mechanisms involved in disruption include sensory adaptation, habituation, competition ("false-trail following") and camouflage of aerial trails from females (14, 15). These mechansims could be working in combination, simultaneously or sequentially, so that some level of disruption can and does occur under a variety of conditions. Without a better understanding of the mechanisms of "attraction" to a pheromone source and the mating disruption process, however, optimization of control methods can proceed only on an empirical basis.

As in most Lepidoptera, spruce budworm males locate conspecific females by flying upwind along a pheromone plume. The blends and release rates of these pheromone components form an important part of a specific communication system for the species. Once the communication system of an insect is understood, especially the pheromone chemistry as it relates to male behavior, it can be used in a variety of ways. For example, pheromones can be used to detect the presence of an insect in an area, to remove males from a population by trapping or poisoning and in air-permeation techniques in which the controlled and continuous release of pheromone components in the forest can disrupt mating. The latter use of pheromones appears to alter the normal male behavioral responses to the natural pheromone (16).

Review of the Pheromone Chemistry of the Spruce Budworm

Over twenty years have passed since it was shown that female spruce budworm can release olfactory cues that attract mates (17). The first attractant chemical identified from female spruce budworm was E11-14:Ald (1) which, by itself, provided inconsistent results in field trapping experiments. Subsequent re-analysis of female volatiles showed that the Z-isomer was present at 4% of the E-isomer (2), and this blend was necessary to maximize trap captures. Further analyses of female pheromone gland extracts revealed the presence of E11-14:OH (18) and E11-14:Ac (19), both of which had been previously shown to reduce field trap efficiency (20, 21). More detailed analyses (3) indicated that female glands contain Δ11-14:Ac (20-40 ng/insect), Δ11-14:Ald (1-2 ng/insect) and Δ11-14:OH (1-2 ng/insect) all in 95/5 E/Z ratios; the saturated analogues of the compounds are also present (at ca. 1% of the corresponding E-isomers). In contrast, we found that effluvia from calling females contains E/Z11-14:Ald (95/5, 10-40 ng/insect/night) along with 14:Ald (at ca. 2% of the E-aldehyde) and traces of E11-14:Ac (at ca. 0.1% of the E aldehyde); no alcohols were detected (3). Preliminary field data indicated that there were no significant differences in trap captures between traps baited with a polyvinylchloride (PVC) rod releasing all four components (in ratios similar to a calling female) compared to traps baited with the primary components, the E/Z-unsaturated aldehydes alone. These tests also verified that addition of the unsaturated acetate to the Δ11-14:Ald reduced trap captures. However, this effect of the acetate was negated by the presence of the saturated aldehyde (3), but it is important to note that this only occurred when these additional components were present with the primary components in female effluvial ratios.

By entraining pheromone from groups (50-100) of freely "calling" virgin females, we found that it was released in the range of 1-5 ng/hour/insect (3). A PVC rod (3X10mm) can be formulated with 0.03% 97/3 E/Z11-14:Ald (aged for ca. 5 weeks) to release these components at approximately the natural female rate (22). A sensitive and specific bioluminescent assay (combined with a Porapak Q trapping technique) has been used to demonstrate that pheromone release by females, as expected, occurs mainly during scotophase in a series of bursts (at rates as high as 50 ng/hour) with considerable individual variability (23-25). The quantity of pheromone in female glands cycled daily with higher levels observed during scotophase (23).

Review of Spruce Budworm Pheromone-mediated Behavior

In sustained-flight wind tunnel experiments, it appeared that synthetic E/Z11-14:Ald's were equivalent in "attraction" to virgin females (22). Furthermore, in response to these two primary components, some males demonstrated a full range of pre-copulatory behaviors, e.g. upwind flight, courtship and copulatory attempts similar to that when they responded to "calling" virgin females (26). Therefore, it seemed unlikely that other chemicals were involved in the "attraction" phase of the mating process (27). The possibility that other chemical cues might be involved in close-range behaviors was ignored until recent laboratory wind-tunnel studies showed that a greater percentage of males initiated upwind flight and continued on to contact the source when 14:Ald was added to 95/5 E/Z11-14:Ald. Similarly, in the field, more males made contact with a 3-component source than with a Δ11-14:Ald source (28). The addition of E11-14:Ac to the primary components decreased the males' responsiveness to the aldehydes, but this effect appeared to be counteracted or altered (when present at low levels with 95/5 E/Z11-14:Ald) by the presence of 14:Ald, confirming earlier trapping data (3, 28). These results were independently confirmed by laboratory wind-tunnel studies (29). In other field observations, unfractionated volatile material from females, added to the 11-14:Ald's + 14:Ald has been shown to increase the percentage of males that contact the pheromone source, and the duration of contacts with the source was significantly longer (30). These observations, however, may be limited to the confines of the experimental conditions and more detailed field and laboratory experiments are required to further elucidate the possible role of these putative short-range pheromone components.

Studies on the precopulatory behavior of males, at close range, have been reported and a basal level of male-to-male homosexual activity has been described (31). This work, however, will have to be re-examined under free-flight conditions especially in light of the possibile involvement of "short-range" pheromone components.

Field Use of Spruce Budworm Pheromone

It is apparent that not all the chemicals involved in female-to-male communication in the spruce budworm are known. In monitoring and mating disruption programs, however, it may not be essential to know every minor component, although as Roelofs has pointed out (16), trap specificity and potency may be greatly increased as the synthetic lure more closely duplicates the natural pheromone and it is presumed that the efficacy of mating disruption would likewise be enhanced by the "more complete pheromone".

Present methods for the detection and population survey of spruce budworm rely on the sampling of egg masses on tree foliage. Pheromone traps could probably detect moths at lower densities than the present method and this information could be used to prevent or decrease the development of an epidemic infestation of spruce budworm. However, a great deal of work is still required to correlate trap capture with moth population densities and with damage to trees.

The spruce budworm is considered a "high density" pest since it occurs at damaging densities of $> 10^4$ adults per hectare. In epidemic situations it occurs in densities sometimes orders of magnitude higher. Under such conditions, it is questionable that pheromone alone could suppress populations. However, recent work has shown some disruptive effects on reproductive behavior even at these high densities and work is underway to clarify whether or not pheromone can play an effective role in controlling high populations of budworm.

Mating disruption experiments with spruce budworm in laboratory, small-scale field tests and "semi-operational" field trials have recently been reviewed (27). Work to date, on the disruption of spruce budworm mating behavior has concentrated on the use of the primary components E/Z11-14:Ald's (95-97% E), and the results indicate that some mating disruption does occur. There appears to be a positive correlation between the applied pheromone concentration and the percent disruption, and based on field cage studies, percent disruption is inversely related to insect density (27) as would be predicted (32).

Previous tests of the aerial application of synthetic sex attractant of the spruce budworm resulted in reductions of up to 90% of males captured in traps baited with virgin females and/or synthetic pheromone. However, there has been no convincing demonstration of reduction in population density in the subsequent generation (33).

In 1975, pheromone-containing microcapsules were applied to 12 ha of spruce/fir forest at 7.4 g active ingredient per hectare (7.4 g AI/ha), in Ontario resulting in a 97% reduction in pheromone trap catches (21). In 1977, again in Ontario, Conrel hollow fibers were applied at a rate of approximately 3 and 30 g AI/ha to two 10 ha plots with low- density populations and at approximately 5 g AI/ha to a 10 ha plot with a moderate population density (34). In all three areas the reduction in trap catches was greater than 97%, but attempts to demonstrate population reduction were inconclusive. In 1978 four different concentrations ranging from 0.2 to 40 g AI/ha were applied in New Brunswick and Nova Scotia (35). The active ingredient evaporated too quickly from the Conrel fibers pointing to problems with the formulation used (36). In spite of this, during the period when the pheromone was detectable, catches in traps were considerably reduced. Also, in cages containing different numbers of male and female budworm, there were significant reductions in the numbers of females mated in presence of the pheromone, with the effects being greatest at the lowest moth densities (37). In 1980, a commercially available sex pheromone formulation was evaluated by RPC in Maine, with joint funding by Canadian Forestry Service (CFS), the State of Maine, and Canada-United States Spruce Budworm Program (CANUSA). The formulation, Hercon flakes, performed satisfactorily; the pheromone was emitted as called for in the specifications. However, even though one treatment consisted of a massive dose of "sex attractant" (500 g AI/ha), biological effects were apparently obscured by invasion of gravid females from other areas (38). A high dose (100 g AI/ha) of synthetic sex attractant of the spruce budworm formulated in Hercon flakes was aerially applied to a 30 ha plantation of white spruce near Sault Ste. Marie, Ontario, in 1981 (33). Mating among caged moths was reduced by 40%, and catches in pheromone-baited traps were reduced 90%. Effects on moth behavior and on population reduction were obscured by a wide-spread population decline (due to disease) but the available data suggested that there was a delay in oviposition, although final egg counts were the same in treated and check plots. Inadequacies were found with the adherence of flakes to foliage and it was clear that more work was required in the laboratory and in small-scale field experiments to evaluate "stickers" and to determine the optimum concentration and distribution of releasers.

In spite of encouraging results obtained to date, as previously stated, none of these tests has shown convincing evidence for reduction in population density in the subsequent generation in the field. There would appear to be three possible reasons for this (27). Firstly, the technique does not work. This seems unlikely because even at high densities, profound reduction in trap catches occurs. Secondly, the concentrations of the attractant were too low or wrongly distributed to be effective. Thirdly, invasion of mated female moths into treatment areas confounded the results. Failures, therefore, are probably related to the latter two points viz., inadequate, poorly designed or sub-optimally distributed releasers and inadequate biological assessment because of invasion of the assessment area by mated egg-laying females. Lack of field data on short and long-range movements of adults in control and treatment field plots, further confounds the issues involved.

Pheromone releaser distributions and/or point-source release rates have pronounced effects on the disruption of trap captures of spruce budworm (39). Small field plot studies with hand-placed releasers in moderate- to-high density budworm populations indicate an increase in trap disruption as the point sources of the synthetic pheromone are increased in release rate and decreased in number per unit area (Fig. 1). Identical pheromone dosages per plot were present in each treatment. Optimizing the releaser spacing and point-source release rate is therefore important and implies the need for a formulation re-design. This effect of releaser distribution and point-source release rate on trap disruption and mating disruption has been demonstrated in several insect species (40).

Experiments using laboratory-reared insects in large screen field-cages have been carried out (41). Using high levels of pheromone and high insect densities, mating disruption was shown to occur. Although the cages alleviate the problem of disruption assessment associated with migrating mated females, the results remain to be substantiated under natural conditions. Laboratory-reared moths may be behaviorally unlike feral moths and the effects of the cage environment on insect behavior is unknown. Additionally, the microclimate in the cage can affect the release rates and aerial concentrations of pheromone. These field-cage constraints make it difficult to extend cage-results to the natural situation.

Until a more detailed understanding of mating behavior, dispersal behavior and a complete identification of additional pheromone components is achieved, further field work on mating disruption with budworm can only proceed on an empirical basis. Additionally, treatment effects will be difficult to interpret unequivocally due to the local and long range movements of budworm adults into and out

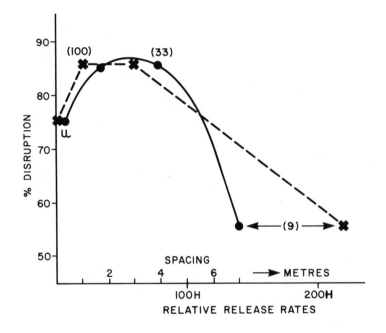

OPTIMUM ꞉ 30 - 50H RELEASE RATE
SPACING 2 - 4m.

Figure 1.   Effect of release rate/distribution on disruption.
All plots had 2000 Hercon flakes per 500 m² H ≡ 1 1/8 x 1/8
flake (≅ 1 µg/h;20 °C @ 0.5m/s.)   x ≡ relative point source
release rates (numbers in parentheses are total release
points/plot).   ˙≡ mean distance between release points.

of pheromone treatment plots. The problem of adult migration requires the development of better techniques for assessing the degree of mating disruption (coupled, of course, with a better knowledge of the moths' field behavior). An improved assessment could be achieved in natural situations by using a label, sprayed or systemically introduced, in a native/treatment population. Rubidium (Rb), for example (42), has been successfully introduced into C. occidentalis by injecting it into its host (Douglas Fir); the Rb was translocated to the growing shoots and incorporated by feeding larvae. The adults retained the Rb label and it was transferred to their eggs. However, this technique required verification for spruce budworm and this is underway in our laboratory.

Mating disruption, in the sense of high-density budworm control, requires a releaser emitting large amounts of pheromone and contact with sources of this sort is not likely because of habituation/sensory adaptation. Controlled-release dispensers releasing the primary pheromone components close to that of a female are highly "attractive" and induce a high degree of contact. The addition of ca. 5% 14:Ald to the blend significantly increases the percent and duration of moth contacts (28) as do unknown, as yet unidentified female-derived components previously mentioned. We have been exploring and optimizing a "male annihilation" approach using pheromone sources to attract and kill spruce budworm males. Since males will fly toward and contact a synthetic pheromone source, it is possible that during contact with the source a lethal insecticide or a chemosterilant could be transferred to the male. Either of these compounds would remove the male from the viable mating population thereby reducing the number of females that will mate and lay fertile eggs. This technique requires contact with a synthetic pheromone source, which, in this case, must closely mimic natural females for optimum results. The two strategies would have to be developed separately although they could be deployed simultaneously; e.g., since male emergence peaks before that of the female, and since males can be activated when females are quiescent, a "male annihilation" application followed by a "disruption" application may be more efficacious than either used separately. It has been shown that contact insecticides can cause quick knockdown of male budworm when added to the sticker (43). This effect, however, has yet to be proven in the field to produce budworm control, although the concept has theoretical appeal (32).

Formulation Assessment

A thorough understanding of the release performance of a controlled-release system under field conditions is essential, in order to have confidence that measurements of mating disruption (or trap capture) are due to biological effects of pheromone treatments and not formulation effects.

We have recently assessed the pheromone release characteristics of a number of commercially available formulations suitable for budworm pheromone delivery, using a laboratory technique which yields good correlation with release characteristics of field-aged formulations (44). However, as mentioned previously, a newly optimized formulation may be required. A specific and sensitive technique for detecting and measuring aerial concentrations of $\underline{E}/\underline{Z}11$-14:Ald's in the field from aerially applied formulations has also been developed and tested (36). This method was recently used (41) to correlate field-caged budworm mating disruption and time-averaged aerial pheromone concentrations.

Conclusions

We now know that some degree of mating disruption can occur under certain circumstances with spruce budworm. The problems now seem to be in the areas of the optimization of the pheromone's blend, dosage and distribution, and the development of the appropriate formulation and application technology for the forest environment. As Daterman (40) has pointed out, what is required, once the system is optimized, is to treat large or isolated areas of budworm populations to avoid the problems associated with migration, and then assess the treatment effects on reproduction and damage in following generations. Also, if a high percentage of disruption can be induced, the interaction of the parasite/predator complex might have an increasingly important role in further controlling budworm populations.

Integrating mating disruption techniques with microbial or chemical pesticides may prove efficacious. Epidemics could be suppressed with the pesticide, with the disruption technique being aimed at preventing reproduction in peripheral areas, keeping the population at low levels. The male annihilation concept, although yet to be proven in the field, offers another approach to population control.

Pheromones could be used to detect and/or predict population trends such that current control practices could be made more effective and an outbreak suppressed before damage is substantial. This could be accomplished by pheromone/mating disruption treatments and/or application of conventional insecticides. However, budworm control measures used when problems are not evident but, perhaps, incipient would require a political change from the practice of crisis management during the epidemics to one of integrated pest management during the entire population cycle.

Pheromones for control of budworm or other potential high-density, migratory defoliators have a role to play, but these epidemic pests present special problems and a great deal more research is required before pheromones will take their place in the integrated pest management of these insects.

Literature Cited

1. Weatherston, J.; Roelofs, A.; Comeau, A.; Sanders, C. J. Can. Entomol. 1971, 103, 1741-7.
2. Sanders, C. J.; Weatherston, J. Can. Entomol. 1976, 108, 1285-90.
3. Silk, P. J.; Tan, S. H.; Wiesner, C. J.; Ross, R. J.; Lonergan, G. C. Environ. Entomol. 1980, 9, 640-44.
4. Cory, H. T.; Daterman, G. E.; Davies Jr., G. D.; Sower, L. L.; Shepherd, R. F.; Sanders, C. J. J. Chem. Ecol. 1982, 8, 339-50.
5. Silk, P. J.; Wiesner, C. J.; Tan, S. H.; Ross, R. J.; Grant, G. G. J. Chem. Ecol. 1982, 8, 351-62.
6. Alford, A. R.; Silk, P. J. J. Chem. Ecol. 1983, in press.
7. Roelofs, W. L. 1981, personal communication.
8. Silk, P. J.; Kuenen, L. P. S.; Roelofs, W. K.; Sanders, C. J., unpublished data.
9. Weatherston, J.; Grant, G. G.; MacDonald, L.; Frech, D.; Werner, R. A.; Leznoff, C. C.; Fyles, T. M. J. Chem. Ecol. 1978, 4, 543-549.
10. Grant, G. G.; Frech, D.; MacDonald, L.; Boyle, B. Can. Entomol. 1981, 113, 449-451.
11. Silk, P. J.; Kuenen, L. P. S.; Tan, S. H.; Alford, A. R., unpublished data.
12. Sanders, C. J. in "Chemical Ecology: Odour Communication in Animals"; Ritter, F. J., Ed.; Elsevier/North-Holland Biomedical Press, Amsterdam, 1979, pp. 427.
13. Daterman, G. E.; Sower, L. L.; Sartwell, C. In "Insect Pheromone Technology: Chemistry and Applications"; Leonhardt, B. A.; Beroza, M., Eds.; ACS SYMPOSIUM SERIES No. 190, American Chemical Society: Washington, D.C., 1982; pp. 260.
14. Cardé, R. T. in "Management of Insect Pests With Semio-chemicals"; Mitchell, E. R., Ed.; Plenum Press, N. Y. and London, 1981, pp. 385-98.
15. Bartell, R. J. Physiol. Entomol. 7, 1982, 353-64.
16. Roelofs, W. L. In Biochemistry of Insects; Rockstein, M., Ed.; Academic Press, New York, 1978, pp. 419-64.
17. Greenbank, D. O. Mem. Entomol. Soc. Can. 1963, 31, 87.
18. Weatherston, J.; MacLean, W. Can. Entomol. 1974, 106, 281.
19. Wiesner, C. J.; Silk, P. J.; Tan, S. H.; Palaniswamy, P.; Schmidt, J. O. Can. Entomol. 1979, 111, 1311.
20. Sanders, C. J.; Bartell, R. J.; Roelofs, W. L. Bi-mon. Bull. Can. For. Service. 1972, 28, 9.
21. Sanders, C. J. Environ. Entomol. 1976, 5, 868.
22. Sanders, C. J. Can. Entomol. 1981, 113, 103.
23. Morse, D.; Sznittner, R.; Grant, G. G.; Meighan, E. A. J. Insect Physiol. 1982, 28, 863-66.
24. Meighan, E. A.; Slessor, K. N.; Grant, G. G. Experientia. 1981, 37, 555-56.

25. Meighan, E. A.; Slessor, K. N.; Grant, G. G. J. Chem. Ecol. 1982, 8, 911-21.
26. Sanders, C. J. Can. Dept. Environ Bi-mon. Res. Notes. 1979, 35, 2.
27. Sanders, C. J.; Seabrook, W. D. In "Insect Suppression With Controlled Release Pheromone Systems. Vol. 2" CRC Press Inc. 1982, pp. 312.
28. Alford, A. R.; Silk, P. J.; McClure, M.; Gibson, C.; Fitzpatrick, J. Can. Entomol. 1983, in press.
29. Sanders, C. J., personal communication.
30. Silk, P. J. "NBDNR Progress Report". 1982-83, unpublished.
31. Palaniswamy, P.; Seabrook, W. D.; Ross, R. J. Ann. Entomol. Soc. Am. 1979, 72, 544.
32. Knipling, E. F. "The Basic Principles of Insect Population Suppression and Management" (USDA, Agriculture Handbook No. 512) 1979, pp. 659.
33. Sanders, C. J.; Silk, P. J. Canadian Forestry Service, Information Report O-X-335 (ISSN 0704-7297). 1982.
34. Sanders, C. J. Dep. Environ. CFS, Report O-X-285. 1979, 32.
35. Miller, C. A. Report of Spruce Budworm Pheromone Trials, Maritimes, 1978. Dep. Environ. CFS, Fredericton. File Report 1980.
36. Wiesner, C. J.; Silk, P. J.; Tan, S. H.; Fullarton, S. Can. Entomol. 1980, 112, 333-334.
37. Schmidt, J. O.; Thomas, A. W.; Seabrook, W. D. Dep. Environ. CFS, Bi-mon. Res. Notes. 1980, 36, 25.
38. Dimond, J., personal communication.
39. Alford, A. R.; Silk, P. J. J. Econ. Entomol. 1983, in press.
40. Daterman, G. E.; Sartwell, C.; Sower, L. L. In "Controlled Release of Bioactive Materials"; Baker, R., Ed.; Academic Press, 1980; pp. 473.
41. Seabrook, W. D.; Valenta, Z., unpublished data.
42. McLean, J. A. Ent. Soc. Brit. Columbia. Sept. 1982.
43. Wiesner, C. J. 1980, 1981, unpublished data.
44. Wiesner, C. J.; Silk, P. J. In "Insect Pheromone Technology: Chemistry and Applications"; Leonhardt, B. A.; Beroza, M., Eds.; ACS SYMPOSIUM SERIES No. 190, American Chemical Society: Washington, D. C., 1982; pp. 260.

RECEIVED September 9, 1983

Mass Trapping of *Ips typographus* with Pheromone-Baited Traps

REIDAR LIE

Borregaard Industries Limited, N-1701, Sarpsborg, Norway

The spruce bark beetle, Ips typographus (L.), is one of the most serious pests threatening Eurasian spruce.
   In the literature we have documentation for destruction of the Norwegian spruce forest by bark beetles in 1850-1860. During the last 10 years there has been a rapid growth in the population of I. typographus in Scandinavia. In 1978 the Norwegian Department of Agriculture estimated the bark beetle attack to be a threat to the whole spruce stand. The Civil Forest Administration faced a possible loss of 70 % of the spruce trees. In the fall of 1978 the Norwegian government recommended several short-term and long-term remedies to reduce the size of the beetle population. The major long-term remedy was to stimulate harvesting of overmature forest stands. The major short-term remedy was a recommendation to mass trap I. typographus.
   In 1976 Bakke (1-2) showed a production of cis-verbenol (I), ipsenol (2-methyl-6-methylene-7-octene-4-ol), ipsdienol (2-methyl-6-methylene-3,7-octadiene-4-ol (II) and 2-methyl-3-butene-2-ol (III) from male I. typographus. Field experiments confirmed (2) that both sexes will respond to a mixture of cis-verbenol, ipsdienol and methylbutenol.

0097-6156/84/0238-0049$06.00/0

Large scale use of pheromones requires a practical dispenser system which must release the pheromone continuously over the prescribed period while, at the same time, being able to withstand the forest environment.
The 3 pheromone components of I. typographus have very different volatilities:

Table I.   Aggregation pheromone for I. typographus

cis-Verbenol (I)	m.p. 64°C
Ipsdienol	b.p. (0,15 torr) 55°C
Methylbutenol (III)	b.p. 97°C

During 1977 and 1978 various dispenser systems were tested in the field. Evaporations rates for these dispensers were measured in the laboratory and under field conditions. The five different dispenser systems tested were:

Vaseline emulsion
Wax emulsion
Hollow fibers
Polyethylene bag
Multilayer strip

The polyethylene bag (produced by Celamerck, West Germany) and the laminated strip (produced by Hercon, USA) proved to be the most suitable dispenser for trapping I.typographus. The evaporation rates of these two dispensers are very temperature dependent. The bark beetle is active at temperature above 18°C. In the field, while trapping, internal trap temperature varied from +5 to 40°C. On sunny days trap temperature was +5 to 10°C above ambient temperature.
Practical use of pheromones started in 1978. That year we used 110.000 trap-trees sprayed with an insecticide (Lindane). The first year we used one dispenser with an initial loading of 70 mg cis-verbenol and 10 mg ipsdienol. A second dispenser was loaded with 100 mg methylbutenol. In 1979 we adjusted the loading and used only one dispenser containing all 3

pheromone components. Initially, each dispenser
contained the pheromone methylbutenol 1500 mg, cis-
verbenol 70 mg and ipsdienol 15 mg.
    Evaporation rates for pheromone components under
field conditions were measured by residual analysis.
In the residual analysis we use gas-chromatography with
internal standard after extraction of the active components.
    Two typical analyses are given below.

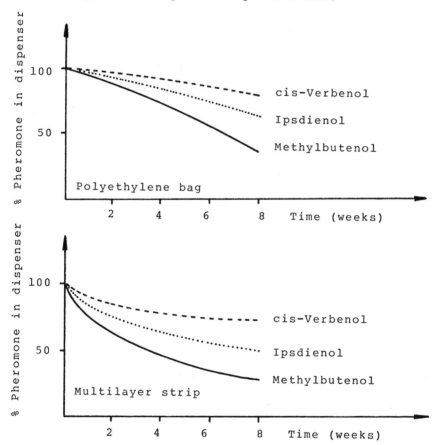

Evaporation from <u>Ips typographus</u> dispenser

Measurement of evaporation rates is interesting, but more important is the correlation between evaporation and actual trap catch. In the field the multilayer and the polyethylene bag attract the same number of beetles. The attractiveness of these dispensers decrease with time also at the same rate. The dispensers have a reduced attractiveness of about 45 % after 2-4 weeks and about 45 % after 2-4 weeks and about 60 % after 6-8 weeks.

The use of insecticide-sprayed trap trees is very labour intensive. For this reason we developed traps for the bark beetles. During the summer of 1978 we tested and evaluated more than 15 different cylindrical traps. The best trap is a black, rigid, drainpipe of polyethylene (12,5 x 135 cm). The pipe has 900 holes (diam. 3,5 mm) ; a lid covers its top while its bottom has a funnel and a collection bottle.

During the summers of 1979-1982 traps were placed in open areas near trees killed previously. To evaluate the efficiency of the mass trapping campaign 1 % of the traps were selected at random and their catch counted. The results are shown in Table I (3)

Table II.   Results from mass trapping I. typographus
             in Norway 1979-1982.

Year	1979	1980	1981	1982
Number of traps deployed	605.000	650.000	530.000	435.000
Average catch of I. typographus per trap	4.850	7.850	3.950	2.200

One result is to capture beetles, but the important question is what impact this has on tree mortality. The Civil Forest Administration has evaluated the number of beetle killed trees each fall from 1977-1981. The results are shown in Table 3.

Table III.   Number of trees killed by I. typographus
             in Norway 1977-1981.

Year	1977	1978	1979	1980	1981	1982
Number of beetle killed trees in millions	2	3,3	3,0	2,7	0,9	0,2

In Norway we have an integrated campaign against
I. typographus. The great decrease in number of beetle
killed trees is mainly attributed to the mass trapping.
We hope this summer's program will bring the beetle
population down to an acceptable level. In the years
to come we plan to continue a low level with sanitation.

Literature Cited

1. Bakke, A., Naturwissenschaften 1976 63, 92
2. Bakke, A. ; Frøye, P. ; Skattebøl, L., Naturwissenschaften 1977 64, 98
3. Bakke A. ; Strand, L., Research Paper Norwegian
   Forest Research Institute 1981 5 4

RECEIVED September 9, 1983

Baculovirus: An Attractive Biological Alternative

MAURO E. MARTIGNONI

U.S. Department of Agriculture, Forest Service, Forestry Sciences Laboratory, Pacific Northwest Forest and Range Experiment Station, Corvallis, OR 97331

Insect pathogens, in general, have less impact on the environment than conventional chemical pesticides because they have high specificity for the target pest and very low or absent mammalian toxicity-pathogenicity. Of the many groups of entomopathogenic viruses, the nuclear polyhedrosis viruses (Baculovirus subgroup A) have shown considerable potential as practical insect control agents in agriculture and forestry. Several of the factors that determine the degree of current development of these biological insecticides and their commercial attractiveness are discussed. Strategies favoring cost-effective production and successful introduction into the forest are examined. Recent approaches to biological standardization of Baculovirus, production control, and toxicity-pathogenicity testing are based on work with baculoviruses registered for use against three insect pests in the United States: the cotton bollworm, the Douglas-fir tussock moth, and the gypsy moth. The Baculovirus used for suppression of the Douglas-fir tussock moth on Douglas-fir and true firs in the Western United States is an example of a successful cycle of research and development, from discovery and identification of the viral agent to registration and use of the viral product.

Most of the major groups or families of animal viruses are represented among the entomopathogenic viruses. More than 20 groups of viruses are known to be pathogenic for insects (Table I). All of these groups are of considerable interest to molecular biologists, biochemists, geneticists, comparative virologists, and invertebrate pathologists. For instance, sigma virus, a member of the Rhabdoviridae and the agent of carbon

Table I. Entomopathogenic Virus Families and Groups, as Proposed
by the International Committee on Taxonomy of Viruses (2)

Poxviridae
   Entomopoxvirinae, entomopoxvirus (Genus A, Genus B, Genus C)

Baculoviridae
   Baculovirus Subgroup A, nuclear polyhedrosis virus
   Baculovirus Subgroup B, granulosis virus
   Baculovirus Subgroup C, nonoccluded virus
   Baculovirus Subgroup D, nonoccluded virus with polydisperse genome

Iridoviridae
   Iridovirus, small iridescent virus
   Chloriridovirus, large iridescent virus

Parvoviridae
   Densovirus, densonucleosis virus

Reoviridae
   Cytoplasmic polyhedrosis virus

Bisegmented dsRNA viruses
   Drosophila X virus

Rhabdoviridae
   Lyssavirus Group, sigma virus, CO_2 sensitivity virus

Picornaviridae
   Bee acute paralysis virus
   Bee slow paralysis virus
   Bee virus X
   Cricket paralysis virus
   Drosophila C virus, A virus, P virus
   Flacherie 1 virus
   Gonometa virus
   Kashmir bee virus
   Sacbrood virus

Caliciviridae
   Calicivirus, Amyelois chronic stunt virus

Nudaurelia β virus Group

Nodaviridae
   Nodavirus, Nodamura virus
   Arkansas bee virus
   Black beetle virus

Unclassified viruses
   Bee chronic paralysis virus
   Bee filamentous virus
   Crystalline array virus

dioxide sensitivity in Drosophila flies, serves as an excellent
model for studies on the hereditary (or vertical) transmission of
animal viruses.
Some groups of entomopathogenic viruses are capable of
causing severe epizootic diseases in insect populations. We
consider these viruses excellent natural pest control agents if
the host insects are destructive species. Natural epizootics of
viral diseases are known to have terminated outbreaks of major
forest pests, such as the nun moth in Europe and the Douglas-fir
tussock moth in the United States.
This paper will focus on the baculoviruses (family
Baculoviridae), a group of viruses reported as pathogens of many
destructive insect species affecting agricultural and forest
production. I will emphasize the role of these pathogens as
introduced microbial insecticides or "living insecticides" (1).
The baculoviruses are known exclusively from arthropods
(Table II). The virions of the Baculoviridae consist of one or
more cylindrical nucleocapsids enclosed within an envelope. The
size of the nucleocapsids is 30-40 nm x 200-350 nm. The nucleic
acid is double stranded DNA of 58-100 x 10^6 dalton. The family
Baculoviridae has four subgroups (A, B, C, and D), characterized
by differences in genome structure, number of nucleocapsids per
virion, and presence or absence of crystalline inclusion bodies
(2).
The virions of subgroups A and B are occluded in a protein
matrix, whereas virions of subgroups C and D have no inclusion
bodies (Figure 1). Because the inclusions of subgroup A
frequently have a polyhedral shape, they are called polyhedral
inclusion bodies (PIB) or, simply, polyhedra; the disease caused
by these viruses is known as nuclear polyhedrosis or
nucleopolyhedrosis. The virions occluded in polyhedra can be
unicapsid (one nucleocapsid per envelope) or multicapsid (more
than one nucleocapsid per envelope, usually from two to seven,
rarely more).
The inclusion bodies of subgroup B are ovoid or cylindrical
with rounded ends and contain a single virion, usually unicapsid
(virions with two nucleocapsids occur rarely). Subgroup B
inclusion bodies are called capsules and the disease caused by
subgroup B baculoviruses is known as granulosis (Figure 1).
In nature, Baculovirus infections (subgroups A, B, and C) are
acquired when insect larvae ingest the virions, along with food,
although under experimental conditions the virus can also be
injected directly into the hemocoel. Transmission of viruses of
subgroup D is probably vertical, through the egg. When occluded
viruses are ingested, the inclusion body protein is solubilized
in the alkaline milieu of the midgut and the virions are soon
released in the midgut lumen. Nucleocapsids penetrate midgut
cells by fusion of the viral envelope with microvilli. A first
cycle of replication begins in midgut cell nuclei. In the
Hymenoptera (sawflies), replication and polyhedron formation

Table II. Host Range of Baculovirus[a]

Baculovirus subgroup	Class	Order	Number of host species
A	CRUSTACEA	Decapoda	2
	INSECTA[b]	Trichoptera	1
		Neuroptera[c]	2
		Diptera	22
		Hymenoptera[d]	26
		Lepidoptera	355
B	INSECTA[e]	Lepidoptera	113
C	INSECTA	Coleoptera	6
D	INSECTA	Hymenoptera[f]	31

[a] From Martignoni and Iwai (26) and from additional entries in MART-FAM computer files (11).

[b] Certain reports indicate Baculovirus subgroup A associated with 4 species of Coleoptera. Since the evidence presented in the reports is incomplete, the host records are not included in this table.

[c] These insects are susceptible in the laboratory to infection with Lymantria dispar NPV. However, there are no records of Baculovirus naturally occurring in neuropteran populations.

[d] Found only in sawflies (suborder Symphyta).

[e] One report indicates Baculovirus subgroup B associated with one species of Hymenoptera. Since the evidence presented in the report is incomplete, the host record is not included in this table.

[f] Found only in braconids and ichneumons.

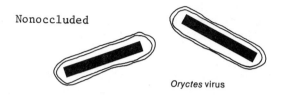

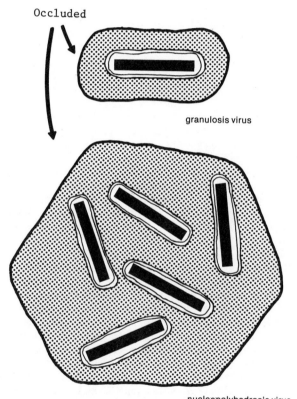

Figure 1. <u>Baculovirus</u> morphotypes. The cylindrical, electron-dense nucleocapsids are about 1/3 micrometer in length. Diagrammatic.

continue in the midgut: the midgut epithelium is the principal
tissue for initial replication as well as polyhedron formation.
In the Lepidoptera, inclusion bodies are not usually formed in
this organ. Progeny virions are released in the hemocoel (viremic
phase), although in some instances enveloped nucleocapsids can
pass directly from the gut to the hemocoel, without a midgut
replication cycle.

Nuclear polyhedrosis viruses or NPVs (subgroup A) replicate
exclusively in cell nuclei. In addition to midgut epithelium,
other tissues affected in the Lepidoptera are fat body, tracheal
epithelium, and epidermis. Hemocytes and silk glands are also
affected in some instances.

Viruses of subgroup B replicate initially in the nuclei and,
later, also in the cytoplasm. Midgut and fat body are the
principal tissues affected, but replication can occur also in
hemocytes, tracheal epithelium, and epidermis.

Nuclei of the fat body are the principal site of replication
of subgroup C baculoviruses. Subgroup D baculoviruses replicate
in nuclei of calyx epithelial cells, in the ovaries of parasitic
Hymenoptera.

Baculovirus diseases (with the exception of subgroup D)
affect mostly the immature stages of insects, particularly
larvae. The infected larvae become sluggish and feed less than
healthy larvae or cease to feed altogether. Usually, this occurs
during the early phase of the disease, but in some hosts (e.g.,
larvae of the gypsy moth) sluggishness and cessation of feeding
are not evident until shortly before death. In the Lepidoptera,
as the disease progresses the chitinous integument becomes
fragile and is easily ruptured. When this happens, usually soon
after death of the sick larvae, high titers of virus are released
in the environment.

Diseases caused by baculoviruses are usually fatal. Nuclear
polyhedrosis is an acute disease with a short, rapid course.
Incubation is from 2 to 3 days at 25 to 30° C, and death occurs
3 to 6 days after appearance of the first symptoms and signs.
Under field conditions, with lower night temperatures, death
is delayed up to 15 days after ingestion of the pathogen.
Granulosis (subgroup B) and diseases caused by nonoccluded
viruses have, in general, a less rapid, subacute course.

A study of the N-terminal amino acid sequence of inclusion
body proteins of Baculovirus subgroups A and B suggests that
these viruses have an ancient association with their host insects
and may have evolved with them (3). The large number of
lepidopteran NPVs and the close genetic relatedness of their
polyhedron proteins indicate that Baculovirus divergence occurred
while the Lepidoptera underwent extensive speciation during their
40-60 million years of existence.

In the remaining pages I shall discuss in greater detail the
NPVs and their applications in biological control of insect
pests. These viruses have been studied intensively during the

last 3 decades, and interest in them has increased substantially
since 1961, when U.S. scientists began practical development of
the NPV of the bollworm, Heliothis zea, an economically important
pest of cotton (4). Several baculoviruses were produced at
pilot-plant and commercial-scale levels during the last 10 years.
Four of these viruses, with proved efficacy against the target
pests, are currently registered in the United States: ELCAR,
registered in 1973 by Sandoz, Inc., for use against the bollworm,
Heliothis zea, and the tobacco budworm, Heliothis virescens;
TM BIOCONTROL-1, registered in 1976 by the U.S. Forest Service,
for use against the Douglas-fir tussock moth, Orgyia
pseudotsugata; GYPCHEK, registered in 1978, by the Forest
Service, for use against the gypsy moth, Lymantria dispar; and
NEOCHEK-S, registered in 1983, also by the Forest Service, for
use against the European pine sawfly, Neodiprion sertifer. In
1982, Sandoz, Inc., applied for and was granted an experimental
use permit for SAN 404 I WDC, the NPV of the alfalfa looper,
Autographa californica, for field tests against the Douglas-fir
tussock moth.
    Additional NPVs have reached the stage of commercial
production in other countries as well, e.g. the United Kingdom,
Finland, the U.S.S.R., and the People's Republic of China.
    Baculovirus formulations are applied in much the same way as
chemical insecticides, i.e., in suitable tank mixes (with
additives that make the virus amenable to spraying and protect
the spray deposits) and with the usual aerial or ground spray
equipment. When target insects feed on sprayed foliage and
ingest a droplet containing the virus, they become infected and
die. Larvae killed by the spray deposits are a source of viral
inoculum for a second passage that will eventually control the
population of the target host (5).

What makes the NPVs so attractive as pest control agents?

    1. Based on our present knowledge, we can safely state that
NPVs occur only in arthropods and that individual NPVs or NPV
strains have a very limited host range (6, 7). NPVs that have
been certified for use as insecticides do not interact with
non-target organisms in forest or agricultural ecosystems. Only
selected host insects are infected and killed; insect predators
and parasites are not harmed by these selective biological
insecticides. Very few NPVs (some isolated from members of the
family Noctuidae) have a relatively wide host range (they infect
species from several families within one order). Most other NPVs
are highly host specific (one host species only) or have a narrow
host range (two or more closely related species from one genus or
one family of insects).
    2. Unlike many chemical insecticides, the NPVs used as
biological insecticides do not contaminate the environment. They
are a superb nonpolluting, biodegradable insecticide. In most

applications in water-based formulations, the amount of pure
inclusion bodies deposited on each acre of forest or agricultural
crop has been one-half to three grams. Rain and melting snow
wash this small amount of organic matter into the duff layer or
the soil, where it is slowly denatured (low soil pH may
accelerate the process). Most of the PIBs that remain above
ground are inactivated by ultraviolet radiation (8).
    3. The effect of a single NPV application can be extended by
natural horizontal and vertical transmission of the pathogen
within the host population. This may affect several generations
of the insect after the pathogen has been introduced in the
host's ecosystem. Furthermore, when adult insects are carriers
of NPV, geographic spread of the disease over several miles has
been observed after introduction of a virus (9).
    4. Packaged as a commercial product, NPVs have a remarkable
shelf life. The occluded virions, within the protective
inclusion-body protein, are among the most stable entomopathogens,
compared with other microorganisms and microparasites, such as
bacteria, fungi, protozoa, and nematodes. In the laboratory,
lyophilized, frozen, or simply refrigerated NPV inclusion bodies,
stored in darkness, remain active for many years, even decades
(8, 10, 11). Only the spores and toxins of certain bacteria
(such as Bacillus thuringiensis, an insect pathogen) have a
comparable shelf life.
    As soon as research results show conclusively that a
Baculovirus is a safe and effective biological insecticide and a
candidate for further development, two important questions must
be answered: a) Can the virus be produced in large scale and at
an acceptable cost, and b) What are the most suitable methods for
potency standardization of the final commercial product?

Virus Propagation

Viruses reproduce exclusively within living cells. Therefore,
successful mass propagation of viruses is linked to successful
mass production of susceptible host cells. Cells are available
in living host organisms or in vitro, as explants or as
established cultured cell lines. At the present time we do not
possess the industrial cell-culture technology needed to produce
baculoviruses in commercial quantities and at a cost comparable
with that of other innovative pesticides. Based on propagation
technology, production cost, and capital investment, living
whole insect larvae are currently the preferred substrate for
production of NPV and other baculoviruses (12, 13).
    NPV production in a susceptible host insect is a relatively
simple process, suitable for development at the industrial scale
or at the "cottage industry" level. There are several
particularly attractive small-scale production processes in
modest facilities: a good example is a production process for
the NPV of the cabbage looper, Trichoplusia ni, with an output of

2 kg of virus-killed larvae per week (14). Small-scale
production of five baculoviruses has been achieved, with good
results, in agricultural communes in the People's Republic of
China (15, 16). These production methods are suitable for
viruses to be used locally rather than marketed regionwide or
nationwide. This type of production may prove particularly
successful in the less mechanized, developing countries.

Industrial production, on the other hand, requires a high
degree of mechanization and automation. For obvious reasons, not
all details of Baculovirus production have been made public by the
industry, but adequate general descriptions of the process are
available (4, 13, 17, 18). The ideal host species is not
fastidious. It can be reared in large numbers on a simple
artificial diet, does not undergo diapause under laboratory
conditions, and has a short generation time. Unfortunately, not
all baculoviruses can be propagated in an ideal host! By
selection techniques, however, it is possible to extend the host
range of certain baculoviruses to include a technically and
economically acceptable production host (19).

The production costs vary considerably and are determined
principally by the cost of rearing the insect species used for
virus propagation. This can account for one-third to two-thirds
of the total production cost. Table III lists some recent cost
estimates for baculoviruses produced in industrial quantities.

A large market, a large product margin, and low research and
development costs are essential to profitability in a production
venture. At first glance, these would not appear to be the
attributes of a Baculovirus production venture. A critical
economic feasibility study by Stanford Research Institute (20)
shows, however, that it could be possible to make this venture
economically attractive on an expected value basis if research
and development were performed or subsidized by an outside agency
(such as governments or growers). The concept that taxpayers
should share the risk of developing environmentally more
desirable—but also more expensive—insecticides has been
analyzed in detail (21). The Federal Government, for instance,
fully supported development of TM BIOCONTROL-1. The Forest
Service performed or subsidized all needed research and
development, including safety evaluation and field efficacy tests
(5, 13).

Potency Standardization

Until recently, the polyhedral inclusion body has been used
conveniently as the "unit" of potency of NPV preparations. Thus,
in the United States, the potency of preparations of NPV of
Heliothis spp. was expressed in "viral units" (1 VU = 10^9 PIB),
in "larval equivalents" (1 LE = 6 VU = 6 x 10^9 PIB), or simply
in billions (10^9) PIB per unit weight or volume of the
preparation. The reproducibility of PIB counts, however, is

Table III.   Costs of Selected Baculovirus Preparations

Virus	Year Computed	Cost[a] per Hectare Dose $ (US)	Literature Reference
NPV of Heliothis spp.	1977	4.45 (P)	20
NPV of Orgyia pseudotsugata	1977	10.93 (M)	13
NPV of Neodiprion sertifer	1978	11.00 (P)	9
NPV of Lymantria dispar	1981	8.65 (M)	18
NPV of Heliothis spp.	1981	7.70 (P)	27
NPV of Orgyia pseudotsugata	1983	42.00 (M)	28

[a]   M, manufacturing cost only (insect rearing, processing, quality control, packaging).

P, plant price (manufacturing cost plus product margin).

known to be poor, especially when one is dealing with technical grade preparations. Variations in counts among operators and among laboratories are large. Because of different storage conditions (packaging, shipping, moisture, temperature, age), PIB counts cannot be used reproducibly as a measure of the killing activity of industrial preparations. Microscopic examinations cannot distinguish fully active from partially active or inactive viral inclusion bodies. Furthermore, there can be considerable variations in polyhedron-to-bioactivity ratios among production batches of a viral product.

To remedy this situation, several procedures have been proposed for standardizing the biological activity of industrial NPV preparations. The U.S. Environmental Protection Agency (22) requires that quantification of Baculovirus preparations "... must be based on bioassays."

Technically, there are two approaches (23) to NPV potency standardization:

    i. Use of standard (reference) preparations, and
    ii. Use of standard response.

i. Adoption of a standard preparation, to be compared with a preparation of unknown activity, is a prerequisite of comparative biological assay. This approach is used for standardization of Heliothis NPV products. Ignoffo (24) proposed a standard preparation of Heliothis NPV and defined an "inclusion insecticidal unit" (IIU) as 2.7 PIB of reference standard/mm^2 of available diet surface, in a prescribed diet-surface treatment assay.

The design of comparative assays requires that the standard preparation and preparations with unknown activity be compared within tests. Thus, the reference standard must be available in sufficient quantity for distribution to testing laboratories and must have a certified level of activity that remains stable for a period of years.

ii. The response of a population of susceptible test insects, in a standardized bioassay, can be used as a reference standard. The response standard is valid only if the test insects are as uniform as possible genetically and if the assays are repeated under the same conditions and with identical materials as those used in the original experiments. Such a procedure has been adopted for the standardization of TM BIOCONTROL-1. Martignoni and Iwai (25) used as a reference standard the response of an inbred strain (GL-1) of O. pseudotsugata established from eggs collected in 1965 near Goose Lake in northern California and propagated since then on a meridic diet. This strain is now in its 23rd laboratory generation.

The response stability of this insect strain is monitored by means of two internal standard preparations. The response of insect strain GL-1 has remained stable since 1975 (11, 25).

Strain GL-1 is maintained in continuous rearing at the Forestry
Sciences Laboratory in Corvallis, and eggs of this strain are
supplied to other laboratories for potency standardization of
viral products.

Concluding Remarks

During the past two decades research has demonstrated that
baculoviruses, in particular NPVs, are effective insecticides.
They are host specific and thus environmentally safe agents. To
this date, no Baculovirus has been found to replicate in
vertebrate organisms.
      Baculoviruses are among the most stable entomopathogens when
we consider their long shelf life as a suitably packaged and
stored commercial product. On the other hand, these viruses are
rapidly inactivated and denatured when sprayed on forests and
agricultural crops, unless protected against inactivating agents.
      The potency of commercial Baculovirus products can be
standardized by means of biological assay. Two procedures are
available and both are acceptable to manufacturers and the
Environmental Protection Agency.
      The production of baculoviruses is technically and
economically feasible in living host organisms, at the commercial
plant level or as a modest "cottage industry." The cost of
commercial production of some viral insecticides is still
relatively high, but a Baculovirus production venture could
become financially attractive if appropriate government agencies
would share research and development costs with the industry.

Literature Cited

1. Steinhaus, E. A. Sci. Am. 1956, 195, 96-104.
2. Matthews, R. E. F. Intervirology 1982, 17, 1-199.
3. Rohrmann, G. F.; Pearson, M. N.; Bailey, T. J.; Becker,
    R. R.; Beaudreau, G. S. J. Mol. Evol. 1981, 17, 329-33.
4. Ignoffo, C. M. Exp. Parasitol. 1973, 33, 380-406.
5. Stelzer, M.; Neisess, J.; Cunningham, J. C.; McPhee, J. R.
    J. Econ. Entomol. 1977, 70, 243-6.
6. Ignoffo, C. M. Proc. Sec. Conf. Proj. 5, Microbiol. Control
    Insect Pests, US/USSR Jt. Work. Group Prod. Subst.
    Microbiol. Means, Am. Soc. Microbiol.: Washington, D.C.,
    1980; pp. 162-75.
7. Miltenburger, H. G. In "Environmental Protection and
    Biological Control of Pest Organisms"; Lundholm, B.;
    Stackerud, M., Eds.; Ecol. Bull. 1980, 31, 57-74.
8. Jaques, R. P. In "Environmental Stability of Microbial
    Insecticides"; Ignoffo, C. M.; Hostetter, D. L., Eds.;
    Misc. Publ. Entomol. Soc. Am. 1977, 10, 99-116.
9. Cunningham, J. C.; Entwistle, P. F. In "Microbial Control
    of Pests and Plant Diseases 1970-1980"; Burges, H. D., Ed.;
    Academic Press: London, 1981; pp. 379-407.

10. Steinhaus, E. A. J. Insect Pathol. 1960, 2, 225-9.
11. Martignoni, M. E., unpublished data.
12. Ignoffo, C. M.; Hink, W. F. In "Microbial Control of Insects and Mites"; Burges, H. D.; Hussey, N. W., Eds.; Academic Press: London, 1971; pp. 541-80.
13. Martignoni, M. E. In "The Douglas-Fir Tussock Moth: a Synthesis"; Brookes, M. H.; Stark, R. W.; Campbell, R. W., Eds.; U.S. Dep. Agric. 1978; Tech. Bull. 1585, pp. 140-7.
14. Lawson, F. R.; Headstrom, R. L. In "Facilities for Insect Research and Production"; Leppla, N. C.; Ashley, T. R., Eds.; U.S. Dep. Agric. 1978; Tech. Bull. 1576, pp. 37-9.
15. Franz, J. M.; Krieg, A. Forum Mikrobiol. 1980, 173-6.
16. Hussey, N. W.; Tinsley, T. W. In "Microbial Control of Pests and Plant Diseases 1970-1980"; Burges, H. D., Ed.; Academic Press: London, 1981; pp. 785-95.
17. Ignoffo, C. M.; Anderson, R. F. In "Microbial Technology"; Peppler, H. J.; Perlman, D., Eds.; Academic Press: New York, 1979; 2nd Ed., Vol. I, pp. 1-28.
18. Shapiro, M.; Bell, R. A.; Owens, C. D. In "The Gypsy Moth: Research Toward Integrated Pest Management"; Doane, C. C.; McManus, M. L., Eds.; U. S. Dep. Agric. 1981; Tech. Bull. 1584, pp. 633-55.
19. Shapiro, M.; Martignoni, M. E.; Cunningham, J. C.; Goodwin, R. H. J. Econ. Entomol. 1982, 75, 69-71.
20. Blue, T. A., Ed. "New, Innovative Pesticides: an Evaluation of Incentives and Disincentives for Commercial Development by Industry"; Stanford Research Institute: Menlo Park, 1977; 318 p.
21. Djerassi, C.; Shih-Coleman, C.; Diekman, J. Science 1974, 186, 596-607.
22. U.S. Environmental Protection Agency. In "Baculoviruses for Insect Pest Control: Safety Considerations"; Summers, M.; Engler, R.; Falcon, L. A.; Vail, P. V., Eds.; Am. Soc. Microbiol.: Washington, D.C., 1975; pp. 179-84.
23. Martignoni, M. E.; Ignoffo, C. M. Proc. Sec. Conf. Proj. 5, Microbiol. Control Insect Pests, US/USSR Jt. Work. Group Prod. Subst. Microbiol. Means, Am. Soc. Microbiol.: Washington, D.C., 1980; pp. 138-53.
24. Ignoffo, C. M. J. Invertebr. Pathol. 1966, 8, 547-8.
25. Martignoni, M. E.; Iwai, P. J. J. Econ. Entomol. 1978, 71, 473-6.
26. Martignoni, M. E.; Iwai, P. J. In "Microbial Control of Pests and Plant Diseases 1970-1980"; Burges, H. D., Ed.; Academic Press: London, 1981; pp. 897-911.
27. Ignoffo, C. M.; Couch, T. L. In "Microbial Control of Pests and Plant Diseases 1970-1980"; Burges, H. D., Ed.; Academic Press: London, 1981; pp. 329-62.
28. Scott, D. W., personal communication.

RECEIVED September 9, 1983

Integrated Pest Management (IPM) in Forestry

JOHN NEISESS

U.S. Department of Agriculture, Forest Pest Management, P.O. Box 2417, Washington, DC
20013

Until about 10 years ago, pest management in forestry was
practiced much like fire management. When insects, diseases,
pocket gophers, competing vegetation, or other pests increased to
outbreak levels, forest managers geared up and put the so-called
fire out. However, over the past few years, forest managers have
been changing their pest management philosophy from a reliance on
direct suppression of pests when they reach damaging levels to an
integrated (or IPM) approach to preventing or reducing the
resource damage caused by pests.

In 1980, an evaluation of Forest Service pest management
programs by the Center for Natural Areas concluded that even
though forest managers did not fully understand IPM terminology
and policies, they were doing an adequate job of implementing the
concepts of IPM, but calling it something else.

What Is IPM?

The Forest Service Manual defines IPM as "a systematic decisionmaking process and the resultant management actions which derive
from considerations of pest-host systems and evaluation of
alternatives for managing pest populations at levels consistent
with resource management objectives." In other words, IPM
consists of two basic elements: the decisionmaking process and
the action program.

The decision process begins with the detection of the pest and
evaluation of its impact on the resource. Detection and
evaluation usually involve site visits by resource or pest
management specialists to determine the density of the pest and
the condition of the site. Aerial photography and pheromone
trapping have improved detection of insect pests. Pheromone traps
are currently being used to help monitor the building Douglas-fir
tussock moth (*Orgyia pseudotsugata* (McDunnough)) populations
in the Northwest.

Early detection permits different action programs than are
used when a pest population reaches outbreak proportions. In 1977,

for example, the Forest Service initiated a project to determine
if early treatment of western spruce budworm (*Choristoneura
occidentalis* Freeman) would reduce the budworm to such a level
that subsequent treatment would not be needed. Measurements of
egg mass densities for 6 years in treated versus untreated areas
have shown the success of this early treatment strategy (Figure 1).
    The decisionmaking process also identifies the resource
management objective and evaluates the cost of pest control
schemes and their impacts on the various resources associated with
the site. The pest control scheme must be compatible with the
overall management and economics of the resources being managed.
An insect outbreak, therefore, would not be controlled on a site
being managed for wildlife if the reduction in the timber resource
improved the site for wildlife without greatly damaging other
resource values.
    The action program consists of a mixture of prevention and
direct suppression activities. Prevention includes those
activities that make the forest less conducive to pest outbreaks.
Direct suppression may involve one or more control tactics
directed at the pest itself. Biological or chemical pesticides,
mechanical methods, use of parasites, and fire are a few of the
available tactics. For example, alternatives used to control
mountain pine beetle (*Dendroctonus ponderosae* Hopkins) in an
IPM program include the following prevention and direct
suppression alternatives: (1) Do nothing, (2) Silvicultural
control to maintain a vigorous stand, (3) Direct control
accomplished by felling and removing infested trees or by felling
and burning or chemically treating infested trees, or (4)
Protective spraying of high-value trees with insecticides.
    Note that chemical pesticides are very much a part of IPM. In
a fully implemented IPM program, however, chemical use patterns
may change because of early detection, which could reduce the
amounts of pesticides used.

Examples of IPM in Forestry

An IPM program undertaken around Dillon, Colorado, in 1982,
exemplifies the combination of treatments used to manage a
mountain pine beetle outbreak in lodgepole pine. Direct
suppression and preventive spraying were important to the Dillon
project because of the high recreational values. But these
activities were only intended to limit immediate tree losses and
allow time to implement cultural or silvicultural treatments.
More than 87,000 infested trees on State, private, and Federal
lands in the Dillon area were either cut and removed or cut and
treated with lindane or ethylene dibromide (Table I). The cut
timber was made available to the public as fuelwood. Slash
disposal was also implemented on 39,000 acres in order to reduce
the possibility of engraver beetle (*Ips* spp.) buildup in the
slash resulting from salvage operations. Carbaryl was applied as

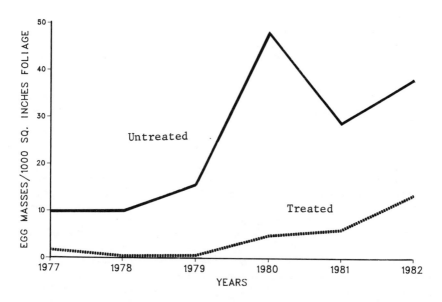

Figure 1. Comparison of average number of western spruce budworm egg masses in treated and untreated areas, New Mexico.

a preventive spray on 26,000 high-value trees in campgrounds and recreational areas. This preventive spraying will be continued in high-use areas while the outbreak persists.

Table I. Mixture of treatment strategies used in the 1982 Dillon, Colorado, IPM project to control mountain pine beetle

Treatment	Units Treated
MPB trees felled/removed	18,455 trees
MPB trees felled/insecticide treated	68,953 trees
Preventive spraying	26,000 trees
Thinning	54 acres
Slash disposal	3,940 acres

The main effort on Forest Service lands will be directed at the 32,000 acres of pine that have been identified as susceptible to beetles and on operable terrain. Plans call for harvesting of the mature and overmature susceptible pines over a 15- to 30-year period. In order to limit the impact on the recreational and esthetic qualities, small clearcuts and patch cuts will be the common treatment used to break up the large continuous areas of susceptible trees into smaller areas. Immature stands will be thinned to prevent stagnation and reduce future susceptiblity.

An action program such as the one around Dillon is based on current knowledge about the pest and its host; research and knowledge are key components in IPM. The role of the pest in the forest ecosystem must be understood when making management prescriptions, and resource managers must be able to predict the effects of various management practices on pest organisms, desired plants, and the environment. It is important to understand that if a pest is treated directly without considering the cause of the outbreak, the pest may reappear once the treatment is finished. If the cause is treated, however, the result will generally be long-term protection.

In developing guidelines for controlling mountain pine beetle, pest management specialists drew on their knowledge of several important biological facts about the beetle and its interactions with the host trees: (1) The mountain pine beetle kills proportionally more large diameter trees than small diameter trees during an infestation, (2) Beetle reproduction is directly related to phloem thickness, (3) Phloem is usually thicker in large diameter trees, and (4) Infestations seldom develop in stands less

than 60 to 80 years of age. Although they disagree about the
effects of stand density on potential beetle outbreaks, most pest
management specialists believe that overstocked, stagnated stands
are more susceptible to beetle attack than vigorous stands.

Another key component to fully implementing IPM in forestry is
integrating pest management into forest management decisionmaking.
This requires resource managers to accept greater responsibility
for pest prevention in their normal activities. Guidelines for
preventing pest outbreaks need to be developed and then used by
the resource managers as they develop and implement management
plans or set priorities for sites needing treatment.

One example where pest prevention is being considered by the
forest manager is the control of dwarf mistletoe (*Arceuthobium*
spp.). Pest management specialists have done their part by
including the understanding of the basic biology and pest/host
relationships into control guidelines so that silviculturists can
determine the severity of an infection in a stand.

When dealing with dwarf mistletoe, the guidelines call for six
action alternatives: (1) No action, (2) Conversion to nonhost
species, (3) Clearcut, (4) Seed tree cuts with subsequent removal
of seed trees, (5) Complete sanitation, or (6) Partial sanitation
which reduces but does not eliminate the pest. Each of these
alternatives is evaluated by the manager in light of the
information about severity of the infestation and basic stand
information (age, stocking density, composition, and growth
potential), the management objective, and the economics of the
situation. Pest management specialists have made the
decisionmaking easier by incorporating the growth impacts of dwarf
mistletoe into a number of models used to predict timber yields.
Given specific stand conditions, these models allow the manager to
predict tree growth following various treatment alternatives.
Generally, one or more of these treatment alternatives can be
accomplished within normal silvicultural practices. Sanitation
cuttings, for example, can be combined with planned thinning or
timber stand improvement operations.

Although research has provided a great deal of knowledge about
pests, and pest management is being integrated into resource
management, many unanswered questions remain. More research is
needed in pest/host relationships and the impact and interactions
of various treatment alternatives. The knowledge base for
implementing an integrated vegetation management program is a case
in point. Research has provided a great deal of information about
the basic biology of the individual crop trees and brush species.
However, little is known about the competitive ability of various
types of vegetative cover. And other than information on the
effects of herbicides, little information exists on the
environmental impacts of direct or cultural treatments or on the
comparative benefits of these treatments. These technical
limitations mean that decisions to control competing vegetation
are generally based on the experience of the manager and are often

made only after the impacts of competing vegetation are clearly evident and some loss in growth or seedling survival has occurred.
    Although the knowledge base for an integrated vegetation management program is limited, much has been learned and put into practice. The manager has a number of direct treatment alternatives, which include using herbicides, mechanical removal, hand cutting or grubbing, burning, as well as doing nothing. Vegetation management specialists have also learned to identify potential weed problems and to prescribe cultural or indirect treatments that may reduce the need for direct treatment. Cultural practices important to an integrated vegetation management program include use of larger, more vigorous growing stock to hasten reforestation, use of shade-tolerant species on sites where competing vegetation is a problem, and shortening the time between harvesting and planting so that the site does not become occupied with brush.
    The treatments used on the Willamette National Forest in Oregon during 1982 to control competing vegetation exemplify the Forest Service effort to integrate the various alternatives in site preparation and release programs (Table II).

Table II. Selected vegetation management alternatives used on the Willamette National Forest, Oregon, 1982

Treatment	Acres
Heavy machinery	123
Hand cutting	320
Hand cutting/burning	162
Hand cutting/herbicide	1,448
Hand pulling and grubbing	463
Herbicides	
Aerial	2,337
Hand	761
No treatment	1,247

    Another problem with implementing IPM in forestry is a reluctance of resource managers to heed the warnings and recommendations of pest management specialists. The current outbreaks of mountain pine beetle typify this reluctance. Most of the stands currently under attack are in areas of the country that have been managed primarily for recreation or wildlife values, not timber production. Therefore, managers have naturally been reluctant to locate clearcuts in areas around ski resorts or favorite camping areas, even though the entomologists predicted

that the unmanaged stands were becoming "beetle bait." Programs
like the Dillon mountain pine beetle project are slowly turning
this reluctance around.

In conclusion, the management of dwarf mistletoe, mountain
pine beetle, and competing vegetation shows that IPM has achieved
some success at becoming a proven option in pest management. IPM
offers indepth evaluations of conditions that cause pest problems
and action programs that are long lasting and environmentally
acceptable. Large advances have been made in integrating pest
management into normal resource management practices, but progress
will continue to be slow. The intensive management required to
prevent pest outbreaks is being practiced on only limited acreage.
As long as our country continues to have vast acres of unmanaged
stands, forest resource managers will still have to rely on direct
treatments to control the damage caused by pest outbreaks. In
these cases, our IPM efforts will be limited to earlier detection
methods and integrated direct suppression when needed.

RECEIVED September 9, 1983

SPRAY DEPOSITION

Technological Progress in Aerial Application of Pesticides

ROBERT B. EKBLAD

U.S. Department of Agriculture, Forest Service, Equipment Development Center, Missoula, MT 59802

JOHN W. BARRY

U.S. Department of Agriculture, Forest Service, Forest Pest Management, Davis, CA 95616

Previous analyses of problems in applying pesticides to forests by aircraft are briefly reviewed. Emphasis is on problems related to meteorological sciences. Several new developments that enhance efforts to minimize drift are described. Models that predict near field effects of aircraft and mesoscale winds are available. The need for additional efforts to describe flow within canopy and description of conditions for inertial deposition on target elements is outlined.

Problems of Wildland Spraying

Let's begin with a brief review of the problems facing the aerial applicator and how we have organized the problems to solve them. The problems are illustrated in figures 1A through

Forest spraying presents many problems not found in normal agricultural spraying:

- Because of the concentrating effect of mountain valleys and canyons, significant concentrations of insecticides can be carried several miles (Figure 1A).
- Instead of falling a few feet as in the case of agricultural spraying, forest insecticides must travel 50 to 150 feet vertically to reach a target. Losses, due to evaporation, become more significant both in terms of greater drift and loss of insecticide (Figure 1B).
- The dense forest foliage may capture all of the insecticide within a few feet, resulting in only one side of the tree being sprayed (Figure 1C).
- On the other hand, the drops may be so small that they are deflected around the target by aerodynamic forces (Figure 1D).
- If the lateral displacement of the spray is excessive the applicator cannot predict where it will reach the forest and has lost effective control of the spray (Figure 1E).
- In his zeal to prevent excessive lateral displacement, the

applicator may select drops so large that too few numbers
of drops are available for effective coverage (Figure 1F).
- It is difficult to fly evenly spaced swaths over large,
  irregular tracts of forest having few roads or identifying
  boundaries (Figure 1G).
- Steep slopes present several problems. The actual surface
  area is greater than shown on a map; the downhill side of
  the boom may be 30 feet higher above the trees than the
  uphill side of the boom. Flight path and direction are
  limited to terrain contours because the aircraft cannot
  climb steep slopes (Figure 1H).
- Rough irregular terrain is usually associated with steep
  slopes. If the applicator flies a level path his altitude
  above the terrain varies continuously; if instead he follows
  the terrain, roller coaster fashion, his speed and
  application rate vary continuously (Figure 1I).
- In an effort to obtain better coverage, the applicator may
  increase the volume of insecticide carried without giving
  adequate consideration to the lethal drop size, requiring
  hundreds of drops to kill a larva rather than one drop
  (Figure 1J).
- The aircraft wake has a major influence on spray behavior.
- Small drops are entrained in this spray cloud and
  transported in a manner similar to smoke ring movement.
- Other larger drops fall independently of the vortex but are
  not readily visible. Thus, the applicator may be misled by
  observing the visible cloud (Figure 1K).
- In two hours of morning spraying, weather conditions
  usually vary from an inversion to neutral or unstable. The
  applicator may not be aware of these changes(Figure 1L).

An Approach to Organizing These Problems

This is a formidable array of problems, and it is a tribute to
aerial applicators that they carry on successful spray projects
despite these problems and lack of knowledge in some of the areas.
     We have devised a scheme to allow us to define each part of
the problem separately, yet consider all parts simultaneously.
     The effect of a droplet being carried so far away that it is
essentially beyond the applicator's control is shown in Figure 1.
Here we have a plot of droplet diameters versus wind speed above
the canopy. The shaded area to the left is where the drops would
be carried too far. We have somewhat arbitrarily chosen 1,000
feet as too far. In some curcumstances it would be more and in
some less. We see that there is an area on the right within which
the drops can be contained and an area to the left that we want
to avoid.
     Large droplets will not penetrate the canopy (Figure 2).
That is they will be filtered out by the first foliage
encountered and cannot be uniformly deposited throughout the

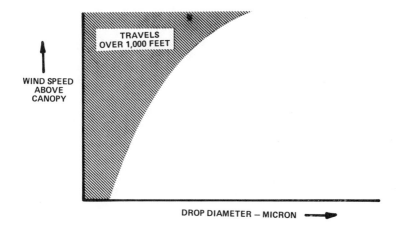

Figure 1. Excessive swath displacement.

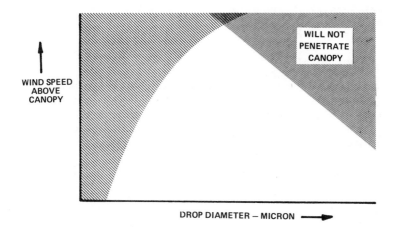

Figure 2. Drops too large to penetrate canopy.

canopy. In this case the permissible area is on the left. The
avoided area is on the right.

In Figure 3, we demonstrate the area in which sufficient
drops are not available to provide adequate coverage. This is
based, of course, on some reasonable amount of total volume of
material being delivered.

The relationship between wind speed and drop size for one
value of turbulence is shown in Figure 4.

The area where drops will not impinge on the target because
the wind speed is too low and the drops are too small is shown
in Figure 5. In this case the target could be either foliage
or insect.

In Figure 6 we show all of the curves on the same graph. In
the center is an area of useful drop sizes bounded by several
areas that are not useful. The range of useful drops can be
divided into two classes. The drops on the left side are so
small they are principally airborne. Their terminal falling
velocity is so low that they are carried wherever the wind and
aircraft wake take them. On the right side are the large drops
that are affected by air movements, but their arrival at the
target is primarily through gravitational settling.

This last figure demonstrates an approach to the entire
problem of predicting spray behavior where a multitude of factors
are involved and must be considered simultaneously. Other
factors, such as evaporation, also can be shown by adding another
axis or dimension to the graph.

What is also demonstrated is the complicating fact that the
physical behavior of the drops in the optimum range are governed
by two different sets of equations; one for the airborne
particles; another for the large particles subject primarily to
gravitational settling. This has led to the development of two
simulation models: AGDISP and FSCBG.

The AGDISP model is based on actually tracking the motion of
discrete particles. The dynamic equations governing the particle
trajectory are developed and integrated. The equations include
the influence of the aircraft dispersal system configuration,
aircraft wake turbulence, atmospheric turbulence, gravity, and
evaporation.

The FSCBG model is based on a line source that is given an
initial disturbance by the aircraft. The line source develops
into a spray cloud that is treated as a tilted Gaussian plume.
The equations track the mean position of the plume as well as rate
of change of its horizontal and vertical variance. Evaporation
effects are included.

Both models can be used independently to track spray from the
time of release until deposition. However, each model has a
range within which it provides the best accuracy and is the most
computationally efficient.

To link the two models for a complete picture of potential
spray behavior, a coupling code, AGLINE, has been developed.

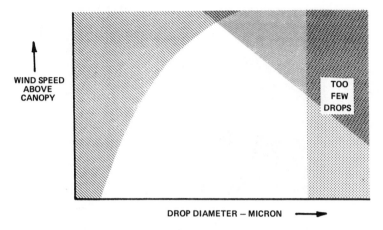

Figure 3.   Too few drops for coverage.

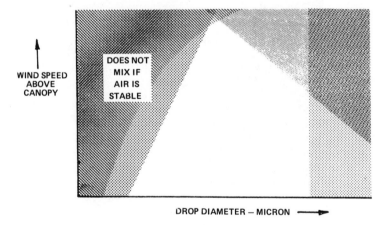

Figure 4.   Lack of turbulence affects deposition.

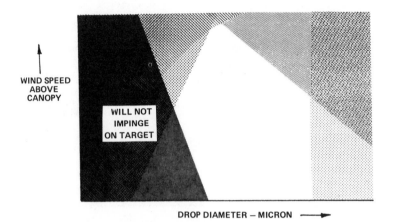

Figure 5.   Drops are deflected around target.

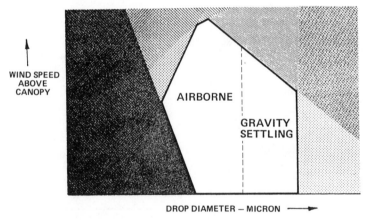

Figure 6.   Envelope of optimum drop size.

The AGDISP model is run until the released material becomes a
spray cloud. Then the FSCBG model uses the AGDISP predictions to
create a Gaussian plume model. This gives a complete predictive
code, accurate from the time of release until long after the
released material can be treated as a cloud. All important
forces influencing the evolution of the released material are
accounted for and the increase in computer time is nominal.
       Again, the two simulation models, AGDISP and FSCBG, can be
used independently or jointly with the coupling code, AGLINE.
       The principal outputs are deposition and drift, but the
models can be programmed to give intermediate information on
drop velocity, evaporation, flow fields, and other factors.
       Inputs to the models describe the aircraft, nozzle,
evaporation rate, meteorology, and biological environment.
Obtaining sufficiently accurate model inputs is as difficult
and challenging as developing the models themselves. The inputs
are estimated, measured, calculated, or selected.
       The relationship of the models' inputs and outputs are shown
in Figure 7. Major inputs concerning aircraft are fixed wing or
helicopter, speed, wing span, weight, wing loading, propeller
characteristics, and wake characteristics.
       The major inputs for the spray system are nozzle, droplet
distribution, number of nozzles, location of nozzles, and flow
rate. Obtaining an accurate description of the droplet
distribution at the aircraft has been difficult. Along with
other groups, the USDA Forest Service sponsored the development
of a wind tunnel and laser measuring device at the University of
California, Davis, Agricultural Engineering Department (Figure 8).
We can now routinely measure droplet size distribution at aircraft
speeds, as shown in Figure 9.
       The major evaporation inputs are temperature, relative
humidity, velocity, and evaporation rate. The evaporation rate
is estimated from mathematical models; for complex mixtures,
solutions, or suspensions, it is measured. The Forest Service
sponsored a project at Colorado State University's Aerosol
Sciences Laboratory to develop a laboratory method to measure
droplet evaporation rate.
       A schematic of the entire system is shown in Figure 10. It
is controlled by a microprocessor and measures evaporation rate
at controlled temperature and humidity while maintaining flow
past the droplet at terminal velocity corresponding to its
changing diameter. An example of results for three different
mixtures is shown in Figure 11.
       The AGDISP and FSCBG models accept the following
meteorological data: vertical wind speed and direction,
temperature profile, relative wind speed, turbulence, depth of
mixing layer, vertical profile of wind speed, vertical profile
of wind direction, effect of canopy, and effect of complex
terrain.
       Information on the biological environment needed for the

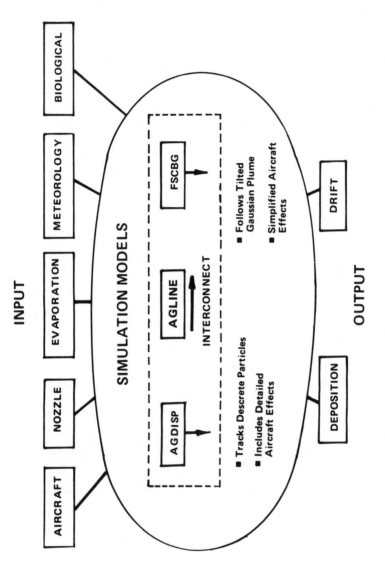

Figure 7. Model relationships.

Figure 8.   Wind tunnel with rotary nozzle.

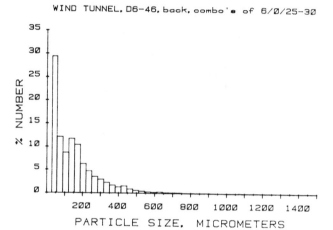

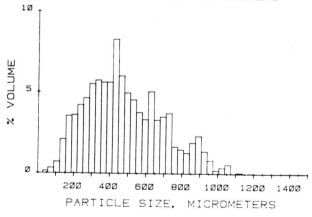

Figure 9.   Particle size distribution measured in wind tunnel.

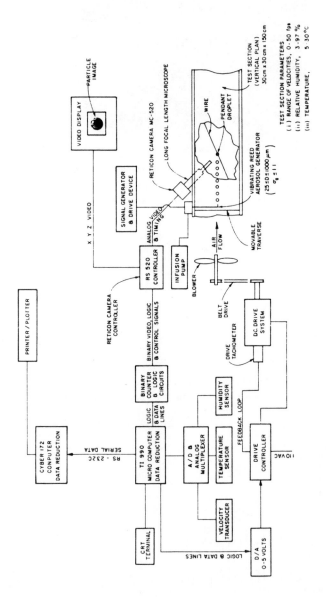

Figure 10. Schematic of data acquisition system for an evaporation rate facility.

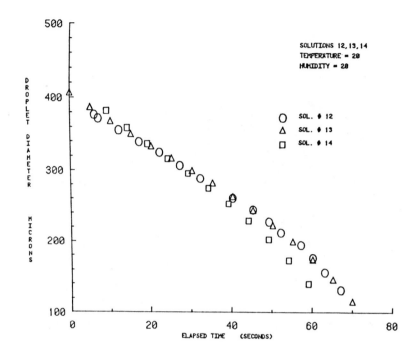

Figure 11. Evaporation rate of water droplets from solutions containing Nalco-Trol.

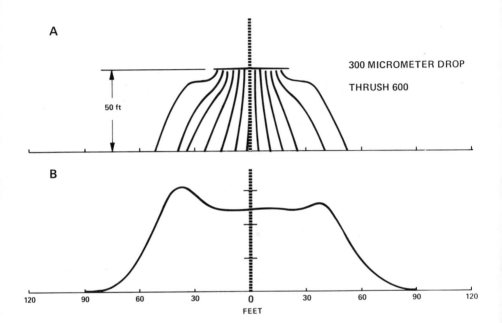

Figure 12.   Computer simulation of drop trajectory and deposit.

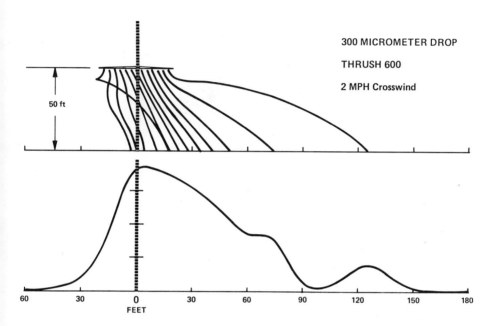

300 MICROMETER DROP

THRUSH 600

2 MPH Crosswind

50 ft

60   30   0   30   60   90   120   150   180

FEET

Figure 13.   Computer simulation with crosswind.

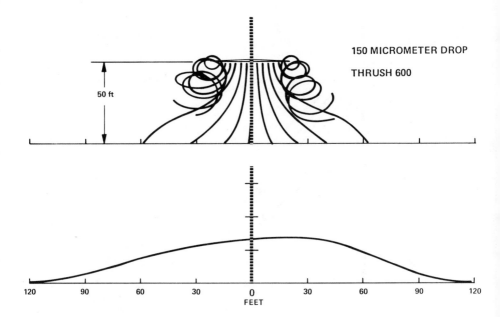

Figure 14.   Computer simulation of small drops.

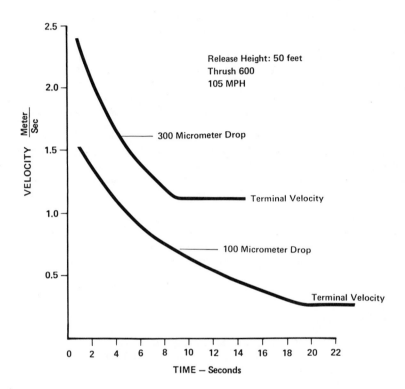

Figure 15.   Vertical drop velocity from wake effects.

models includes details of the forest type, terrain classification, and pesticide toxicity.

The FSCBG model is the older of the two models and has been
described in detail in various publications (1). The AGDISP model
is in the final stages of development and verification and will
be available this fall (2).

A graphic output of the AGDISP model is shown in Figure 12.
The trajectory of 300-micrometer droplets released from 13 nozzle
locations of a Thrush 600 airplane flying 105 mph at 50 feet
above the terrain is shown in Figure 12A. The ground deposition
of spray across the aircraft flight path is shown in Figure 12B.
The same configuration with a 2-mph crosswind is shown in
Figure 13. The same configuration without a crosswind but with
150-micrometer droplets, half the diameter of the droplets in
Figure 12 is given in Figure 14. This shows the droplet
entrainment in the wing tip vortices that aggravates the problem
of drift. An example of other information that is available
from the model is the droplet's vertical velocity (Figure 15).

We believe the major shortcoming of these models is
inadequate meteorological input. In particular we need better
descriptions of flow within the canopy and vertical flow profiles
generated by drainage flow rather than mesoscale winds. We also
need a fully operational three dimensional, complex terrain winds
model.

In summary, we now have models that account for all
important forces influencing the dispersion and deposit of
aerial sprays. We have estimates of inputs to make the models
useful to forest managers. Further improvement in model results,
particularly drift estimation, depends on better meteorological
input.

Literature Cited

1.   Dumbauld, R.K., Rafferty, J.E., and Bjourklund, J.R.,
     "Prediction of Spray Behavior Above and Within a Forest
     Canopy"; special report under contract 19-276. USDA For.
     Service, Pacific N.W. For. and Range Exp. Sta., Portland,
     Oreg., and For. Pest Management, Davis, Calif., 1977.
2.   Bilanin, A.J., Teske, M.E., and Morris, D.J., "Predicting
     Aerially Applied Deposition by Computer"; SAE Paper No.
     810607, April 1981.

RECEIVED September 9, 1983

Physical Parameters Affecting Aircraft Spray Application

NORMAN B. AKESSON and WESLEY E. YATES

Department of Agricultural Engineering, University of California, Davis, CA 95616

The several physical parameters affecting aircraft spray applications for (1) deposit in flagged swath, (2) deposit in extended downwind swath and (3) airborne portions of the released spray are discussed. The drop size spectrum (usually expressed as a volume median diameter) is the most significant factor affecting the spray movement. Drop size is most easily attained by using different type atomizers, or various sizes of a given type such as the hollow cone and fan series. The formulations used are custsomarily either a water base or an oil base. Considerable interest is being generated in vegetable oil sprays which are less phytotoxic to crop plants and trees than petroleum oils. Aircraft swath data and total recovery of deposited sprays as a percent of the released material are presented for a few selected systems and formulations.

Physical parameters which control the dispersion, deposit, coverage (of target plants) as well as drift losses of liquid pesticides released from aircraft in mountainous forest land are (1) spray drop size and spray formulation, (2) local meteorology, (3) local terrain at spray site and (4) type of application aircraft.

1. The transport phenomenon for any spray material released in the air is foremost a function of the particle size and size distribution of the released spray. The particle density plays a minor role, the settling rate from Stokes law for example varies as the square root of the density. Further, the density differences between liquids commonly used for pesticides is very little, varying only slightly from water at density of 1 gm/ml. Other formulation physical factors of surface tension, viscosity and viscoelasticity play significant roles in the atomization process. These are altered by the addition of petroleum and vegetable oil as solvents and carriers as well as a host of adjuvants in varying

0097–6156/84/0238–0095$06.50/0
© 1984 American Chemical Society

amounts of the total spray to 100% use of vegetable oils as
carriers for certain specific spray formulations. The vapor
pressure, or partial pressure of the various multi-phase formulations can affect the rate of vaporization loss of the finished
spray.

The atomizers may vary in design from hydraulic, and two-fluid
to spinning screen and disc types. The direction of the released
spray relative to the airstream and the airstream velocity
(aircraft velocity) relative to the liquid emission velocity also
play a fundamental role in the atomization process.

2. The local meteorology, principally the temperature and wind
velocity gradients from ground level, through the forest canopy to
the spray release height, and to 300 m (1000 ft) or more above the
release height, can have a dramatic effect on the spray dispersion
and deposit in the target area and can influence the drift losses
downwind for several miles. For instance, a temperature inversion
ceiling will prevent small drop size spray released below the
ceiling height from dispersing upward, thus having the characteristic of confining this spray and permitting it to concentrate
below the ceiling and be transported for considerable distances on
ambient winds. On the other hand, larger drops over 75 to 100
microns diameter are less affected by air motion and have sufficient fall velocity to deposit nearby, usually within 60 to 152
m (200 to 500 ft) of the release. For convenience we have
designated drops less than 100 microns diameter as being capable
of air transport for 1 to several miles while those above 100
microns can be expected to fall out in an extended swath pattern
downwind. Obviously the latter will be influenced by the height
of release and the wind velocity while the airborne drops will
actually have decreased concentration with higher wind and more
turbulent mixing type air conditions. The temperature inversion
condition acts principally on the small drift prone drops producing undesirable concentrations downwind. However, it should be
noted that certain aerosoling applications such as adulticiding
for mosquitoes requires the inversion in order to maintain a
lethal downwind concentration. Relative humidity alters spray
drop size by its effect on spray evaporation.

3. The type of terrain, mountains, hills and valleys which
constitute air drainage systems exerts a significant influence on
the concentration in the downwind area from a spray release. The
terrain along with local weather problems can act to concentrate
airborne particles such as in a valley, especiallly when combined
with an inversion ceiling less than the height of the valley
walls. Such a phenomenon is quite common in mountainous forest
land areas and may contribute to high concentrations of pesticides
appearing in the air and collected by water, soil and plants downwind in a valley.

4. The type, size and configuration of the aircraft equipment can
of itself have a significant effect on swath patterns and downwind

transport of spray drops. Larger aircraft create greater vorticity in wing tip and propeller areas and also because of safety requirements the larger aircraft must usually be flown higher than small aircraft; at 1600 to 3200 m (500 to 1000 ft) elevations instead of the more desirable 165 to 328 m (50 to 100 ft) above the canopy. Helicopter equipment generally is flown at slower speed, 80 to 125 km/hr (50 to 75 mi/hr) in comparison with fixed wing aircraft at 165 to 200 km/hr (100 to 120 mi/hr) for smaller aircraft and 250 to 500 km/hr (150 to 300 mi/hr) for larger multi-engine types. The air wake created by either fixed or rotary wing aircraft is basically a function of the aircraft weight, wing or rotor disk loading (higher loading usually means higher speed and greater vorticity) and aircraft speed. The effect of increased vorticity and air wake is to move the spray release to a greater altitude which in turn produces a wider swath displacement for the ballistic size drops and greater dispersion for airborne size drops.

Studies on swath deposit and airborne drift losses have followed a basic pattern or protocol as accepted by State and Federal regulatory agencies. For example, sprays are collected on (a) artificial collection sheets, such as Mylar, Teflon, glass, metal or other materials from which residues are readily removed; and (b) plant samples are taken either of the trees or crop plants in the area or from plants in flats or pots which are used either for specific plant response (herbicides) or plant spray deposit (6). Air samples for airborne portions may be taken with high volume air samples $0.67-0.85$ m^3 (20-30 ft^3/min.) through a glass fiber filter backed up with a resin type (Rohm and Haas XAD) absorbing column or liquid bubbler for gas phase trapping where desired. Any type application may be monitored downwind with these type of collectors at ground level, or vertical tower collection can be provided for impacted drops or for those drawn into air samplers.

The manner of site selection and weather monitoring is generally related to the specific material to be used or forest crop in which it will be applied. Progressive passes may be made across the target area or where a study is designed for maximum return of information it is frequently desirable to apply all of the material with the test aircraft to a single line or pass, making 5 to 10 passes to build up a sufficient concentration for increased downwind sampling sensitivity. A typical layout (Figure 1) could thus be with a sampling line on a logrithmic pattern such as 12, 25, 50, 100, 200, 300, 800, 1600 and 3200 m (40 ft to 2 mi. downwind) with the fallout, plants and air collectors located at each of these stations. The application line would be at 90 degrees to the sampling line and should be of a length equal to the sampling line in order to insure deposits on the furthermost station when small wind variations occur. If a vertical tower collector is used, it should be located within 45 to 75 m (150 to 250 ft) of the application line and be of sufficient height to

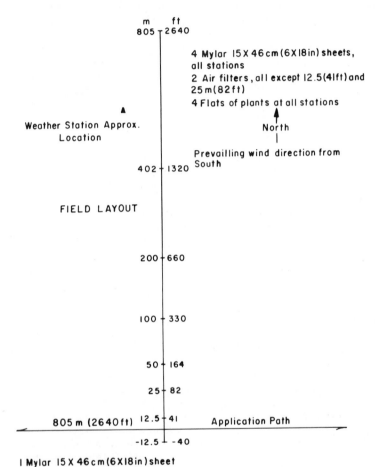

Figure 1. Field layout for aircraft spray tests.

extend above the released cloud. A 15 to 30 m (50 to 100 ft) tower at this distance will handle most applications applied within 2.5 to 7.5 m (10 to 25 ft) of the ground, higher towers would be needed for greater application heights such as above a forest canopy.

The deposit of active chemical, the drift losses and drop size range can be found and would be functions of the spray formulations and application equipment which are under test in a given weather and application terrain. In order to compare different test run data, the results may be plotted as a series of 2nd degree polynomial regression curves (6). Actual chemical analysis of the released spray caught on the samplers provides the most accurate measure of deposit and airborne losses, but calculation of these functions from the drop sizes found can also be done. A total deposit recovery as a % of the amount released can be determined.

By replicating these tests under a series of differing weather conditions and differing terrain, we are able to observe the effects these and other parameters have on the amount of deposit in the target area, burden in the air and residues on the fallout collectors located at the downwind stations (2).

There are many studies published on both field collection data as obtained in actual field measurements of drift-loss (1,2) as well as from predictive models of varying sophistication. The latter are derived basically from single drop size behavior coupled with the basic atmospheric diffusion parameters (3,4). The references listed are not all inclusive but will assist the reader in obtaining a broader view of aerial application studies.

Spray Drop Size Evaluation

Because so much of the aerial spray operation is related to and dependent on drop size characteristics it follows that more accurate knowledge of drop size and size range of the released sprays would be desirable. Also specific effects on drop size from atomizer type, formulations and installation on the aircraft would not only enable more accurate evaluation of specific systems and spray releases, but could also be used to aid in prediction of the swath and downwind transport regime for these releases.

One of the newest instruments available for drop size studies is the Particle Measuring Systems ruby laser. This instrument has a wide range of probe units for different size ranges. The imaging probes will measure from a minimum of around 20 microns to several millimeters diameter while the forward light scatter units will measure downward from 100 to about 0.1 microns. We are presently using this instrument for evaluation of aircraft sprays either by mounting the probe on the aircraft for in-flight studies of individual atomizers or by use of a wind tunnel where a wide variety of atomizers and formulations can be readily handled.

The use of various formulation additives and straight vegetable oil base sprays has been considered many times in the past.
With the present favorable cost relationship of vegetable to
petroleum oils, a renewed interest has prompted us to examine the
potential benefits as well as possible problems that vegetable oil
carriers might produce.

The advantages that may occur from use of vegetable oil base
sprays are primarily (1) the potential for reduction in total
volume applied (low or ultra-low volume) and (2) the potential for
better adherence, longer residual and possible increase in biological activity. The oils may be more compatible with certain
types of active pesticide formulations where solubility or misci-
bility may be increased and flowable particulate type formulations
may be better adaptable to the oils than the customary water-base.
But, in order to obtain a reduction in total volume of application
the drop size of the released spray must be reduced in order that
coverage and contact of the spray with the target insect be maintained. Physically this is not difficult to do. For example, if
the water-base spray has an average drop size of 300 microns and
we reduce this by one-half to 150 microns the total number of
drops is increased by a factor of 8 (2 cubed). If the applied
volume is then reduced from 19 ℓ (2 gal/acre) to 2.3 ℓ/ha (1
qt/acre) the volume decrease is also by a factor of 8 which means
that 2.3 ℓ/ha (1 qt/acre) can be applied with drop numbers or
equal coverage to the 19 ℓ/ha (2 gal/acre) water-base spray. But
this is not all of the story. Figure 2 shows the graphic drop
size distribution of a spray from a D6-45 (.24 cm or 6/64 in.
orifice, #45 whirl plate) cone type nozzle directed with a 165
km/hr (100 mi/hr) airstream. The vmd (volume median dia. - half
the drop volume is in drops above the vmd, and half below this
size) is 327 microns, there are 2% of drop volume is in drops less
than 122 microns dia. (the drift-prone drops) and the R.S. or
width of the spray drop size distribution is 0.71 where:

$$RS = \frac{90\% \text{ size} = 10\% \text{ size}}{50\% \text{ size}}$$

Figure 3 shows data for a spinner atomizer in a 110 mi/hr
airstream. The vmd is 140 microns, the % volume in drops less
than 122 microns is now 24% while the relative span has increased
to 1.23. It is this tremendous increase of drops (less than 122
microns dia.) from 2.0% for the 300 microns spray to 24% for the
150 microns spray that is a potential source of trouble from airborne transport of these small drops. These are carried away from
the treatment area and a potential exists for contact with humans
and animals as well as unwanted deposit on non-target crops.
These small drops have been found at distances of several miles
from the actual applications (5). If the material being released
is of low toxicity, or in a remote area, the problem is not
serious. But for high toxicity materials the 24% loss which is
not controlled, poses a serious problem.

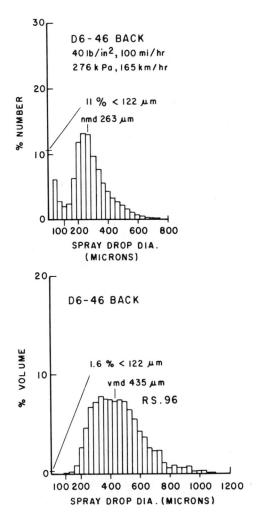

Figure 2. Drop size from hollow cone, D6-46 nozzle.

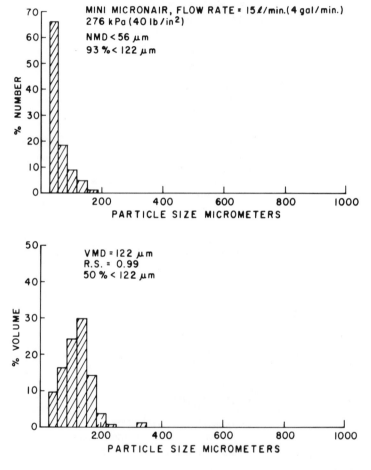

Figure 3.   Drop size from Micronair spinner atomizer.

It is to be noted that an increased pesticide efficacy can frequently be obtained with the small drop size sprays over the larger; this in spite of the 24% loss potential that smaller drop size sprays may have. Thus the inference has been drawn that small drop size sprays, where they can be used safely, are potentially more biologically active than large drop size sprays. Just how far this theory can be carried remains a function not only of the basic toxicity of the applied spray to the target organism, but also is highly dependent on application parameters. In general, fine sprays and aerosols are more difficult to control than larger drop size sprays. Another factor difficult to rationalize occurs when a spray cloud moves downwind. The leading edge close to the crop canopy is turned under while the upper portions move forward thus producing a rolling motion at the boundary of the cloud and the crop. Different crop canopies would induce different degrees of rolling and contact with the cloud. Larger drops may be shattered upon contact with the canopy and this turbulent mixing motion undoubtedly aids in obtaining better target coverage as well as filtration of spray drops from the cloud.

The total deposit recovery of aerially applied sprays can be plotted as in Figure 4. Here Mylar plastic fallout sheets were located at 0.6 m (2 ft) intervals from 12 m (40 ft) upwind to 25 m (82 ft) downwind and at greater intervals out to 800 m (1/2 mi.) (see Fig. 1). These were analyzed for deposit of chemical and cumulatively plotted by computer to obtain the curves of Figure 4. The two curves, one for a water-base ec and the other is oil-base spray, had drop diameters of approximately 300 microns vmd for the water and 150 microns vmd for the oil. As can be seen, the recovery out to 106 m (350 ft) is low at around 66% for the oil and 80% for the water and is related basically to the drop size being produced. Figure 5 shows a series of recovery curves for sprays of different drop sizes commencing at the top for Curves A, B, C of very large drop size of 500 to 1,000 microns vmd used for herbicides. These are produced with simple orifice-jet and large hollow cone nozzles such as D6-46 and D6-56 (Spraying Systems Co.). The addition of a polymer thickener to a water-base spray will also produce very large drop size. Curve D for a 200 microns spray and Curve E for a spinner at 150 microns vmd show recoveries out to 660 ft of 90% and 59% respectively. These latter curves are for the drop sizes commonly used for insect control sprays.

Figure 6 shows the resulting downwind drift-loss pattern when an oil and a water-base spray of the same drop size is used. Here the evaporation of the water reduces the deposit at points closer to the application while the non-evaporative oil shows a higher deposit out to about one mile, where the two curves cross. The characteristic of non-evaporative oil sprays is to deposit in greater amounts out to about one mile distance when compared with water base sprays, also the oil appears to have less material left to deposit beyond the one mile. Thus a low evaporative base spray produces a wider extended swath and requires wider buffers than a water-base application.

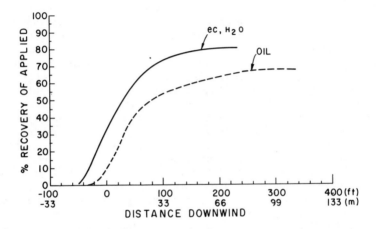

Figure 4. Deposit recovery, oil and water base sprays.

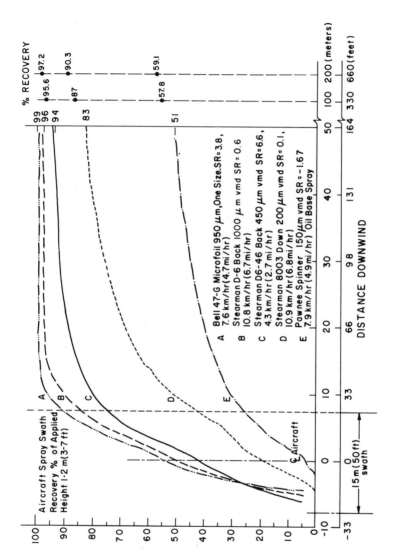

Figure 5.   Deposit recovery from five different drop sizes.

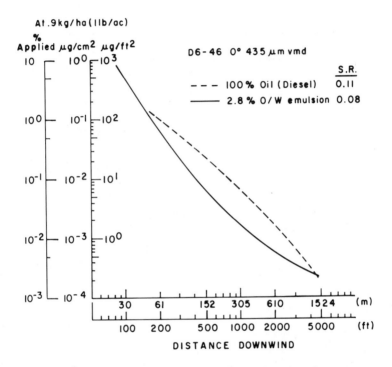

Figure 6.   Spray deposit from oil and water base sprays.

Figure 7 illustrates the relationship of the (A) flagged swath width (B) actual total downwind or extended swath and (C) the airborne or what we identify as the drift-loss portion. Allowance must be made (such as buffer zones) for the swath displacement which actually is desirable in smoothing out the frequently rough distribution patterns in an aircraft swath (Figure 8). The portion of Figure 7 with which we should always be concerned is the airborne drift-loss from drops of 100 microns dia. and smaller.

Figure 8 illustrates the swath pattern resulting from the use of a polymer viscoelastic material added to the water-base spray. As can be seen the swath width is reduced from 15 to 13 m (60 to 42 ft) and deposit in the flagged swath increased from 29% to 70%. But the drop size has increased from around 400 microns vmd to 800 microns. This is quite satisfactory as long as the material being used remains biologically effective in such large drops. But the use of polymer additives is basically limited to herbicides and is not normally suited to fungicides and insecticides where smaller drops are needed for biological effectiveness. A further complication in polymer use is illustrated in Table 1. Here a D6-46 nozzle is operated at 275 kPa (40 lb/in^2) in a 165 km/hr (100 mi/hr) airstream. The vmd for water when directed with the airstream (0 degrees) is 451 microns. When directed at 90 degrees to the air it is 286 microns. When the polymer is added, the drop size at 0 degrees increases to 850 and at 90 degrees to 538 microns. But note what happens to the % volume in drops under 122 microns. With water this was 1.2 and 3% for 0 and 90 degrees, but when polymer was added it was 1% for 0 and 4% for 90 degrees. Thus there would be no reduction in the airborne losses with the polymer added even though the swath width was narrowed and deposit in this measured or flagged swath was up from the water spray. This point must carefully be considered before adding a polymer to any spray. Also shown in Table 1 is drop size data on sprays with Bivert a spray adjuvant and chlordimeform, an insecticide. These showed a small increase in vmd when Bivert was added and reduced vmd with chlordimeform. The % volume in drops less than 122 μm is increased above that of water.

Table 2 shows the results of drop size studies on an 8001 fan nozzle spraying oil and water at 0 and 90 degrees to the airstream of 100 mi/hr. Liquid pressure was maintained at 275 kPa (40 lb/in^2). As can be seen the oil (cottonseed) caused the vmd to be reduced somewhat, and increased the % volume in drops less than 122 microns dia. The chlordimeform-Pydrin-oil mixture increased the vmd slightly. Table 3 shows a serrated cup spinner operated at different air speeds with water and with oil. Again the drop size decreases with the oil, but even more impressively the drops below 122 microns have gone up significantly due to the characteristic of this spinner to produce small drops. The changes in rotational speed and liquid flow rate alter the drop size significantly. Table 4 presents data on the Micronair AU 5000 operated

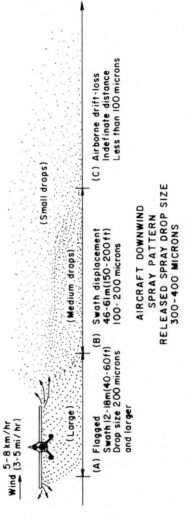

Figure 7. Aircraft spray patterns.

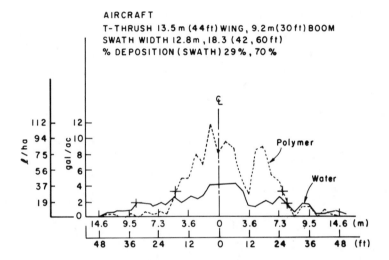

Figure 8.   Aircraft swath pattern, water and water plus polymer.

TABLE I. D6-46 Cone Nozzle
275 kPa (40 lb/in^2) 165 km/hr (100 mi/hr)

Formulation	Direction degrees to airstream	nmd	% < 122 μm	vmd	% < 122 μm
H$_2$O	0	125	49	451	1.2
H$_2$O	90	100	56	286	3
13.3 mℓ (.5 oz) Polymer/19 ℓ (5 gal) H$_2$O	0	86	62	850	1.1
Bv .47% (1 pt) 19 ℓ (5 gal) H$_2$O	90	94	61	299	4
237 mℓ (.5 pt) Ch/19 ℓ (5 gal) H$_2$O	90	88	60	268	4
13.3 mℓ (.5 oz) Polymer/237 mℓ (.5 pt) Ch/19 ℓ (5 gal) H$_2$O	90	78	69	538	4
13.3 mℓ (.5 pt) Bv 13.3 mℓ (.5 pt) Ch/19 ℓ (5 gal) H$_2$O	90	64	70	231	6

Ch - Chlordimeform

Bv - Bivert

TABLE II. 8001 Fan Nozzle
275 kPa (40 lb/in^2) 165 km/hr (100 mi/hr)

Formulation	Direction degrees to airstream	nmd	% < 122 µm	vmd	% < 122 µm
H$_2$O	0	123	49	219	5
H$_2$O	90	<60	78	179	15
cs oil	0	<60	83	174	19
cs oil	90	<60	84	175	18
chlordimeform pydrin cs oil	0	66	73	200	11
	90	<60	81	187	14

TABLE III. MW Spinning Serrated Cup

Air Vel. km/hr	mi/hr	rpm	pressure kPa	ℓ/min	gal/min	nmd	% < 122 μm	vmd	% < 122 μm
Water									
165	100	3700	138	1.63	.43	60	85	128	41
165	100	3600	275	2.27	.6	82	63	169	10
115	70	2100	275	"	"	156	21	226	3.
82	50	—	275	"	"	119	51	387	1.26
Cottonseed Oil									
165	100	3700	138	.15	.04	<60	99.5	72	92
165	100	3600	275	.47	.125	<60	96	104	64
165	100	3000	480	.68	.18	<60	93	128	44
115	70	2200	275	.47	.125	<60	86	144	29

TABLE IV. Mini-Micronair AU 5000, Ex1772
Air Speed 165 km/hr (100 mi/hr), 9.22 cm (3.63 in.) blade, 35 degrees

Flow rate gal/min	ℓ/min	rpm	$D_V.5$	R.S.	% vol. < 122 μm
4	15	8,000	122	0.99	50
2	7.5	9,100	94	1.27	81
.4	1.5	9,500	94	1.06	92

at 3 flow rates. This shows the normal distribution of drop sizes for this spinner is similar to the data of Table 3 not unlike the hydraulic nozzles when operated in the 165 km/hr (100 mi/hr) airstream.

In summary, a wide range of parameters affect the aerial application of pesticides, biological and chemical in the forest areas. The role of spray drop size is dominant and this paper has tried to evaluate the drop size characteristics of a few customary nozzles as well as some data on additives and vegetable oil-base sprays. The volume reduction that is usually offered when an oil-base spray is considered must be matched or at least approached by a reduction in drop size in order to maintain biological efficacy. But in reducing drop size we also increase drift-losses and the potential problems these in turn can cause on non-target crops and the general habitat. Obviously what is needed is an atomizer that produces all of the drops near an ideal 200 microns average size and cuts off the small drift-prone drops as well as the wasteful large ones. Such a device is shown in Figure 9 which is called an Aerodynamic nozzle. The drop distribution is shown in Figure 10 The limitations on this are the requirement for an orifice diameter of 1/2 the drop size being produced, or about 127 microns or 0.0127 cm (0.005 inches) for the 200 microns diameter drop. We haven't found a way to keep such an orifice from blocking as yet. But there are other means which we are investigating which we hope will enable us to get that narrowed drop size range without which the future of reduced volume sprays will remain under the cloud of the drift-loss problem. The potential for vegetable oil-base sprays in reduced or ultra-low volumes, 1 to 2 ℓ/ha (1/2 to 1 qt/ac), is excellent and with better drop size controls this valuable technique will find broader favor for a wide variety of forest and agricultural spraying.

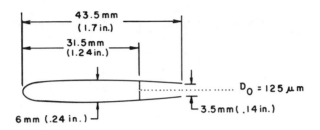

Figure 9.   Aerodynamic monodisperse atomizer.

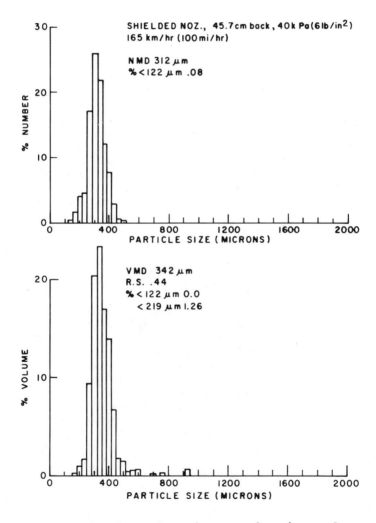

Figure 10.   Spray drop size, aerodynamic nozzle.

Literature Cited

1. Ghassemi, Masood, Page Painter, Michael Powers, Norman B. Akesson and Michael Dellarco. 1982. Estimating drift and exposure due to aerial application of insecticides in forests. Environmental Sci. and Tech. 16(8):510-514.

2. Akesson, N.B., W.E. Yates, N. Smith and R.E. Cowden. 1981. Rationalization of pesticide drift-loss accountancy by regression models. ASAE Paper 81-1006, St. Joseph, MI.

3. Dumbauld, R.K., J.R. Bjorklund and S.F. Saterlie. 1980. Computer models for predicting aircraft spray dispersion and deposition above and within forest canopies. User's Manual for the FSC BG Computer Program. Report 80-11, H E. Cramer Co., Inc., Salt Lake City, Utah.

4. Miller, Conrad O.M. 1980. A mathematical model of aerial deposition of pesticides from aircraft. Environmental Sci. and Tech. 14(7):824-831.

5. Akesson, N.B , W.E. Yates and R.E. Cowden. 1977. Procedures for evaluating the potential losses during and following pesticide application. ASAE Paper 77-1504, St. Joseph, MI.

6. Yates, W.E., N.B. Akesson and D.E. Bayer. 1977. Drift of glyphosate sprays applied with aerial and ground equipment. Weed Science 26(6):597-604.

RECEIVED September 9, 1983

Deposition of Chemical and Biological Agents in Conifers

JOHN W. BARRY

U.S. Department of Agriculture, Forest Service, Forest Pest Management, Davis, CA 95616

Accounting for aerially released pesticides
involves techniques for sampling and assessing
pesticide drops within and below the canopy. The
USDA Forest Service (FS) in its effort to account
for pesticide sprays has supported research to
quantify deposition in the canopy, on foliage, and
beneath the tree. This paper reviews results of
several FS aerial spray projects. Field methods
included spray deposit sampling with cards and
assessing foliage for presence of pesticide drops
and tracers. Results show that conifers are
relatively efficient collectors of spray drops and
that deposits decrease from the upper to the lower
crown. The majority of drops observed on
coniferous foliage are below 60 μm in diameter.
Results indicate that recovery of spray is
influenced by application rate, drop size, tree
species, and density of foliage.

The ban on the chlorinated hydrocarbon pesticides during the
early 1970's resulted in a search for methods to improve the
efficiency of aerial application of pesticides to forests. It
soon became apparent that the use of less persistent chemical and
biological agents to control defoliators such as the tussock
moth and spruce budworm, would require a higher degree of
application precision than previously had been practiced.
Candidate agents required more attention to application timing,
atmospheric conditions, and the target's physical and behavioral
characteristics. Emphasis was given to developing methods which
would increase pesticide deposit on the target.
 Concurrent with the need to improve aerial application, needs
have been expressed for techniques which will assist in
accounting for pesticides released over forests. While a total
accountancy or mass balance of aerially released spray may be an
unattainable goal, 90 percent accountancy may be attainable.

Accountancy is a complex process as it includes the entire tank mix—carrier, dilutent, adjuvant and the active ingredient. The forest pest manager has a need for information on how much spray reaches the tree crown and the forest floor, or drifts off the target. Understanding interaction of spray within the tree crown, quantifying the collection of drops by foliage elements, and determining how much spray deposits on the forest floor are part of the accountancy process.

Consistent with the concern to improve the efficiency of aerial application there has been an attempt over the past 20 years to determine where spray drops deposit in coniferous forests. Researchers such as Hurtig et al. (1), Snowden et al. (2), Thompson et al. (3), Barry et al. (4), Joyce et al. (5), Armstrong and Yule (6), and Sundaram (7), have reported on the deposit of pesticide drops on conifers. Himel and Moore (8), reported that the highest mortality of western spruce budworm was caused by particles less than 50 m in diameter. Their work prompted others to look at what was being deposited directly on target following conventional application methods. These and similiar studies have helped to provide us an understanding of the behavior and deposition of spray drops in coniferous forests. The rationale for these studies is based on the assumption that once we have determined what is deposited in trees, steps can be taken to apply the proper number and size range of drops to achieve results. Safe, effective, and economical applications are dependent upon information generated by such studies.

Several factors are known to influence deposition of drops on foliage and insects. These include drop size, wind speed, target shape and size, density and type of foliage, and velocity of the falling drops. Other factors have a less defined role such as the microenvironment surrounding the target, physical and chemical aspects of the drops, and characteristics of the target surface, including its electrical charge (9). Research is needed to understand the contribution of these factors to drop deposition, impaction, and retention on foliage.

This paper reviews observations on the deposition of spray drops on trees, foliage, and the floor of coniferous forests. The data presented provides some insight into our knowledge of spray behavior in coniferous forests.

Deposition on Forest Floor

The filtration of drops by coniferous foliage has a pronounced affect on what reaches the forest floor. Maksymiuk (10) suggested that ground samplers should be placed three or more tree heights from the nearest tree to avoid filtering of drops. Typically as part of the spray cloud descends to the ground after release, it descends at an angle due to wind. In the absence of wind the spray tends to descend perpendicularly with the smaller drops expanding laterally. Our observations indicate that under

low wind velocities (<6 mph) fine drops (<50 μm) and large drops
(>400 μm) tend to penetrate open spaces in Douglas-fir canopies
and deposit on the forest floor. Small drops, which do not
deposit on foliage, apparently meander around objects within the
crown eventually settling and coming to rest on the ground.
Large drops have a more direct fall angle and pass by fewer
objects in their course to the ground. Under higher wind
velocities or atmospheric instability the penetration pattern of
drops may change significantly.
     To estimate amount of spray penetrating the canopy and
depositing on the ground, we collected spray on Kromekote paper
cards. Tables I-IV provide deposit data from several aerial
application projects. As expected more spray was recovered on
the ground in the open forest than was recovered beneath trees.
To estimate what might be in the crown or lost to the atmosphere,
we subtracted deposits obtained beneath the tree from deposits
obtained in the open. Although deposits as a percent of the
application rate range widely, it is apparent that conifers
collect a large portion of the spray. These data reflect the
spray deposit which might be expected from conventional chemical
and biological forest spray operations. The oil base sprays
showed higher recoveries than the water-base spray. We assume
that a significant volume of the water-base spray was lost to
evaporation. For comparison purposes recoveries of spray
released over flat, open terrain are shown in Table V.
     Data from Tables I-V show that deposits in the open from
low-volume aerial sprays range from 8 percent to 82 percent; and
beneath trees from 3 percent to 39 percent. The percentages vary
due to drop size of the spray, meteorology, properties of the
tank mix, and release height. Improved formulations, uses of low
volatile tank mixes, attention to atmospheric conditions which
support deposition, and improvement in sampling methods should
increase accountancy.

Deposition in the Crown

Researchers (Armstrong and Yule (6), and Snowden (2)) provided
information on distribution of spray in the crown; however, data
often has been lacking on quantifying the pesticide spray
immediately before it penetrates the canopy.
     In 1980 the FS conducted an aerial spray test in a Florida
seed orchard to obtain data on penetration of spray into the
canopy (16). As part of the test design, spray was sampled on

Table I. Volume recoveries on Kromekote cards beneath sample trees and in open forests.

| Treatment Block | Mexacarbate (Zectran) Application 1 gallon/acre | | | | | |
| | Volume Recovered (gal/acre) | | | Volume Recovered (%) | | |
	Outer Ring[2]	Inner Ring[3]	Open Area[4]	Outer Ring	Inner Ring	Open Area
1	0.216	0.181	0.345	22	18	35
2	0.412	0.370	0.389	41	37	39
3	0.271	0.198	0.678	27	20	68
4	0.329	0.298	0.225	33	30	23
5	0.307	0.263	0.351	31	26	35
6	0.232	0.189	0.388	23	19	39
Average	0.295	0.250	0.396	30	25	40

Bacillus thuringiensis (Dipel WP) Application 2 gallons/acre

Treatment Block	Volume Recovery (gal/acre)		Volume Recovered (%)	
	Inner Ring	Open Area	Inner Ring	Open Area
1	0.237	1.102	12	55
2	0.227	0.566	11	28
3	0.218	0.630	11	32
4	0.068	0.248	3	12
5	0.096	0.294	5	15
6	0.228	0.577	11	29
Average	0.179	0.570	9	29

1 Table from Barry et al. (11).
2 Cards placed at dripline of tree.
3 Cards placed halfway between trunk and dripline.
4 Cards placed in open forest.

Table II. Recovery of aerially applied carbaryl (Sevin 4-oil) tank mix on Kromekote cards at tree dripline and in the open of a spruce/fir forest.

Treatment Block	Application Rate	VMD (μm)²	Ounces/Acre Trees	Ounces/Acre Open	Percent Trees	Percent Open
1	30 oz.	157	3.88	11.53	13	38
2	40 oz.	134	5.19	14.88	13	37
3	30 oz.	157	4.59	11.32	15	38
6	40 oz.	171	4.58	17.94	12	45
7	40 oz.	147	1.83	5.56	5	14
8	30 oz.	127	1.42	5.16	5	17

[1] Table from Barry et al. (12).
[2] VMD is volume median diameter. Half the spray volume is in drops smaller than the VMD and half is in drops larger than the VMD.

Table III. Recovery of aerially applied acephate (Orthene FS) tank mix on Kromekote cards applied at 0.5 gallons per acre.

Treatment Block	Location[2]	VMD (μm)	Gallons/acre	Percent
1	Trees	273	0.14	28
	Open	290	0.33	66
2	Trees	306	0.09	18
	Open	260	0.41	82
3	Trees	281	0.12	24
	Open	325	0.32	64
4	Trees	267	0.18	36
	Open	263	0.24	48

[1] Stipe et al. (13).
[2] Tree samples taken at tree dripline. Open samples taken in open forest areas.

Table IV. Recoveries on Kromekote cards as percent of the 0.5 gallon per acre application rate of dyed fuel oil.

Turbo Thrush Aircraft

Block	Forest Sampling Line								VMD (μm)	Mean Volume (gal)	Mean (%)
	A		B		C		D				
	gal	%	gal	%	gal	%	gal	%			
1	0.022	4.4	0.029	5.8	0.041	8.2	0.072	114.4	147	0.041	8
2	0.061	12.2	0.052	10.4	0.048	9.6	0.038	7.6	129	0.049	10
3	0.067	13.4	0.074	14.8	0.109	21.8	0.107	21.4	127	0.089	18
4	0.030	6.0	0.067	13.4	0.059	11.8	0.082	16.4	128	0.059	12
5	0.040	8.2	0.041	8.2	0.071	14.0	0.065	13.0	131	0.054	11
6	0.096	19.2	0.089	17.8	0.071	14.2	0.105	21.0	131	0.091	18

Bell 206 Jet Ranger Helicopter

| Block | Forest Sampling Line | | | | | | | | VMD (μm) | Mean Volume (gal) | Mean (%) |
| | A | | B | | C | | D | | | | |
	gal	%	gal	%	gal	%	gal	%			
1	0.131	26.2	0.083	16.6	0.108	21.6	0.151	30.2	297	0.118	24
2	0.149	29.8	0.138	27.6	0.148	29.6	0.125	25.0	290	0.140	28
3	0.110	22.0	0.101	20.2	0.113	22.6	0.136	27.2	253	0.115	23
4	0.116	23.2	0.159	31.8	0.136	27.2	0.158	31.6	264	0.142	28
5	0.171	34.2	0.128	25.6	0.160	32.0	0.212	42.4	286	0.168	34
6	0.192	38.4	0.188	37.6	0.188	37.6	0.221	44.2	270	0.197	39

[1] Table from Barry et al. (14).

Table V. Recoveries of Bacillus thuringiensis (Thuricide 16B)
          and carbaryl (Sevin 4-oil) on Kromekote cards
          over flat open terrain.

Trial	Time	Insecticide	Drops/cm	VMD (μm)	Recovery[2] Volume G/A	Volume (%)
2	1820	Thuricide 16B	32	156	0.124	12
3	1842	Thuricide 16B	29	148	0.0827	8
4	0647	Thuricide 16B	39	167	0.237	24
5	0710	Thuricide 16B	52	190	0.2263	23
6	0733	Thuricide 16B	37	189	0.3125	31
7	0753	Thuricide 16B	45	120	0.078	8
8	0804	Thuricide 16B	40	130	0.076	8
9	0815	Thuricide 16B	65	144	0.131	13
11	1845	Sevin 4-oil	34	133	0.1527	31
12	1912	Sevin 4-oil	45	125	0.1777	36
13	1923	Sevin 4-oil	40	133	0.1998	40

[1] Table from Barry et al. (15).
[2] Recovery is expressed as a function of application rate (1
gallon/acre for Thuricide 16B, and 0.5 gallon/acre for Sevin
4-oil) and amount recovered on ground. Volume (%) is the %
recovered of the application rate.

Mylar sheeting immediately above the canopy, at three levels in
the crown, and at each cardinal position in the canopy. A salt
($MnSO_4$) was added to the tank mix as a tracer (17). One spray
application was made at tree top by a Hughes 500C helicopter and
two applications by a Stearman fixed-wing aircraft.

Analysis of $MnSO_4$ tracer from cylindrical samplers revealed
that a high percentage of the spray was unaccounted for only a
few feet below the canopy top. A few feet below the canopy top,
67 to 75 percent of the spray was unaccounted for in the slash
pine, and 75 to 83 percent was unaccounted for in the Ocala sand
pine. Approximately 20 feet below the canopy top 77 to 90
percent of the spray was unaccounted for in the slash pine, and
85 to 95 percent in the Ocala sand pine. This trend was
consistent from trial to trial and tree to tree. Results are
given in Table VI.

The high percent of unaccounted spray is likely due to
filtration of the spray by foliage, and not to drift or
evaporation. The effect was pronounced in the Ocala sand pine, a
more densely foliated species than the slash pine. Dense foliage
acts as fibers in a filter. As the number of fibers increase
there are fewer open spaces for drops to penetrate without
colliding with a fiber, in this case a needle. As the foliage
collects drops at the upper crown there are fewer available to
the lower crown levels. These results suggest that pines, even
with their sparse foliage compared to spruce and fir, are
efficient collectors of spray drops.

Deposition of Foliage

Himel and Moore (8), observed mostly small drops on western
spruce budworm larvae. They used a fluorescent particle tracer
in the mexacarbate spray. The question following their study was
whether the drops from other pesticide tank mixes would behave in
a similar manner. Was the deposition of drops on larvae
influenced by physical properties of the tank mix, application
technique, or other factors? These and other questions provided
the basis for investigations. In 1971 the FS initiated studies
on an opportunity basis, to pursue the question of drop
deposition on coniferous foliage.

One study (18) showed that aerially applied pigmented
mexacarbate particles observed on western spruce budworm larvae
and Douglas-fir needles were minute (Table VII). Eighty-seven
percent of the particles found on western spruce budworm larvae
were less than 16 μm in diameter while 87 percent of the
particles found on Douglas-fir needles were less than 11 μm in
diameter. It is noteworthy that 76 percent of the particles
observed on the larvae were 6 to 15 μm in diameter. We assume
that the particle size distribution in the field was similar to
the particle size distribution measured in the laboratory.

Table VI. Recovery of spray at three crown levels in slash and Ocala sand pine, relative to spray recovered at canopy top.

Trial/ Aircraft	Tree No.[2]	Mean Recovery $MnSO_4$ at Crown Levels (Micrograms)	Percent Loss/Distance Percent[3]	Percent Loss/Distance Distance[4] (feet)
5 Stearman biplane	1	Canopy top 199	—	—
		Upper crown 49	75	3
		Middle crown 32	84	11
		Lower crown 20	90	19
5	12	Canopy top 194	—	—
		Upper crown 32	83	5.5
		Middle crown 14	93	11.6
		Lower crown 10	95	21.5
7 Stearman biplane	1	Canopy top 46	—	—
		Upper crown 15	67	3
		Middle crown 15	67	11
		Lower crown 10	78	19
7	12	Canopy top 32	—	—
		Upper crown 8	75	5.5
		Middle crown 6	81	11.6
		Lower crown 3	91	21.5

Equipment	Tree				
10 Hughes 500C helicopter	1	Canopy top	105	–	–
		Upper crown	34	68	3
		Middle crown	40	62	11
		Lower crown	24	77	19
10	12	Canopy top	96	–	–
		Upper crown	17	82	5.5
		Middle crown	14	85	11.6
		Lower crown	14	85	21.5

1 From Barry et al. (16).
2 Tree 1 was slash pine, tree 12 was Ocala sand pine.
3 Percent determined from ratio of material recovered at top of canopy on Mylar sheets to that recovered at each of three crown levels.
4 Vertical distance descending from top of canopy to each crown level.

Results suggest that the observation of a high percentage of small particles on larvae and needles was not overly influenced by a high percentage of minute particles in the particulate cloud.

Table VII. Distribution by percent of particles found on three collection surfaces.

Particle size [1]		Collection surfaces		
Categories (μm)	Size distribution (%)	Impaction plates	Western spruce budworm larvae	Douglas-fir needles
<6	94.54	15.2	10.7	60.8
6-10	3.92	6.5	50.7	25.8
11-15	0.14	9.6	25.3	9.3
16-20	0.28	13.5	8.7	2.6
21-25	0.14	6.8	3.3	0.5
>25	0.7	48.4	1.3	1.0

[1] Particle size distribution of the tank mix.

(Reproduced with permission from Ref. 18. Copyright 1977, Entomological Society of America.)

    In another study (19) we evaluated dyed drops which had been applied aerially by helicopter over a Montana forest. Three tank mixes were studied, a wettable powder tank mix of Bacillus thuringiensis (B.t.), carbaryl, and trichlorfon. The VMD of the spray was 320 μm for B.t.; 261 μm for carbaryl; and 281 μm for trichlorfon. Results (Table VIII) showed that 86 to 94 percent of the drops observed on Douglas-fir needles were less than 61 μm in diameter, and 71 to 40 percent were less than 16 μm in diameter. Drop stains on needles were corrected for spreading by applying a spread factor to calculate their airborne drop diameters.
    Other studies were conducted by the FS in 1976 to expand the data base on the size of drops which deposited on Douglas-fir needles. These studies provided an opportunity to determine if the drop size distribution would be similar to drop size distributions of tank mixes studied earlier. The 1976 study involved aerial application of acephate and trichlorfon, and the 1981 study involved Bacillus thuringiensis (Dipel 4L and Thuricide 16B). These data have not been published or reported previously. The chemical tank mixes were applied by helicopter and the B.t. tank mixes were applied by fixed-wing aircraft. Each tank mix was applied at one gallon per acre to three

Table VIII. Number of drops observed on needles by size categories.

Drop size category (m)	Bacillus thuringiensis				Carbaryl		Trichlorfon	
	Trial 2		Trial 3		Trial 6		Trial 8	
	No. drops	Cum. percent	No. drops	Cum. percent	No. drops	Cum. percent	No. drops	Cum. percent
<4	96	12.15	108	15.86	137	11.40	353	18.85
4–10	226	40.76	239	50.96	236	31.03	323	36.10
10–15	172	62.63	139	71.37	106	39.85	200	46.78
15–21	43	67.97	28	75.48	139	51.41	228	58.95
21–31	114	82.40	90	88.70	254	72.54	338	77.00
31–41	31	86.32	10	90.17	76	78.86	116	83.19
41–61	45	92.02	24	93.69	88	86.18	57	86.23
61–81	27	95.44	25	97.36	73	92.25	108	92.00
82–121	16	97.47	7	98.39	45	95.99	87	96.64
121–151	8	98.48	8	99.56	26	98.15	21	97.76
151–200	9	99.62	1	99.71	17	99.56	24	99.04
>200	3	100	2	100	5	99.98	18	100
Totals	790		681		1202		1873	

(Reproduced with permission from Ref. 19. Copyright 1978,
American Society Agriculture Engineers.)

separate spray blocks. Needles were collected from 75 trees in
each block and examined under the microscope for presence of drop
stains. The majority of drop stains observed on needles were
measurable. The drop stain sizes were not converted to drop
sizes; however, drops were estimated to spread on needles roughly
2 times their airborne diameter. Results (Table IX) showed 73
percent of the trichlorfon drop stains and 63 percent of the
acephate drop stains were less than 101 μm in diameter.

The B.t. drop stain sizes from the 1981 study were assessed
in a similar manner as the chemical tank mixes. Results (Table
X) differed, however, from the 1976 chemical applications. Sixty
percent of the Dipel 4L drop stains were less than 42 μm in
diameter and 42 percent of the Thuricide 16B drop stains were
less than 31 μm in diameter. Differences between the chemical
and biological spray drop size distribution, however, may be due
to variation in spreading of the drop after it deposits on the
needle. There was no statistical difference in percent
distribution of the drop stain sizes between the two B.t. tank
mixes or between the two chemical tank mixes.

Table IX.   Distribution of chemical stains on Douglas-fir needles
by drop stain size, Montana, 1976.

Chemical/ spray block		Drop/stain size distribution (μm)							
		50	51– 100	101– 150	151– 200	201– 250	251– 300	301– 350	351– 400
Trichlorfon	7	686	391	214	121	85	44	16	22
	2	2311	1028	596	171	106	43	21	34
	1	784	569	234	177	94	49	32	46
Totals		3781	1988	1044	469	285	136	69	102
Percent		48.0	25.2	13.3	6.0	3.6	1.7	0.9	1.3
Acephate	8	613	440	210	176	75	62	27	30
	5	280	285	186	129	95	47	28	59
	3	919	797	333	210	132	71	18	65
Totals		1812	1522	729	506	302	180	73	154
Percent		34.4	28.8	13.8	9.6	5.7	3.4	1.4	1.9

From these two studies we concluded that the majority of
drops depositing on Douglas-fir needles are less than 60 μm in
diameter. This conclusion is significant to the efficacy of
spray operations. Most low-volume applications (1 gallon per
acre) have consisted characteristically of spray VMD's in the 225

Table X. Distribution of Bacillus thuringiensis drop stains on Douglas-fir needles by stain size, New Mexico, 1981.

Biological/ spray block	Drop stain size distribution (μm)											
	<15	16–30	31–45	46–60	61–80	81–100	101–125	126–150	151–200	201–300	301–400	400
Dipel 4L												
1	320	107	49	31	26	13	33	19	24	34	22	21
2	273	144	92	45	24	12	16	17	12	13	5	4
3	302	130	79	49	37	25	34	29	24	34	32	8
Totals	895	381	220	125	87	50	83	65	60	81	32	33
Percent	42.4	18.0	10.4	5.9	4.1	2.4	3.9	3.1	2.9	3.8	1.5	1.6
Thuricide 16B												
4	218	107	83	58	34	23	49	21	32	37	9	4
5	90	30	38	35	29	28	42	43	56	28	29	1
10	129	54	31	11	16	12	20	19	26	30	10	9
Totals	437	191	152	104	79	63	111	83	114	95	48	14
Percent	29.3	12.8	10.2	7.0	5.3	4.2	7.4	5.6	7.7	6.4	3.2	0.9

to 350 μm range. This places 50 percent of the spray volume in
drops below 113 to 175 μm. It can be seen that little of the
volume is in drops which deposit on needles. Until the droplet
spectrum of pesticide sprays applied to the canopy top is
characterized by number and size of drops, we can only speculate
as to why we are observing mostly small drops on needles.
Reduction of drop diameters by evaporation is not a likely
explanation as the phenomena is observed under conditions of high
relative humidity and when using low volatile oil sprays. One
explanation might be that large drops, with high fall velocities,
may shatter into numerous small drops upon colliding with tree
elements. It has been calculated (18) that Douglas-fir will
collect particles mostly in the 11 to 35 μm size under wind
velocities of 0.5 to 4.5 meters per second; however, the best
explanation is explained by probability. Although we have not
characterized the small end of the droplet spectrum, there are
probably a greater number of small drops in spray clouds than
previously believed. If this is the case there is a large
population of drops <50 μm available in pesticide spray clouds
and thus a higher probability of one colliding with a needle.

Spray Drop Density on Conifer Needles

The Florida seed orchard project conducted in 1980 (16) provided
an opportunity to study drop deposit on needles of two distinct
pine species. Five gallons of a dyed water base tank mix was
applied per acre by aircraft. Drop stains were counted on
needles microscopically. The VMD of the spray as determined on
Kromekote cards was approximately 350 μm. Depending upon tree
species and crown level, drop stains per centimeter length of
needle ranged from 0.5 to 17.7 drops. A higher drop density was
observed on the sparsely foliated slash pine than on the dense
foliated Ocala sand pine (Table XI). A significantly greater
density of drops was observed in the upper crown of both species
as compared to the lower crown.

Table XI. Deposit of drop stains on pine needles expressed as
           number of drops per cm length of needle.

Location	Slash pine		Sand pine	
	Tree 1	Tree 2	Tree 9	Tree 10
Upper crown	6.8	15.6	1.8	0.8
Middle crown	3.9	17.7	1.3	1.3
Lower crown	3.4	10.7	1.0	0.5

(Reproduced with permission from Ref. 4. Copyright 1981,
Verlag Paul Parey.)

The 1981 New Mexico study previously discussed also provided
an opportunity to study drop deposits on Douglas-fir needles.
One gallon of tank mix per acre was applied aerially. The VMD of
the Dipel 4L spray was 239 μm and for the Thuricide 16 B spray it
was 221 μm. Needle samples were collected from branch tips 5
feet above ground. Approximately 900 needles from the three
Dipel blocks and 900 needles from the three Thuricide blocks were
examined microscopically. We found from 0.31 to 0.55 drop stains
per centimeter length of needle from the Dipel treated blocks,
and 0.20 to 0.44 drop stains per centimeter length of needle from
the Thuricide treated blocks (Table XII).

Table XII. Deposit of drop stains on Douglas-fir needles,
New Mexico, 1981.

Spray block	Drop stain/cm length of Douglas-fir needle
1 Dipel	.31
2 Dipel	.53
3 Dipel	.55
4 Thuricide	.44
5 Thuricide	.39
6 Thuricide	.20

Conclusion

The data sets reviewed, document our knowledge on the deposition
of aerial sprays released over coniferous forests. Conifers are
relatively efficient collectors of spray drops as more drops are
consistently observed on the ground in open areas than beneath
trees. Spray which penetrates the upper canopy, and is
unaccounted for on samplers in the lower canopy, probably was
filtered out by foliage. More deposits are observed in the upper
crown than in the lower crown. Data are lacking, however, on the
fate of drops which do not penetrate the canopy. There is a
potential for these drops to penetrate the canopy downwind or to
drift off target.

The majority of drops observed on needles usually are less
than 60 μm in diameter. We have no scientific explanation as to
the fate of large drops or why mostly small drops are found on
needles. Technology is needed which will reveal the physical
changes of spray drops as they leave the atomizer and enter the
canopy. Large drops may be shattering when they collide with
conifers or they may be too few to detect. After spraying we
also observe a high percentage of small drops on the forest

floor. This suggests that there initially was a large population of small drops. Shattering of large drops by foliage also may add to the small drop population. Field research is needed to provide information on atomization and behavior of spray in tree canopies.

The assumption that spray which is unaccounted for on the forest floor is lost by drift processes is not supported by data presented in this paper.

Literature Cited

1. Hurtig, H.J.; Fettes, J.J.; Randall, A.P.; Hopewell, W.W., "Field and Laboratory Investigations of the Effectiveness of Insecticidal Sprays Applied from Aircraft in Controlling Larvae of Spruce Budworm (Chroistoneura fumiferana (Clem))", Rep. No. 176, Suffield Exper. Sta., Alberta, Canada, 1953; pp. 11-33.
2. Snowden, P.; Andrews, W.; Sufley, G., "Spray Deposit Distribution within Balsam Fir Crown", Report P-77-6, USDA Forest Service, NA Area, S&PF, Upper Darby, PA., 1977.
3. Thompson, C.; Neisess, J.; Batzer, H., "Field Tests of Bacillus thuringiensis and Aerial Application Strategies on Western Mountainous Terrain", USDA Forest Service Research Paper PNW-230, Pacific Northwest Forest and Range Experiment Station, Portland, Oregon. 1977; p. 12.
4. Barry, J.; Wong, J.; Kenney, P.; Barber, L.; Flake, H.; Ekblad, R. Zeitschrift fur angewandte Entomologie. 1981, 92, pp. 224-232.
5. Joyce, R.J.V.; Beaumont, J. "Collection of Spray Droplets and Chemical by Larvae, Foliage and Ground Deposition" In: Control of Pine Beauty Moth by Fenithrothion in Scotland 1978. A.V. Holden and D. Beva, Eds., Forestry Commission. The Nuffield Press Ltd.: Oxford, England, 1978; pp 63-80.
6. Armstrong, J.A.; Yule, W.N. Can. Ent. 1978, 110, 1259-67.
7. Sundaram, A.; Proc. 1982 Summer Meeting Amer. Soc. Agri. Engr. 1982, Paper No. 82-1006.
8. Himel, C.M.; Moore, A.D., Science, 1967, 156, 1250-1251.
9. Ekblad, R.; Armstrong, J.; Barry, J.; Bergen, J.; Miller I.; Shea P., "A Problem Analysis-Forest and Range Pesticide Application Technology"; U.S. Dep. of Agriculture, Forest Service, Missoula Equipment Development Center, Missoula, MT. 1979; pp. 107.
10. Maksymiuk, B. J. of Forestry. 1963, 61, No. 2 143-144.
11. Barry, J.W.; Sutton, G.L.; Grim, B.S.; Ekblad, R.B.; Ciesla, W.M.; Dewey, J.E.; "Aerial Spray Evaluation Pine Butterfly Test Bitterroot National Forest, Montana 1973"; U.S. Army Dugway Proving Ground, Dugway, UT, USDA For. Serv., Region 1, S&PF, and Missoula Equipment Development Center, Missoula, MT, 1975; pp. 170 and Apdx.

12. Barry, J.; Ciesla, W.; Ford, R.; Luebbe, R.; Whitcombe, L.;
    Young, R., "Spray Deposit Maine 1976 Operational Project for
    Control of the Eastern Spruce Budworm Comparing Effectiveness
    of Sevin 4-oil 3/4 and 1 pound per acre"; USDA For. Serv.,
    Methods Application Group, Davis, CA. 1976.
13. Stipe, L.; Knopf, J.; Livingston, L.; Young, R.; Markin, G.P.
    "A Cooperative Pilot Project to evaluate Orthene Forest Spray
    for Control of the Western Sruce Budworm, Choristoneura
    occidentalis Freeman, McCall, Idaho 1977"; USDA For. Serv.,
    Intmtn. Region, Ogden, Utah, in coop. with State of Idaho
    Dept. of Lands and Boise Cascade Corp. 1977.
14. Barry, J.; Markin, G.; Knopf, J.; Wong, J. "Demonstration of
    the Marsh Turbo Thrush to Deliver Pesticides to Coniferous
    Forests, Phase 2 - Forest Spraying"; Rpt. No. 79-2. USDA
    For. Serv., FI&DM/Methods Application Group, Davis, CA.,
    1978.
15. Barry, J.; Whyte, G.; Hofacker, T. "Evaluation of the Marsh
    Turbo Thrush for Forest Spraying, Phase 1 - Spray
    Characterization"; Rpt. No. 79-1, USDA For. Serv., Methods
    Application Group, Davis, CA. 1978.
16. Barry, J.; Kenney, P.; Wong, J.; Barber, L.; Ekblad, R.;
    Dumbauld, R.; Flake, H. "Aerial Application to Southern Pine
    Seed Orchards"; USDA For. Serv., Southern Region, Forest Pest
    Management, Asheville, NC. 1982.
17. Akesson, N. and Cowden, R. Metallic Salts as Tracers for
    Spray Deposit Applications. In: USDA Tech. Bull. 1596.
    Methods for Sampling and Assessing Deposits of Insecticidal
    Sprays Released over Forests. USDA, Washington, DC., 1978;
    pp. 107-112.
18. Barry, J.; Ciesla, W.; Tysowsky, M.; Ekblad, R. J. Econ.
    Entom. 1977, 70, No. 3, 387-388.
19. Barry, J.; Ekblad, R. Trans. ASAE. 1978, 21, 438-441.

RECEIVED September 9, 1983

Droplet Deposition and Drift in Forest Spraying

CHARLES J. WIESNER

Research and Productivity Council, P.O. Box 6000, Fredericton, New Brunswick, E3B 5H1, Canada

This paper presents the results of recent experiments aimed at elucidating relationships between atmospheric stability and spray deposition on conifer foliage. While the aerial application parameters which were used are specific to the New Brunswick spruce budworm operation, the conclusions should be applicable to problems of spray accountability in general.

The spruce budworm, Choristoneura fumiferana (Clem.) is one of the most widely established of all coniferous forest defoliators. This pest presents a particular threat in New Brunswick which is 80% forested with largely budworm-prone species. A sequence of epidemic outbreaks has affected these regions for at least 200 years. It appears that large scale outbreaks tend to develop where extensive areas of susceptible host stands approach maturity, possibly triggered by several seasons of weather especially conducive to budworm survival. Historically, the result of such outbreaks in New Brunswick has been the death of large tracts of spruce/fir forests in 30-50 year cycles (1). The tremendous growth of the pulp and paper industry in this century has made these soft woods a highly valued resource and has put New Brunswick's forest industry and socio-economic well-being in direct competition with the budworm.

  Based on studies of the 1912-1920 epidemic, forest entomologists predicted another outbreak in the 1940's. Nature did not disappoint them and by 1951 heavy infestation was recorded over 2,200 square miles in northern New Brunswick. In view of the immense losses experienced in the earlier outbreak, the pulp and paper industry and the provincial government in 1952 initiated, on a cost-shared basis, a spraying operation using DDT over 75,000 hectares of prime forest. On the basis of that operation, it was concluded that a large proportion of the larvae were indeed killed and a significant degree of foliage was saved. At the same time it was clearly demonstrated that the insect could not be "eradicated" since long range re-invasion by mated females ensured a significant re-infestation of the sprayed area the following year.

Following the 1968 decision to discontinue the operational use in
New Brunswick of DDT (a decision which predated both federal and
provincial regulatory bans), a number of alternatives have been used
including phosphamidon, fenitrothion, aminocarb and Bacillus
thuringiensis.

In the last several years of the current outbreak, approximately
1.6 million hectares of forest land have been sprayed per year. The
areas to be treated in any given season are selected by means of a
rating system based on population forecasts, previous defoliation and
stand vigour. The same stands are usually not sprayed in successive
years (1).

In spite of numerous studies attesting to negligible environmental
impact of spray operations in New Brunswick, public pressure has
resulted in the need for ever-increasing sophistication in the
monitoring of off-target insecticide drift and the ability to
understand and predict such drift. Consequently, the province has
provided extensive support for research into various aspects of spray
drift and efficacy. In order to help coordinate research and to
develop the necessary interdisciplinary approach, the New Brunswick
Spray Efficacy Research Group (NBSERG) was formed. NBSERG is not
a centralized research group or institution but an association of
scientists representing those disciplines which are implicated in the
mechanistic definition of spray drift and efficacy. These include
chemists, physicists, engineers, meteorologists, foresters,
entomologists and spray operators.

The present study illustrates one segment of the cooperative and
multidisciplinary spray research being carried out under the aegis of
NBSERG.

Background

A widely held doctrine has been that both wind and small droplets are
an anathema to aerial spraying in that both significantly enhance
drift. While "common sense" appears to support these convictions,
analysis of the mechanisms of droplet transport and impaction reveals
that, under most circumstances, quite the opposite is true.

Qualitative evidence in support of the effectiveness of
turbulent, small droplet spraying has been available for some time but
has largely been ignored. For example, studies at the Cranfield
Institute of Technology, and the CIBA-GEIGY Agricultural Aviation
Research Unit in England have demonstrated that turbulent eddies
immediately above the canopy provide an efficient mechanism for
vertical transport of small droplets into the canopy (2). In the
absence of such turbulence - that is under stable atmospheric
conditions, small droplets having relatively slow sedimentation
velocities tend to drift slowly off target.

Deposit assessment methodology has been a major obstacle to the
advancement of our understanding of the spray process. It is now
largely accepted (3) that droplet deposit on cards (the most common

assessment tool) is an inadequate measure of deposition on the real target - pest habitat foliage. Under conditions of increased wind and turbulence, when the sedimentation component of even large droplets diminishes in importance, this technique may fail entirely.

It is important to realize that while assessment of spray efficacy by larval mortality or foliage saved provides a measure of the overall result of the operation, it yields no insight into the reasons for success, variability or failure. In other words, it is not a diagnostic research tool. Such a tool is essential to the interpretation of results. Consequently, several methods have been developed to enable counting and sizing of drops impacted on foliage and insects. For example, in 1967 using his newly developed fluorescent particle method, Himel (4) was able to demonstrate that no significant numbers of spray droplets larger than 50 μ in diameter impacted on western spruce budworm larvae during a test in Montana although the spray spectrum was broad, with droplets ranging beyond 300 μ. Himel estimated that the biologically effective portion of the spray, that is the portion having diameters below about 100 μ, constituted only a few percent of the emitted spray volume.

In 1978 Barry and Ekblad (5) used dyed spray mixes with volume median diameters between 250 and 350 microns to determine the droplet spectrum deposited on conifer needles. Two applications of Bacillus thuringiensis and one each of carbaryl and trichlorphon gave remarkably similar results. Approximately 95% of all drops observed on foliage were less than 82 microns in diameter, with an average deposit close to 2 drops per needle. The conclusion again was that only those drops significantly smaller than 100 μ are effective in reaching and depositing uniformly on the target. Large drops, while carrying the bulk of the insecticide, are very few in number and are found on such a small percentage of needles that they can contribute little to insect mortality.

In 1979 Crabbe et al (6) investigated the effect of meteorological conditions on long-range drift in New Brunswick (Table I) and were able to demonstrate a significant increase in drift with increasing atmospheric stability at both 7.5 and 24 km downwind.

As a follow-up to these and other pioneering studies recent efforts in New Brunswick have been aimed at establishing quantitative relationships between meteorology, droplet spectrum and foliar deposit.

One such experiment was conducted in July 1982 near Dunphy air field in central New Brunswick. This was a collaborative effort involving the University of New Brunswick (UNB), Forest Protection Ltd. (FPL), the National Research Council (NRC), the Atmospheric Environment Service (AES) and the Research and Productivity Council (RPC). The aim was to provide more quantitative data on the relationships between atmospheric stability or structure and target deposition.

Experimental Design

The layout of the Dunphy experiments is shown in Figure 1. The experiment consisted of a single swath cross-wind application with various sampling and measuring devices deployed from the swath line to 3600 m downwind.

The objective was to measure both foliar deposit and drift at distances downwind under several well characterized meteorological conditions.

A Grumman Avenger TBM flying approximately 20 m above the forest canopy applied the dyed spray with an emitted volume median diameter (vmd) close to 100 μ. The spray mix, an aqueous fenitrothion emulsion, was applied at a rate equivalent to 1.5 l/ha and had a residual volume of 20% after evaporation of the water. Consequently, the evaporated vmd was approximately 58 μ.

$$d_2 = d_1 \ (v_2/v_1)^{1/3}$$

Meteorological measurements were made by cooperators from NRC, AES and UNB using an instrumented 46 m mast situated 400 m downwind of the spray line as well as balloonborne mini-sondes and tether-sondes. Spray drift samplers (7) were deployed at 400, 1200 and 3600 meters while vertical flux profiles were provided to a height of 200 m by light weight dosimeters suspended from tethered balloons. This sampling system was designed to provide data necessary to enable calculation of a total mass budget for drifting spray at the three downwind distances.

Our role at RPC was to determine the size and frequency of spray droplets deposited on foliage at various distances downwind. Four sampling lines were established at 100, 200, 400 and 600 m from the spray line. On each line three trees, 30-50 m apart, were selected for sampling. As we were conducting successive experiments, we could not use the native foliage on the trees for deposit analysis since after the first run it would have been contaminated. Instead, wooden brackets were constructed in the mid-crown of each tree with the brackets oriented parallel to the wind direction. Fresh balsam fir boughs were then mounted at each end just prior to the spray application. Following each spray these boughs were returned to the laboratory for both droplet and gas chromatographic (GC) analysis. Stains were counted and sized on eighty needles taken at random from each bough, while ten gram samples of needles and twigs were macerated, solvent extracted and column chromatographed in preparation for GC analysis. This system provided us with three replicate upwind and downwind mid-crown samples for each distance from the spray line.

We investigated a number of systems in the laboratory to determine how best to size droplets on conifer needles. It soon became obvious that, from a technical point of view, dyes provided the simplest means; however, we found that oil soluble dyes are ineffective for the visualization of droplets on foliage. The dye is very quickly absorbed into the waxy surface of the needle and loses its visibility within minutes. On the other hand, various water soluble dyes were found to retain their clarity on the needle surface indefinitely. We found that we could store foliage in the freezer for months without affecting stain visibility. Since the stain is water soluble, foliage samples had to be removed from the freezer in hermetically sealed containers and brought to room temperature so as to prevent moisture condensation smearing the stains.

The stains were then sized in 10 µ ranges using a Fleming particle size micrometer as well as microscopes fitted with eye piece micrometers.

The diameter of any stain is always larger than that of the impinging droplet, the relationship between the two diameters is referred to as the spread factor. The spread factor is an empirical value which must be a determined anew for each formulation and each target surface. The droplet size data in the present study were derived using an assumed spread factor on fir foliage of 2.5. Recent measurements (8) using a mono-disperse droplet generator have shown the true factor to be 2.66.

Results

Drift Budget. Four tests were conducted in atmospheric conditions which ranged from slightly stable through neutral to moderately unstable but with very similar mean wind speeds at 46 m above ground. The results of Crabbe et al. (7) for the airborne fraction of the applied spray are shown in Table II. At 400 m downwind of the swath 31% of the material is still airborne while under neutral and unstable conditions the drifting fraction decreased to 12% and 9%, respectively. This trend is supported by measurements at 1200 m where under neutral atmospheric conditions 10% of the spray is still drifting while in the unstable case, no airborne droplets were detectable at this distance.

Foliar Deposit Analysis. Figures 2 and 3 represent droplet deposits on fir needles located on upwind and downwind aspects of the sample trees as a function of distance from the spray swath. The peak droplet density was found to average near one drop per needle on the upwind aspect with downwind deposits significantly lower in keeping with the findings of Armstrong and Yule (9). The position of the peak, however, varies systematically with atmospheric conditions. Under unstable conditions (tests #3 and #4) the peak deposit is found closer to the swath (100 m) than under neutral or stable conditions (200 m). This result is in accord with the turbulent deposition hypothesis and is further supported by GC analytical results as shown in Figure 4. These curves represent overall average deposit on foliage expressed as parts per million of fenitrothion related to downwind distance. Clearly, under unstable conditions the spray gets down sooner and is deposited more effectively than under stable or even neutral atmospheric conditions.

TABLE I

Peak Axial Concentration at Tree-top in Long Range Drift Study (6)

Test	Distance (km)	Peak Axial Concentration (ng/l)	
I	7 .5 24	1.4 0.15	(Neutral Conditions)
II	7.5 24	2.0 0.37	(Slightly Stable)
III	7.5 24	5.6 1.1	(Moderately Stable)

(Reproduced with permission from Ref. 6. Copyright 1980,
National Research Council Canada.)

TABLE II

Airborne Fraction in Fenitrothion Budget Trials (7)

Test	Stability Class	Mean Wind$_1$ (ms^{-1})	Fraction Airborne @		
			200 m	400 m	1200 m
1	Stable	4.41	0.3	0.31	–
2	Neutral	4.32	0.24	0.12	0.1
3	Unstable	4.30	–	0.09	0

(Reproduced with permission from Ref. 7. Copyright 1983,
National Research Council Canada.)

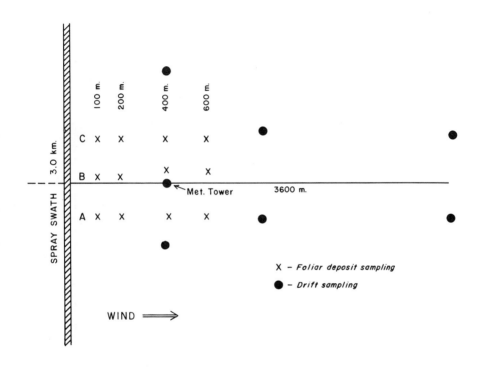

Figure 1. Dunphy experimental layout and sampling scheme used
to measure drift and deposit under various meteorological
conditions.

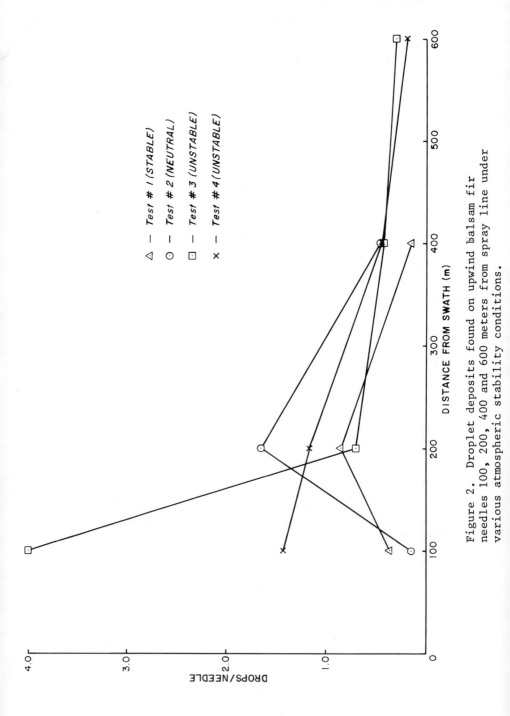

Figure 2. Droplet deposits found on upwind balsam fir needles 100, 200, 400 and 600 meters from spray line under various atmospheric stability conditions.

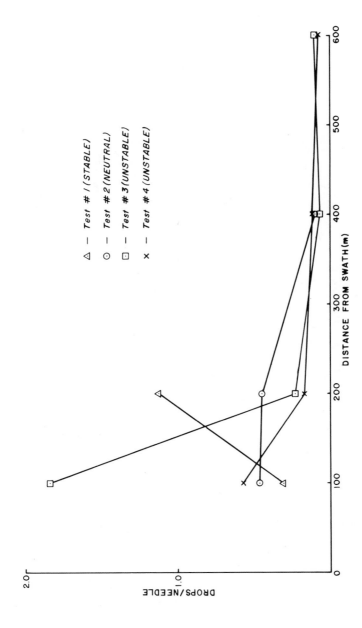

Figure 3. Droplet deposits found on downwind balsam fir needles 100, 200, 400 and 600 meters from spray line under various atmospheric stability conditions.

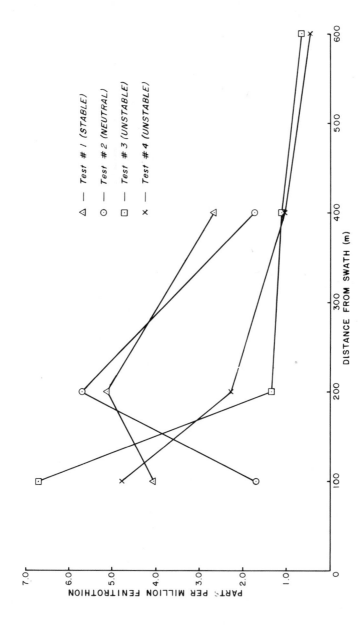

Figure 4. Fenitrothion concentration in balsam fir needles as determined by gas chromatography. Average of upwind and downwind concentrations at each distance.

We found that the spectrum of droplet sizes on needles was remarkably uniform, both within a given sample line and between lines. While we anticipated classification to smaller drop sizes with increasing distance, this was not observed. Future experiments will include a 50 m sample line, which should show some increase in the proportion of larger droplets.

Figure 5 shows representative spectra for test #4, an unstable case. The maximum of the deposited spectrum occurs at 10 µ. Since 10 µ droplets have quite poor impaction efficiency, this finding suggests that the proportion of very small drops emitted by the aircraft must be very large indeed. Earlier studies (10) of the TBM emitted spectrum have severely underestimated these numbers due to problems associated with measuring in-flight drops smaller than about 30 µ. Recent studies using a laser spectrometer are expected to clarify this point (11).

Discussion

In summary, this work has provided further, quantitative evidence that wind and turbulence are not a priori detrimental to forest aerial spraying; on the contrary they tend, within limits, to improve deposit and reduce drift. The drift budget studies of Crabbe et al. (6, 7) compellingly demonstrate the presence of more drift at both medium and long ranges under classical stable spray conditions than in the neutral or somewhat unstable cases. Similarly, the foliar deposit study has shown that peak deposit in the mid-crown is located closer to the swath line under unstable conditions. The inference is that total deposit in these cases must also be improved; however, given the natural heterogeneity of the forest and the consequent variability of deposit, our sampling regime was insufficient to permit integration of foliar deposit over the entire field. Further experiments planned for the spring of 1983 will provide more detailed drift and deposit data. These forthcoming trials will also include sprays carried out under extreme conditions of stability and instability so as to define effective meteorological limits to the spray operation.

One aspect of the deposited spectrum which is of particular practical significance is its relationship to the evaporated emitted spectrum. We have seen that the evaporated vmd is approximately 58 µ a value considerably lower than is commonly used with ultra low volume applications. Yet, of 5000 droplets sized on fir needles 90.4% were smaller than 60 µ. Since this method of application has proven efficacious over millions of hectares of New Brunswick forest, one must conclude, yet again, that small drops are not merely effective but, in all likelihood, are responsible for the bulk of insect mortality.

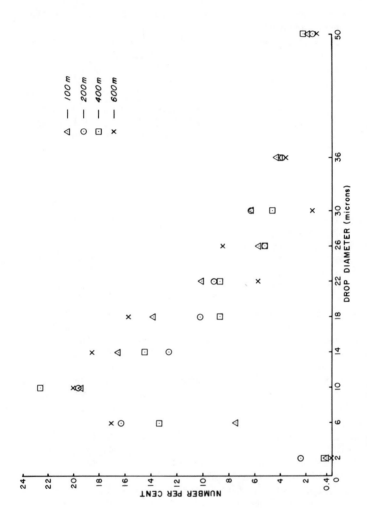

Figure 5. Droplet spectra deposited on balsam fir needles under unstable conditions 100, 200, 400 and 600 meters from swath.

Acknowledgements

The work discussed here has formed only a small part of the overall project and I would like to stress that the collaboration of Drs. R. S. Crabbe and L. Elias of the National Research Council of Canada, and Professors J. J. C. Picot, D. D. Kristmanson and R. B. B. Dickison of the University of New Brunswick, and Dr. R. E. Mickle of the Atmospheric Environment Service was essential. Dr. F. E. Webb has provided invaluable perspective and advice. The genuine interest in and unstinting support of this research by Forest Protection Ltd. is gratefully acknowledged.

Literature Cited

1. Irving, H. J.; Webb, F. E. Pulp and Paper Canada 1981, Jan., 3-8.
2. Joyce, R. J. V.; Spillman, J. J. in "Control of Pine Beauty Moth by Fenitrothion in Scotland, 1978"; Holden, A. V.; Bevan, D., Eds.; Forestry Commission: Edinburgh, 1979; Chap. 2. pp. 13-24.
3. Barry, J. W. in "Method for Sampling and Assessing Deposits of Insecticidal Sprays Released Over Forests" U. S. Department of Agriculture. Technical Bulletin No. 1596, 1978, p. 8.
4. Himel, C. M.; Moore, A. D. Science 1967, 156, 1250-1.
5. Barry, J. W.; Ekblad, R. B. Trans. ASAE 1978, 21, 438-41.
6. Crabbe, R.; Elias, L.; Krzymien, M.; Davie, S. Report No. LTR-UA-52 1980, National Aeronautical Establishment, National Research Council Canada.
7. Crabbe, R. S.; Elias, L.; Davie, S. J. Report No. LTR-UA-65 1983, National Aeronautical Establishment, National Research Council Canada.
8. Henderson, G., personal communication.
9. Armstrong, J. A.; Yule, W. N. Can. Entmol. 1978, 110, 1259-67.
10. Tomney, T. D.; Smedley, J. B.; Kristmanson, D. D.; Picot, J. J. C. NRC Report No. 0SU77-00155 1978, University of New Brunswick, Fredericton, N. B., Canada.
11. Picot, J. J. C., personal communication.

RECEIVED September 9, 1983

12

Modeling of Aerial Spray Drift and Canopy Penetration

RICHARD K. DUMBAULD

H. E. Cramer Company, Inc., P.O. Box 8049, Salt Lake City, UT 84108

The FSCBG aerial spray computer program is the
result of more than a decade of refinement and
verification of spray dispersion models used by
the USDA Forest Service and the U. S. Army for
predicting the drift, deposition and canopy penetration of particles and drops downwind from
aircraft releases. This paper describes the
mathematical framework of the models and selected
applications of the models to military and Forest
Service projects.

The FSCBG aerial spray models and computer program are a result
of more than a decades effort in the development, refinement
and application of models for use by the U. S. Army and USDA
Forest Service in predicting drift, deposition and canopy penetration from aerial releases. During the 1960's, the U. S.
Army extended generalized modeling techniques developed for the
aerial release of aerosols near ground level (1) based on the
results from field measurement programs (2-5) conducted over a
variety of terrain. By the late 1960's, provision had been
made in the modeling techniques to account for the loss of
material by gravitational settling of drops from spray clouds
and for predicting ground-level deposition patterns of spray
drops (6). Increased concern about the environmental effects
of spray material in the early 1970's led to further development and application of models to predict the dispersion and
deposition of pesticides applied by aircraft. The U. S. Forest
Service began the use of aerial spray models, with cooperation
from the U. S. Army (7), to determine optimum swath widths and
application rates for pilot tests of insecticides under consideration for control applications in western forests. The
implications of these early efforts in the use of mathematical
models to improve the planning, conduct and analysis of spray
programs were reviewed in a paper presented at the USFS Workshop

0097-6156/84/0238-0153$06.50/0
© 1984 American Chemical Society

for Aerial Application of Insecticides Against Forest Defoliators, held in Missoula, Montana, 23-29 April 1974 (8). In 1977 mathematical spray dispersion models were used to assist the State of Maine Bureau of Forestry (9) in determining offset distances required for various aircraft to ensure that drift from spray blocks posed no environmental hazards to exclusion areas (waterways, homes, etc.). Under the sponsorship of the USDA Expanded Douglas-Fir Tussock Moth Research Program, work began in 1977 on the refinement and adaptation of existing models to predict spray behavior above and within forest canopies. This work led to the development of the FSCBG computerized spray dispersion model (10) which contained algorithms for considering the penetration of drops into canopies, simple expressions for considering the wake effects of aircraft and provision for considering finite line-source releases when the winds are not perpendicular to the release line. Development of the aerial spray dispersion model has continued to date. Recent improvements include provision for considering the evaporation of spray material (11). Currently a more sophisticated treatment of aircraft wake effects is under development in work performed under the sponsorship of the U. S. Forest Service Equipment Development Center.

Considering the continued development, verification and improvement of these aerial spray modeling techniques and their acceptance by the U. S. Army and U. S. Forest Service, we believe the concepts deserve wider use in civil spray operations, pesticide development programs and environmental assessment studies. We therefore welcome the opportunity presented by this symposium for discussing the mathematical framework of the models and to illustrate their applications.

Mathematical Framework of the Spray Dispersion Model. The mathematical spray dispersion model ideally provides a framework for describing the fate of spray from the time the material is released from the aircraft spray nozzle until it impacts on the target or drifts to distances where deposition or drift are no longer important. In simplest terms, the model uses mass continuity concepts to describe aircraft wake and atmospheric effects on the transport and dispersion of the spray material. The FSCBG model to our knowledge represents the state-of-the-art in aerial spray models. The model is based on Gaussian atmospheric dispersion formulas which are peerless as practical diffusion modeling tools (12). Thus, in unbounded space, the distribution of spray material about a mean cloud axis is assumed to be Gaussian distributed. Appropriate modifications to the Gaussian distribution are made in the model to account for the reflection or loss of material at the earths surface and reflection at the bases of elevated thermal inversions. The FSCBG model and computer program are modular in concept to permit the updating of model components and to facilitate the choice of options in applications to specific problems. Figure 1 is a schematic diagram showing the major components of the model and program.

Model Input Requirements. As can be seen from examination of the model inputs required (or provided under certain options) by the FSCBG model shown in Table I, specification of the inputs requires both problem organization and an interdisiciplinary effort between aircraft and spray system engineers, meteor-ologists, foresters, chemists, biologists and entomologists. The importance of some of these elements is discussed in other papers presented in this Symposium. The importance of others are briefly defined in the discussion below of the various FSCBG program modules.

Aircraft Wake Module. Spray emitted from aircraft spray nozzles is quickly engulfed in the propellor slipstream and the vortices formed by the body and wings of fixed wing aircraft or the rotor tip-vortices of helicopters. The dimensions and turbulent velocities within these vortices are governed by some of the aircraft characteristics in Table I. Depending on the magni-tude of the vortex motions and the ambient turbulence and wind velocity, these vortices control the growth and spatial position (except for translation by the ambient wind) of the cloud from seconds to minutes after the spray is released. For very low-altitude releases in light wind conditions used to spray some crops, the aircraft wake vortex can determine the swath width and deposition pattern although drift of smaller drops may still occur. As aircraft release altitude increases, the direct impact of the wake vortices on the deposition pattern decreases and the atmospheric transport and dispersion of the spray cloud becomes more important in determining the characteristics and spatial position of the deposition pattern as well as the drift of the spray cloud. The development of models describing the deposition patterns produced by wake effects has increased over the last decade (13-14). The effects of aircraft wakes on the release of agricultural materials and the resulting development of criteria for improved aircraft design have been studied at NASA Langley Research Center (15). The study has resulted in the development of models characterizing the near-field deposi-tion patterns produced by wake effects (16). In an effort to improve the capabilities of the FSCBG model which now contains only an elementary wake model, the U. S. Forest Service Missoula Equipment Development Center has recently participated with NASA in initiating the adaptation of the wake model for use in the FSCBG model (17-18).

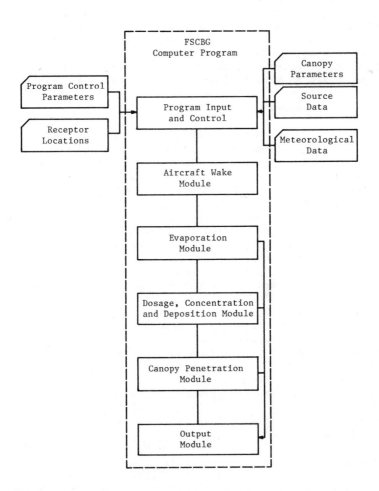

Figure 1.   Schematic diagram showing major modules of the FSCBG computer program.

Table I. Model Input Requirements

Functional Category	Major Elements
Spray System Characteristics	o Application rate, swath width, spray altitude
	o Aircraft speed, wing span and chord, weight and other characteristics
	o Spray boom and nozzle locations, type of nozzle
	o Physical and chemical properties of the spray material (molecular weight, density, heat of vaporization, molal concentration, etc.)
	o Drop-size distribution
Meteorological Factors (Above and Below Canopy)	o Temperature and wind-speed structure
	o Relative humidity
	o Turbulence structure
	o Wind direction and shear
	o Depth of the surface mixing layer
Forest Characteristics	o Typical tree height and diameter at 1 m vertical intervals
	o Tree foliage density
	o Tree spatial distribution (stem density)
	o Probability of penetration, collection efficiencies
Target Characteristics	o Pest-pesticide relationships (LD_{50}, etc.)
	o Topography and other surface features
	o Spray block dimensions
	o Exclusion areas

Evaporation Module. Evaporation can significantly alter the
aerosol size distribution as the spray cloud descends from the
aircraft release height to deposit on the ground. The net
effect of evaporation, because of reductions in the drop size
and thus a decrease in gravitational settling velocity, is to
decrease deposition near the source and increase the downwind
drift of spray drops or vapor. The FSCBG model has two options
that can be used to account for the evaporation of material.
In all modules of the program, the time-rate change in drop
diameter for up to 20 drop-size categories is expressed in the
form of a quadratic equation. The constants a, b and c of the
quadratic can either be directly input to the program or, given
sufficient information, be calculated. The theoretical calculation uses expressions developed by Frossling (in 19) for drops
moving through the atmosphere. Unfortunately, some of the
input parameters required to exercise the Frossling model are
difficult to specify for the complex organic structures of some
pesticides or the mixture of the pesticide and carrier. In
some cases wind-tunnel experiments (20) are conducted to determine the appropriate constants for the pesticide. If the
carrier is water and the pesticide is biological or non-
evaporative, the program uses constants developed from the work
by Pruppacher and Rasmussen (21). The evaporation module also
calculates the centroid height of drops in each category and
other pertinent data as a function of time and distance from
the source for use in other program modules.

Dosage, Concentration and Deposition Module. As noted above,
the FSCBG dosage, concentration and deposition models are based
on Gaussian modeling concepts designed for application to elevated, nearly instantaneous and finite line-sources and include
provision for gravitational settling and evaporation of spray
material. In the models, the axis of the spray cloud is assumed
to be inclined at an angle from the horizontal plane that is
proportional to $(V_j f\{E_j\}/\bar{u})$, where $V_j f\{E_j\}$ is the gravitational
settling velocity for the jth drop size category and $\bar{u}$ is the
mean cloud transport speed above the canopy (6, 22). Because
V_j is functionally dependent on the evaporation rate E_j, this
inclination angle varies with time or distance. The lateral
and vertical extent of the cloud axis are governed by power-law
expressions yielding the standard deviation of the distribution
in the form

$$\text{Lateral:}\quad \sigma_y \sim \sigma_A x^\alpha$$

$$\text{Vertical:}\quad \sigma_z \sim \sigma_E x^\beta$$

where x is downwind distance from the point of cloud stabilization, σ_A and σ_E are measures of the lateral and vertical

turbulence intensity in the atmosphere and α and β depend   on
the thermal stratification of the atmosphere. For nearly
instantaneous sources, α and β can usually be assumed equal to
unity. The point of cloud stabilization for aerial line sources
refers to the point at which aircraft wake effects are no longer
dominant in spray cloud dispersal. Small drops or vapor borne
aloft by turbulence are reflected downwards at the base of
elevated thermal inversions. Drops that reach the ground or
canopy top are either deposited or reflected, depending on
their settling velocity. For example, water drops with diameters less than about 5 micrometers are assumed to be 90 percent reflected at the ground and drops with diameters greater
than about 120 micrometers in diameter are captured. The dosage
(mass x time/unit volume) is a measure of the total amount of
material passing through a unit volume of air at a particular
point in space. In the case of an evaporating pesticide, both
drops and vapor produced by evaporation must be considered in
the calculation. In this case the program generates sources of
vapor material between the aircraft and canopy top or ground,
for each initial drop-size category, with strengths proportional
to the amount of material that evaporates in small vertical
intervals. The transport and dispersion model is exercised for
each of these sources and the total dosage calculated by summing
the contributions from all drop-size categories and vapor
sources. The FSCBG model also calculates the peak concentration
(mass/unit volume) at any user designated point in space as the
spray cloud passes. Time profiles of concentration are not
presently calculated. Deposition (mass/unit area) is calculated
at either the canopy top or, in the absence of vegetation, at
the ground. The deposition calculation results at the canopy
top are used as input to the canopy penetration model. Finally,
the user can select an output option which determines the horizontal area covered by the dosage, peak concentration or deposition levels of interest. However, the accuracy of the area-
coverage calculations depend on the density of the calculation
grid in the area encompassing the expected path of the spray
cloud.

Canopy Penetration Module. The canopy penetration module calculates the amount of spray reaching a given height within the
canopy or the ground beneath the canopy by considering losses
of material due to impaction on vegetative elements. The mathematical framework of the module is based on a Monte Carlo technique developed by Grim and Barry (23) in which a large number
(~1000) of drops in each drop-size category are passed along a
path through a simulated canopy. The inclination of the drop
trajectory with a horizon is treated in a similar manner to
that used above the canopy. Trees in the simulated canopy are
located in equal areas corresponding to the density (stems per

hectare) estimated or measured for the forest. A cross-
sectional height profile or tree envelope of the typical tree
in the forest must also be specified from measurements or from
relationships between the diameter at breast height (DBH) and
canopy height that have been developed for some species.
Finally, an estimate of the foliage density is required. As a
drop "proceeds" along the trajectory, each tree is randomly
displaced within its assigned area in the plane of the horizon
and the program determines if the drop intersects the tree
envelope. If an intercept occurs, the program then determines
if the drop impacts on a tree element using the probability of
penetration based on the foliage density and the impaction
efficiency calculated for the typical tree elements. When the
drop passes through a tree it continues along the trajectory
until it either impacts on another tree or deposits on the
ground. A tally is recorded when a "hit" occurs in a given
height interval for that height interval and all lower height
intervals. After the total user specified number of drops has
been passed along the trajectory, the tally in each height
interval is divided by the total number of drops to form a
cumulative frequency distribution for the particular drop-size
category. The canopy penetration module also calculates the
point, for each receptor calculation point at ground-level and
for each drop-size category, where the drop within the category
entered the forest canopy. Given these coordinates the program
calculates the amount of material "deposited" at the entry
point using the deposition model described above and multiplies
the result by the appropriate percentage obtained from the
cumulative frequency distribution to yield the amount of material deposited within each height interval below the canopy.
The total number of drops passed along the trajectory required
to achieve a stabilized cumulative frequency distribution
depends on the steepness of the trajectory with more drops
required for size categories with large settling velocities
because the path lengths are smaller.

Target Characteristics. Except for the dimensions of the spray
block (target area), the receptor or calculation points and the
description of the canopy structure, the input format does not
explicitly contain further information concerning target-
characteristics, although the meteorological inputs implicitly
reflect the influence of topography (roughness) on atmospheric
turbulence and wind structure. The model output can usually be
easily adapted to user requirements provided a relationship can
be established between mass per unit area or mass per unit
volume and the amount of pesticide required to achieve the
desired control. The model can provide this information as a
function of drop-size category when the drop size is an important factor in achieving control.

Applications of Spray Dispersion Models. Spray dispersion
models are useful in all phases of spray technology. Typical
applications of models in the support of military and civil
spray operations are listed in Table II. More of the example
applications of the FSCBG program described below are for military applications because we have wider experience in this
area. The U. S. Army, Air Force and Navy conduct frequent test
programs involving aircraft releases of material at U. S. Army
Dugway Proving Ground, UT (DPG). Model simulations are routinely conducted for all major tests at DPG where material is
released to the atmosphere and are used to develop meteorological and other criteria for the safe conduct of the trials.
More important to the overall military mission of DPG is the
use of models to assist in the analysis of trial data, the
comparison of weapon performance, systems development, and in
the projection of trial results to examine the tactical and
strategic use of weapons systems.

System Characterization. The Chemical Logistics Evaluation
Test Series conducted at DPG in 1979 provides an example of
trials designed to characterize a spray system. Seven trials
were conducted to test the effectiveness of the AERO 14/B spray
tank filled with non-evaporating simulant and mounted on an A4D
jet aircraft flying at speeds to 0.8 Mach. The aircraft flew
approximately perpendicular to the wind direction along one
edge of a 22.6 km^2 grid at altitudes from 23 to 72 m above the
surface. Deposition measurements were made at 183 m intervals
within the grid using filter paper and Printflex cards as samplers. The dyed simulant drops spot the Printflex cards which
are analyzed using automatic spot and size analyzers. A known
relationship between stain size and drop diameter provides
estimates of the mass deposition and the drop-size distribution.
The filter paper samplers are washed and the leached material
analyzed to obtain an independent estimate of mass deposition.
Meteorological measurements were made near grid center on a
48-m tower. Wind speed and temperature were measured at heights
of 0.5, 1, 2, 4, 8, 16, 32 and 48 m on the tower. Horizontal
and vertical wind directions were measured at heights of 2, 8,
16, 32 and 48 m on the tower. Wind speed and direction were
also measured at 2-m at locations on the upwind and downwind
edges of the grid and by the tracking of Pibals (pilot balloons)
released immediately following the aircraft flight. All meteorological data is digitally recorded during trials and routinely
analyzed to provide means and standard deviations of measured
parameters for the appropriate averaging times and time periods
required to characterize the event. A summary of the meteorological model input parameters for Trial 3 obtained from the
measurements is presented in Table III. The mean wind direction
is a 10-min mean from measurements at 16 m (~half the release

Table II.   Applications of Aerial Spray Dispersion Models

Function	Military Operations	Civil Operations
Development and Planning	Weapons design, development, and comparison of weapons effects	Design develop and select spray delivery systems
	Weapons expenditure data; strategic and tactical offensive and defensive strategies	Determine emission rate, flight altitude, flight path and swath width requirements
	Design specifications for warning system deployment and system requirements	Develop "Buffer zone" requirements
	Selection and comparison of spray materials	Design specifications for sampling networks
	Test design	Determine optimum schedules for spray operations
	Evaluation of intelligence reports	Prepare environmental impact statements
Spray Operations	Schedule flight operations, designate target and system requirements	Schedule flight operations (spray blocks, flight patterns, emission rates, buffer zone requirements)
	Estimate effects on "friendly" forces	On-site sampling data quality checks
	Evaluation of intelligence reports	Public warning and information requirements
Post-Analysis	Compare predicted casualty levels with intelligence reports	Compare spray patterns and measurements levels with mortality data
	Refinement of modeling techniques	Compare predicted spray patterns with measurements
		Assessment of data quality
		Environmental hazard analysis
		Refinement of modeling techniques

Table III. Meteorological Inputs for Trial 3 of the
Chemical Logistics Evaluation Trial Series

Parameter	Value
Mean Wind Direction (deg)	322
$\bar{u}_R\{z_R = 2\ m\}$ (m s^{-1})	3.99
p	0.14
$\bar{\sigma}_A\{10\ min\}$ (deg)	14.8
σ_E (deg)	7.4
H_m (m)	414

height). The wind speed $\bar{u}_R$ measured at a reference height of
z_R equal to 2 m is also measured over a 10-min period beginning
at the time of release. The value of $\bar{u}_R$ and the coefficient p
in the table are used to define the increase of wind speed with
height above ground in a power-law expression of the form

$$u\{z\} \;=\; \bar{u}_R \left(\frac{z}{z_R}\right)^p$$

where z is a calculation height. The value of p is obtained by
fitting the power-law expression to the 10-min mean wind speed
measured at all heights on the tower using least-square regres-
sion techniques. The turbulence parameter $\bar{\sigma}_A\{10\text{-min}\}$ is the
standard deviation of the fluctuations in the horizontal wind
direction for the 10-min sampling period and the turbulence
parameter σ_E is the corresponding standard deviation of the
fluctuations in the vertical wind direction. The values for
$\bar{\sigma}_A\{10\text{-min}\}$ and σ_E in Table III represent mean values between
2 m and the release height obtained from power-law fits to the
values measured in the 48-m tower. The value of H_m in Table
III represents the depth of the surface mixing layer for Trial
3 and was obtained from an analysis of Pibal data.
     High-speed photographic data obtained during the trials
and the deposition data indicated that the release rate along
the aircraft flight path was non-uniform. For example, Figure
2 shows the results of deposition measurements made along the
downwind sampling row with the maximum crossgrid integrated
deposition for Trial 3. As indicated in the figure, the spray
tank release rate decreases exponentially with distance after

Figure 2.   Solid line shows deposition measurements along
the sampling row with the maximum crossgrid integrated
deposition for Trial 3 of the Chemical Logistics Evaluation
Trial Series. Dashed line represents a least-squares to fit
to the data.

activation. Similar results were obtained for the other 6
trials. The drop-size distribution at ground-level was obtained
from the analysis of the Printflex card data measurements made
during the 7 trials. The trial-to-trial variation in mass-
median diameters ranged from 125 to 164 µm. The measurements
from all seven trials were averaged to obtain the cumulative
drop-size distribution shown in Figure 3, where the mass-median
diameter is 150 µm.

Model Verification. For comparison of the results of these 7
trials with previous trials conducted at lower aircraft speeds
and with the results of trials conducted using other systems
requires that dispersion models be used to remove the variability in the results due to the environmental conditions under
which the trials were conducted. The model performance for
these trials and the other trials must be verified before a
comparison can be accomplished. Figure 4 shows measured and
modeled crossgrid integrated dosage for Trial 3 of the Chemical
Logistics Evaluation Trial Series as a function of downwind
distance from the flight path. The sharp peak in the model
curve near 350 m occurs because model calculations were made
only at sampler positions and a straight line used to connect
the points. As is normal for deposition from aerial line
sources, the deposition decreases rapidly with increasing distance from the flight path. Note however the relatively constant
deposition level between 2.5 to 5 km downwind from the flight
path shown in the figure for both the model-calculated and
measured crossgrid integrated deposition. Measurements of
deposition made at long distances from flight paths often show
the influence of an elevated inversion in reflecting material
back towards the surface for subsequent deposition (24). The
deposition area-coverage, or area covered by specific deposition levels, are of interest in military and civil spray operations. Figure 5 shows measured and model calculated deposition
area coverage for Trial 3. For a deposition level of 100 mg m^{-2}
the figure shows a model calculated area-coverage of 4.3×10^5 m^2
and the measured area-coverage is 3.4×10^5 m^2. The calculations for the 7 trials indicated that, for the deposition levels
of interest, the model on average overestimated the measured
area-coverage by about a factor of 1.7. Since the model calculations were made under the assumption that the spray tank was
100 percent efficient, the results indicated an efficiency
factor of 60 percent should be used for future model
calculations.

Post-Analyses of Forest Spray Operations. The Withlacoochee
spray trials were planned and conducted (25-26) as a pilot
project by the Southeastern Area-Forest Pest Management and the
Forest Pest Management-Methods Applications Group, U. S. Forest

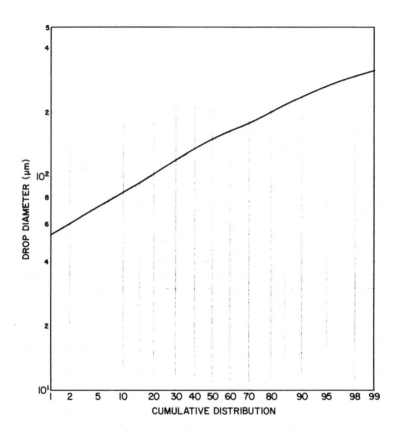

Figure 3.   Cumulative drop-size distribution based on measurements made during the Chemical Logistics Evaluation
Trial Series.

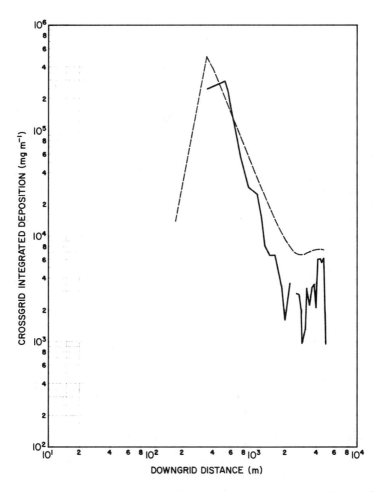

Figure 4.   Crossgrid integrated deposition versus downwind distance for Trial 3 of the Chemical Logistics Evaluation Trial Series.   The heavy solid line represents measured values and the dashed line is model calculated.

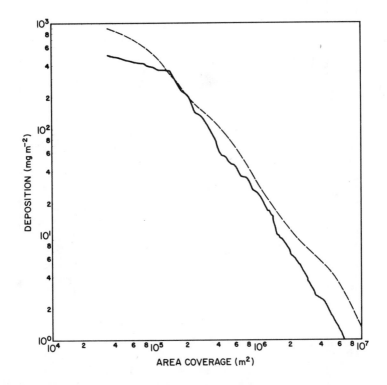

Figure 5.   Deposition area coverage for Trial 3 of the
Chemical Logistics Evaluation Trial Series.   The heavy
solid line is calculated from the deposition measurements
and the dashed line refers to the model calculations.

Service to evaluate the feasibility of using aerial spray application techniques in the control of cone losses due to coneworm
in pine seed orchards. The Withlacoochee orchard near
Brooksville, FL contains uniform stands of slash and Ocala sand
pines planted every 4.6 m in north-south rows separated by a
distance of 9.1 m, or a density of 96.8 stems per acre. The
branches at the bases of the trees along the rows were inter-
twined and the top of the canopy at 12 m was nearly uniform.
Deposition measurements were made at the orchard canopy top,
within sample trees and on the ground beneath the trees in
designated sampling areas. Sampling at the canopy top was
accomplished by stretching a 36.6 m line with aluminum soft-
drink cans attached at 1.8 m intervals between four rows of
trees at up to 6 locations in the orchard. The sampling cans
were also placed within the canopy on sample trees in the upper
crown, mid-crown and in the lower crown facing the four cardinal
directions (north, east, south and west). The soft-drink cans
were wrapped with sampling cards and a cut-out circle of card
placed on the top of each can. Sampling cards were also placed
on the ground at 0.91-m intervals beneath the sampling lines
stretched across the canopy top. Other ground-sampling lines
were placed in the open along a service road cut through the
orchard and along the orchard perimeter. The sampling cards
along the service road were used to obtain the ground-level
drop-size distribution, again accomplished using an automated
image analyzer to count and size the stains produced by drops.
    There were 12 aircraft spray trials; 7 trials were sprayed
by a modified Stearman crop-spraying aircraft at a speed of
40 m s^{-1} and 5 trials were sprayed by a Hughes 500-C helicopter
flying at speeds from 11 to 14 m s^{-1}. Both aircraft sprayed
water containing dye from an altitude of 1.5 m above the canopy
top. A surfactant was added to the water on all but one trial
and manganese sulfate was added to the tank mix as a tracer for
subsequent mass deposit analyses on 4 trials. Mass-median diameters ranged from 353 to 604 μm for the trials, with a slight
indication that the helicopter spray system produced larger
drops. Meteorological measurements of wind speed and horizontal
and vertical wind directions were made at 2- and 16-m on a
tower located near the center of the slash pine orchard. Wind
direction, wind speed, temperature and relative humidity were
measured to heights to 70 m using a tethered balloon
(Tethersonde) placed in a small open area near the spray plot.
An additional measurement of wind speed and direction was made
at a height of 2-m in an open field adjacent to the orchard.
    Figure 6 shows observed and model calculated deposition at
the top of the slash pine canopy for Trial 6. The mass median
diameter drop for Trial 6 was 583 μm. The ratio of the average
measured deposition to the average model-calculated deposition
is about 1.3 for this trial. Observed and model calculated

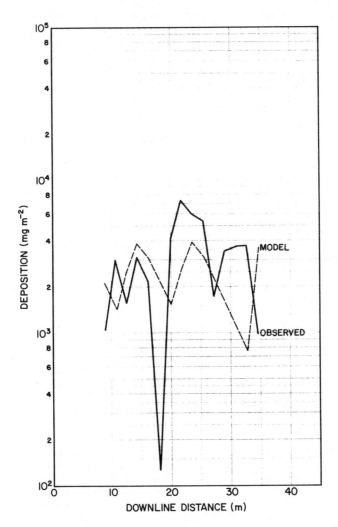

Figure 6.   Observed and model calculated deposition at the
top of the slash pine canopy for Trial 6, Withlacoochee
Spray Trials.

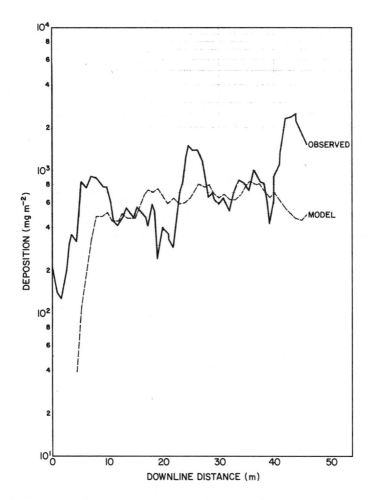

Figure 7.   Observed and model calculated ground-level deposition below the slash pine canopy for Trial 6, Withlacoochee Spray Trials.

deposition at ground-level beneath the slash pine canopy for
Trial 6 are shown in Figure 7, where the ratio of measured to
model calculated mean deposition is about 1.5. The results
shown in Figures 6 and 7 for Trial 6 represent some of the best
agreement achieved between model calculated and measured deposition levels for the Withlacoochee trials. The mean wind speed
for Trial 6 was 4.2 m s^{-1} at the 16 m level on the tower, next
to the highest wind speed recorded at this height during the 12
trials. At low wind speeds observed during many of the trials,
the expected aircraft wake effects were more dominant than the
wind in dispersing the spray. The simplified wake model now
contained in the FSCBG model did not adequately account for the
broader spread of drops caused by the wake turbulence. As
mentioned above, work in improving the models capacity for
considering wake effects, particularly for low-flying aircraft,
is underway.

<u>Summary</u>

The mathematical framework of the FSCBG aerial spray models and
computer program and selected applications of the program have
been presented to demonstrate the potential of transport and
dispersion models for providing assistance to scientist and
engineers in the development of spray systems, the planning and
conduct of spray programs and the assessment of the environmental effects of aerial spray activities. The mathematical
construct of the FSCBG program accounts for the major processes
affecting the atmospheric transport and dispersion of sprays
released from aircraft. The program output has been verified
through comparison with measurements made over open terrain and
to a limited extent within and below forest canopies. There is
no reason to doubt that similar successes cannot be achieved in
predicting the deposition and drift associated with crop-
spraying activities. We believe that the community of pesticide
scientists and engineers require aerial spray dispersion models
to assist them in making the scientific and economic decisions
they confront.

Literature Cited

1. Milly, G. H. "Atmospheric diffusion and generalized muni-
    tion expenditures." <u>ORG Study NR17</u>, U. S. Army Chemical
    Corps, Operations Research Group, Army Chemical Center,
    MD, 1958.
2. Smith, T. B.; M. A. Wolf "Further analysis of Windsock
    data." Final Report, Contract No. DA-42-007-CML-504,
    U. S. Army Dugway Proving Ground, UT, 1961.

3. MacCready, P. B., Jr.; T. B. Smith; M. A. Wolf "Vertical diffusion from a low altitude line source-Dallas tower studies." Final Report, Contract No. DA-42-007-CML-504, U. S. Army Chemical Corps, Dugway Proving Ground, UT, 1961.

4. Smith, T. B.; M. A. Wolf "Vertical diffusion from an elevated line source over a variety of terrains." Final Report, Contract No. DA-42-007-CML-545, U. S. Army Dugway Proving Ground, UT, 1963.

5. Vaughan, L. M.; R. W. McMullen "Intermediate-scale aerosol cloud travel and diffusion from low-level aerial line releases." Technical Report No. 97, U. S. Army Chemical Corps Contract No. DA-42-007-CML-543, 1963.

6. Cramer, H. E.; J. R. Bjorklund; R. K. Dumbauld; J. E. Faulkner; F. A. Record; R. N. Swanson; A. G. Tingle "Development of dosage models and concepts." Final Report Contract No. DAAD09-67-C-0020(R), Deseret Test Center, Ft. Douglas, UT, 1972.

7. "Model estimates of deposition and concentration for the 1973 field tests of insecticides on Pine Butterfly Larval population in the Bitterroot National Forest," Tech. Note, H. E. Cramer Company, under Contract No. DAAD-09-71-C-0003, U. S. Army Dugway Proving Ground, UT, 1973.

8. Dumbauld, R. K.; H. E. Cramer; J. W. Barry "Application of meteorological prediction models for forest spray problems." Report No. TECOM 5-CO-403-000-051, U. S. Army Dugway Proving Ground, UT, 1975.

9. Dumbauld, R. K.; J. R. Bjorklund "Deposition profile calculations for the State of Maine 1977 spray program." Prepared for Litton Aero Products, Woodland Hills, CA and State of Maine Bureau of Forestry, Augusta, ME, 1977.

10. Dumbauld, R. K.; J. E. Rafferty; J. R. Bjorklund "Prediction of spray behavior above and within a forest canopy." Special Report, Contract No. 19-276, Methods Application Group, USDA Forest Service, Davis, CA, 1977.

11. Dumbauld, R. K.; J. R. Bjorklund; S. F. Saterlie "Computer models for predicting aircraft spray dispersion and deposition above and within forest canopies: User's manual for the FSCBG computer program." Report No. 80-11, USDA Forest Service, Methods Application Group, Davis, CA, 1980.

12. Gifford, F. A. in "Lectures on Air Pollution and Environmental Impact Analyses"; D. A. Haugen, Ed.; American Meteorological Society, Boston, MA, 1975, p. 40.

13. Trayford, R. S.; L. W. Welch "The simulation of aerial spray trajectories." Div. Mech. Eng. Commonw. Sci. and Ind. Res. Organ., Melbourne, Aust. Internal Rep. 110, 1972.

14. Wickens, R. H. "A technique for simulating the motion and ground effect of aircraft wake vortices-with particular reference to the spraying of insecticides." LTR-LA-186, Natl. Aeronaut. Establ., Natl. Res. Counc. Can., Ottawa, 1975.

15. Holmes, B. J.; D. K. Morris; K. Razak "Data and analysis
     procedures for improved aerial applications mission
     performance." Paper No. AA 79-001, Natl. Agricultural
     Aviation Meeting; Las Vegas, NV, 1979. Am. Soc. Agri.
     Eng., St. Joseph, MI 49085.
16. Teske, M. E. "Numerical studies of the deposition of agri-
     cultural materials from fixed and rotary wing aircraft:
     AGDISP (MOD 1.0)." Tech. Note 81-14, Contract No. NAS1-
     16031, NASA Langley Res. Ctr., VA, 1982.
17. Teske, M. E. "Numerical studies of the deposition of agri-
     cultural materials from fixed and rotary wing aircraft:
     FSCBG conversion AGLINE (Mod 0.0)." Tech. Note 82-23,
     Contract No. NAS1-16031, NASA Langley Res. Ctr., VA, 1982.
18. Rafferty, J. E. "Review of the AGLINE code compatibility
     with FSCBG code requirements." USDA Forest Service Equip-
     ment Development Center, Missoula, MT, 1983.
19. Fuchs, N. A. "Evaporation and Droplet Growth in Gaseous
     Media"; Pergamon Press, New York, NY, 1959.
20. Dennison, R. S.; J. B. Wedding "Determination of evapor-
     ation rates of pesticide droplets." Aerosol Science
     Laboratory, Ft. Collins, CO, 1982.
21. Pruppacher, H. R.; R. Rasmussen J. Atmos. Sci., 1979, 36,
     1255-1260.
22. Pasquill, F. "Atmospheric Diffusion (Second Edition)."
     Ellis Horwood Limited, Sussex, Eng.
23. Grim, B. S.; J. W. Barry "A canopy penetration model for
     aerially disseminated insecticide spray released above
     coniferous forests." Final Report MEDC Project No. 2425,
     USDA Forest Service Equipment Development Center, Missoula,
     MT, 1975.
24. Dumbauld, R. K.; J. E. Rafferty; H. E. Cramer Proc. 3rd
     Symp. on Atmos. Turbulence, Diffusion and Air Quality, Am.
     Meteorol. Soc., 1976.
25. Barry, J.; J. Wong; P. Kenney; L. Barber; H. Flake; R.
     Ekblad Zeitschrift fur angewandte Entomologie, 1981, 92,
     224-232.
26. Rafferty, J. E.; R. K. Dumbauld; H. W. Flake; J. W. Barry;
     J. Wong "Comparison of modeled and measured deposition for
     the Withlacoochee spray trials." Final Report, Contract
     No. 53-91S8-9-6260, USDA Forest Service Method Applications
     Group, Davis, CA, 1981.

RECEIVED September 9, 1983

Air Circulation in Forested Areas
Effect on Aerial Application of Materials

LEO J. FRITSCHEN

College of Forest Resources, AR 10, University of Washington, Seattle, WA 98195

During summer, the forested areas of the
Northwest and Southwest United States are dominated
by high pressure systems which are characterized by
subsiding air. The combination of subsiding air
and marine or local inversions yield very stable
conditions. Circulation in valleys capped by inversions is characterized by turbulent upslope,
upvalley winds during heating periods and laminar
downslope, downvalley winds during cooling periods.
Interception of radiant energy by vegetative canopies produces an inversion at the crown closure
level while radiant cooling raises the inversion
above the canopy at night. Materials released below these inversions tend to drift below the inversion until a thermal chimney is encountered.

The success of any aerial application depends in part upon the
meteorology and the micrometeorology (both will be referred to as
meteorology) of the area to be treated. The meteorology is in
turn related to the general location within the continent, topography, time of year and time of day. The combination of these
features yield specific environmental conditions which can be
predicted successfully in some areas at certain times of the
year. The purpose of this paper is to describe the combination
of features and the resulting climatic conditions in the Pacific
Northwest during summer periods as they may relate to aerial application of materials.

General Circulation

The excess heating in the tropical regions of the earth, relative
to other regions, causes rising air over the tropics. This warm
air moves both north and south. Due to the rotating earth, the
northward moving air is deflected to the right and becomes a
westerly flow, thus the northward flow is slowed and air piles up

at about 30 degrees N. Because of the pile up of air and the
heat loss by radiation, some of the air starts to descend forming
a high pressure zone. Air that descends flows radially outward.
Again the northward flowing air is deflected to the right and
becomes the prevailing westerlies in the middle latitudes while
the air that flows to the south is deflected to the west and becomes the northeasterly trades of the low latitudes.

At the surface, air that flows outward from a high pressure
zone is replaced by sinking air originating high in the tropo-
sphere. This sinking is referred to as subsidence and gives rise
to the upper air stability that dominates the Pacific Northwest
during the summer. The sinking air warms at the dry adiabatic
lapse rate and, without the addition of moisture, has a very low
relative humidity. Because of the warming and drying of the air,
subsiding air is characteristically very clear and cloudless.
Subsidence may occur in stages giving rise to two or more inversions. The subsiding air has a westerly or northwesterly trajectory in the Pacific Northwest. The number and intensity of
inversions increase at Seattle while their height decreases from
spring to fall as the Pacific High intensifies (Figure 1) (1).

Along the west coast at lower levels, warm moist air over
the Pacific Ocean is advected over the cold upwelling coastal
currents giving rise to cool moist air and frequent fog. This
layer, 300 to 600 m thick, is overlain with the warm dry subsiding air resulting in extremely stable conditions. The cool moist
air frequently invades the lower coastal valleys and the Puget
Sound lowland while the higher topography is exposed to the warm
dry air. Strong surface heating may finally wipe out the lower
or marine inversion leaving the higher subsidence inversions.
When the cool marine air is dammed by the Coastal and Cascade
mountains (Figure 2) and if the pressure is greater on the west
side than on the east side, a foehn wind may result on the east
side (2-3). The foehn winds are warm dry descending winds which
result in clear sky conditions and may induce inversions.

Topography

Topography also influences stability at the lower atmospheric
levels. Night time radiational cooling of the surface produces
low inversions which grow deeper during the night. Strong surface heating during the day usually eliminates the radiational
inversions. Additionally, air in mountain valleys and in basins
heats faster during the day and cools more rapidly at night than
air over the plains. The amount of heating or cooling depends
upon the steepness and orientation of the sloping surfaces, and
the degree of vegetative cover. East facing slopes heat earlier
in the day than do west facing slopes, however southerly slopes
reach greater temperatures and produce greater instability than
northerly slopes, Figure 3 (3). Cooling of these surfaces is
also dependent upon slope, orientation and vegetative cover.

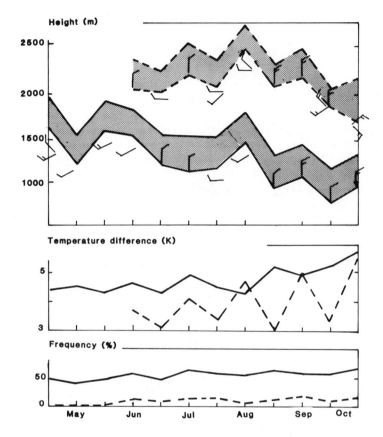

Figure 1. Afternoon inversions at Seattle during May to October 1957-61. Mean inversion heights (base and top): magnitude (potential temperature difference); percentage frequency of inversion occurrence; wind speed and direction at the inversion base for the principal (solid lines) and secondary inversions (dashed lines). (Adapted from Ref. 1.)

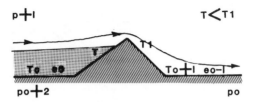

Figure 2. Anticylonic foehn with damming of cold air: T,
air temperature; p, air pressure; and e, vapor pressure;
suffix o, values at the ground level; and 1, values on the
leeside slope. (Reproduced with permission from Ref. 3.
Copyright 1975, University of Tokyo Press.)

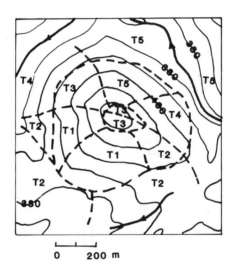

Figure 3. Temperature on a conical shaped mountain.
Values are ranked from Tl (warmest) to T5 (coldest)
(Reproduced with permission from Ref. 4. Copyright
1967, Harvard University Press.)

Slope and valley winds

The result of solar heating on upper slopes as contrasted to
lower slopes produces less dense air which rises up the side
slope, Figure 4, b (4). The steeper sunlit slopes act as natural
chimneys especially if they are barren and associated with draws
or ravines.

Similarly about midmorning, the head of valleys are heated
with respect to the base which promotes air flow up the major
axis of the valley (Figure 4, c). Usually this flow starts after
the slope flows. However, both depend upon the orientation of
the valley and the vegetation cover. The upslope or upvalley
flows are usually turbulent.

Later in the day, as the solar heating becomes less intense
on the side slopes, upper portions cool quickly by radiational
loss to the clear cold sky. Vegetated surfaces cool more quickly
than bare rock surfaces. The air associated with the cool surfaces becomes dense and starts to drain down the slope taking the
path of least resistance (Figure 4, e). This process occurs on
easterly slopes early in the afternoon. These downslope or
drainage winds are laminar in nature and tend to flow like water,
usually through the stem space if trees are present. They can be
dammed momentarily by any obstruction like vegetation, road
fills, fences or narrowing of valleys. Later in the evening, the
head of the valley cools with respect to the base and the cold
dense air begins to flow down the central portion of the valley
usually above the vegetation (Figure 4, g). The downvalley winds
tends to be stronger than the downslope winds having a maximum
speed some distance above the vegetation. Note that the drainage
winds persist during the hours of darkness and until enough solar
heating causes a reversal. These up- and down- slope, and valley
winds are cyclic in nature, specific for a given drainage, and
can be very predictable in the absence of frontal systems.

Winds were studied in the Carbon River Valley near Mount
Rainier (5). The longitudinal sectional winds are shown in Figure 5 a and b. The down-valley or mountain wind persisted until
midafternoon on 9 and 10 August. The up-valley or valley winds
started at the base of the valley at 1200 on 10 August and increased in thickness during the afternoon. Above these valley
winds were anti-valley and anti-mountain winds which varied in
direction from the lower winds by 90 to 180 degrees.

Another example of up- and down-valley winds along the Rio
Grand River near Los Alamos, N.M. is shown in Figure 6 (6). During June, the drainage winds start about 1900 (WNW to NNW through
the night) and give way to the downvalley winds about 0530. The
upslope winds (SE) start around 0900. Note the sudden change in
wind direction that occurs shortly after sunrise with increasing
air temperatures.

In north-south valleys, the east-facing slopes are sunlit
early in the morning while the west-facing slopes are sunlit lat-

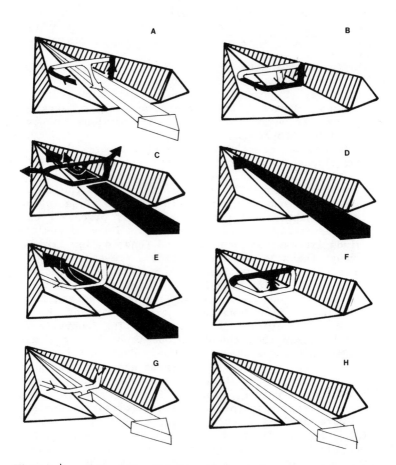

Figure 4. Schematic illustration of the slope and valley
winds where: A, is about sunrise; B, about midmorning; C,
about noon; D, afternoon; E, early evening; F, early
night; G, midnight; and H, dawn. (Reproduced with permission from Ref. 4. Copyright 1967, Harvard University
Press.)

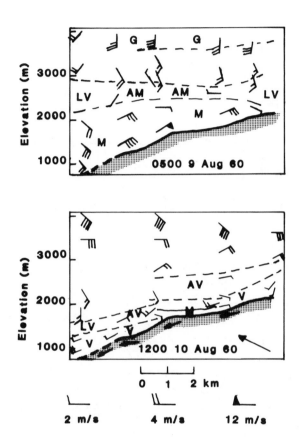

Figure 5. Mountain and valley winds in the Carbon River Valley near vicinity of Mount Rainier, Washington. Local down valley direction ←; AV, antivalley wind; AM, anti-mountain wind; M, mountain wind; V, valley wind. (Reproduced with permission from Ref. 5. Copyright 1966, Springer Verlag.)

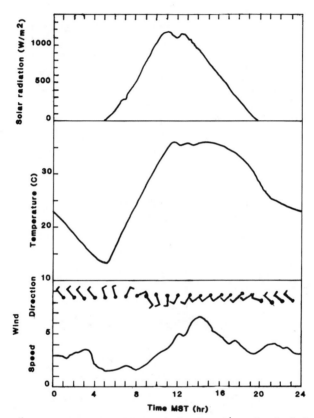

Figure 6.   Slope and valley winds for 14 selected days in
June 1980.   (Reproduced with permission from Ref. 6.   Copyright 1981, Brent M. Bowen.)

er in the day. This may cause upslope winds on the easterly slopes early in the day and downslope winds on the westerly slopes. The thickness of the warmed air layer increases upslope reaching maximum thickness near the top of the slopes. The generalized slope and valley winds are dependent upon the shape and orientation of the valley and the vegetative cover. Therefore, winds in mountain valleys can be extremely complex being influenced by regional and local conditions. The general circulation may reinforce or oppose these local convective winds. Their relationship may change suddenly and over short distances--sometimes winds differing by 90 degrees are separated by the tree crowns. Drainage wind systems for specific valleys have been presented by (7-13). The wind field of a large valley in France was discussed by (14).

Valley inversions

As the cool dense air associated with slope and valley winds accumulates in the bottoms of the valleys, warmer air is pushed up in the center of the valley creating an inversion which increases in depth and strength during the night. This inversion usually occurs at 2/3 to 3/4 of the height of the valley and gives rise to the thermal belt. The strength of this inversion is dependent upon the configuration, orientation and vegetative cover of the valley, Figure 7 (15, 4). Temperature inversions in other valleys have been studied by (16-18).

Canopy inversions

During daylight periods, strong radiant heating produces a warmed zone of air near the height of crown closure and another inversion (0948 through 1608, Figure 8) (19). At night, radiant cooling of the vegetation cools the layer of air associated with the vegetation which moves the inversion above the plant canopy (2028 through 0556, Figure 8). These canopy inversions produce a distinctive microclimate either within the stem space during the day or within the canopy during the night. During night time hours the canopy inversion may be strengthened by cold air draining down the slopes within the stem space.
        The strength of the canopy inversion depends upon the density of the stand. They tend to be more pronounced in dense stands than in sparse stands. Likewise the windspeed within dense stands is usually less than in more open stands (Figure 9) (19). The low level jet in the stem space is stronger if an understory is absent. Furthermore, when the wind is blowing into a forest from a clearing, the windspeed is reduced to a low constant speed in two to three heights (Figure 10) (19). The standard deviation of the reduced canopy windspeed is low indicating a more or less constant windspeed regardless of the external wind. Thus the

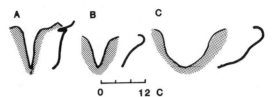

Figure 7. Schematic temperature profile (right hand)
showing the position of the thermal belt on the slope in
relation to the shape of the valley cross section.
(Reproduced with permission from
Ref. 3. Copyright 1975, University of Tokyo Press.)

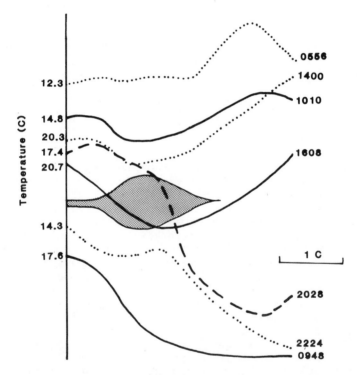

Figure 8. Average air temperature profiles in a 27 m
Douglas fir forest. Shaded area represents vertical vegetation density.

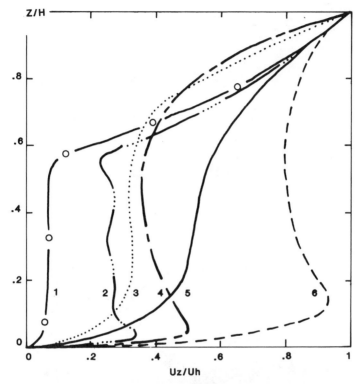

Figure 9. Comparison of normalized wind profiles of various vegetative canopies where Z is the height above the ground, H is the height of the top of the canopy and U is wind speed. 1, dense cotton (21); 2, Douglas fir forest (19); 3, dense conifer with understory (22); 4, moderately dense conifer stand with no understory (20); 5, dense hardwood jungle with understory (23); and 6, isolated conifer stand (24).

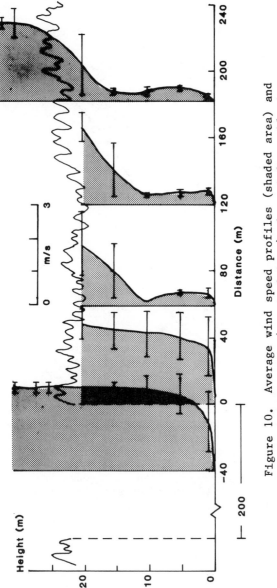

Figure 10. Average wind speed profiles (shaded area) and standard deviations (vertical bars) when wind was blowing from a clearcut into a 27 m Douglas fir forest.

combination of the canopy inversion and low wind speed creates a different microclimate in the stem space.

In addition to the canopy inversions, heating of the forest floor creates an unstable zone (Figure 8) which tends to inhibit deposition of the less dense materials. Again, this effect is more pronounced in more open forests.

Implication to aerial spraying

Inversions tend to inhibit mixing of air below the inversion with that above the inversion. The combination of the Pacific high pressure, topograpy and generally clear sky conditions found in the Pacific Northwest during the summer months results in multi-level inversions (e.g. subsidence, marine air, valley and canopy inversions). All of these could affect a particular site. However, the valley and canopy inversions are the most common. These, in combination with slope and valley winds, greatly affect the distribution of particle and gaseous dispersoids.

Fluorescent particles (3 μm in diameter, density of 4 and settling velocity of 1.3 mm/sec) released within the canopy, below canopy inversion, tended to remain below the inversion regardless of the release height and drift with the flow until they reach some sort of a thermal chimney, Figure 11 (25). Openings in the canopy, streams and lakes could act like thermal chimneys. Furthermore, low density material released above these inversions tends to remain above the inversions and drift with the flow (25). Spread of materials released within the canopy was more rapid than materials released above the canopy. They tended to spread laterally faster and fill the space below the inversion. The vertical extent of plume mixing was determined by stability and vegetative density.

In a study where 5.1 μm diameter fluorescent particles (deposition velocity, 54 mm/sec) were released at 26 m over a sage brush and grass site, 93 percent (an average of 2.1 percent per unit height up to 45 m) of the material remained airborne at 842 m from the release point (26). The temperature differential between 10 and 6 m was 0.5 C and the windspeeds were 2.0 and 6.7 m/s at 2 and 30 m, respectively.

Based upon the above statements, it appears that the best time of day for aerial application in valley situations is when the laminar drainage winds are present either in the early morning (daylight plus 2 hours on easterly slopes) or late afternoon. Drainage wind persists longer on westerly slopes. Late afternoon may be undesirable because of the possibility of either up-slope or valley winds being present. To be effective, materials applied should have a large enough terminal gravitational settling velocity to penetrate the canopy inversion; otherwise they may drift for long distances above the inversion. The material should be of a nature that when it impacts upon vegetation it does not break up in smaller particles or droplets which can be

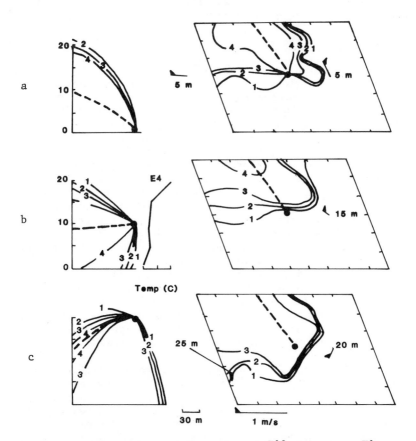

Figure 11. Dosage intensities $\propto 10^{-12}$ (min liter^{-1}) in a horizontal plane (at 1 m) and in vertical planes along the plume center lines of fluorescent particles released in a 27 m Douglas fir forest. Isolines are in powers of 10. Release points, and plume center lines are shown • and – – –, respectively. (a) release at 1 m; (b) release at 10 m; and (c) release at 20 m. Average temperature profiles and wind direction (↰) and speeds are shown for selected towers and heights. (From 20).

carried on the drainage winds. If drops are used, an evaporation
retardant should be used to maintain drop size and thus reduce
drift.

Literature Cited

1. Clarida, K. W., M.S. Thesis, University of Washington.
    Seattle, Wa., 1970.
2. Cadez, M. Veroff. Schweiz. Met. Zentralanstalt 1967, 4,
    155-175.
3. Yoshino, M. M. "Climate in small area"; University of Tokyo
    Press: Tokyo, Japan, 1975; p. 549.
4. Geiger, R. "The climate near the ground"; Harvard University
    Press: Cambridge, Mass., 1967; p. 611.
5. Buettner, K. and Thyer, N. Arch. Met. Geophys. Biokl. 1966,
    B. 14, 125-147.
6. Bowen, B. M. and J. M. Deward. in "Proceedings of the Second
    Conference on Mountain Meteorology"; Am. Meteor. Soc., 1981;
    p. 408.
7. Gudiksen, P. H. and J. J. Walton. in "Second Conference on
    Mountain Meteorology"; Am. Meteor. Soc., Boston, Mass.,
    1981; p. 408.
8. Horst, T. W., and J. C. Doran. in "Second Conference on
    Mountain Meteorology"; Am. Meteor. Soc., Boston, Mass.,
    1981; p. 408.
9. King, C. W. in "Second Conference on Mountain Meteorology";
    Am. Meteor. Soc., Boston, Mass., 1981; p. 408.
10. Martner, B. E. and J. D. Marwitz. in "Second Conference on
    Mountain Meteorology; Am. Meteor. Soc., Boston, Mass., 1981;
    p. 408.
11. Orgill, M. M., R. I. Schreck, and C. D. Whiteman. in "Second
    Conference on Mountain Meteorology"; Am. Meteor. Soc.,
    Boston, Mass., 1981; p. 408.
12. Sommers, W. T. in "Second Conference on Mountain
    Meteorology"; Am. Meteor. Soc., Boston, Mass., 1981; p. 408.
13. Wooldridge, G. L., and D. G. Fox. in "Second Conference on
    Mountain Meteorology"; Am. Meteor. Soc., Boston, Mass.,
    1981; p. 408.
14. Pettre, P. in "Second Conference on Mountain Meteorology";
    Am. Meteor. Soc., Boston, Mass., 1981; p. 408.
15. Koch, H. G. Zeitsch. Met. 1961, 15, 151-71.
16. Whiteman, C. D. in "Second Conference on Mountain
    Meteorology"; Am. Meteor. Soc., Boston, Mass., 1981; p. 408.
17. Banta, R. M. in "Second Conference on Mountain Meteorology";
    Am. Meteor. Soc., Boston, Mass., 1981; p. 408.
18. Schroeder, T. A. in "Second Conference on Mountain
    Meteorology"; Am. Meteor. Soc., Boston, Mass., 1981; p. 408.

19. Fritschen, L. J., C. H. Driver, C. Avery, J. Buffo, R. Edmonds. R. Kinerson and P. Schiess. Grand No. DA-AMC-28-043-68-G8. DA Task No. 1T061102B53A-17. U.S. Army Electronics Command, Atmospheric Sciences Laboratory, Fort Huachuca, Arizona. 1970.
20. Fons, W. L. J. For. 1940, 38, 481-6.
21. Fritschen, L. J. in "Atmospheric and soil-plant-water relationships." Tech. Rept. ECON 2-66P-A. U.S. Army Electronic Command, Ft. Huachuca, Ariz. 1966.
22. Gisborne, H. G. 11th Rocky Mt. For. Range Expt. Sta. 1941, p. 14.
23. Latimer, W. M. in "Handbook on aerosols"; Atomic Energy Comm. Washington, D.C. 1950; p. 170.
24. Reifsynder, W. E. For. Sci. 1955, 1, 289-97.
25. Fritschen, Leo J. and Robert Edmonds. in "Atmosphere-surface exchange of particulate and gaseous pollutants"; ERDA Symposium Series 38; Technical Information Center, Energy Research and Development Administration, 1976; p. 988.
26. Nickola, P. W. and G. H. Clark. in "Atmosphere-surface exchange of particulate and gaseous pollutants"; ERDA Symposium Series 38; Technical Information Center, Energy Research and Development Administration, 1976; p. 988.

RECEIVED September 9, 1983

TARGET AND NONTARGET
RESIDUE DISTRIBUTION

Importance of Volatilization as a Pathway for Pesticide Loss from Forest Soils

W. F. SPENCER

U.S. Department of Agriculture, Agricultural Research Service, University of California, Riverside, CA 92521

W. A. JURY and W. J. FARMER

Department of Soil and Environmental Sciences, University of California, Riverside, CA 92521

The importance of volatilization of pesticides in the forest environment has not been established by direct measurement. Considering the high rates of pesticide volatilization from foliage and moist soil surfaces under agricultural conditions, it is apparent that volatilization of the more commonly used forest pesticides will be relatively high from canopy foliage and from litter or grass on the forest floor. A dynamic model based on the physical and chemical factors controlling pesticide concentrations at the soil surface was used to estimate the susceptibility of pesticides to volatilization loss from soil in the forest environment. Calculations indicated that volatilization from soil of the more commonly used forest herbicides and insecticides with the exception of carbaryl, will be relatively low or insignificant because of their low volatility, low Henry's constants, K_H, and/or their high rates of degradation in the soil environment.

Volatilization of pesticides is an important pathway for their loss from treated agricultural lands. The importance of volatilization in the forest environment has not been established by direct measurement, but can be inferred from volatilization rates of the same pesticides under agricultural conditions and from other data on their behavior in the forest environment. In recent years, several studies of actual volatilization rates of pesticides under field conditions have provided an assessment of the rate of input to the air under typical conditions of use (1). These studies showed that volatilization rates from plant or moist soil surfaces can be very large with losses approaching 90% within 3 days for more volatile pesticides. Volatilization losses from dry soil or from incorporated chemicals are much less.

The forest environment is quite different from the agricultural environment. Pesticide applications occur at infrequent

0097–6156/84/0238–0193$06.00/0
© 1984 American Chemical Society

intervals in forest lands. Applications are usually made on a
rotational basis with only a small fraction of the total land
area receiving chemicals at any one time. During a 30- to 80-year
period, each acre may receive applications only 2 or 3 times.
Forest soils are more typically shallow, have a high infiltration
rate, low pH, and relatively high organic matter content. In the
undisturbed state, forest soils are usually overlain by forest
floor material consisting of a litter layer over a partially de-
composed layer which is on top of a humus layer.

The forest floor is one of the major receptors of spray
materials (2). Most pesticides in forests are aerially applied.
Initially, they will be distributed among the air, vegetation,
forest floor and surface waters (3). The proportion of chemical
entering any of the four compartments will depend on the chemical,
its application method, climatological factors and site factors,
such as vegetation type and density. Pesticides reach the ground
during application or later by the washing action of rain or in
leaf fall from treated plants. The distribution of the chemicals
between the overlying litter layers and the mineral soil is
obviously affected by the density and thickness of the litter
layer and amounts or timing of rainfall.

Herbicides and insecticides are the main pesticides used in
the forest. The phenoxy herbicide 2,4-D is the most commonly used
herbicide. Other phenoxy herbicides, such as 2,4,5-T, silvex,
dichlorprop, and MCPA, along with picloram, and dicamba constitute
the bulk of the other herbicides used in US forests (4). Insecticides are generally not used in most of the forest, although
they find some limited used in intensively managed areas and
occasionally on very large blocks of forest land where certain
species of insects have been the object of large scale spraying
operations. Treatments against the western and eastern spruce
budworm and the gypsy and douglas fir tussock moth accounted for
over 95% of the acreage sprayed by the US Forest Service between
1945 and 1974 (5). Carbaryl is by far the most widely used
insecticide in forests at the present time with the organophosphate insecticides fenitrothion, trichlorfon, and malathion being
used in much lesser quantities (6).

No direct measurements of volatilization losses of any pesticide has been made following applications to forests. However,
Grover et al. (7) recently measured the volatilization of 2,4-D
after application as the isooctyl ester to a wheat field. This
same low-volatile ester is used in forest vegetation control. The
total vapor loss within 3 days after application of the isooctyl
ester of 2,4-D was 20% of the amount applied. The applicability
of these findings to volatilization of like pesticides in the
forest environment will be discussed. We will indicate how
volatilization in forests may differ from that reported from
agricultural applications to open fields. The paper also will
discuss the transfer of pesticides into the atmosphere from the
standpoint of mechanisms involved, factors influencing rates of

vapor transfer and the use of a screening model in predicting
relative volatilization rates. Recent reviews on volatilization
include those by Hamaker (8), Spencer et al. (9), Wheatley (10),
Guenzi and Beard (11), Plimmer (12), Taylor (1), and Spencer
et al. (13).

The Volatilization Process

Volatilization is defined as the loss of chemicals from surfaces
in the vapor phase, that is, vaporization followed by movement
into the atmosphere. The rate at which a pesticide moves away
from the surface is diffusion controlled. Close to the evaporating surface, there is relatively no movement of air and the vaporized substance is transported from the surface through this
stagnant boundary layer to the region of turbulent mixing only by
molecular diffusion. The actual rate of mass transfer away from
the surface by diffusion will be proportional to the diffusion
coefficient and to the vapor density of the pesticide at the
evaporating surface. Since the thickness of the stagnant boundary
layer depends on air flow rate and turbulence, vapor loss is
influenced strongly by the type of soil cover and the atmospheric
conditions, i.e., wind in the vicinity of the soil surface. In
general, under a given set of conditions as air exchange rate or
air turbulence increases, volatilization rate increases.
     Volatilization rates of chemicals from surface deposits are
directly proportional to their relative vapor pressures. The
actual rates of loss, or the proportionality constant relating
vapor pressure to volatilization rates, are dependent upon
external conditions that affect movement away from the evaporating surface, such as wind speed and air turbulence. Initial
volatilization of pesticide deposits from leaf surfaces and grass
or litter on the forest floor are examples of this type of volatilization. Factors controlling volatilization rates from plants
was discussed by Taylor (1).
     In comparing the factors governing volatilization from soil
and plant surfaces, the dominant effect of adsorption that reduces
the vapor pressure of pesticides adsorbed on dry soil becomes
apparent (9). Vapor pressures of pesticides are greatly decreased
by their interaction with soil, mainly due to adsorption.
Spencer et al. (14) reported that the degree of reduction in
vapor pressure in soil due to adsorption is dependent mainly upon
soil water content, the nature of the pesticide, its concentration and soil properties, particularly soil organic matter content. The concentration of the desorbed pesticide in the soil
water dictates the vapor density of the pesticide in the soil air
in accordance with Henry's law. Hence, soil water adsorption
coefficients can be used to calculate relative vapor densities
in the soil atmosphere.
     Studies by Spencer et al. (9, 14) and Spencer and Cliath

(15, 16) have shown that the adsorption of many pesticides is
very strongly influenced by soil moisture. Vapor pressures of
weakly-polar pesticides decreased markedly when the soil water
content decreased below 1 molecular layer of water. Consequently,
under very dry conditions, strong adsorptive forces reduce the
vapor pressure of the pesticide residues to negligible values.
However, when sufficient soil water is present to cover the surface of the soil colloids to a depth of a molecular layer or more,
pesticide vapor pressures increase to values near those of the
pure compounds. This indicates that greater volatilization from
wet than from dry soils is due mainly to an increased vapor pressure resulting from displacement of the chemicals from the soil
surface by water. An example of the effect of pesticide concentration and water content on vapor density of a weakly-polar
pesticide, dieldrin, is shown in Figure 1. Similar relationships
hold for other relatively non-polar pesticides and for other soils
over the temperature ranges normally encountered in the field.
While water contents above 1 molecular layer may have little or
no effect on pesticide vapor densities in soil, higher water contents do greatly affect volatility through their effects on pesticide movement through the soil. Even though the vapor density or
volatility of most weakly polar chemicals are very low in dry
soil their volatility increases to higher values when the dry soil
is rewetted indicating that the drying effect is mostly reversible.
        Volatilization of soil-incorporated pesticides involves de-
sorption of the chemicals from the soil, movement to the soil
surface, and vaporization into the atmosphere. The initial
volatilization rate will be a function of the vapor pressure of
the chemical at the surface as modified by adsorptive interactions with the soil. The small fraction of exposed material
that remains on the surface after mixing is readily lost. Volatilization then becomes dependent upon the rate of movement of the
pesticide to the soil surface by diffusion or convection in
evaporating water. When water is not evaporating, volatilization
rate depends upon rate of movement to the soil surface by diffusion only. Usually both mechanisms, diffusion and convection work
together in the field where water and the pesticide vaporize at
the same time. Movement of pesticides to the surface by bulk
flow or convection in the soil water is the dominant mechanism
controlling volatilization of pesticides incorporated in moist
soils. Volatilization rates due to convection can be estimated
from the water flux and the concentration of the chemical in the
water. The magnitude of the so-called "Wick Effect" will depend
upon the adsorption characteristics and water solubility of the
pesticide and other factors affecting partitioning between the
air, water, and soil (17).

Volatilization of Pesticides Under Field Conditions

Measurements of pesticide volatilization in the field have been
made by several researchers using microclimate techniques. Vapor

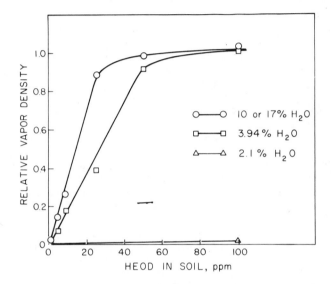

Figure 1.   Relative vapor density of dieldrin (HEOD) versus concentration in Gila silt loam as affected by soil water content.

fluxes were calculated from measured pesticide vapor concentration profiles and supporting meteorological data as described by
Caro et al. (18) and Parmele et al. (19). Taylor (1) in his
review of post-application volatilization of pesticides under
field conditions, summarized the data from several field experiments on pesticide volatilization from vegetation and soil. He
concluded that volatilization rates from plant or moist soil surfaces can be very large. In moist soils, volatilization rates
from surface applications were similar to volatilization from
foliage surfaces, i. e., up to 90% loss in 3 days for the more
volatile chemicals (1, 20, 21). When soil surfaces were dry
volatilization was greatly reduced or negligible even for surface
applied pesticides (22, 23).
    Volatilization rates were much less where the pesticides were
incorporated even to shallow depths in soil. Incorporation of
heptachlor, dieldrin, or trifluralin to the 7.3 cm depth reduced
losses to less than 7% in 90 to 167 days--volatilization rates 3
orders of magnitude less than those for exposed residues of the
same pesticides.
    Willis et al. (24) measured volatilization of toxaphene from
a mature cotton canopy following an aerial application at 2.24
kg/ha. They found less than 20% of the applied toxaphene present
in the canopy one hour after application. Measured volatilization
rates were equivalent to 25% of the remaining toxaphene within 5
days. Willis et al. (25) also measured volatilization of toxaphene and DDT from a cotton field following their application by
ground equipment. Total toxaphene and DDT volatility losses
during the 32 day test period were 53 and 58% of the amounts on
the plants, respectively. Because of dry weather, no measurable
pesticide volatilization occurred from soil. They concluded that
post-application volatilization from plants is a major pathway of
pesticide loss. Cliath et al. (26) reported volatilization
losses of 74% of the applied herbicide, EPTC, from irrigation
water and moist soil within 52 hours following its application in
irrigation water to an alfalfa field.
    Grover et al. (7) recently measured the volatilization of
2,4-D isooctyl ester after application to a wheat field at 0.5
kg/ha (acid equivalent). He reported that total vapor losses
of the isooctyl ester over a 5-day sampling period were 93.5 g/ha
or 20.8% of the amount applied. The crop canopy intercepted 77%
of the applied ester and thus acted as the major source of vapor
loss. He found that the 2,4-D ester losses from the soil surface
occurred only when the soil surface was moist, i.e., after a
rainfall event or in the early hours of the morning following the
disposition of dew. The ester was rapidly hydrolyzed to the acid
on the wheat plants and in the soil, particularly when surface
soil moisture was available.
    Volatilization of pesticides from various components of the
forest environment, foliage, forest floor, or soil should follow

somewhat the same pattern as that reported by Taylor (1), Willis et al. (24, 25) and Grover et al. (7) in that volatilization of deposits on foliage and on grass or litter on the forest floor should be much greater than from within the soil. Even though pesticides applied to forest soils are seldom incorporated, pesticides on the forest floor, or washed off foliar surfaces, may move into the soil by rainfall instead of by incorporation. Subsequently, they will move to the soil surface and volatilize by the same mechanisms as for soil-incorporated pesticides. However, air circulation under the forest canopy may be quite different from that in an open field. The forest canopy provides more of a closed environment with a fairly stable atmosphere in the daytime and relatively unstable at night (27). Consequently, we expect pesticide turnover under the forest system to be lower than that in a more open environment such as a bare soil or wheat field. Specifically, volatilization rates from the forest floor will probably be lower than from surface applications in an open field; whereas, volatilization from the top of the canopy might be somewhat similar to that reported for agricultural crops.

The length of time pesticides persist in the forest floor and soil bears strongly on the probability they will be lost by volatilization (28-31). The phenoxy herbicides are commonly applied to forests as the low-volatile esters. These esters are readily hydrolyzed to their respective acids in soil or on the forest floor. For example, Smith (32) reported that no traces of 2,4,5-T and 2,4-D esters were observed in any of four moist soils after 48 and 72 hours, respectively, and most of them were hydrolyzed in less than 24 hours. The vapor pressures of the acids are much lower than the esters and this hydrolysis, along with subsequent degradation of the acids, results in a very low potential for volatilization of these materials from soil.

Estimating Volatilization Rates from Soils

Vaporization of pesticides from soil can be estimated from a consideration of the physical and chemical factors controlling their concentration at the soil surface. These factors have been discussed in the section on the volatilization process. When pesticides are present in the soil matrix, they can move to the surface by gaseous or liquid diffusion or by convection (mass flow) with the soil water moving upward to the surface during evaporation. Most models developed for estimating volatilization rates are based upon equations describing the rate of movement of the chemicals to the surface by diffusion and/or by convection and away from the surface through the air boundary layer above the surface by diffusion. In addition, the proportion of a pesticide in soil that will be lost by volatilization depends on the resistance of the chemical to degradation.

Screening Model. In a series of papers, Jury et al. (33-36) described and applied a model for assessing relative volatility, mobility, and persistence of pesticides and other trace organics in soil. The model describes movement in both the liquid and vapor phases for chemicals which partition between liquid, vapor, and adsorbed phases in the soil. The soil surface boundary consists of a stagnant boundary layer connecting the soil and air through which pesticide and water vapor must move to reach the atmosphere. The model assumes that gas and liquid concentrations are related by Henry's law, and that the adsorption isotherms relating liquid and adsorbed concentrations are linear over the range of concentrations encountered. It is also assumed that degradation occurs by a first order rate process. The model [presented in detail in Jury et al. (33)] is intended to classify and screen organic chemicals for their environmental behavior. Each chemical simulated must have values provided for its vapor pressure and solubility or Henry's constant, K_H, and its organic carbon partition coefficient, K_{oc}, and its degradation rate, μ. The purpose of the model is not to simulate chemical transport in a given field situation, but rather to estimate how a pesticide will move under a given set of imposed circumstances or to evaluate the susceptibility of a chemical to a given loss pathway and to classify chemicals into groups.

Jury et al. (35) applied the screening model to a set of 20 pesticides and 15 other trace organic chemicals for which benchmark properties were obtained from the literature or calculated. Results were presented in a series of classifications rating the susceptibility of the chemicals to a given loss pathway. The model indicated that volatilization behavior of a chemical was controlled mainly by the ratio of its solution to vapor concentration or Henry's constant, which determined the extent to which the air boundary layer restricted volatilization from soil. The extent to which this boundary layer limits the volatilization flux can be used as a criterion for classifying pesticides into general categories, based upon whether control of volatilization is within the soil or within the boundary layer (34). When a boundary layer is present, it will act to restrict volatilization fluxes only if the maximum flux through the boundary layer is small compared to the rate at which chemicals move to the soil surface.

The 20 pesticides were divided into one of three categories depending on whether Henry's constant (K_H) (in units of μg/ml air per μg/ml solution) is much greater (Category I), approximately equal to (Category II), or much less (Category III) than the value 2.65×10^{-5}. Category I chemicals are not affected by the boundary layer and Category III chemicals are dominated by the boundary layer properties. This independence of or dependence on boundary layer properties has clear cut implications for volatilization of soil-incorporated pesticides. For example, Jury et al. (34) were able to show from the model that (for no water flux) the dependence of pesticide flux J_p on physical and chemical parameters was as follows:

Category I

$$J_p \propto C_{T_0} K_H^{\frac{1}{2}} a^{5/3} K_{oc}^{-\frac{1}{2}} f_{oc}^{-\frac{1}{2}} t^{-\frac{1}{2}} e^{-\mu t} \tag{1}$$

Category III

$$J_p \propto C_{T_0} K_H K_{oc}^{-1} f_{oc}^{-1} d^{-1} e^{-\mu t} \tag{2}$$

where C_{T_0} = M/L is initial pesticide concentration, M is initial pesticide mass, L is initial depth of incorporation, a is volumetric soil air content, t is time, d is thickness of air boundary layer, and f_{oc} is soil organic carbon fraction.

Figure 2 shows volatilization flux rates versus time for three prototype chemicals under conditions of 1) no water evaporation, 2) steady evaporation at 2.5 mm/day, and 3) steady evaporation at 5.0 mm/day (34). A clear distinction is apparent between the behavior of Category I and Category III chemicals. For Category I, the volatilization flux shows a characteristic decrease with time in all three cases whereas the flux rate of the Category III chemical tends to increase with time when upward water flow is occurring and to decrease slowly with time when water is not evaporating. The Category II volatilization flux decreases with time when no evaporation occurs and increases with time when high evaporation occurs. The Category III compound with a low Henry's constant moves to the surface in evaporating water faster than it can volatilize into the atmosphere, consequently, its concentration increases at the soil surface under evaporative conditions and volatilization rate increases with time. Volatilization rate of Category III chemicals depends upon the depth of the stagnant air layer and control of volatilization rate is within the atmosphere as well as within the soil.

Model Application to Herbicides and Insecticides Commonly Used in Forestry. The screening model described by Jury et al. (33) was applied to four herbicides and four insecticides commonly used in the forest environment for the purpose of determining their susceptibility to loss from soil by volatilization compared with degradation. Table I gives the parameters at 25°C of vapor density, C_V; water solubility, C; organic carbon partition coefficient, K_{oc}; Henry's constant, K_H; and half-life, $t_{\frac{1}{2}}$; for the four herbicides and four insecticides commonly used in forests along with lindane as a comparison Category I pesticide. The parameters were either obtained directly from the literature or estimated from various relationships. In the case of the phenoxy herbicides 2,4-D and 2,4,5-T, the properties of the acids were used instead of the more volatile esters. Even though they may be applied as low volatile esters, the phenoxy herbicides rapidly hydrolyze to the acids on contact with the soil (2, 32). The vapor pressure of 2,4,5-T acid was estimated from the vapor pressures of the hexylethyl esters of 2,4-D and 2,4,5-T and the vapor pressure of 2,4-D acid.

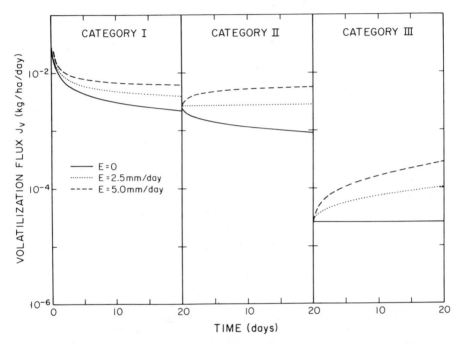

Figure 2. Volatilization flux rates for a prototype chemical from each category of volatilization behavior as
affected by water evaporation (E).

Table I.   Chemical and Physical Properties of Forest Pesticides
Used in Simulations

Chemical	Vapor Density[1] (mg/L)	Solu- bility (mg/L)	Henry's Constant, (K_H)	K_{oc}, (mL/g)	$t_{\frac{1}{2}}$ (days)	Category (34), (No.)
HERBICIDES						
2,4,5-T (Acid)	1.9E-06[2]	268	7.2E-09	53	25	III
2,4-D (Acid)	5.0E-06	900	5.6E-09	20	15	III
Picloram	8.0E-06	430	1.9E-08	25	100	III
Dicamba	2.4E-04	4500	5.3E-08	2	25	III
INSECTICIDES						
Carbaryl	3.2E-03	40	8.1E-05	230	12	I
Fenitrothion	1.8E-04	30	6.0E-06	670	12	II
Trichlorfon	2.2E-04	150000	1.5E-09	6	3	III
Malathion	3.6E-04	145	2.4E-06	280	1	II
Lindane	1.0E-03	7.5	1.3E-04	1300	266	I

[1]/ Vapor Density (C_V) calculated from vapor pressue (P) using
the equation C_V = PM/RT where M is molecular weight, R the
gas constant, and T absolute temperature.

[2]/   E-06 = x10^{-6}, etc.

The simulations of volatilization were conducted using the
complete model described by Jury et al. (33) where each chemical
is present in the soil at a uniform concentration of 1 kg/ha to a
depth, L, in the soil and is allowed to volatilize through a
stagnant air boundary layer for a specified time period in the
presence or absence of water evaporation. The standard conditions
or common properties assumed in the simulations are the same as
those indicated in Jury et al. (35, 36), i.e., air diffusion
coefficient, 0.43 m^2/d; water diffusion coefficient, 4.3 X 10^{-5}
m^2/d; atmospheric relative humidity, 50% temperature, 25°C;
soil porosity, 50%; bulk density, 1.35 g/cm^3; soil water content,
0.30; organic carbon fraction, 0.0125; amount of pesticide in
soil, 1 kg/ha; depth in soil, 1 or 10 cm; water evaporation rate,
0, 0.25, or 0.50 cm/d.
   The resulting volatilization fluxes and cumulative losses
are used to categorize the relative susceptibility to atmospheric
loss of the nine chemicals. The four herbicides have very low
Henry's constants and fall into Category III (34) from the standpoint of their volatility characteristics. Two of the four insecticides have intermediate Henry's constants and fall into Category
II, while trichlorfon is a Category III chemical because of its
very high water solubtility and carbaryl and lindane are Category
I chemicals.
   Figure 3 shows calculated volatilization fluxes versus time
over a 20-day period for the nine pesticides present in the

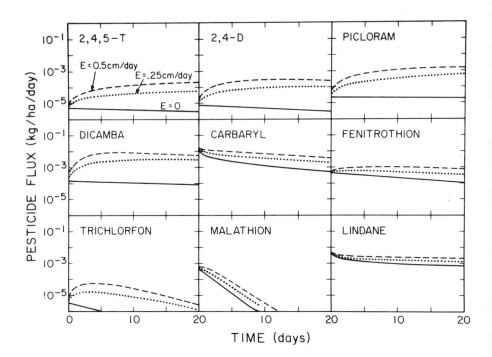

Figure 3. Calculated volatilization flux versus time for
selected forest pesticides as affected by water evaporation
(E) at soil depth L = 10 cm.

0 - 10 cm soil depth as affected by water evaporation. The boundary layer thickness (d) for the three water evaporation rates (E),
calculated using Equation 28 of Jury et al. ($\underline{33}$), were d = 4.75
mm when E = 0 and 0.25 cm/d and d = 2.38 mm when E = 0.5 cm/d.
The shapes of the curves indicate the effect of water evaporation
on changes in volatilization with time for the various pesticides.
The herbicides fall into Category III chemicals and their volatilization rates increase with time when water is evaporating. The
volatilization rates of lindane and carbaryl, the Category I
chemicals, decrease with time under all conditions. The Category
II insecticides are intermediate in their response to water evaporation rate. The chemicals with high degradation rates, such as
malathion and trichlorfon degrade so rapidly that their volatilization rate decreases with time under all conditions.

Figure 4 shows pesticide volatilization as affected by soil
depths of 1, 5, and 10 cm with water evaporation (E) equal to
0.25 cm/d. Since the concentration is inversely proporational
to the depth of soil containing the 1 kg/ha of pesticide, the
ratio of the concentrations roughly explains the initial relative
volatilization rates. The very water soluble (Category III) compounds appear to approach a constant volatilization rate regardless of depth because their volatilization is controlled by diffusion of the chemical through the boundary layer above the soil
surface as well as by the rate of movement upward to the soil
surface.

Table II shows the calculated cumulative volatilization after
10 days as affected by depth of pesticides in soil (L) and water
evaporation rate (E) expressed as a percent of the 1 kg/ha
initially present in the soil at t = 0. Soil water content (θ)
was assumed to be equal to 0.30, and the organic carbon content of
the soil (f_{oc}) equal to 0.0125. The volatilization rates shown
in Table II are for the ideal conditions and high water evaporation rates assumed in the simulations. They are undoubtedly the
upper limits of volatilization to be expected from forest soils.
Volatilization was increased greatly by evaporating water, particularly for the compounds with low K_H values and increasing soil
depth decreased volatilization.

The amounts volatilized in 10 days were extremely low in most
cases. Dicamba was the only herbicide exhibiting significant
volatilization and that only in the presence of high water evaporation. Apparently the insecticide carbaryl, has the potential
to volatilize significantly from the soil with or without water
evaporation, particularly when it is present near the soil
surface. The reference insecticide, lindane, will appreciably
volatilize when it is present near the soil surface, but its
volatility decreases markedly when present within the entire
0 - 10 cm depth. Volatilization of the other insecticides will
be essentially insignificant due either to their rapid degradation
rate or low K_H.

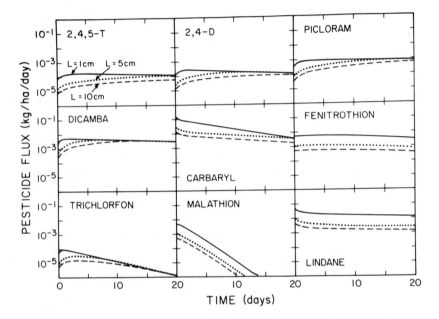

Figure 4. Calculated volatilization flux versus time for
selected forest pesticides as affected by depth (L) within
the soil at water evaporation rate E = 0.25 cm/day.

Table II.   Cumulative Volatilization After 10 Days as a Function
of Evaporation (E, cm/day), and Soil Depth (L, cm),
Expressed as a % of the 1 kg/ha Initially in Soil
(With θ=0.3; f_{oc}=0.0125)

	L = 1 cm		L = 10 cm	
Chemical	E=0.0	E=0.25	E=0.0	E=0.25
HERBICIDES				
2,4,5-T	0.05	0.31	<0.01	0.05
2,4-D	0.06	0.45	<0.01	0.10
Picloram	0.20	1.60	0.02	0.35
Dicamba	0.94	9.07	0.13	3.73
INSECTICIDES				
Carbaryl	24.2	51.2	2.44	5.40
Fenitrothion	3.98	6.65	0.30	0.67
Trichlorfon	0.01	0.09	<0.01	0.02
Malathion	0.62	1.24	0.06	0.12
Lindane	12.6	18.8	1.26	1.88

Table III shows the percent of each pesticide remaining in
the soil after 10 days of volatilization and degradation. The
percentage of the chemicals not accounted for by volatilization
disappeared by degradation at a rate reflected by the half-life,
$t\frac{1}{2}$, in Table I. A comparison of the data in Tables II and III
provides an insight into the relative rates of volatilization
and degradation of the nine pesticides. With the exception of
lindane at the 0 - 1 cm depth and carbaryl at 0 - 1 cm depth with
water evaporating, degradation is a much more important pathway
for loss of the nine chemicals from soil than is volatilization.

Table III.   Percent Mass (M) Remaining in Soil After 10 Days as
Affected by Evaporation (E, cm/day) and Soil Depth
(L,cm) (With θ=0.3, M_0=1 kg/ha and f_{oc} = 0.0125)

	L = 1 cm		L = 10 cm	
Chemical	E=0.0	E=0.25	E=0.0	E=0.25
HERBICIDES				
2,4,5-T	75.7	75.5	75.8	75.7
2,4-D	63.0	62.6	63.0	62.9
Picloram	93.1	91.7	93.3	93.0
Dicamba	75.0	67.9	75.7	72.4
INSECTICIDES				
Carbaryl	39.5	19.7	54.5	52.5
Fenitrothion	53.9	51.1	55.9	55.6
Trichlorfon	9.9	9.9	9.9	9.9
Malathion	0.1	0.1	0.1	0.1
Lindane	85.0	79.0	96.2	95.6

Conclusions

Extrapolating to the forest environment from field measurements
of pesticide volatilization in agricultural environments, along
with output from the screening model using benchmark properties,
we conclude that volatilization from the canopy foliage will be
relatively high for the more commonly used forest pesticides.
Their volatilization from litter on the forest floor will also be
appreciable. With the possible exception of carbaryl, their
volatilization after being washed into the soil will be relatively
low or insignificant because of their low volatility, low Henry's
constants, K_H, and/or their high rates of degradation in the soil
environment. The rapid disappearance of the phenoxy herbicides
(2, 31) and the insecticide, fenitrothion (28) from vegetation
and the forest floor is supporting evidence that volatilization
is an important pathway for loss of applied pesticides from the
forest canopy and litter on the forest floor.
        The screening model developed by Jury et al. (33) should
provide a useful mechanism for determining the relative importance
of volatilization and other pathways for loss of applied chemicals
from soils. The model should also be useful for assessing the
relative loss by volatilization of new compounds based on their
physico-chemical properties.

Literature Cited

1. Taylor, A. W. J. Air Poll. Control Assoc. 1978, 28, 922-7.
2. Norris, L. A. Residue Reviews 1981, 80, 63-135.
3. Norris, L. A.; Moore, D. G., in "Forest Land Uses and Stream
    Environment"; Oregon State University, Corvallis, Oregon,
    1971; pp 138-158.
4. "The Biologic and Economic Assessment of 2,4,5-T," U. S.
    Department of Agriculture, Technical Bulletin No. 1671, 1982.
5. "Pest Control: An Assessment of Present and Alternative
    Technologies, IV Forest Pest Control." National Academy of
    Sciences, 1975.
6. Crisp, C. E. in "Biodegradation of Pesticides," Matsumura, F.
    Crishna Murti, Eds.; Plenum: New York, 1982, pp 157-91.
7. Grover, R.; Schewchuk, S. R.; Cessna, A. J.; Smith, A. E.;
    Hunter, J. H. J. Environ. Qual. 1983, (in press).
8. Hamaker, J. W. in "Organic Chemicals in the Soil Environment";
    Goring, C.A.I.; Hamaker, J. W., Eds.; Marcel Dekker: New York,
    1972; pp 341-97.
9. Spencer, W. F.; Farmer, W. J.; Cliath, M. M. Residue Reviews
    1973, 49, 1-47.
10. Wheatley, G. A. in "Environmental Pollution by Pesticides";
    Edwards, C. A., Ed.; Plenum Press: London, 1973; pp 365-409.
11. Guenzi, W. D.; Beard, W. E. in "Pesticides in Soil and Water";
    Guenzi, W. D., Ed.; Soil Science Society of America, Inc.
    Madison, WI, 1974; pp 108-22.

12. Plimmer, J. R. in "Herbicides: Chemistry, Degradation, and Mode of Action," Vol. 2; Kearney, P. C.; Kaufmann, D. D., Eds. Marcel Dekker: New York, 1976, pp 891-934.
13. Spencer, W. F.; Farmer, W. J.; Jury, W. A. Environ. Toxic. Chem. 1982, 1, 17-26.
14. Spencer, W. F.; Cliath, M. M.; Farmer, W. J. Soil Sci. Soc. Amer. Proc., 1969, 33, 509-11.
15. Spencer, W. F.; Cliath, M. M. Soil Sci. Soc. Amer. Proc. 1970, 34, 574-8.
16. Spencer, W. F.; Cliath, M. M. J. Agric. Food Chem. 1974, 22, 987-91.
17. Spencer, W. F.; Cliath, M. M. J. Environ. Qual. 1973, 2, 284-9.
18. Caro, J. H.; Taylor, A. W.; Lemon, E. R. in "Proc. Int. Symp. on Measurement of Environ. Pollut.," National Research of Canada: Ottawa, 1971, pp 72-7.
19. Parmele, L. H.; Lemon, E. R.; Taylor, A. W. Water, Air, Soil Poll. 1972, 1, 433-51.
20. Taylor, A. W.; Glotfelty, D. E; Turner, B. C.; Silver, R. E.; Freeman, H. P.; Weiss, A. J. Agric. Food Chem. 1977, 25, 542-8.
21. Glotfelty, D. E. Ph.D. Thesis, University of Maryland, College Park, MD, 1981.
22. Turner, B. C.; Glotfelty, D. E.; Taylor, A. W.; Watson, D. R. Agron. J. 1978, 70, 933-7.
23. Harper, L. A.; White, A. W., Jr.; Bruce, R. R.; Thomas, A. W.; Leonard, R. A. J. Environ. Qual. 1976, 5, 236-42.
24. Willis, G. H.; McDowell, L. L.; Smith, S.; Southwick, L. M.; Lemon, E. R. Agron. J. 1980, 72, 627-31.
25. Willis, G. H.; McDowell, L. L.; Harper, L. A.; Southwick, L. M.; Smith, S. J. Environ. Qual. 1983, 12, 80-5.
26. Cliath, M. M.; Spencer, W. F.; Farmer, W. J.; Shoup, T. D.; Grover, R. J. Agric. Food Chem. 1980, 28, 610-3.
27. Fritschen, L. J. "Air Circulation in Forested Areas," paper presented at the 185th ACS National Meeting, Seattle, WA, March 20-25, 1983 (Abstracts).
28. Yule, W. N.; Duffy, J. R. Bull. Environ. Contamin. Toxic. 1972, 8, 10-8.
29. Altom, J. D.; Stritzke, J. F. Weed Sci. 1973, 21, 556-60.
30. Norris, L. A.; Montgomery, M. L.; Johnson, E. R. Weed Sci. 1977, 25, 417-22.
31. Radosevich, S. R.; Winterlin, W. L. Weed Sci. 1977, 25, 423-5.
32. Smith, A. E. Weed Research 1976, 16, 19-22.
33. Jury, W. A.; Spencer, W. F.; Farmer, W. J. J. Environ. Qual. 1983 (in press).
34. Jury, W. A.; Farmer, W. J.; Spencer, W. F. J. Environ. Qual. 1983 (in press).
35. Jury, W. A.; Spencer, W. F.; Farmer, W. J. J. Environ. Qual. 1983 (in press).

36. Jury, W. A.; Spencer, W. F.; Farmer, W. J. in "Hazard
     Assessment of Chemicals, Current Developments, VOL II";
     Saxena, J., Ed.; Academic: New York, 1983,; pp 1-43.

RECEIVED September 9, 1983

Vapor Phase Redistribution of Aminocarb and Transformation Products from Leaf Surfaces

W. D. MARSHALL—Department of Agricultural Chemistry and Physics, Macdonald College of McGill, Ste. Anne de Bellevue, Quebec, H9X 1C0, Canada

W. N. YULE—Department of Entomology, Macdonald College of McGill, Ste. Anne de Bellevue, Quebec, H9X 1C0, Canada

D. J. ECOBICHON—Department of Pharmacology and Therapeutics, McGill University, Ste. Anne de Bellevue, Quebec, H9X 1C0, Canada

The process of pesticide volatilization from a leaf surface is considered first in terms of the component physical processes of sublimation and molecular diffusion through a saturated boundry layer. Predicted volatilization rates based solely on pesticide vapour pressures often bear little relation to field observations due to myriad interactions of the pesticide with the leaf and the surrounding microenvironment. Observed pesticide fluxes above sprayed agricultural fields together with microclimatological characteristics of coniferous forests are then used to predict general patterns of pesticide volatilization from a treated coniferous stand.

The multiplicity of abiotic transformation products which have been detected for aminocarb has prompted a comparison of the anticholinesterase activity, in vivo insect toxicity and relative volatility of a series of oxidation products. Successive oxidations of the aryldimethylamino group resulted in increased toxicity whereas oxidation of the arylmethyl group or of the carbamate N-methyl group considerably reduced toxicity. Saturated vapour concentrations of the toxic transformation products were only slightly lower than the parent carbamate.

Within the forest environment pesticides are limited to a relatively few specific use patterns; however in terms of area treated (and quantity of active ingredients applied) these restricted patterns still represent usage on a rather massive scale. Herbicides are used

0097-6156/84/0238-0211$06.00/0
© 1984 American Chemical Society

for brush control along "rights of way" and for the selective control of vegetation (broad leaf and woody plants) which may compete with young conifers for limited resources. The use of phenoxy herbicides (mainly 2, 4-D and 2,4,5-T with lesser amounts of dichlorprop, silvex and MCPA) in forestry has been reviewed recently)(1).

Insecticides are also used on a large scale to control a few lepidopterous defoliators of mature conifers including spruce budworm. The strategy in these spray programs is to protect the current years foliage only and as a consequence insecticides are applied aerially at very low rates (52 to 87 g active ingredient per hectare (2). Spraying programs commence in mid-May and are completed by early June. Insecticides currently used for these purposes include aminocarb and fenitrothion with lesser amounts of carbaryl. It has been estimated that over 1,000 tons of aminocarb alone were applied to eastern North American spruce-fir stands during the decade 1970-1980 (2).

Upon release the formulated control agent is partitioned between the air, the forest vegetation and the forest floor. It is the post application loss of insecticides from conifers which is the subject of the following discussion. Volatilization has become increasingly recognized as a significant factor which limits the efficiency of pesticides and provides a major pathway to general environmental contamination.

Volatilization

Volatility is a measure of the tendency of a chemical to escape from the solid (or liquid) phase into the gaseous phase; a measure of its tendency to evaporate or sublime. This process can be considered as an equilibrium phenomenon in which the concentration in the vapour phase is independant of the chemical composition of the vapour phase or of the pressure, however it is directly related to the temperature. This equilibrium is modified by the rate of escape of the vapourized pesticide from the stagnant boundary layer of saturated vapour into the bulk of the air. The boundary layer is a very thin blanket of stagnant air which lies just above the leaf surface. This boundary layer is unaffected by eddy currents from the more turbulent air above due to the buffering action of several intervening layers of air which are successively less turbulent as one approaches the evaporating surface. Although eddy diffusion is a much more rapid mechanism for transport it is inoperative at the boundary layer interface. Thus escape from the solid (or liquid) phase is subject to a rate limiting step which is the diffusion (a random molecular motion) of vaporized pesticide through the boundary layer. The thickness of the boundary layer (and thus the overall volatilization rate) is a function of environmental and meteorological conditions. This subject has been considered in depth in several excellent reviews (3,4,5).

A key parameter used to estimate or model volatilization processes is the pesticide vapour pressure; a fundamental property of the chemical agent which is uniquely defined by the temperature. This parameter is readily and reproducibly measured in the laboratory. Two approaches have been widely used. The most popular technique (6,7) involves the creation of a saturated vapour of the pesticide in an inert atmosphere and determining the saturated vapour concentration (SVC).

$$SCV = \frac{n}{V} = \frac{p}{RT} \qquad p = \text{vapour pressure of the pesticide}$$

A less widely used approach (8,9) has been to expose a surface of pesticide to an air flow under conditions of a rapid rate of air change such that the concentration of the pesticide in the air surrounding the stagnant boundary layer is far below saturation. Under these conditions the relative rates of diffusion of two pesticides will be inversely related to the square root of their respective molecular weights (Graham's law of Diffusion) and directly related to their saturated vapour concentrations in the boundary layer.

$$\frac{rate_1}{rate_2} = \frac{\sqrt{M.W.}_2}{\sqrt{M.W.}_1} \quad x \quad \frac{SVC_1}{SVC_2} = \frac{\sqrt{M.W.}_2}{\sqrt{M.W.}_1} \quad x \quad \frac{n_1/V}{n_2/V}$$

and if the rates are expressed in units of mass transferred

$$\frac{rate_1}{rate_2} = \frac{\sqrt{M.W.}_2}{\sqrt{M.W.}_1} \quad x \quad \frac{n_1 \cdot MW_1}{n_2 \cdot MW_2} = \frac{p_1\sqrt{MW_1}}{p_2\sqrt{MW_2}}$$

If the rates are determined experimentally and the vapour pressure for one pesticide is known the vapour pressure of the second pesticide may be determined.

Neither procedure requires pure compound(s): thus technical products, spray formulations or multi-component pesticide mixtures may be assayed. Both techniques are as sensitive as the chemical procedure(s) used to determine the quantity of pesticide trapped (SVC technique) or lost (volatilization rate technique). In both techniques mixtures must be uniform, of sufficient thickness to attenuate any interactions with the surface and the entraining gas should be unreactive to the test chemicals.

Processes which Attenuate Volatilization Rates in the Field

Although saturated vapours can be reproduced precisely in the laboratory the application of equilibrium vapour pressures to the prediction of field volatilization rates are fraught with difficulties. The pesticide may interact with other spray components to change the physical characteristics of the deposits. As pointed out by Hartley (4) a pesticide which can exist in a supercooled state (eg. impure DDT in thin films) will be more volatile and more soluble than if it is crystalline. As a rough approximation a crystalline substance becomes one-third to one-fourth as volatile as the supercooled liquid for each

50° C below the melting point. The nature and the size of the exposed surface of the deposit on the leaf surface can be modified by spray adjuvants such as wetting agents, thickeners or particulating agents. The deposited pesticide may also interact with the target surface, with leaf exudates or with the polymeric wax-like surface of cutin. It may also physically penetrate the surface of the leaf.

If a uniform coating is ever achieved initally the quantity of pesticide will be dissipated with time. Eventually a point will be reached where so little remains that it no longer uniformly covers the surface. Discrete point sources will result. This time dependent retreat of the pesticide into crevices and less exposed surfaces will serve to further attenuate the volatilization process. The target leaves can also be serveral degrees warmer than the air temperature (if receiving solar radiance) or several degrees cooler if at night. Volatilization rates will be modified accordingly. Meteorological conditions will also profoundly influence volatilization rates. Wind profiles and temperature profiles will provide conditions of instability leading to forced convection currents and buoyant thermal currents of air which will efficiently transport vapourized pesticide away from the stagnant boundary layer resulting in bulk air with a high "saturation deficiency" of pesticide. Moreover the resulting turbulence will directly reduce the thickness of the boundary layer. Calculations by Hartley (5) are illuminating. A ten meter depth of air over one hectare would be saturated by 500, 12 and 0.01 g of dichlorbenil, lindane and simazine respectively. In completely calm conditions the saturation process would require several months (if by molecular diffusion alone) but only a few minutes in conditions of normal wind and turbulence. The topography and aerodynamic roughness of the leaf surface will also contribute significantly to the degree of turbulence.

Humidity has also been demonstrated to influence volatilization rates. Although the mechanism of interaction remains obscure the loss of BHC from bean leaves was lower under conditions of high relative humidity than under conditions of low relative humidity (10). The effect of humidity upon volatilization however is generally considered to be small (11).

Field Measurements of Pesticide Volatilization

In the absence of direct field measurements of pesticide fluxes eminating from a sprayed forest a series of suppositions may be drawn from similar observations of losses from treated agricultural crops. The volatilization of dieldrin and heptachlor from a grass pasture was characterized by rather marked diurnal variations in vertical flux intensities of both insecticides during the initial days post application (12). The authors concluded that the volatilization ceased or was greatly reduced with decreased solar radiance. Estimated relative vapour concentrations of dieldrin rapidly declined from saturation 2 hours post application to 10% by evening. This parameter reached a maximum of 30 - 40% on day 2 and 20 - 25% on day 3. Although the saturated vapour concentration of heptachlor is approximately fifty times greater than dieldrin estimated relative vapour concentrations of the former remained much lower throughout this study. Declination curves for both pesticides were characterized by a biphasic response suggesting an initial period of rapid volatilization followed by slower rates of loss in the latter parts of the study. Nonetheless direct volatilization, as measured by pesticide fluxes in the air above the treated plots was sufficient to account for all the decreases in residues found in the grass and in the soil. The losses of 90% of the dieldrin and 95% of the heptachlor within the first week contrast the small losses of these two insecticides (3 and 7% respectively when incorporated to a depth of 7.5 cm) from soil over a growing season. Maize subsequently grown in plots treated with these insecticides accumulated a maximum of 1.8 ppm pesticide in the lower leaves by late October (13). Upper leaves contained considerably less. The authors interpret these results as being due primarily to a redistribution process in which deposition from the vapour phase accounts for accumulation by the maize plants. Even at distances of 30 m downwind from the treated plot corn leaves had accumulated 5 to 10% of the residues found in plants from the treated plots.

Volatilization losses of toxaphene and DDT from cotton plants decreased exponentially with time and were linearly related to the pesticide load on these plants (14,15). Although typical volatile loss patterns suggested that flux densities were highest during mid-afternoon evidence was also obtained for high volatilization rates when leaves were drying after a heavy dew or a light rain (15).

There are relatively few studies which relate to volatilization of pesticides from conifers. Yule et al.(16) have monitored the level of phosphorus in air (both vapours and particulate material) at five sites in New Brunswick during a spraying season in which 300 tons of fenitrothion were applied to over 10^6 ha. Average daily concentrations ranged up to 3 ug/m^3 and were generally between 0.5 and 1.5 ug/m^3 (background 0.5 ug/m^3). The atmosphere contamination was due partly to local application and partly to downwind drift of pesticide.

Addison (17) has measured vapour pressures for technical aminocarb of 3.0 - 5.0 x 10^{-10} mm Hg (at $13°C$ and 0-35% relative humidity) when sprayed on Balsam fir foliage and a vapour pressure of 7.5 to 9.5 x 10^{-9} mm Hg (16-18$°C$) was determined for fenitrothion.

Microclimate of a Coniferous Stand

As a consequence of the very rough surface of a coniferous canopy (which in no way approaches a plane structure) thermal fluxes from these surfaces are relatively small ie. forest canopy surfaces are relatively cooler than the surfaces of farm crops (18). The spire like structure of the crown result in daytime temperature gradients immediately above the canopy surface which are small and wind speed gradients which are relatively large. It should he anticipated that buoyant (free convective) eddies generated by vertical temperature gradients will be relatively unimportant and that wind speed gradients will provide the major source of eddy currents.

The loading of pesticide in the lower canopy and in the sub canopy region will depend on the denseness of the stand. The microclimate within these lower regions are characterized by calmer conditions with only occasional bursts of wind. It is generally cooler (with less diurnal variation) and somewhat moister than the upper canopy. Nonetheless most wind profiles which have been measured are not monotonic within the canopy and subcanopy regions. There are regions within the stand of preferred downdraft, horizontal pressure gradients and regions of preferred uplift (18). Despite a very complex pattern of convective air flows it seems reasonable to anticipate that pesticides will be volatilized most rapidly from the crown and the upper canopy but that diurnal variations in the pesticide flux from these regions will be relatively less intense than from a similarly treated agricultural field. Since dew deposition is mainly limited to the upper canopy and crown of the forest profile early morning fluxes from this region may be augmented during this period of rapid drying of the leaf surfaces. Heavy dew deposits would be anticipated during the spray season. Volatilization losses from the lower canopy and sub canopy regions will be considerably less rapid thus providing conditions for redistribution of the control agent into the upper canopy.

Volatility of Aminocarb Transformation Products

Despite several monitoring studies for aminocarb (under field conditions and in laboratory simulations) our knowledge of the environmental fate of this control agent remains far from complete. Laboratory studies and field trials do indicate that a multiplicity of products can be formed (2). A consideration of the structure of aminocarb suggests that all three functional groups (aryl dimethylamino, aryl methyl and carbamate N-methyl) will be susceptible to oxidation. Because abiotic transformations in the environment are mainly oxidative and because the carbamate functionality is at least as resistant to oxidation as the other two functional groups, several transformation products may be anticipated. A partial oxidative decommposition scheme is outlined in Figure 1. Each of the products of Figure 1 retains a carbamate functionally intact and thus is likely to inhibit cholinesterases in vitro. In this decomposition scheme hydrolysis (which is competitive with oxidation in terms of rates) has been deemphasized because the products are considered to be relatively non-toxic. Further the scheme arbitrarily emphasizes separate routes of oxidation; viz (1) the sequential oxidation of the aryl dimethylamino group to result in the N-Methyl, N-Hydroxymethyl derivative (II), N-formyl N-methyl (III), N-methyl (IV), N-hydroxymethyl (V), N-formyl (VI) and amino (VII) analogs. Route 2 delineates a sequential series of oxidations of the aryl methyl group to result in the aryl hydroxymethyl (VIII), aryl formyl (IX) and aryl carboxy (X) products. Route 3 emphasizes the oxidation of the carbamate N-methyl group to result in the carbamate-N-hydroxymethyl (XI), carbamate N-formyl (XII) and the unsubstituted amino carbamate (XIII) analogs. There does not seem to be any good reason why any one route should predominate over the other two, therefore cross-products should be anticipated.

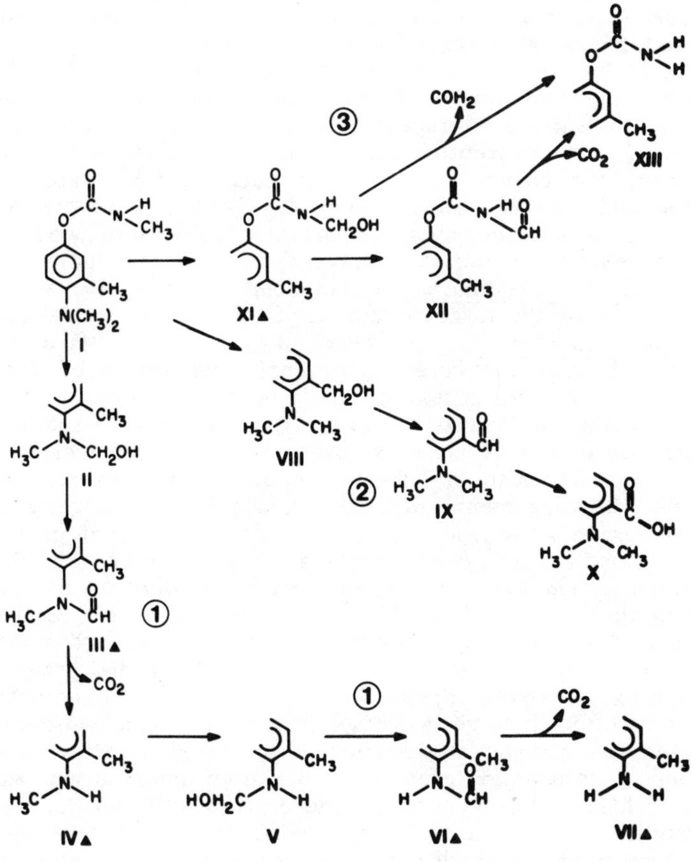

Figure 1.   Hypothetical oxidative decomposition scheme for aminocarb.

Our approach to this problem has been to synthesize several of these potential transformation products, to test their ability to inhibit acetylcholinesterase in vitro as well as their toxicity to a suitable insect indicator species and to begin an assessment of their stability under environmental conditions. In this connection it was deemed necessary to measure the volatility of the more potent inhibitors.

Figure 2 represented a log-probit plot of the observed inhibition of purified bovine erythrocyte acetylcholinesterase as a function of concentration for several of the transformation products of aminocarb. The observation that these inhibition curves are parallel suggests a similar mechanism of interaction for the various derivatives. The parameter I_{50} (the concentration of inhibitor required to achieve 50% inhibition of the enzyme activity) for each of the inhibitors were calculated and are recorded in Table 1. These values are reported relative to the parent compound aminocarb = 1. Also included in Table 1 are the relative toxicities of several of these products to house crickets (Acheta domesticus). It had been our intention to develop bioassay tests using the target insect itself, the eastern spruce budworm (Choristoneura fumiferana). However, spray tower results were quite variable and it was considered that genetic variability of the stock culture made the production of uniform test batches difficult to achieve. Using the house crickets, an LD_{50} of 130-155 ppm for aminocarb standard was observed over the course of more than 25 bioassays. Also included in Table 1 are observations by Abdel-Wahab and Casida (19) using human plasma or house fly head cholinesterases. We were very much envouraged by the close agreement of the four assay systems. The results indicated that oxidation of the aryl dimetylamino group increased toxicity modestly whereas oxidation of the aryl methyl functionality reduced toxicity. Moreover as the level of oxidation increased the capacity to inhibit was correspondingly reduced. Similarly oxidation of the carbamate N-methyl group to the corresponding aldehyde or further to result in the unsubstituted carbamate resulted in large decreases in activity. Our synthetic work and related spectrosopic studies further indicated a relatively strong interaction of para amino group (or substituted amino group) with the neighboring hydroxymethyl (or aldehyde or carboxylic acid). Based on these studies it was arbitrarily decided to concentrate on those transformation products which retained at least one one-hundreth of the activity of the parent compound in the bioassays. Among the studies it was considered prudent to determine the equilibrium vapour pressures of several of these products.

SVCs of Aminocarb Oxidation Products

The system used to generate a saturated vapour of each of these products was essentially as described by Grayson and Fosbracy (20) in which a gas chromatograph was modified to accept a U-tube saturator which was filled with glass beads. Nitrogen was used to entrain volatiles from the saturator through a detector port in the roof of the

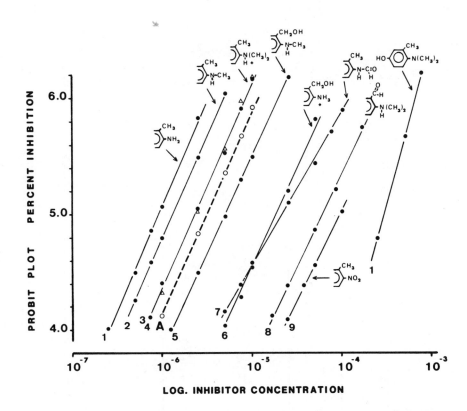

Figure 2. Log-probit plot of acetylcholinesterase inhibition as a function of concentration of aminocarb and transformation products.

Table I. Biological Activity of Aminocarb and Transformation Products[a]

R_1	R_2	R_3	Inhibition of Cholinesterase			Toxicity to House Crickets (LD_{50})
			Acetyl-cholinesterase	Human Plasma[b]	Housefly heads[b]	
$NHCH_3$	CH_3	NH_2	3.3	4	1.6	2.4
"	"	$NHCH_3$	2.9	3.2	1.0	0.79
"	"	$(+)NH(CH_3)_2$	1.4			1.2
"	"	$NHC(O)H$	0.14	0.5	0.2	0.23
"	CH_2OH	NH_2	0.17			0.15
"	CH_2OH	$NHCH_3$	0.63			0.17
"	$C(O)H$	$(+)NH(CH_3)_2$	0.05			<0.01
"	CO_2H	$N(CH_3)_2$				<0.01
$NHC(O)H$	CH_3	$N(CH_3)_2$				<0.01
NH_2	CH_3	$N(CH_3)_2$				<0.01

[a]Relative to aminocarb = 1
[b]Data taken from Ref. 19

chromatograph overn and into a series of collectors. These collectors consisted of small glass coil condensors filled with glass beads and immersed in liquid air. The portion of the gas train between the top of the oven and the first collector was wrapped with heating tape and maintained at 50°C. No product could be detected in the third trap during any of our trials. The flow-rate of nitrogen was controlled via a needle valve and the entraining gas was passed through a heat exchanger consisting of an eight foot coil of copper tubing positioned inside the chromatographic oven. Quantitation of the trapped volatiles was performed by gas chromatography (17,2) or by high pressure liquid chromatography (21). The system was exhaustively silylated prior to commencing these trials.

Results are presented in Table II. Observations at 30° or 40°C represent the average of at least three observations performed at separate flow rates. Included in this table is the correlation coefficient (r) for linear regression analysis of log P vs the inverse of temperature (degrees Kelvin) and estimates of the heat of sublimation which represents the slopes of these plots.

Table II - Equilibrium Vapour Pressures for Aminocarb and
Transformation Products as a Function of Temperature

Equilibrium Vapour Pressure (mm Hg x 10^6)

		20°C	30°C[a]	35°C	40°C[a]	r	Hs[b]
Aminocarb	I	9.7	28.9±3.0	58.2	83.9±8.6	0.997	20.80
N-methyl	VI	2.7	10.1±0.9	21.2	29.1±3.3	0.994	22.51
N-formamido	VI	4.0	17.5±2.1	38.9	47.2±5.1	0.993	23.71
Amino	VII	2.0	5.3±0.5	13.9	24.7±2.2	0.992	23.40
m-hydroxymethyl p-methylamino		6.8	18.2±2.1	35.9	55.4±5.8	0.997	19.53

[a] average of three replicates

[b] heat of sublimation in kcal/mole

Our observations are in relatively good agreement with those of Addison (17) who observed vapour pressures between 7.4 and 33.2 x 10^{-6} mm Hg at 30°C and relative humidities between 0 and 59 percent. Apparently the volatility of aminocarb is profoundly affected by changes in the humidity of the entraining gas. In our assays no changes in the chemical composition of the test substance in the vapour saturator could be detected after six hours of operation. Each of the four transformation products was somewhat less volatile than the parent compound; however, the environmental implications remain unclear. The persistence of these products remains to be studied.

Redistribution of Aminocarb

In a final series of experiments we wished to begin studies on possible redistribution via the volatilization mechanism. In a closed system it is intuitively clear that aminocarb would be redistributed throughout the system. However if deposits of aminocarb on a flat poorly-adsorbing surface were exposed to turbulent air the results would be less certain. Aminocarb (ring $1^{14}C$) dissolved in acetonitrile was spotted (1 uL) on the plastic backing from a thin layer chromatography plate using the spotting template in Figure III. Each spot was determined to contain 40-45 ng of the pesticide. About the labelled deposits were placed a series of potential trapping agents. These consisted of carbowax 20-M (quandrant 1), SE-30 (quandrant 2) Nujol (quandrant 3) and olive oil (quandrant 4). Each of the potential trapping agents was applied as a 1 uL droplet of a 2 percent solution in hexane or acetonitrile. The open symbols of Figure III denote deposits of trapping agent (different symbols for different mean distances from each deposit of pesticide). Four plates were spotted and placed in a fume hood. After 1 hour or 1, 3 1/2 or 7 days a spotted plate was removed and exposed to X-ray film in a light-tight cassette for 4 days. Figures IV (after 3 1/2 days) and V (seven days) are photographs of the resulting autoradiograms. The 'comet tails' associated with each of the aminocarb deposits indicate the prevailing wind direction. The flow had been measured previously at 0.8 meters/sec. Trapping of activity is clearly evident in quadrants 1 and 2 but not evident in quandrant 3 of each of these photographs. Moreover, there is an increase in activity in the trapping zones with time (Figure IV vs Figure V) and a gradient of activity with distance from the pesticide deposit. It is considered that translocation of activity must have occurred either in the gas phase or as a result of radioactive microcrystals being physically transported as crystalline material. The fact that there was no detectable redistribution of activity after one hour of laminar air flow, that only the closest traps contained detectable activity after one day and that the activity in corresponding traps increased after three and seven days would seem to mitigate against the physical transfer of microcrystals; i.e. the time frame is too long. Moreover the activity is more or less evenly distributed across the surface of each trap. If a crystal had impinged on the trapping surface a concentration gradient across the surface of the trap might have been anticipated. Although the mechanism of transfer remains equivocal the redistribution of activity is clearly evident. It is suggested that similar mechanisms operate on leaf surfaces. A predictive model for uptake of volatilized pesticide by leaves as a function of distance from the spray tract has recently been published (22).

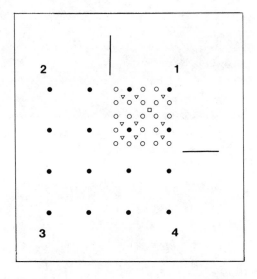

Figure 3.   Spotting template for redistribution trials.

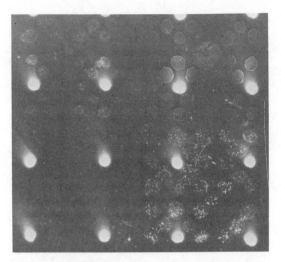

Figure 4. Autoradiogram of aminocarb on plastic sheet
after 3-1/2 days exposure to laminar flow of air.

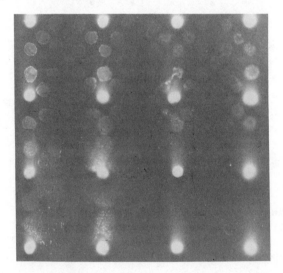

Figure 5. Autoradiogram of aminocarb on plastic sheet
after 7 days exposure to laminar flow of air.

Acknowledgments

The excellent technical assistance of R. Simpson and financial support from the National Science and Engineering Research Council is greatfully acknowledged.

Literature Cited

1. Norris, L.A. Residue Reviews 1981, 80, 65 - 135.
2. "Aminocarb: The Effects of its Use on the Forest and Human Environment, National Research Council of Canada, Document 18979 of the Environmental Secretariat, Ottawa, Canada.
3. Plimmer, J.R., in "Herbicides"; Kearney, P.C. and Kaufman,a D.D. Eds., Marcel Decker Inc., New York, N.Y. 1976 p 891-934.
4. Hartley, G.S. in "Pesticide Formulation Research"; Gould, R.F. Ed.; ADVANCES IN CHEMISTRY SERIES No. 86 American Chemical Society; Washington, D.C. 1969, p 269.
5. Wheatley, G.A. in "Environmental Pollution by Pesticides"; Edwards, C.A. Ed.; Plenum Press, New York, 1973; pp 365-408.
6. Spencer, W.F. and Claith, M.M. Residue Reviews 1983, 85: 57-71.
7. U.S. Environmental Protection Agency: Proposed environmental standards and proposed good laboratory practice standards for physical chemical persistence and ecological effects testing, Fed Register 1980, 45 (227) 77345.
8. Gueckel, W.; Synnatschke, G.; Rittig, R. Pestic.Sci. 1973, 4, 137.
9. Dobbs, A.J.; Grant C., Pestic. Sci. 1980, 11, 29.
10. Starr, R.I. and Johnsen, R.E. Agric. Fd. Chem. 1968, 16, 411.
11. Phillips, F.T. Chem. and Ind. 1974, 193.
12. Taylor, A.W.; Glotfelty, D.E.; Turner, B.C.; Silver, R.E.; Freeman, H.P. and Weiss, A. J. Agric. Food Chem. 1977, 25, 542.
13. Caro, J.E. J. Agric. Food Chem. 1971, 19, 78.
14. Willis, G.H.; McDowell, L.L.; Harper, L.A.; Southwick, L.M.; Smith, S. J. Environ. Qual. 1983, 12, 80.
15. Willis, G.H.; McDowell, L.L.; Smith, S.; Southwick, L.M. Agron. J. 1980, 72, 627.
16. Yule, W.N.; Cole A.E.W.; Hoffman, I. Bull. Environ. Contam. Toxicol 1971, 6, 289.
17. Addison, J.B. Chemosphere 1981, 10, 355.
18. P.G. Jarvis,; James, G.B.; Landsberg, J.J. in Vegetation and the Atmosphere, Vol. 2, Monteith, J.L. Ed., Academic Press, New York, N.Y. 1976 pp 171-239.
19. Abdel Wahab, A.M.; Casida, J.E. J. Agric. Food Chem. 1967, 15, 479.
20. Grayson, B.T,; Foirbraey, L.A. Pestic. Sci. 1982, 13, 269.
21. Brun, B.L.; MacDonald, R.M. Bull. Environ. Contam. Toxicol. 1978, 24, 886.
22. Thompson, N. Pestic. Sci.: 1983, 14, 33.

RECEIVED October 12, 1983

Implications of Pesticide Photochemistry in Forestry Applications

DONALD G. CROSBY

Department of Environmental Toxicology, University of California, Davis, CA 95616

Pesticides, widely applied for modern forest
management, become distributed on leaf surfaces, as
airborne particles, and as atmospheric vapor. Forest
applications usually coincide with the most intense
solar ultraviolet light, and many of the pesticides
can be expected to undergo photochemical degradation.
Photodegradation actually has been observed, for example in the photoreduction of 2,4,5-T esters. While
photolysis under the leaf canopy is limited, most
applications result in exposure of the chemicals to
sunlight on canopy surfaces, where formulation plays a
major part in degradation. Photodegradation in airborne drift may be more important than previously
recognized, and photodegradation in vapor produced
from spray or treated surfaces probably provides a
major sink for most chemicals. The resulting losses
lead to overapplication, with its consequent hazard
and expense, but might be substantially reduced and
efficacy improved by appropriate formulation and
timing. Photodegradation also can contribute a
desirable nonpersistance to environmental pesticide
residues. Despite these important implications,
quantitative supporting data generally are lacking.

Forestry now represents a major area of pesticide use. In
North America and, increasingly, worldwide, herbicides are being
applied for site preparation, brush control, conifer release
(defoliation of competing vegetation), and control of resprouting.
A large forest acreage also is sprayed for insect control, and a
market for disease-control chemicals is developing. "Minor uses,"
still involving a large tonnage of pesticides, include Christmas
tree farms, nurseries, and firebreaks. The subject has been
reviewed in a recent handbook (1) as well as in other papers in
this Symposium.

0097-6156/84/0238-0227$06.00/0
© 1984 American Chemical Society

All together, these applications consume millions of pounds of pesticides annually. Where does it all go? What part does sun-light play in its environmental fate? What does this imply for forest management? These will be the subjects addressed in this paper.

Pesticide Fate in the Environment

There still seems to be little specific information on the fate of the pesticides used in forestry. However, it is reasonable to expect that application methods and their physical and chemical consequences will not differ greatly from those relating to other forms of agriculture. The major applications are made by air-craft, especially in rugged terrain; the coverage will be largely on open foliage—economics minimizes application to bare soil, and water contamination usually is excluded specifically by law; the chemicals most often are applied between April and November, coinciding with maximum temperatures and sunlight; and most are not applied neat but as a diluted spray of formulated materials dispersed in water or oil.

As a result of almost any forest application, a pesticide will take three forms:

1. Airborne particles. Droplets with diameters less than about 100 μm may remain aloft for considerable periods of time and move over many kilometers, continually losing volume to become minute solid or semisolid particles.
2. Deposits on leaf surfaces. Considerable ingenuity has been directed toward formulating pesticides so that they will adhere to leaves, and aerial spraying (especially from conven-tional aircraft) generally results in a large proportion of the spray remaining on the sunlit upper surfaces of the canopy. Comparatively little spray reaches the forest floor (2).
3. Atmospheric vapor. Vapor results from pesticide volatiliza-tion during spray release, vaporization from leaf deposits, and, over a longer time period, desorption from the soil and litter of the forest floor. Several reviews of this subject appear elsewhere in this Symposium volume.

To illustrate this distribution, Figure 1 shows the result of an actual aerial application of a typical pesticide spray to a broadleafed tree species (3). The "application level" (A) simply assumes that all the spray leaving the aircraft becomes uniformly distributed over the target area (1.12 kg/ha), and the curve shows the parathion levels analytically detected on a statistical samp-ling of leaves. A major part of the applied pesticide (B) fails to reach the canopy, as corroborated by Barry (2) with conifers, and is assumed to represent airborne drift, volatilization, and, to a lesser extent, penetration to the ground. Once on the

leaves, a further amount (C) is lost by volatilization, chemical
transformation, and eventual absorption into the tissue. Whether
suspended in air, vaporized, or residing on a surface, the pesticide is most likely to meet conditions favoring any possible
action of sunlight.

Pesticide Photochemistry

There now exists a sizable body of literature to demonstrate that
many—perhaps most—pesticides are subject to photochemical degradation energized by the ultraviolet (UV) portion of sunlight, at
least under laboratory conditions. Background information and
numerous examples have been provided in the review by Crosby (4).
The most important UV energy generally is that provided between
the lower-wavelength cutoff imposed by the atmosphere's ozone
layer, about 290 nm, and the point near 350 nm above which the
quantum energy is insufficient to break the interatomic bonds
commonly found in pesticides. This UV energy varies with wave-
length and solar angle (and hence with the time of year), although
at least as much of it is derived from open sky as from direct
sunlight (Figure 2) (5).

Penetration of this UV radiation to ground level depends upon
the type of forest stand and canopy (6). A clumped stand and
erectophile canopy admit the greatest proportion (about 35% of the
UV incident at the top), as expected. However, in either normal
or planophile canopies in any type of stand, penetration always is
less than 15% and often is on the order of only 2%. Almost all
photodegradation will be expected to occur at or above the top
contour of the sprayed foliage.

The first law of photochemistry states that a substance must
absorb light energy in order for photochemical transformation to
occur, and many pesticides do react in this way. However, the
importance of environmental reagents and the specific surrounding
chemical microenvironment in pesticide photodegradations now is
becoming apparent. In water and aqueous spray, for example, not
only H_2O but OH^-, other nucleophiles, and other ionic reagents can
react photochemically with appropriate pesticides (7), especially
in photonucleophilic substitution reactions (8). In the presence
of organic solvents such as those employed in emulsifiable
concentrates, spray oils, or even natural leaf waxes, a reducing
environmental exists which can result in light-energized replace-
ment of functional groups by H (9). As atmospheric vapor, pesticides react principally with oxidants such as O_2, O_3 and HO • (10);
the presence of air pollutants increases oxidant levels substantially (Table 1). In aqueous media, especially, several such
type-reactions may occur simultaneously (11), and it is not essential that the pesticide itself absorb the UV energy for some
transformation—expecially oxidation—to take place, as long as
appropriate light-generated reagents are present. Under some
circumstances, the phenomenon of "photosensitization" also can

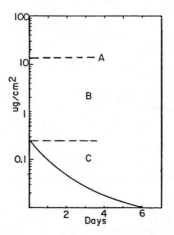

Figure 1. Distribution of parathion emulsion spray applied
(1.12 kg/ha) to peach trees (3). A = application level,
B = atmospheric dispersion, C = leaf residue.

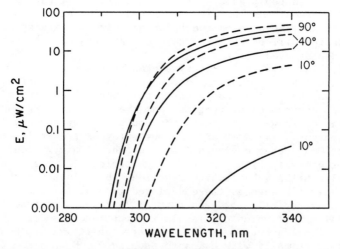

Figure 2. Spectral energy distribution of sunlight at the
earth's surface for solar angles of 10°, 40°, and 90°, from
direct sun (---) or reflection from open sky (---) (5).

Table I.   Atmospheric Reagents (Moles/km^3) (10)

Reagent	Normal Atmosphere[a]	Polluted Atmosphere[a]	Percent Increase
Oxygen (triplet, $^3\Sigma$)	8.0×10^9	8.0×10^9	0
Oxygen (singlet, $^1\Delta$)	1.0	20	2,000
Oxygen (atoms, ^{3}P)	1.2×10^{-4}	8×10^{-4}	670
Ozone	1,200	20,000	1,670
Hydroxyl	0.003	0.08	2,670
Nitrogen dioxide	150	8,000	5,330
Nitric acid	600	7,000	1,170

[a]Ground level

occur, in which the UV energy absorbed by another substance can be passed on to the pesticide and so result in its chemical reaction while the sensitizer returns to its inactive state.

With so many opportunities, one cannot be surprised that many pesticides are found to undergo photochemical reactions. However, few photochemical investigtions have been made with forestry pesticides under practical field conditions, and illustration of the possible consequences requires a certain amount of extrapolation.

Environmental Photodegradation

Airborne droplets. Upon release from the aircraft, a large proportion of the spray droplets—expecially those with diameters below 100 μm—become airborne, and, within minutes, water and other volatile solvents evaporate. In most cases, it is doubtful that appreciable pesticide photodegradation occurs during this short time. However, MCPA (4-chloro-2-methylphenoxyacetic acid), applied as an aqueous solution of the dimethylamine salt (12, 13), underwent photodegradation even in the remaining, hydrated, semi-solid particles. The resulting products (Figure 3) represented processes of oxidation (by dissolved oxygen), photonucleophilic "hydrolysis" to replace Cl by OH (from water), and some reduction (presumably by H-abstraction from the organic solutes present). In instances where a high-boiling petroleum fraction were to be present, less oxidation and hydrolysis and more photoreduction might be expected.

In model (laboratory) experiments, the half-life of MCPA was about 3 days, suggesting that particles might have to be airborne for appreciable time periods in order for breakdown to occur. However, atmospheric drift of emulsified parathion ($\underline{O},\underline{O}$-diethyl $\underline{O}$-p-nitrophenyl phosphorothionate) underwent substantial photooxidation, isomerization, and p-nitrophenol formation within a few minutes (Figure 4) (14).

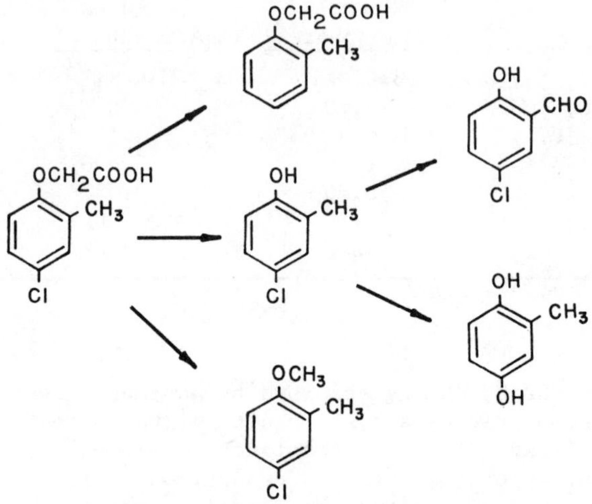

Figure 3. Sunlight degradation products of commercial MCPA dimethylamine salt formulation in aqueous spray droplets.

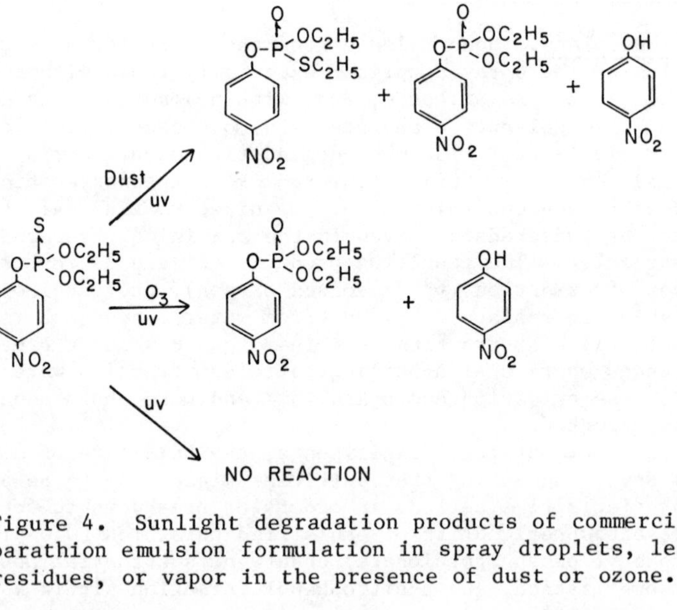

Figure 4. Sunlight degradation products of commercial parathion emulsion formulation in spray droplets, leaf residues, or vapor in the presence of dust or ozone.

Leaf surfaces. Photoreduction is a prominent reaction on leaf
surfaces, with either formulation, pesticide, or the surface
itself providing the necessary hydrogen atoms. For example,
Sundström, et al. (15), reported the reductive dechlorination of a
2,4,5-T (2,4,5-trichlorophenoxyacetic acid) ester formulation to a
complex mixture of successively less-chlorinated phenoxyacetic
esters, and Que Hee, et al. (16) reported a similar dechlorination
of 2,4-D (2,4-dichlorophenoxyacetic acid). The toxic 2,4,5-T
impurity, TCDD (2,3,7,8-tetrachlorodibenzo-p-dioxin), was dechlorinated in a herbicide ester deposit on a sunlit leaf surface
within a few hours (Figure 5) (17).

Photooxidation of parathion also occurred on leaf surfaces
(18), together with isomerization and other reactions. Fenitrothion (0,0-dimethyl 0-3-methyl-4-nitrophenyl phosphorothionate)
and other phosphorothionate insecticides behaved similarly (19).
Some pesticides do not require external reagents for photodegradation on surfaces; carbamate insecticides such as carbaryl
(1-naphthyl N-methylcarbamate), aminocarb (4-dimethylamino-3-
methylphenyl N-methylcarbamate), and mexacarbate (4-dimethylamino-
3,5-dimethylphenyl N-methylcarbamate) photodecomposed by elimination of methyl isocyanate to give the corresponding phenol (Figure
6) (20), and dieldrin formed the isomeric (and more toxic) photodieldrin (21), a reaction which can be photosensitized (22).
Hydrolysis and other ionic reactions seem unlikely unless the
formulation can somehow provide water.

Atmospheric Vapor. As emphasized elsewhere in this volume, most
forest pesticides can be expected to volatilize. Even those with
seemingly low vapor pressures (less than 10^{-6} torr) are observed
to vaporize from soil, leaves, and especially from aqueous solutions and suspensions (23-25). Consequently, a significant and
perhaps major proportion of applied chemicals—pesticides, solvents, and adjuvants—can be expected to move eventually into the
atmosphere.

Oxidation is, of course, the dominant reaction. For example,
vaporized trifluralin (α, α, α-trifluoro-2,6-dinitro-N,N-dipropyl-p-
toluidine) was demethylated (Figure 7) (26), and its atmospheric
half-life was found to be 8 minutes (27). However, the reaction
occurred to a small extent even at night, and oxidation by ozone
was implicated. In fact, there is evidence (28) that parathion
photooxidation actually required the presence of ozone or other
highly reactive oxidants. Degradation not requiring external
reagents also may proceed rapidly; trifluralin was cyclized to a
substituted benzimidazole (11, 26), and dieldrin again formed
photodieldrin (29).

Although the herbicide, molinate (S-ethyl hexahydro-1H-
azepine-1-carbothioate), does not absorb appreciable sunlight UV
energy, its vapor still was photooxidized by atmospheric ozone
(Figure 8) (30). We, and others, have observed the same phenomenon with a number of other non-absorbing chemicals such as

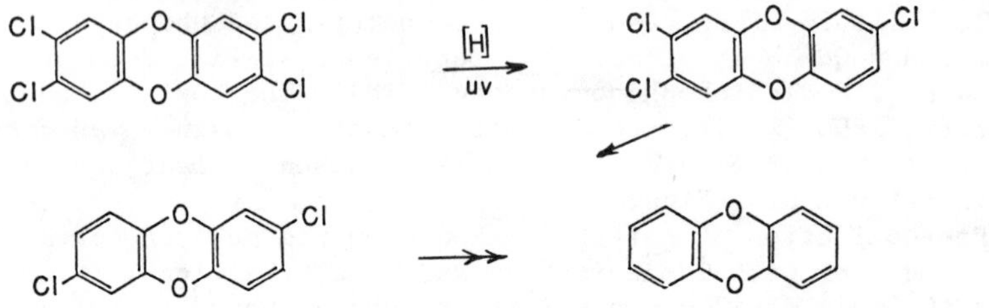

Figure 5. Sunlight degradation products of TCDD in mixed butyl esters of 2,4-D and 2,4,5-T as a deposit on a leaf surface.

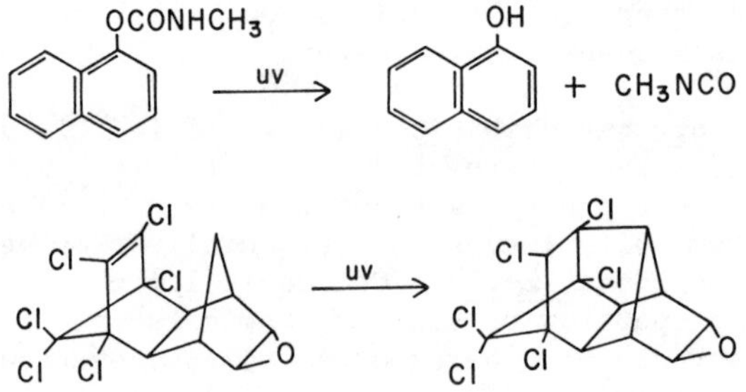

Figure 6. Sunlight degradation products of carbaryl and dieldrin on surfaces or as vapor.

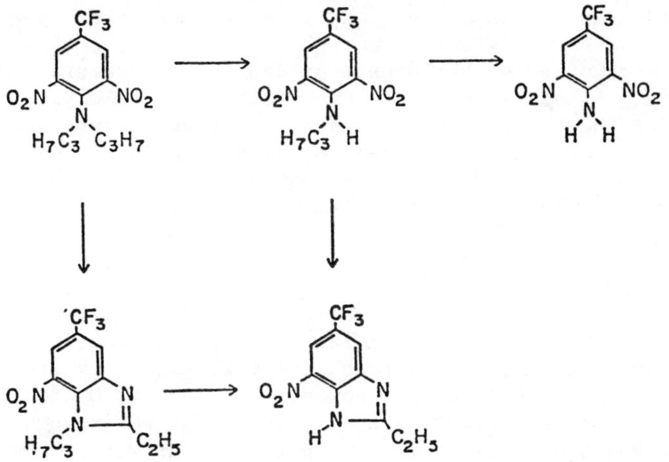

Figure 7. Sunlight degradation products of trifluralin as atmospheric vapor.

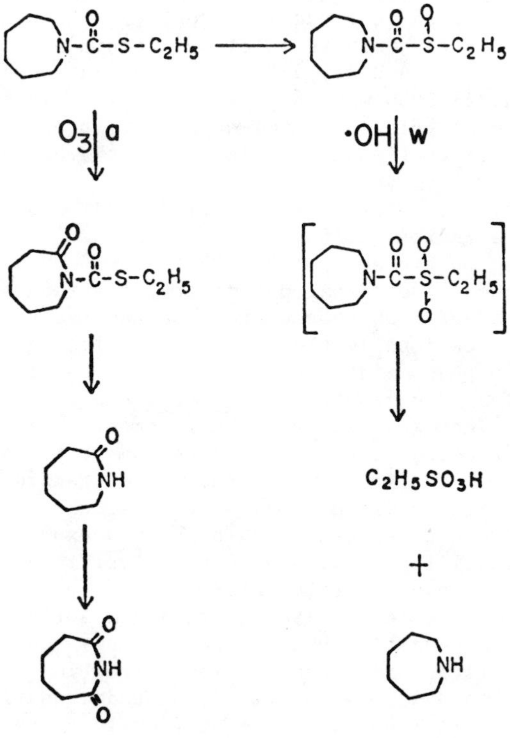

Figure 8. Sunlight degradation products of molinate as atmospheric vapor (a) compared to natural water (w) containing oxidant.

chlorinated aliphatic hydrocarbons, some of them otherwise
considered to be highly persistent (31, 32). Consequently, the
type and level of atmospheric photooxidants--both natural and
manmade "smog"--may assume major significnce in their role as
reagents for the transformation and destruction of many and
perhaps most pesticides. The apparently high oxidant levels
observed to be generated over forest areas (33, 34) actually may
exert a profound influence on vaporized pesticides.

Implications

Despite the diverse chemical types represented by forest pesticides, the variety of their formulations, and the many rates and
routes of application, two factors remain consistently present in
their environment--sunlight and powerful reagents. Quite apparently, these forces are active and acting. The well-known "blue
haze" observed over forests in many parts of the world remote from
man's chemical wastes is a result of photooxidation reactions of
volatile natural chemicals similar to those which generate manmade
smog.
    We can expect the forest pesticides similarly to respond to
such natural forces, and our very limited knowledge indicates that
they do. 2,4,5-T applied to a sunlit forest was photoreduced; our
recent experiments at the University of California's Blodgett
Forest with a standard 2,4-D/2,4,5-T ester application showed that
the trace of contained TCDD was largely photolyzed within a single
sunlit day and undetectable after two days; forest application of
fenitrothion produced continuous low levels of the expected oxon
and nitrocresol on foliage.
    Photolysis reflects oxidation, reduction, hydrolysis, and
occasional characteristic elimination or isomerization reactions,
although even those pesticides which do not absorb UV light can
react in the presence of external photochemical oxidants. As in
the case of 2,4,5-T and TCDD, these processes most often imply
detoxication, but occasionally the result is toxicological activation instead, as in photooxidation of parathion and fenitrothion
or the isomerization of dieldrin. The actual health significance
of such transformations in the forest environment remains unknown;
for example, the products of vapor photolysis must be so dilute as
to present negligible respiratory hazard, while transformations on
Christmas trees or frequently-handled nursery stock might have
unexpectedly dangerous consequences through skin exposure.
    Our frequent inability to account for a significant proportion
of applied pesticides even shortly after application (Figure 1) is
bothersome and unsatisfactory. Vaporization and surface photolysis may be partly responsible, but it seems likely that airborne
drift of minute particles represents a large fraction of such
losses. From our own evidence, pesticide photodegradation in such
dispersions may be more important than previously suspected, and
the consequences--especially in terms of inhalation toxicity--

remain unexplored. However, these losses, plus those from subsequent surface photolysis, mean that a considerable proportion of applied chemical is simply wasted—worse than wasted, as people must be concerned over possible adverse effects of the "missing" pesticide or its degradation products. Use of formulation additives has proved successful in controlling both surface volatilization and photodegradation (35), and such an approach could lead to substantial reductions in the level of pesticides needed and the frequency of application. As simple an expedient as properly regulating the diurnal timing of applications and the formulation could help to take advantage of a particular pesticide's photochemical reactivity.

Surprisingly and unfortunately, information on the photochemical fate of almost all major forest pesticides still is sparse indeed—2,4-D, 2,4,5-T, picloram, and fenitrothion have received the most attention—and practical measurements in the forest environment are even rarer. Limited laboratory experiments imply that photodegradation can occur and may be significant, but field investigation will be necessary. Release of existing manufacturer's analytical data also would be scientifically helpful and might reduce the expense of others' repetitious investigations. Far from being undesirable, photochemical instability can provide the nonpersistence now considered the hallmark of an environmentally compatible product.

It appears likely that vapor-phase photolysis provides the ultimate destruction of many pesticides, including those now so important to forest management. However, most pathways, processes, and intermediates which separate a pesticide's release at the spray nozzle and its eventual environmental fate still demand our best scientific attention.

Literature Cited

1. Newton, M.; Knight, F. "Handbook of Weed and Insect Control Chemicals for Forest Resource Managers;" Timber Press: Beaverton, OR, 1981.
2. Barry, J.W. in "Implications of Chemical and Biological Control Agents in Forestry Applications;" Garner, W.Y.; Harvey, J., Jr., Eds.; ACS SYMPOSIUM SERIES, American Chemical Society, Washington, D.C., 1983.
3. Winterlin, W.L.; Bailey, J.B.; Langbehn, L.; Mourer, C. Pestic. Monit. J. 1975, 8, 263–69.
4. Crosby, D.G. in "Herbicides: Chemistry, Degradation, and Mode of Action;" Kearney, P.C.; Kaufman, D.D., Eds; Dekker: New York, NY, 1976; pp 835–890.
5. Shettle, E.P.; Green, A.E.S. Appl. Optics 1974, 13, 1567–81.
6. Allen, L.H., Jr.; Gausman, H.W.; Allen, W.A. J. Environ. Qual. 1975, 4, 285–94.

7. Crosby, D.G. in "Fate of Organic Pesticides in the Aquatic
    Environment;" Faust, S.D. Ed.; ADVANCES IN CHEMISTRY SERIES
    No. 111, American Chemical Society: Washington, D.C., 1972;
    p 173-88.
8. Crosby, D.G.; Moilanen, K.W.; Nakagawa, M.; Wong, A.S. in
    "Environmental Toxicology of Pesticides;" Matsumura, F.;
    Boush, G.M.; Misato, T. Eds.; Academic Press: New York, NY,
    1972; pp 423-434.
9. Crosby, D.G.; Hamadmad, N. J. Agr. Food Chem. 1971, 19, 1171-
    74.
10. Crosby, D.G. in "Proceedings of the Fifth International
    Congress of Pesticide Chemistry;" Hutson, D.H. Ed.; Pergramon
    Press: London, 1983; Vol. 3.
11. Moilanen, K.W.; Crosby, D.G.; Soderquist, C.J.; Wong, A.S. In
    "Environmental Dynamics of Pesticides;" Haque, R.; Freed,
    V.H., Eds.; Plenum Publ. Corp.: New York, NY, 1975; pp 45-
    60.
12. Crosby, D.G.; Li; M.-Y.; Seiber, J.N.; Winterlin, W.L.
    "Environmental Monitoring of MCPA in Relation to Orchard
    Contamination;" Report to the California Department of Food
    and Agriculture: Univ. of California, Davis, Calif., 1981,
    146 pp.
13. Freiberg, M.; Bowers, J.B.; Crosby, D.G. Abstr. 185th
    National Meeting, Amer. Chem. Soc., Seattle, WA, Mar. 24,
    1983; PEST 89.
14. Woodrow, J.E.; Seiber, J.N.; Crosby, D.G.; Moilanen, K.W.;
    Soderquist, C.J.; Mourer, C. Arch. Environ. Contam. Toxicol.
    1977, 6, 195-91.
15. Sundström, G.; Jensen, S.; Jansson, B.; Erne, K. Arch.
    Environ. Contam. Toxicol. 1979, 8, 441-48.
16. Que Hee, S.S.; Paine, S.H.; Sutherland, R.G. J. Agr. Food
    Chem. 1979, 27, 79-82.
17. Crosby, D.G.; Wong, A.S. Science 1977, 195, 1337-38.
18. Joiner, R.L.; Baetcke, K.P. J. Agr. Food Chem. 1973, 21,
    391-96.
19. Yule, W.N.; Duffy, J.R. Bull. Environ. Contam. Toxicol.
    1972, 8, 10-18.
20. Crosby, D.G.; Leitis, E.; Winterlin, W.L. J. Agr. Food Chem.
    1965, 13, 204-207.
21. Rosen, J.D.; Sutherland, D.S.; Lipton, G.R. Bull. Environ.
    Contam. Toxicol. 1966, 1, 133-40.
22. Ivie, G.W.; Casida, J.E. J. Agr. Food Chem. 1971, 19, 410-
    16.
23. Hartley, G.S. in "Pesticidal Formulations Research;" Van
    Valkenburg, J.W., Ed.; ADVANCES IN CHEMICAL SERIES No. 86;
    American Chemical Society: Washington, D.C., 1969; p. 115-
    34.
24. Spencer, W.F.; Farmer, W.J.; Cliath, M.M. Residue Reviews
    1973, 49, 1-47.

25. Mackay, D.; Leinonen, P.J. Environ. Sci. Technol. 1975, 9, 1178-80.
26. Soderquist, C.J.; Crosby, D.G.; Moilanen, K.W.; Seiber, J.N.; Woodrow, J.E. J. Agr. Food Chem. 1975, 23, 304-309.
27. Woodrow, J.E.; Crosby, D.G.; Seiber, J.N. Residue Reviews 1983, 85, 111-25.
28. Moilanen, K.W.; Crosby, D.G. Environ. Qual. and Safety 1975, 3, 308-12.
29. Crosby, D.G.; Moilanen, K.W. Arch. Environ. Contam. Toxicol. 1974, 2, 62-74.
30. Crosby, D.G., Moilanen, K.W., Woodrow, J.E., Seiber, J.N. Fourth International Congress of Pesticide Chemistry, Zürich, 1978.
31. Crosby, D.G.; Moilanen, K.W. Chemosphere 1977, 6, 167-72.
32. Dilling, W.L.; Bredeweg, C.J.; Tefertiller, N.B. Environ. Sci. Technol. 1976, 10, 351-56.
33. Miller, P.R.; McCutchan, M.H.; Milligan, H.P. Atmos. Environ. 1972, 6, 623-33.
34. Research triangle Institute. "Investigation of Ozone and Ozone Precursor Concentrations at Nonurban Locations in the Eastern United States;" EPA-450/3-74-034; Research Triangle institute: Research Triangle Park, NC, 1974, 141 pp.
35. Aller, H.E.; Dewey, J.E. J. Econ. Entomol. 1961, 54, 508-10.

RECEIVED September 9, 1983

Fate of Chemical Insecticides
in Foliage and Forest Litter

J. A. ARMSTRONG

Canadian Forestry Service, Environment Canada, Place Vincent Massey, Hull, Quebec, Canada

The spruce budworm programs in Eastern Canada result in the annual application of carbamate (aminocarb), organophosphate (fenitrothion) and biorational (Bacillus thusingiensis) insecticides to several million hectares of spruce-fir forest. Accountability of the pesticide deposit requires an understanding of the fate of the pesticide on and into foliage. Studies show a longer residual life of the insecticide on old than new foliage. There is also a greater retention of the oil base than the water base sprays. Decidous foliage yielded measurable deposits for 15 days post treatment. The insecticide aminocarb has a very short residual life. The insecticide residues found in the forest litter appear to have relatively little impact on the biota of the forest floor.

The current outbreak of the spruce budworm (Choristoneura fumiferana Clem.) in Eastern Canada has resulted in the significant loss of softwood resource in that area. The larval form of the insect attacks the tree by feeding on the foliage and when the population is sufficiently high there can be a significant decrease in increment growth and, under extreme pressure for several years, death of the tree. To protect their forest resources, and to ensure a continuing supply of raw maeterial to the mills, the provinces of New Brunswick, Quebec, Newfoundland and Nova Scotia have used either chemical or biological insecticides to prevent unacceptable defoliation. The province with the longest history of continuous spray application is New Brunswick, with Quebec next followed by Newfoundland and Nova Scotia. Over the years DDT (1,1,1-Trichloro-2,2-bis-(p-chlorophenyl)ethane), phosphamidon (2-chloro-N,N-diethyl-3hydroxycrotonamide dimethyl phosphate) fenitrothion (O,O-dimethyl O-(4 nitro-m-tolyl)

0097-6156/84/0238-0241$06.00/0
© 1984 American Chemical Society

phosphorothioate), aminocarb (4-dimethylamino-m-tolyl methylcarbamate), mexacarbate (4-dimethylamino-3,5 xylyl methylcarbamate), Trichlorfon (dimethyl (2,2,2-trichloro-1-mydroxyethyl)
phosphonate) and acephate (O,S-dimethyl acetylphos-phoramido-
thioate) have been used operationally in these areas with the
major use being the first four (DDT, phosphamidon, fenitrothion
and aminocarb). Table I shows the use pattern of these products
in terms of area treated. Prior to 1967, the insecticides used
were DDT (only product used up to 1960) and DDT and phosphamidon
(used exclusively for the period 1961 to 1966).

The awareness of the effect of the chemical insecticides
on the forest ecosystem resulted in the initiation of research
programs within the Canadian Forestry Service to not only
record the presence of the insecticide and its metabolites,
but also to try to gain some understanding of the biological
significance of the residues. In addition regulatory authorities
now demand more information on the ultimate fate of the
insecticides in Canadian forests; thus although a product
may be registered and have a forestry use in other countries,
data must be generated to answer the specific questions
pertaining to tree types, soils and temperature regimes
experienced in Canada.

In the aerial application of an insecticide the target
is the tree, however the realities of aerial application
are that areas other than the tree receive a dose of insecticide. Norris (1) has indicated that the pesticide
ends up in 4 main compartments, air, vegetation, soil and
water. The insecticide that is deposited on the vegetation
may be washed off to fall to the forest floor or, if it is
absorbed into the foliage it will remain there until such
time as the foliage itself falls to the forest floor. Once the
insecticide is on the forest floor it may remain in the
litter-soil compartment to be ultimately broken down or it may,
through leaching or run-off, end up in the water of streams
running through or emanating from the forest. This paper
reviews a portion of the literature on the fate of insecticides
in foliage and forest litter.

The Fate of Insecticides on Foliage

The droplet of insecticide on the foliage of fir (Abies
balsameae (L) Mill.) and spruce (Picea spp.) may be in the
form of a deposit on the surface or it may be absorbed
into the foliage depending on the physical-chemical properties
of the insecticide, the insecticide mix applied, and the foliage.
Some insecticides suffer an initial rapid loss due to washing
off and weathering of the deposit while others are absorbed
and held in the foliage for periods of up to several months.
GLC analysis of virtually all aspects of trees after aerial
application of insecticide showed the maximum amounts on outer
portions of the tree (2).

Table 1.   Insecticides used operationally and areas treated
aerially for control of the spruce budworm in E.
Canada during the period 1967-1982[1]

Year	Insecticides	Area treated [2,3] ha[4] (000's)
1967	DDT	311
	Fenitrothion	80
	Phosphamidon	30
1968	Fenitrothion	234
	Phosphamidon	96
	DDT	84
1969	Fenitrothion	1262
	Mexacarbate	5
	DDT	1.4
1970	Fenitrothion	1736
	Phosphamidon	124
	Aminocarb	3
	Trichlorfon	1.7
1971	Fenitrothion	3303
	Aminocarb	15
	Mexacarbate	10
1972	Fenitrothion	1612
	Mexacarbate	70
	Aminocarb	31
	Phosphamidon	3.2
1973	Fenitrothion	4682
	Phosphamidon	890
	Aminocarb	121
	Mexacarbate	36
1974	Fenitrothion	2673
	Phosphamidon	1406
	Aminocarb	486
	Mexacarbate	424
	Trichlorfon	13
1975	Fenitrothion	2537
	Phosphamidon	2121
	Trichlorfon	94
	Aminocarb	64

Continued on next page

Table I. Continued

Year	Insecticides	Area Treated[2,3] ha[4] (000's)
1976	Fenitrothion	5829
	Aminocarb	2017
	Phosphamidon	200
	Trichlorfon	107
1977	Fenitrothion	1920
	Aminocarb	1683
	Phosphamidon	978
	Trichlorfon	138
1978	Aminocarb	2132
	Fenitrothion	1412
	Mexacarbate	52
1979	Aminocarb	2158
	Fenitrothion	158
	Acephate	2
1980	Fenitrothion	1529
	Aminocarb	313
1981	Fenitrothion	2038
	Aminocarb	794
1982	Fenitrothion	1934
	Aminocarb	1069

1. Data Summarized from Nigam and P.C. and P. Shea in Managing Spruce Budworm in E. America USDA Ag. Handbook. in Press; and reports to the Canadian Forestry Service Annual Forest Pest Control Form.

2. Areas less than 1000 ha not included.

3. Areas shown are not the total area treated but the areas to which each insecticide was applied.

4. To convert area to acres multiply ha by 2.47.

In measurements of the fate of phosphamidon applied as an aqueous solution on spruce trees (Picea glauca spp) (3) it was shown that while there were measurable residues on the trees a rapid loss of the chemical occured. The rapid decrease in concentration (ppm wt/wt) was partially attributed to a dilution effect from the rapidly expanding new foliage. The half-life of the phosphamidon was a few days and by 4 days post spray, the insecticide was no longer detectable. The rapid loss of the material was attributed to weathering, breakdown, growth dilution, absorption and translocation within the tree.

Sundaram (4) found that, due to the geometry of the needle fir (Abies balsamea) acted as a better receptor of phosphamidon than spruce foliage. The fir collected about 75% more insecticide than the spruce. In comparing the relative amounts of the cis and Trans isomers, it was found that the Trans isomer was preferentially absorbed into the foliage while the cis form remains on the surface. The surface residue is then more rapidly lost by physical and metabolic processes.

Fenitrothion (applied as a water emulsion) also showed an initial rapid loss from the foliage with approximately 50% of the initial deposit being lost within 4 days of spray and 70–85% lost in 2 weeks (5,6). The study by Yule and Duffy (5) included several varieties of trees, they reported that the rate of loss was greater on spruce than on fir and that the insecticide persisted for a longer time on coniferous foliage than on "crop" plants. (Crop plants not specified, but these probably include rice, on which fenotrothion is used.) The study showed a long persistance of fenitrothion with 0.5 ppm present 336 days after application. Extension of this work to other areas of New Brunswick showed measurable amounts of fenitrothion one year after application. Analysis of older foliage showed an accumulation of fenitrothion in proportion to the number of years sprayed and the dosage applied (6).

The insecticide aminocarb has also been used extensively in eastern Canada on budworm control operations. Fenitrothion has been applied as a water emulsion (New Brunswick) and an oil solution (Quebec), but aminocarb because of its formulation characteristics, has been only applied operationally as an oil solution. Analysis of spruce foliage (7) showed aminocarb had a half life of 5 to 6 days with complete disappearance by 64 days post spray. Subsequent work (8) confirmed the short half life of aminocarb on coniferous foliage (3.2 to 6.9 days), and showed that the half life was dependant on the initial concentration of the insecticide. The material was found to be highly labile and dissipated rapidly and the authors made the statement that with these characteristics

this product was not likely to harm the forest environment.
In the last year a new formulation of aminocarb has appeared
on the insecticide market. It is finely ground aminocarb
suspended in an oil and it has the advantage that it can
be tank mixed to give either an oil or a water suspension.
Studies (10) show that, like the oil solution, this product
has a half life in the same range (3.2 to 6.0 days). There
was an indication of a variation in the initial rate of loss
due to the physical characteristics of the water emulsion spray
(in a series of repeat studies the evaporation rate was not
constant). The presence of the emulsifier inhibited evaporation
resulting in a higher initial foliar deposit than with the
oil base spray. The occurence of the lower rate of deposit
of the oil spray can be attributed to the particular oil used
in the Canadian budworm sprays. To meet the concerns of the
health authorities the standard No. 2 and No. 4 fuel oils
which had been used are now prohibited. The accepted product,
known as Insecticide Diluent 585 is volatile with an
evaporation rate approaching that of water.

    The insecticide Gardona (2-chloro-1(2,4,5-trichloro-
phenyl)-vinyl dimethyl phosphate) has been used experimentally
on white pine (Pinus strobus L.) to protect it from attack
by the white pine weevil (Pissodes strobi Peck.) (11). The
insecticide, applied in the form of a wettable powder, showed
an initial rapid loss with 50% being lost within 4 days of
application. By 9 days, 72% was lost and at 50 days post
spray only 4% remained. Residue analysis of both "oven dry"
and "wet" (fresh) foliage samples showed the initial rapid
loss of insecticides being very small. It is suggested that the
initial loss was due to wash-off and weathering (a problem of
wettable powders that are not properly tank-mixed) and that a
small portion of the insecticide was probably absorbed into the
surface waxes of the foliage. This absorbed material, being
protected from the weather is then subjected to different
pathways of dissapation and is lost at a much slower rate.

    The insecticide acephate, applied as a water spray has
a very short life in terms of biological activity and for
this, as well as economic reasons, it is not used on large
scale operations in Canada (12). Residue analysis of acephate
foliar deposits (13) showed that more than half of the
insecticide was lost within one day of spraying, and that by
32 days post spray, the amount of insecticide had decreased
to lessthan 0.01 ppm (the detection limit for 20 gm of
substrate). The metabolite of acephate known as Ortho 9006
(0,S-dimethyl phosphoramidothioate) was also assessed
in this study but was found to be present only in very small
amounts. At 2 hours post spray the average acephate concentration on spruce foliage was 55.15 ppm, and the average
concentration of the Ortho 9006 was 0.12 ppm. There was no
increase with time in the amount of the metabolite. The rapid

loss of acephate from the foliage suggests that the external
factors of photodecomposition volatilization and rainfall
were key agents in its disappearance. Although acephate is
reported to have some systemic action when applied to the
trunk of the tree or the surrounding soil (4) there was no
indication of any translocation when the insecticide was
applied to the foliage (aerial spray of 0.28 kg AI/ha).
Presumably at these rates there was no penetration of the waxy
epicuticular layer and hence virtually all of the insecticide
was susceptible to wash off and weathering.

The insecticide chlorpyrifos-methyl also suffered a
rapid initial loss from balsam fir foliage with only about
50% of the initial deposit remaining 5 to 8 hours post spray
(15). By 4 days post spray only 5% of the original deposit
remained; but there was then a low level of residue that
persisted at detectable levels (minimum level of detection
1.5 ppb wet wt.) for up to 125 days post spray. The current
year's foliage had a higher level of insecticide than did the
new foliage (i.e. it was shown that on a weight basis, the
new foliage (i.e. new shoot plus needles) had more needles than
did the old foliage, i.e. more surface area to result in a
higher collection efficiency (2).

The Fate of Insecticides in Forest Litter

A review of the literature pertaining to insecticide
deposits in Canadian forests reveals that there are very
few studies on the litter alone; most studies deal with soil
residues in which a soil sample consisting of litter plus soil
to a certain depth was taken. This sample was usually screened
to remove the larger bits and pieces i.e. stones, sticks,
mixed uniformly and then processed for residue study using
the appropriate techniques for analysis.

In studies on DDT residues in forest soil (16) soil
profiles were dug at intervals across the study area, and
horizontal samples were then taken from the exposed face
of each profile at measured intervals down from the surface.
All DDT residues were found in the surface 15 cm of the
profile which was the region which contained the litter.
There was no indication of any leaching of the insecticide
down into the subsoil. Analysis of the samples taken
at intervals across the study area showed a lack of
uniformity in the pesticide deposit. This lack of uniformity
can be attributed to several factors; unevenness in the original
spray deposit on the forest floor, caused by the screening
effect of trees or conversely the lack of trees to give more
exposure to the ground; terrain characteristics and an uneven
spray application. The study indicated that the larger residues
were lost at a greater rate and that the DDT residues levels
were maintained for several years after cessation of DDT
application by the continued fall of contaminated foliage.

A study of phosphamidon residues (3) in soil which was
again made up of the litter layer plus soil to a depth 15 cm
showed a rapid loss of the insecticide with the last measurable
deposit (level of detection 0.025 ppm) being recorded at
4 days post spray and non-detectable levels after 8 days post
spray. This particular study compared the deposits in both
coniferous and deciduous areas and similar results were found
in each location, thus indicating that litter from coniferous
and deciduous trees acted as a common base for the insecticide
deposit.

The early work on fenitrothion residues in soil also
used the soil-litter mix as the sample base (5). Following
operational sprays of fenitrothion (2x210 g AI/ha) only
traces of the insecticide were found in the surface layer;
at an average depth of 15 cm the level was less than 0.04 ppm.
This study also recorded the presence of the fenitrothion
metabolite fenitro- or feni-oxon. As with the foliage
study, low level deposits persisted with measurable amounts
being found at 64 days post spray. With the analytical
procedures being at the limit of sensitivity (0.04 ppm) no
significant loss of fenitrothion could be measured. In a
later study (17) the litter-soil layer was analysed for the
presence of fenitrothion and the breakdown products fenitrooxon and 4-nitrocresol. In two plots with initial measurable
amounts of fenitrothion (0.10 and 0.03 ppm) there was a
similar pattern of insecticide loss. For the first 10
days the deposit levels were fairly uniform in the 0.02
to 0.03 ppm range. By 20 days post spray the level of the
deposit was 0.01 to 0.015 ppm and by 30 days post spray
the amounts were 0.005 ppm to trace (<0.005 ppm). From this
time period to 90 days post spray (the end of the sampling
period) the insecticides was either not detectable or was
only found at levels less than 0.005 ppm. During the
same time period there was only one sample in which the oxon
metabolite was found (0.01 ppm); that was at 30 days post
spray in the plot with the high initial concentration of
fenitrothion (0.10 ppm). At 45 days post spray it was present
in trace (<0.005 ppm) amounts only.

In studies on the residue levels of aminocarb in a
litter-soil mixture (samples taken to a depth of 10 cm)
there was no detectable material even at the first post spray
sample which was 14 hours after application (7). In this
particular study the aminocarb had been applied at 70 g AI/ha
in 0.42 1/ha. Aminocarb was found in foliage and water.
However background interference in the foliage samples resulted
in a minimum detectable limit of 0.5 ppm in a 10 g sample.
In the litter-soil sample, the limit of detection was 0.1
ppm. Thus even if aminocarb had reached the litter layer,
it was probably not present at levels that could be detected.

In a subsequent study (12) there was a rapid loss of aminocarb
with more than 75% of the initial amount of the chemical having
disappeared from the soil-litter sample by 7 days post spray.
In this particular study a second application of the insecticide
was made on day 7 (of the first spray application), and again
there was 60-75% loss from the immediate post spray high in the
following 7 days. By 27 days post spray, the aminocarb was
found at trace levels only (limit of detection 0.1 to 0.2 ppm)
and from day 40 post spray to the end of the sample period
($\neq$69 days) residue levels were not detectable.

A true litter residue study was carried out in New
Brunswick in 1982 (10). The research was part of a program
to assess the environmental behavior of the new aminocarb
formulation known as Mactacil 180 F. In this particular
study, trees and screening vegetation in the spray block were
removed to give a plot of 25 m^2 (5 x 5m) completely exposed
to the spray. Litter only was collected from areas of 240
cm^2 (15.5 x 15. cm) to a depth of 1 cm for residue analysis.
Sample units consisting of flat aluminum plates supporting
Kromekote cards (10 x 10 cm) and two microscope slides
(7.5 x 15 cm) were placed in the plot at ground level to record
the amount and droplet spectrum of the spray deposit (18).
Following normal operational spray procedure two applications
of aminocarb were made each at 70 g AI in 1.46 1/ha of spray
mix. The total deposit recorded on the ground sample units
for the two sprays ranged from 10.37 to 40.86% of the material
emitted (7.23 to 28.6 g AI/ha). The maximum spray deposit
in the litter (1 hour post application) ranged from 40 to 70
ppb. From 3 hours to 12 days post spray the aminocarb level
never exceeded the detection limit of 10 ppb. with the
exception of 3 samples (total number of samples-17) in one
of the blocks in which levels of 10, 50 ppb were found in
the "as sampled" litter. The authors suggest that the rapid
loss of aminocarb from the litter was due to volatilization
photolysis and biodegradation.

Bioavailability of Insecticide Residues

In all the studies referred to, the presence of the insecticide
is determined by chemical means. The major concern is the
biological effect of the material on the ecosystem. In a
classical study, Yule (19) determined DDT residues in forest
soils and litter using GLC and TLC techniques. Bioassays
using Drosophila spp insects were then done on these samples
and the mortality equivalent in terms of ug of DDT was determined.
The mortality equivalent level of DDT was 50 to 250 times lower
than the chemical analysis level. Thus, although the insecticide
may be present in the substrate for a period of time extending

to several years (20) its biological activity is at a much
lower level. If this argument is extended to the residues
of fenitrothion and aminocarb, one might assume that, although
these compounds are present, their biological significance
is highly questionable. In fact they may be present at
such low levels that when their bioavailability is taken into
consideration, the residues are of no significance.

Summary

The aerial application of insecticides for budworm control
results in the deposition of insecticide on the foliage and
on the forest litter; the proportions of the spray being
deposited can be related to tree species (fir collecting more
than spruce) and the fate of the insecticide. DDT became
a problem of concern partially because of its long residual
life, since its withdrawal from use the presently used
insecticides, fenitrothion and aminocarb are characterized
by their rapid initial disappearance. Although aminocarb
cannot be found chemically relatively shortly after the
spray application, fenitrothion residues at very low levels
can be found for a long time (up to one year) after spray
application. Gardona, acephate and chlopyrifos-methyl are
also characterized by a rapid initial loss.

   A similar behavior pattern is found in the insecticide
residues in the litter-soil complex; partly as a result of needle
fall fenitrothion residues persist for an extended period (up
to one year). Phosphamidon and aminocarb disappear very
quickly.

   The pattern of disappearance of the insecticides from
foliage and litter appears to be an initial loss by wash-off
then degradation by weathering, photolysis and biodegradation.
The insecticides that have a longer residual life (DDT and to
a limited extent phosphamidon) do so because they are absorbed
into the waxy layer of the cuticle and are protected from the
environment. This protection from the environment may also
remove the insecticide as a biological hazard.

Literature Cited

1. Norris, L. The Behavior of Chemicals in the Forest   in
   Pesticides, Pest Control and Safety on Forest Range Lands.
   1971 Proc. Short Course for Pesticide Applicators, Oregon
   State University 1971: 90-106.
2. Armstrong, J. A. and W. N. Yule. Can. Ent. 1978, 110:
   1259-1267.
3. Varty, I. W. and W. N. Yule. Bull. Environ. Contam. and
   Toxicol. 1976, 15 (3): 257-264.
4. Sundaram, K. M. S. Environment Canada, Canadian Forestry
   Service Information Report CC-X-95. 1975, 22 pp.

5. Yule, W. N. and J. R. Duffy. Bull. Environ. Contam. and
    Toxicol. 1972, 8 (1): 10-18.
6. Yule, W. N. Bull. Environ. Contam. and Toxicol. 1974,
    12 (2): 249-252.
7. Sundaram, K. M. S., Y. Volpe, G. G. Smith, and J. R. Duffy.
    Environment Canada, Canadian Forestry Service Information
    Report CC-X-116. 1976, 44 pp.
8. Sundaram, K. M. S. and W. W. Hopewell. Environment Canada,
    Canadian Forestry Service Information Report FPM-X-6.
    1977, 41 pp.
9. Sundaram, K. M. S. in "Advances in Pesticide Science, Part 3"
    Geissbuhler, Pergamon Oxford and New York. 1979, 416-419.
10. Sundaram, K. M. S., J. Feng, R. Nott and C. Feng, unpublished
    data. Environment Canada, Canadian Forestry Service. 1983.
    File Report No. 47: 82 pp. Forest Pest Management Institute
    Sault Ste. Marie, Ont. Canada.
11. Sundaram, K. M. S. Environment Canada, Canadian Forestry
    Service Information Report CC-X-62. 1974: 32 pp.
12. Armstrong, J. A. and P. C. Nigam. Environment Canada,
    Canadian Forestry Service Information Report CC-X-82. 1976,
    29 pp.
13. Sundaram, K. M. S. and W. W. Hopewell. Environment Canada,
    Canadian Forestry Service Information Report CC-X-121. 1976,
    25 pp.
14. Lyon, R. L. Reports from the Insecticide Evaluation Project
    PSW-2203 USDA F. PSW 400. and Range Experimental Sta. 1973,
    Berkeley, CA.
15. Szeto, S. and K. M. S. Sundaram. J. Environ. Sci. Health
    1981, B16 (6): 743-766.
16. Yule, W. N. Bull. Environ. Contam. and Toxicol. 1973, 9 (1):
    57-64.
17. Sundaram, K. M. S. Environment Canada, Canadian Forestry
    Service Information Report CC-X-64. 1974, 43 pp.
18. Randall, A. P. Can. For. Serv. Bi-monthly Res. Notes. 1980
    36 (5): 23.
19. Yule, W. N. Bull. Environ. Contam. and Toxicol. 1970, 5 (2):
    130-144.
20. Tarrant, R. F. "Persistence of Some Chemicals in Pacific
    Northwest Forests" in Pesticides, Pest Control and Safety
    on Forest Range Lands. 1971. Proc. Short Course for Pesticide
    Applicators, Oregon State University, 1971: 133-141.

RECEIVED September 9, 1983

Fate of Chemical Insecticides in Aquatic Environments

Forest Spraying in Canada

K. M. S. SUNDARAM, P. D. KINGSBURY, and S. B. HOLMES

Forest Pest Management Institute, Canadian Forestry Service, Environment Canada, 1219 Queen Street East, Sault Ste. Marie, Ontario, P6A 5M7, Canada

The environmental behavior of some forestry insecticides in aquatic systems was studied under controlled conditions in laboratory model ecosystems
and in forest streams following experimental stream
injections or operational forest spraying. Insecticides studied were representative of organophos-
phorus and carbamate groups. In aquatic model systems consisting of sediment and natural water, the
mobility of the chemicals was usually from water to
sediment even though the insecticides studied were
very different in chemical structure. Results indicated that adsorbed insecticides were lost primarily due to microbial action. Studies in stream
ecosystems showed that the distribution and fate of
insecticide residues varied with physicochemical
properties of the material, additives present in
tank mixes, mode of application, stream discharge
and other site conditions. Disappearance of residues from stream waters was rapid due to downstream
transport and dilution, movement into other substrates and chemical processes. Stream sediments,
aquatic plants, fish and aquatic invertebrates accumulated residues to varying extents and showed a
wide range of retention times with different insecticides under different exposure conditions.

Chemicals have been an important means of controlling forest
insect pests in Canada for the past four decades. They have been
used to limit the impact of some of the most destructive forest
pests, such as spruce budworms (*Choristoneura* spp.), on forest resources essential to the production of fibre and other forestry
products. With growing demand for these products, pest control

0097-6156/84/0238-0253$07.00/0
© 1984 American Chemical Society

chemicals, because of their efficacy and economy, will continue to be our primary weapon of defense against insect pests and their usage will constitute an integral part of the current control strategies.

In order to evaluate the potential hazards chemical insecticides pose to forest environments, it is essential that adequate and reliable research data be generated on their environmental chemistry (distribution, persistence, movement, metabolic degradation, toxicity, fate, etc.). This paper gives a brief account of some laboratory and field research activities carried out at the Forest Pest Management Institute, Canadian Forestry Service to meet this requirement. Using two chemical insecticides which are extensively used now in forest insect control programs in Canada *viz* aminocarb [Trade name, Matacil; 4-dimethylamino-m-tolyl N-methylcarbamate] and fenitrothion [0,0-dimethyl 0-(3-methyl-4-nitrophenyl) phosphorothioate], studies conducted at the Institute to elucidate the environmental behavior and fate of forestry insecticides in general will be discussed.

Materials and Methods

Two research programs were conducted to examine the fate of aminocarb and fenitrothion insecticides in aquatic environments. In laboratory experiments, the dissipation of these chemicals in simple model ecosystems were studied. In the second experiment, the fate and persistence of these two chemicals were studied in forest streams following a semi-operational spray program in New Brunswick in 1982.

Laboratory Studies on Insecticide Degradation. Degradation in natural waters: Stream water (pH 6.0) and sediment (organic content 36%) were taken from a small shallow stream (depth *ca* 20 cm, width *ca* 1.5 m) in the Goulais River watershed, a mixed conifer-deciduous forest area, *ca* 50 km northeast of Sault Ste. Marie, Ont., Canada. Two degradation studies in duplicate (one for aminocarb and another for fenitrothion) were set up according to Sundaram and Szeto (1). Aminocarb and fenitrothion (100 µg/L in acetone) were added separately to 1000 mL aliquots of sterilized (Ameco Sterilizer 1 h) and unsterilized stream water in either open or closed 1500 mL Erlenmeyer flasks. The latter were sealed with polyethylene snap caps which were removed once a day for about 1 min. to allow air exchange. The flasks were incubated at 15 ± 0.2°C in an environmental chamber. Unfortified water samples, treated similarly, served as controls. Artificial light (400 W multivapor discharge lamps) with a photoperiod of 16 h light and 8 h dark was used during incubation to simulate sunlight. At designated intervals of time, aliquots of the control, sterilized (open and closed flasks) and unsterilized (open and closed flasks) water samples were collected, the pH was adjusted to *ca* 7 by Na$_2$CO$_3$ (aq.), solvent extracted (3 x 50 mL pesticide grade CH_2Cl_2), passed through a Na_2SO_4 column, flash-evaporated gently to dryness, dissolved in C_6H_6 and analyzed only for the active ingredients (AI) using gas-liquid chromatography (GLC). Partial and fully demethylated aminocarb as well as aminocarb phenol, as metabolites in aminocarb flasks, and demethylated (partial and complete) fenitrothion, amino-fenitrothion, and nitrocresol in fenitrothion flasks, were identified as breakdown products. None of the metabolites were quantified. No GLC responses corresponding to the active materials were found in the control flasks.

Dissipation in stream water with sediment: In a concurrent study, a series of 120, 100 g aliquots of coarsely sifted stream sediment were placed in 500 mL Erlenmeyer flasks containing 200 mL of stream water each. One half of the samples, i.e., 60 flasks, were autoclaved as before in an Ameco sterilizer for 1 h. After they were cooled to room temperature, all samples including the 60 non-autoclaved samples were separated into two sets (20 autoclaved + 20 non-autoclaved for each set) and one set was fortified with aminocarb and the other with fenitrothion in acetone to a level of 100 ppb (30 µg/ 300 g) and incubated in an environmental chamber as described above. The remaining 40 flasks served as controls for both experiments. Samples of both the autoclaved and the non-autoclaved water and sediment in open and closed flasks as well as control samples were analyzed for the active ingredients 1.0 h after fortification (zero time) and thereafter at intervals of time up to 75 h.

Extraction, clean-up and analysis of water and sediment: At the end of incubation, the entire water sample in each flask was filtered under aspiration through Whatman No. 1 filter paper in a Buchner funnel. The filter paper was later extracted along with the corresponding sediment. Each filtrate was quantitatively transferred into a 500 mL separatory funnel and repeatedly extracted with CH_2Cl_2 after adjusting to pH 7 as before and analyzed by GLC ($\underline{2}$, $\underline{3}$). Aliquots (40 g) of sediment samples from each flask were extracted in a Sorvall homogenizer using ethyl acetate (2 x 150 mL) as the solvent. The pooled extracts were concentrated to 40 mL (1 mL = 1 g) using a Buchii Rotovapor. The extracts (1 g equivalents) after passing through Na_2SO_4 were cleaned ($\underline{2}$, $\underline{3}$) using neutral charcoal (Nuchar SN)-cellulose (Whatman CF11) ($\overline{4}$:$\overline{10}$, w/w, 3 cm length) mini columns (Fisher 13-678-8) topped with Na_2SO_4. The columns were eluted with 35 mL of ethyl acetate: toluene (1:3) (fenitrothion) or 35 mL of CH_3OH:EtOAc (1:4) (aminocarb). The eluates were concentrated under reduced pressure and finally brought to a known volume under a stream of dry N_2 and stored at 4°C until analysis by GLC. A Hewlett-Packard 5710A GC/NPD was used for both aminocarb and fenitrothion residue analysis. The GC conditions were:

Detector temp: 250°C H_2 flow rate: 4 mL/min.
Injector temp: 200°C   Air flow rate: 70 mL/min.
Oven temp: 180°C   He flow rate: 35 mL/min.
R.T. (Min.):   aminocarb 3.5; fenitrothion 5.0
Column: 1.2 m x 4 mm glass column packed with
                   1.5% OV-17 + 1.95% OV-210 on Chromosorb
                   W, H.P., 80/100 mesh

Natural water (pH 6.0) and sediment (organic content 36%) used in this study were fortified with both the insecticides and subsequently analyzed by the described methods. No response that interfered with the detection of active ingredients was found in any of the untreated controls during incubation. The recoveries for water were 93 ± 4% at 400 ppb and 97 ± 7% at 20 ppb; for sediment they were 86 ± 6% and 91 ± 9%, respectively, at the same fortification levels. The minimum detection limit (MDL) for both insecticides was 0.1 ppb in water and 10 ppb in sediment (as sampled).

Except demethylated fenitrothion, all other metabolites found in water in the earlier study, were also identified in sediments for both the insecticides. Amino-fenitrothion, nitrocresol and monodemethylated aminocarb (MA) were most frequent compared to other metabolites.

Field Studies in Forest Streams. Insecticide treatments: The fate and persistence of fenitrothion and aminocarb were studied in 1982 in small headwater trout streams within the Nipisiguit River watershed near Popple Depot, New Brunswick. Three study streams were treated with different insecticide tank mixes, receiving two applications at a 6 to 8 day interval sprayed by Agcat or Agtruck aircraft equipped with Micronair spray emission systems. Each stream later received a point source injection by hand-held sprayer of the same insecticide tank mix which had been previously applied to it from the air.

Two fenitrothion and one aminocarb tank mixes were studied, all containing Triton X-100 (p-tert-octylphenoxynonaethoxy-ethanol), a nonionic surfactant, and water. One fenitrothion tank mix also contained cyclosol, a petroleum distillate. The percent (vol.) composition of different ingredients present in the tank mixes, the streams sprayed with them and their discharge, and dates and rates of application are summarized in Table I.

Aerial applications were conducted by Forest Protection Ltd. (FPL), the crown corporation responsible for budworm spraying in New Brunswick. Spotter planes were used to ensure that spray lines were followed and the streams and sampling sites received good coverage. Stream injections from the ground were applied *ca* 100 m upstream from the selected sampling sites using a "Micron ULVA Sprayer". According to the manufacturer's specifications, this ultra-low volume applicator is capable of producing a narrow

spectrum of droplet sizes with a VMD (volume-median diameter) of
70 μm. Treatment rates were adjusted by diluting the tank mixes
with water so that the residue levels obtained in stream water
were higher than in normal aerial applications and variations
between streams with different discharges were reduced. Details
of the insecticide formulations and applications are summarized in
Table I.

Residue sampling, preparation and analysis: Water, aquatic
moss, stream insect and fish samples were collected from some or
all study streams for residue analysis after each insecticide
treatment. In light of the dynamic nature of the systems studied
and the relatively small treatment areas, sampling was concentrated into the initial 24 hours after insecticide applications.

Water samples (ca 1 L) were collected by immersing clean
mason jars to a depth of 1 cm in midstream. Water samples were
extracted immediately with dichloromethane as described earlier.
Moss samples (ca 300 g) were collected from rocks on the stream
bed and packed in polyethylene bags after gently squeezing out adsorbed water. Samples were later cut into small pieces, thoroughly mixed in a Hobart bowl chopper and stored in sealed plastic
bags at -20°C until analyzed.

Samples (<1 g) of mayfly nymphs, *Ephemerella* sp., were collected after the first application of aminocarb to Portage Brook
by picking individual insects from moss on rocks picked from the
stream. Samples (10-110 g) of resident brook trout, *Salvelinus*
fontinalis Mitchill, were sampled from Portage Brook after each
aminocarb treatment using electrofishing equipment. Stomachs were
removed from the fish and they were placed in plastic bags and
frozen at -20°C until analyzed, as were mayfly nymph samples.

The procedures used for extraction, clean-up and GLC analysis
of aminocarb and fenitrothion residues in moss, insects and fish
were similar to the ones described earlier for sediment. Each
fish sample was ground by chopping with a large knife and mixing
thoroughly, then taking triplicate subsamples for analysis.
Entire mayfly samples collected were analyzed in most cases.
Moisture content of moss and mayfly nymph samples was determined
by collecting the pre-weighed ethyl acetate extracted material on
a weighed filter, drying it for 16 h at 105°C and reweighing.
Very large variations in moisture content were observed in these
samples.

Results and Discussion

Model Ecosystem Studies. Dissipation of aminocarb and fenitrothion in stream water: Measurements of the concentrations (ppb)
of fortified aminocarb and fenitrothion in the stream water as a
function of time (t [h]), and graphing of the data (Figure 1 and
2) showed that the concentration of these two insecticides decreased exponentially with time and followed the first-order rate

Table I. Details of insecticide

Ingredients (% by volume) in tank mixes applied to streams		Stream applied to and discharge on 5 July
Matacil 180F[1]	26.7	Portage Brook
Triton X-100[2]	3.0	179 L/sec.
Water	70.3	
Fenitrothion technical[3]	10.9	Ransom Brook
Triton X-100	10.7	58 L/sec.
Water	78.4	
Fenitrothion technical	10.9	Sixty-three Mile Brook
Triton X-100	3.0	23 L/sec.
Cyclosol 63[4]	24.0	
Water	62.1	

[1] Chemagro Ltd., Mississauga, Ont.

[2] Rohm and Haas Canada Inc., West Hill, Ont.

[3] Novathion (tech.) supplied by Cheminova, Lemvig, Denmark.

[4] Shell Canada Chem. Co. Ltd., Toronto, Ont.

treatments of study streams.

Dates of aerial treatment	Aerial application rate	Date of ground injection	Injection mix tank mix: water
17 June AM 25 June AM	70 g AI/ha in 1.46 L/ha	7 July	650 mL:0 mL
17 June AM 24 June PM	210 g AI/ha in 1.46 L/ha	7 July	75 mL:575 mL
22 June PM 28 June PM	210 g AI/ha in 1.46 L/ha	7 July	30 mL:620 mL

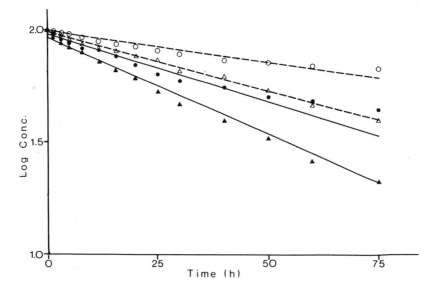

Figure 1.   Degradation of aminocarb in fortified natural
and sterile stream water in open and closed flasks.

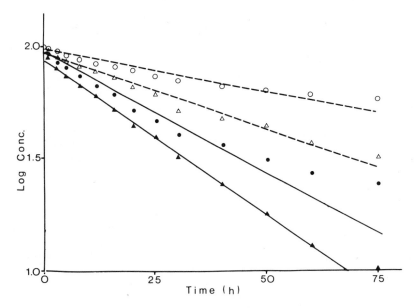

Figure 2. Degradation of fenitrothion in fortified natural and sterile stream water in open and closed flasks.

law. On integration and rearrangement, we obtained the concentra-
tion-time relation expression as:

$$\log \frac{x_o}{x} = \frac{kt}{2.303}$$

where x and x_o are the residual (at time t [h]) and initial (t =
0) concentrations of the insecticide and k is the rate constant
(t^{-1}). Plots of log x vs t (h) are linear and the half-life
$(t_{\frac{1}{2}})$, the time required for half of the insecticide to disappear, is obtained from 0.693/k.

The rate constants (t^{-1}) and half-lives $(t_{\frac{1}{2}})$ for both autoclaved and non-autoclaved aminocarb and fenitrothion samples in
open as well as closed flasks varied considerably (Figures 1 and
2). Rate constants were higher (more rapid degradation) in open
flasks and half-lives were longer in closed flasks, showing that
the loss of chemicals was higher in the open flasks due to volatilization compared to the closed ones. Half-lives for non-autoclaved aminocarb and fenitrothion samples in open and closed
flasks differed by 38% and 50% respectively, i.e., loss rates were
higher by those amounts in open flasks compared to the closed ones
because of volatilization. Similar trends in half-lives were also
observed for the autoclaved samples confirming the significance of
volatilization and codistillation in the dissipation of these two
insecticides from water.

The decrease in concentration of fenitrothion from spiked
stream water samples was faster compared to aminocarb. The concentration of the former decreased to 10 ppb in non-autoclaved
open flasks in 75 h, while aminocarb concentrations fell to 21 ppb
in the same period. A similar increased loss for fenitrothion was
also found in closed flasks (32 ppb vs 39 ppb) as well as in autoclaved (open, 24 ppb vs 44 ppb and closed 57 ppb vs 67 ppb)
flasks, indicating that at pH 6.0, fenitrothion is more readily
lost than aminocarb. Increased stability of aminocarb in acidic
waters is probably due to its nucleophilicity leading to protona-
tion and forming an aryldimethylammonium cation

$$(CH_3)_2-\overset{\underset{\displaystyle H}{|}}{\overset{\displaystyle (+)}{N}}-\underset{}{\bigcirc}\!\!\!\!\!\!\!-\overset{CH_3}{}\!\!\!\!-O-\overset{\overset{\displaystyle O}{\|}}{C}-N\overset{\displaystyle H}{\underset{\displaystyle CH_3}{}}$$

which resists degradation. Very likely the N-methylcarbamoyl part
of the molecule is also stabilized by the delocalization of elec-
trons on N, carbonyl and ester oxygens. Formation of such
cationic species and stabilization due to delocalization of elec-
trons is not possible for fenitrothion, consequently the molecule

is susceptible to hydrolysis. The preponderance of demethylated aminocarb (methylamino (MA) and amino (AM) Matacil) metabolites found in the incubated water samples also confirm that the chemical retained the intact carbamate ester group for a while. It seems therefore, that in an open system, both chemicals are lost from water by volatilization and co-distillation and the rate of loss for fenitrothion is ca 37% higher than for aminocarb, although the latter has a higher $(ca$ 12 fold) vapour pressure (1 x 10^{-2} Pa at 20°C) than the former (8 x 10^{-4} Pa at 20°C), ($\underline{4}$, $\underline{5}$). Both chemicals persisted longer in closed, non-autoclaved flasks ($t_{\frac{1}{2}}$ for aminocarb 56.64 h and for fenitrothion 44.05 h) further supporting the suggestion that volatilization and co-distillation are primarily responsible for the dissipation of these chemicals.

The prolonged persistence of aminocarb and fenitrothion in autoclaved water samples shows that both were amenable to biological degradation in stream water as a result of the activities of microorganisms. After an incubation of 75 h, 79% of aminocarb was degraded in non-autoclaved open flasks and 61% in closed vessels, while for autoclaved samples, the respective values were only 56% and 33%. The half-lives for the autoclaved samples were correspondingly longer (49.45 h vs 35.14 for open and 104.14 h vs 56.64 for closed flasks). The primary step in the microbial degradation of aminocarb seems to be the demethylation of the dimethylamino group forming MA and AM followed by hydroxylation of the aryl ring and eventual hydrolysis of the ester group yielding the phenol (AP). Similar trends of lower rate constants (0.025 vs 0.032 and 0.009 vs 0.016) and half-lives (28.00 vs 21.91 and 77.92 vs 44.05) were also observed for autoclaved vs non-autoclaved fenitrothion samples. Compared to aminocarb, we speculate that the dissipation of fenitrothion from stream water under controlled laboratory conditions is primarily due to volatilization followed by enzymatic hydrolysis of the P-O-aryl bond to yield $\underline{p}$-nitro-$\underline{m}$-cresol (FP). The formation of amino-fenitrothion (AF) through microbial reduction of the NO_2^- group is also apparent. Photo and bio-oxidations converting (1) the aryl $-CH_3$ group to -COOH to form carboxyfenitrothion and (2) P=S to P=O to form isomeric products as intermediates are additional possibilities, but none were identified. Other physicochemical processes such as photolysis, ionic strength, i.e., salt content of stream waters, suspended solids (because of their large surface area) and chemical hydrolysis could have played minor roles in the dissipation process. Several research groups ($\underline{6}$) have reported that such processes did not contribute significantly to the dissipation of forestry chemicals from aquatic environments.

Movement and degradation of aminocarb in water/sediment model: The concentrations of aminocarb in water and sediment at different intervals during incubation are presented graphically in Figure 3. During the experimental period, the concentration of aminocarb in water in non-autoclaved flasks decreased from 92 (open) and 95 (closed) ppb to 11 and 21 ppb respectively, while

WATER

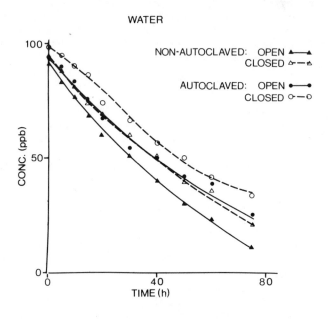

SEDIMENT

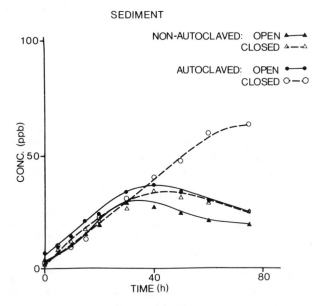

Figure 3. Movement and degradation of aminocarb in a
water/sediment model.

increasing in autoclaved sediment from 4 ppb (0 h) to a maximum of 29 ppb in 30 h (open flask) and from 2 ppb (0 h) to a maximum of 36 ppb in 40 h (closed flask). Concentrations in sediment decreased after these times to 19 (open) and 25 (closed) ppb after 75 h. The rate of decrease in water as well as in sediment was higher in open flasks compared to closed ones because of the escape of the chemical into the atmosphere by volatilization. After 75 h, 30 (11 + 19) ppb or 30% of the fortified aminocarb in the open flask *vs* 46 (21 + 25) ppb or 46% of it in the closed flask remained. The 70% loss in the open flask is attributable to volatilization and microbial degradation and the 54% loss in the closed flask is purely due to microbial degradation in water and sediment.

Residual concentrations of aminocarb in water as well as in sediment were higher in autoclaved samples because of the absence of microbial activity. The pattern of mobility of the chemical from water to sediment was similar to that observed in non-autoclaved samples, but its overall persistence was higher and because of this, a gradual buildup of the active ingredient in sediment occurred in the closed flask. Most of the aminocarb was likely adsorbed onto particulate matter in suspension and then gradually settled in the sediment. Nearly 97% of the fortified aminocarb remained in the autoclaved sample (closed flask) at the end of experiment; out of this 34% was in water and 63% was adsorbed onto sediment. In contrast, 51% of the fortified amount of aminocarb remained in the open flask, of which 26% was in water and the rest in sediment. Sediments, like water, contained detectable levels of demethylated aminocarb moieties as well as the phenol, but among them, the monodemethylated derivative (methylamino Matacil) was predominant compared to the other two metabolites.

Movement and degradation of fenitrothion in the water/sediment model: The concentration of fenitrothion in non-autoclaved and autoclaved stream waters in the presence of sediment are shown in Figure 4. The concentration of fenitrothion decreased rapidly in water and increased rapidly in sediment, showing that fenitrothion has a greater tendency than aminocarb for translocation from water to sediment. Within 15 h, 94% (open flask) and 89% (closed flask) of the chemical in the non-autoclaved samples was lost from the aqueous phase and the corresponding concentrations in sediment were 43% and 66% respectively. The rapid translocation of this compound from water to sediment was probably due to its lipophilic nature (7, 8). Such a phenomenon was not very significant for aminocarb because it was present in water as a cationic species at pH 6.0. At the end of the experimental period (75 h), only 0.2% and 0.5% of the chemical remained in water whereas the sediments contained 19% and 31% of the fortified levels respectively. The rapid loss in the open flask is primarily attributable to volatilization coupled with some microbial degradation. In the absence of volatilization (closed flasks), the decrease in concentration in both the phases was lower. The presence of sediment therefore,

WATER

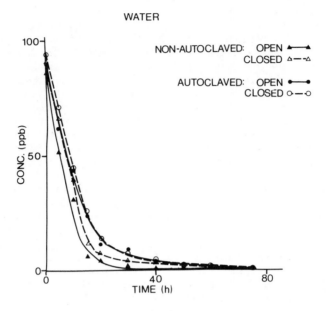

SEDIMENT

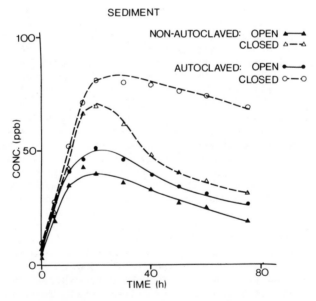

Figure 4. Movement and degradation of fenitrothion in a
water/sediment model.

reduces the loss of fenitrothion from stream water (open flasks) through surface volatilization and co-distillation.

Fenitrothion persisted longer in autoclaved water/sediment samples compared to the non-autoclaved ones because of the absence of microbial activity. The peak concentrations of 51 ppb (open flask) and 81 ppb (closed flask) of fenitrothion in sediments were reached 20 h after fortification and the decrease was significant in the open flask compared to the closed one because of desorption followed by volatilization. No serious attempt was made to identify and quantify all the breakdown products in sediment, but a casual study confirmed the presence of aminofenitrothion (initial stages) and the cresol, both of which were strongly adsorbed to the sediment. Sediments in rivers and streams act as sinks for chemicals and are important in decontaminating natural waters through adsorption. Much of the sediments contain colloidal organic and inorganic materials with large surface areas. They act as good adsorbents for pesticides provided the following equilibrium is shifted far to the right, *i.e.*, $k_1 >>> k_2$:

$$\text{Adsorbate} + \text{Adsorbent} \underset{k_2}{\overset{k_1}{\rightleftharpoons}} \text{Adsorbate:Adsorbent}$$

$$\text{(Pesticide) (Sediment)}$$

Microbes
(Aquatic
Environment)

$$\downarrow$$

Metabolite(s) + Adsorbent

The magnitude of k_1 depends upon the nature of the chemical under investigation. In the present study, it is evident that fenitrothion has a higher degree of adsorption ($k_1 >> k_2$) compared to aminocarb although it is claimed that aminocarb is strongly adsorbed to soil particles (9). In acidic waters (pH 6.0), aminocarb exists as a protonated cation

and under such conditions, the moiety will be less lipophilic, consequently the adsorptive processes will be less significant. The present study demonstrates this difference.

In conclusion, water/sediment model studies suggest that the dissipation pathways for aminocarb and fenitrothion would be primarily *via* volatilization and microbial action as schematically represented in Figure 5.

Field Studies. Fenitrothion was detected in ppb levels in all pre-spray water samples, although it is impossible to trace the

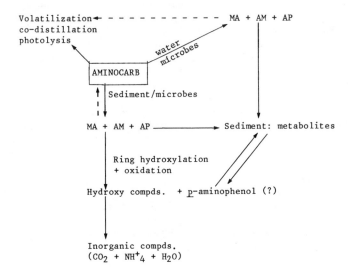

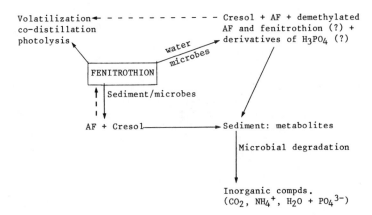

Figure 5. Dissipation pathways of aminocarb and fenitrothion in water/sediment model systems.

exact source. It may have resulted from aerial drift from operational sprays in adjacent areas, or have resulted from long-term persistence at low levels in the forest ecosystem due to extensive use over the past two decades. Previous studies (10-13) have reported such a phenomenon.

The disappearances of fenitrothion and aminocarb from stream waters are documented in Table II. Following aerial spraying, peak levels ranging from 0.10 to 2.26 ppb were found in 1 h samples. Residues decreased rapidly with time, probably primarily due to studies with more than 85% of the amount found at 0.5 h post-spray lost within 5 h. The half-lives $(t_{\frac{1}{2}})$ were below 1 h. There is no known explanation for the increases in concentrations of fenitrothion during the last sampling period (24 h) after some aerial treatments. The very rapid loss of aminocarb from Portage Brook following aerial applications reflects its relatively high stream discharge compared to the other streams.

It is difficult to deduce whether the additives present in the formulations studied had significantly influenced the persistence of the insecticides in stream water, because the system was so dynamic such subtle points were difficult to evaluate. Usually aminocarb and fenitrothion are hydrophobic in nature, while Triton X-100 is hydrophilic because of its hydroxyl and ethoxy groups. It is soluble in water on agitation. The presence of petroleum distillate in Matacil 180F very likely made it more hydrophobic compared to fenitrothion. The observed persistence of fenitrothion in water beyond the 24 h period at concentrations ranging from 0.03 to 0.33 ppb may be attributable to the hydrophilic nature of the emulsifier. Triton X-100, being water soluble and a polar cosolvent, may have caused partial mixing of fenitrothion in the water column which in conjunction with the low stream discharge in fenitrothion treated streams resulted in longer persistence of fenitrothion in stream water than for aminocarb. No metabolites (aminocarb: MA, AM and AP; fenitrothion: AF and FP) were found in any of the water samples analyzed.

Moss samples from the three brooks varied greatly in their uptake and degradation or release of the insecticides (Table III). Peak concentrations of aminocarb (98 and 152 ppb) along with detectable levels of AM and MA were found in moss 3 h after the 1st and 2nd aminocarb applications and persisted at measurable amounts (16 and 19 ppb) beyond the 24 h sampling period. The bioaccumulation ratios [aminocarb concen. in moss (as sampled)/aminocarb concen. in water] for moss in Portage Brook after the 1st and 2nd applications were 33 and 211, respectively at peak water concentrations. Small amounts (ca 20 ppb) of aminocarb persisted in moss over the 8-day period from the 1st application to the pre-spray sample in 2nd application. Persistence of aminocarb in aquatic vegetation has not been reported previously and future investigations should be made to determine the possible ecological ramifications.

Table II. Insecticide concentrations
aerial applications of aminocarb and

Time after application (h)	Portage Brook (aminocarb)				
	1st application			2nd application	
	Moss*	Mayfly nymphs*	Brook trout*	Moss*	Brook trout*
Pre-spray	ND	ND	ND	20 (72)	ND
1	75 (290)**	20 (34)	25.1	112 (399)	84.6
3	98 (349)	<20 (<35)	6.9	152 (535)	3.7
6	61 (196)	<20 (<35)	2.3	83 (307)	0.6
12	44 (111)	<20 (<35)	1.1	31 (138)	ND
24	16 (56)	<20 (<35)	ND	19 (71)	ND

*Pre-spray and all the post-spray moss and brook trout samples and
some mayfly nymph samples from Portage Brook contained fenitrothion.
Values in parentheses are for oven-dry samples (105 $^{\circ}$C for 16 h;
AOAC 1955).

(ppb) in stream waters following
fenitrothion containing TRITON X-100.

Ransom Brook (fenitrothion)		Sixty-three Mile Brook (fenitrothion)	
1st application	2nd application	1st application	2nd application
Moss	Moss	Moss	Moss
62 (179)	100 (354)	128 (579)	176 (646)
140 (560)	143 (442)	60 (390)	152 (609)
160 (970)	168 (471)	40 (230)	116 (342)
90 (580)	177 (469)	30 (160)	133 (397)
100 (450)	160 (452)	20 (140)	71 (260)
56 (300)	66 (259)	70 (252)	130 (516)

The uptake of fenitrothion by aquatic moss was to some extent directly relatable to the insecticide concentrations in the stream water. The first application to both streams did not produce comparatively high levels of fenitrothion in water, with peak concentrations of only 0.10 and 0.17 ppb. The maximum corresponding concentrations in moss samples were 60 and 160 ppb (Table III) yielding bioaccumulation ratios of 600 and 941. Similar bioaccumulation ratios for fenitrothion in aquatic plants have been reported elsewhere (12, 14, 15). Higher peak concentrations of fenitrothion (1.84 and 0.25 ppb) in stream water following the 2nd fenitrothion treatment did not result in higher peak residues in moss (70 and 152 ppb) or bioaccumulation ratios (83 and 708). Fenitrothion content in all moss samples studied from the two brooks did not rapidly decrease with time, contrary to the case observed earlier in aminocarb. This may be partly due to the longer persistence of fenitrothion in stream waters, but high prespray residues in moss and the presence of fenitrothion residues in moss from the aminocarb treated stream suggest that fenitrothion may accumulate and persist in moss for some time. It is also possible that the substrates studied were exposed and contaminated with fenitrothion drift from operational spray programs in surrounding areas. Some moss samples did contain trace levels of FP and AF along with the parent material.

Table III shows the levels of aminocarb present in mayfly nymphs sampled from Portage Brook following the 1st application. Aminocarb concentrations found in insects were not high and no breakdown products of the insecticides were found. The peak concentration detected is only 20 ppb (1 h post-application) exposed to a maximum of 2.26 ppb aminocarb in water, representing a concentration factor of *ca* 9. Residues declined to below detection limits (< 20 ppb) rapidly afterwards coinciding with the disappearance of residues in stream water indicating that the uptake and bioconcentration potential by the insects for aminocarb were not high. Further work is necessary to confirm this observation since Penny (16) reported that the other insecticide, fenitrothion, is readily bioaccumulated by aquatic insects yielding a concentration factor of about 60.

Residues of aminocarb found in brook trout sampled at intervals of time from Portage Brook following the two aerial applications are recorded in Table III. Maximum levels of aminocarb (25.1 and 84.6 ppb) in fish were observed at the first sampling period (1 h post-treatment) after both applications, indicating a rapid uptake of the insecticide. Concentration factors of 11 and 160 were obtained for 1st and 2nd treatments, respectively, indicating high variability because of the inherent variables involved in the stream ecosystems. Residues in the fish declined rapidly, coinciding with the disappearance of residues in the stream water. A few of the samples analysed contained the monodemethylated aminocarb (MA) as a metabolite; AM and AP were not identified. After 12 h, none of the fish samples analysed contained

Table III. Insecticide residues (ppb) found in moss, mayfly nymph and brook trout samples collected from streams.

Time after spraying (h)	Portage Brook (aminocarb)			Ransom Book (fenitrothion)		
	aerial applications 1st	2nd	ground application	aerial applications 1st	2nd	ground application
Pre-spray	ND*	ND*	ND*	-*	-*	0.04
0.5	-	-	6.15	-	-	4.06
1.0	2.26	0.53	2.98	0.17	0.25	1.33
3.0	0.38	0.06	1.01	0.13	0.15	0.16
5.0	-	-	0.75	-	-	0.04
6.0	0.06	ND	-	0.09	0.12	-
12.0	0.03	ND	-	0.07	0.09	-
24.0	ND	ND	-	0.03	0.11	-

Continued on next page

Table III. Continued

Time after spraying (h)	Sixty-three Mile Brook (fenitrothion)		
	aerial applications		ground application
	1st	2nd	
Pre-spray	-*	-*	0.07
0.5	-	-	21.45
1.0	0.10	1.84	4.06
3.0	0.03	0.61	0.32
5.0	-	-	0.14
6.0	0.01	0.40	-
12.0	0.01	0.15	-
24.0	0.09	0.33	-

*Pre-spray samples of water in all the three blocks and the post-spray water samples in Portage Brook contained detectable levels of fenitrothion. The usual concentration levels varied from 0.01 ppb to 0.06 ppb. No rigorous attempt was made to quantify fenitrothion from all water samples analyzed from Portage Brook.

detectable (0.5 ppb) levels of aminocarb, which is in agreement with the study reported by Holmes and Kingsbury (17).

In summary, we speculate that in dynamic stream ecosystems such as the ones we have studied, applied chemicals reaching stream surfaces are rapidly lost by transport, dilution, volatilization and co-distillation. The small fraction that persists in water disappears partly by absorption by aquatic organisms such as plants, insects and fish, and also by adsorption onto suspended particulates, where it likely degrades by microbial reduction. In the light of this, if current use patterns are rigidly adhered to and where necessary, improved and modified, these chemicals could seldom pose any significant long-term harm (biomagnification and resultant damage) to the aquatic ecosystem. We must however, continue to improve our knowledge regarding, and our criteria for evaluation, the ecotoxicity of these chemicals and their transformation products, especially when they are present at low levels in various environmental compartments as we have seen in the present field study.

Acknowledgments

The authors wish to thank Mr. Ed. G. Kettela of the Maritimes Forest Research Centre (Environment Canada) in Fredericton, N.B. for field work assistance, S.Y. Szeto and J. Feng for technical advice, C. Feng and R. Nott for the technical assistance and Cindy Beith for her excellent help in the preparation of this manuscript.

Literature Cited

1. Szeto, S.; Sundaram, K.M.S. J. Environ. Sci. Health 1981, B16, 743-766.
2. Sundaram, K.M.S.; Feng, J.; Nott, R.; Feng, C. "Distribution, dynamics, persistence and fate of aminocarb and fenitrothion formulations containing Triton X-100 in a New Brunswick forest environment"; File Report 44, Forest Pest Management Institute: Sault Ste. Marie, Ont., 1982.
3. Sundaram, K.M.S.; Feng, J.; Nott, R.; Feng, C. "Environmental chemistry studies on Matacil 180F formulations following their semi-operational applications over a New Brunswick forest during 1982"; File Report 47, Forest Pest Management Institute: Sault Ste. Marie, Ont., 1982.
4. "Mobay Tech. Inf. Rept. on Matacil"; Mobay Chem. Co.: Stilwell, Kansas, 1982.
5. Worthing, C.R. "The Pesticide Manual"; British Crop Protection Council: Croyden, England, 1979.
6. Maguire, R.J.; Hale, E.J. J. Agric. Food Chem. 1980, 28, 372-378.
7. Sundaram, K.M.S.; Szeto, S. J. Environ. Sci. Health 1981, B16, 767-776.

8.   Szeto, S.; Sundaram, K.M.S. J. Agric. Food Chem. 1982, 30, 1032-35.

9.   "Aminocarb: The effects of its use on the forest and human environment"; Publication No. 18979, National Research Council of Canada: Ottawa, Ont., 1982.

10. "Assessment of the effects of the 1977 New Brunswick spruce budworm control program on fish food organisms and fish growth"; Montreal Engineering Co. Ltd.: Fredericton, N.B., 1978.

11. "Effects on fish of the 1979 New Brunswick spruce budworm control program"; Montreal Engineering Co. Ltd.: Fredericton, N.B. 1979.

12. "Fenitrothion accumulation by plants and invertebrates in two experimentally sprayed streams in New Brunswick"; Montreal Engineering Co. Ltd.: Fredericton, N.B., 1981.

13. Pearce, P.A.; Brun, G.L.; Witteman, J. in "Environmental Surveillance in New Brunswick, 1978-79"; Varty, I.W., Ed.; University of New Brunswick: Fredericton, N.B., 1980; pp. 68-69.

14. Moody, R.P.; Greenhalgh, R.; Lockhart, L.; Weinberger, P. Bull. Environ. Contam. Toxicol. 1978, 19, 8-14.

15. Weinberger, P.; Greenhalgh, R.; Moody, R.P.; Boulton, B. Unpublished data.

16. Penney, G.H. "Summary report of the effects of forest spraying in New Brunswick in 1971 on juvenile Atlantic salmon and aquatic insects"; Environment Canada Fisheries Service, Resource Development Branch: Halifax, N.S., 1972.

17. Holmes, S.B.; Kingsbury, P.D. "Comparative effects of three Matacil field formulations on stream benthos and fish"; Report FPM-X-55, Forest Pest Management Institute: Sault Ste. Marie, Ont., 1982.

RECEIVED September 26, 1983

Fate of Fenitrothion in Shaded and Unshaded Ponds

GREG P. MALIS[1] and DEREK C. G. MUIR

Department of Fisheries and Oceans, Freshwater Institute, 501 University Crescent, Winnipeg, Manitoba, R3T 2N6, Canada

Fenitrothion (^{14}C-ring-labelled) was applied to two outdoor ponds (3.6 m^3 water volume) at a rate of 165 g/ha on two consecutive years. One pond was shaded from direct sunlight with black polyethylene for the first 17 days of the experiment to simulate a forest pond. Initial concentrations of the insecticide in water were about 70 µg/L. Half-lives (t 1/2's) of fenitrothion were 1.0 and 1.6 days under unshaded and shaded conditions, respectively, indicating the importance of photolysis in the degradation of the compound in water. T 1/2's of the major degradation product, 3-methyl-4-nitrophenol were similar under shaded and unshaded conditions. Concentrations of fenitrothion in air above the ponds, at 10 cm height, averaged 0.020 and 0.098 µg/m^3 over the shaded and unshaded water, respectively, during the first 24 hours after application (Year 1). Levels in air represented a flux estimated to be 5.5 µg/m^2 hour in the unshaded pond or less than 1% of the insecticide applied. Aquatic macrophytes (Lemna and Typha species) and fish accumulated 3 to 6% of added (^{14}C)-fenitrothion by two days post-treatment. Levels of ^{14}C-fenitrothion in sediment (0-3 cm depth) reached a maximum after 5 days and were higher in unshaded conditions (27% of added ^{14}C) than under shaded conditions (8.5%) during both years of the study. Greater than 90% of the radioactivity could be accounted for at 2 days post-treatment, however, by 21 days overall accountibility was reduced to <30%.

[1]Current address: Agriculture Canada, Laboratory Services Division, Mass Spectrometry Laboratory, Ottawa, Ontario, L1A 0C5, Canada

0097-6156/84/0238-0277$06.00/0
© 1984 American Chemical Society

The fate of fenitrothion in the environment has been a subject of great interest in Canada since the late 1960's because of its use for control of the Spruce Budworm (Choristoneura fumiferana). Laboratory and field experiments have established that fenitrothion persists for only 1 to several days in natural waters and is degraded primarily by photolysis and microbial activity (1-4). Sorption by sediments, aquatic macrophytes and microphytes are also important paths of loss of the insecticide from the water column (2-5).

Although the paths of dissipation of fenitrothion in aquatic systems are well known, their relative importance needs to be established at the µg/L concentrations observed in field studies. For example, volatilization has been suggested as a major path of loss from lakes (6) but has not been measured directly. The relative contribution of photolysis under shaded and unshaded conditions has also not been studied.

The objective of this study was to follow the dissipation of fenitrothion under conditions resembling a stagnant forest pond. Fenitrothion has frequently been detected at µg/L concentrations in stagnant waters following aerial spray operations (5)(7) since the spray deposit is not diluted as it is in a flowing system. The study was designed to examine the effect of sunlight intensity, the importance of volatilization and the extent of partitioning of fenitrothion and degradation products into sediment, plants and fish under field conditions.

Materials and Methods

Analytical standards. Fenitrothion (^{14}C-ring-labelled, sp. act. 73.7 µCi/mg) was provided by Sumitomo Chemical Co. Ltd.. Fenitrothion, fenitrooxon (FO), S-methyl fenitrothion (SMF), and amino-fenitrothion (AF) were obtained from R. Greenhalgh (Agriculture Canada, Ottawa). The hydrolysis product 3-methyl-4-nitrophenol (MNP) was obtained from Aldrich Chemicals, St. Louis. Standards were prepared in ethyl acetate or methanol.

Experimental design. Three small ponds (4.08 m x 2.6 m x 0.48 m) depth were used in the study. One pond was maintained as a control and one was shaded from direct sunlight with a shelter (5.3 m x 4 m x 1.5 m height) of black polyethylene (4 mil thickness) erected 2 days prior to the start of the experiment. The shelter was open at the north end which allowed entry of reflected light and silts in the plastic allowed circulation of air. Sunlight intensities in the two ponds (400-700 nm) during the first week post-treatment and some chemical characteristics of the pond water are given in Table I. The ponds were constructed one year prior to the experiment by covering a 10 mil polyethylene plastic liner with silty clay sediment and clay based sod as described previously (8). The ponds were eutrophic with abundant macrophytes (duckweed (Lemna minor), cattails

(Typha sp.)). A bloom of filamentous green algae (Spirogyra sp.)
occurred in the unshaded pond during Year 2. Fathead minnows
(Pimephales promelas) were added to the ponds one week prior to
the study each year.

The shaded and unshaded ponds were each treated on two
consecutive years (July, 1979 and again in June, 1980) with
fenitrothion at a rate of approximately 165 g/ha similar to
commonly used rates of aerial application (1). The formulation
consisted of fenitrothion (175 mg Year 1 and 163.4 mg Year 2;
technical grade), ^{14}C-fenitrothion (100 μCi Year 1; 90 μCi Year
2), 33 mg Aerotex 3470 (Texaco Canada Ltd.) and 34 mg Atlox
(Atlas Chemical Co.) in 500 mL water. The formulation was
stirred into the upper 10 cm of the water column with a metal
rod.

Water (0-30 cm depth), sediment (0-3 cm depth cores), fish,
duckweed, algae, and cattail shoots (portion of the plant above
sediment) were collected once pre-treatment each year and at
various time intervals up to 77 days post-treatment. All samples
except water were stored at -50^0C in sealed containers until
analysis.

Table I. Water chemistry parameters and light intensity in
outdoor ponds following fenitrothion treatment - Year 1.

Pond	Time (days)	pH	TSS[a] (mg/L)	Chloro (μg/L)	Susp. C (mg/L)	Light Intensity $(\mu E/m^2 sec)$[b] +4cm	−15cm
Shaded	1	n.s	8	32.0	3.5	45	20
Unshaded		8.06	10	97.0	8.0	1450	775
Control		7.52	28	208.0	17.1	--	--
Shaded	14	--	--	--	--	30	14
Unshaded		--	--	--	--	1700	800
Shaded	35	8.02	8	15.1	1.4	1300	750
Unshaded		8.80	16	11.2	3.4	1550	800
Control		7.94	9	37.8	4.89	--	--

a - TSS = Total suspended solids; Chloro = chlorophyll a; Susp. C
    = suspended carbon.
b - Light intensity measured with a quantum sensor. The shelter
    over the unshaded pond was removed on day 17.

Analytical methods. a. Water. Depth integrated water samples
(0.9 L duplicates) were collected by attaching a screw-cap with
inlet (6mm i.d. glass) and outlet nozzles (6 mm i.d. U-tube) to

each sample jar and lowering the container slowly through the water column (0-30 cm depth). Dichloromethane (DCM)(10mL) was added to the sample immediately after collection and the sample was stored at 4^0C until analysed. Water samples were acidified (pH 2.0) and extracted with DCM (150, 75, 75 mL). Portions of the extract were analysed by liquid scintillation counting (LSC) and by gas chromatography (GLC). The extracts were also assayed by thin-layer chromatography (TLC) and radioactivity was detected by autoradiography.

b. Sediment. A portion of each sediment sample (0.5 g triplicates) was combusted on a Packard 306 oxidizer (Packard Instruments, Chicago) and the $^{14}CO_2$ analysed by LSC. Samples (20 g wet wt) were refluxed with 150 mL acetonitrile-water (9:1) for 17 hours. The mixture was filtered, the filtrate evaporated to 10 mL and transferred to a separatory funnel with water. The aqueous phase was extracted with DCM and the organic phase was evaporated to small volume. Aliquots of the DCM extract were assayed by LSC to determine total extractable radioactivity. Portions of the extract were dissolved in methanol-water (9:1) and cleaned up by reverse phase chromatography on C18 Sep-Pak (Waters Associates, Mississauga, Ont.) and then analysed by HPLC. Unextractable radioactivity in sediment was determined by combustion of a small portion of the residuum. Selected samples were also re-extracted by refluxing with 1N HCl (17 hrs) and the acidic extract partitioned with DCM to recover additional radioactivity. Recoveries of (^{14}C)-fenitrothion from 4 pre-treatment sediment samples spiked at 0.75 ng/g averaged 90.2 ± 18.7% using the 17 hour reflux with acetonitrile-water.

c. Aquatic plants and fish. Duckweed, cattail and fish samples were combusted (0.5 g)(duplicates Year 1, triplicates Year 2) and the $^{14}CO_2$ assayed by LSC. Whole fish (average wt 3 g) were initially ground and sub-sampled. Dry weight of plants was determined by air-drying to constant weight. Duckweed samples (20 g wet wt) were extracted by blending with methanol (10 min). The extract was then evaporated to remove most of the methanol. The residue was partitioned with DCM and cleaned up on C18 Sep-Paks as described for sediment.

d. Air. Polyurethane foam plugs (50 mm dia.) were prepared for use by extraction with hexane:acetone (1:1) for 84 hours (9). The foam plugs were placed in glass tubes located above the center of each pond. The tubes were located 10 cm above each pond (Year 1) or at 2, 5 and 10 cm heights (Year 2). Air-flows were maintained at 10L/min. Foam plugs were changed every 24 hours (days 1-3) and then every 2-3 days for the next 18 days post-treatment. The foams were placed in wide-mouth glass jars and hexane was added immediately. Further extraction was carried out on a Soxhlet apparatus and the extracts were assayed by LSC and GLC.

e. GLC, TLC and HPLC conditions: GLC was carried out with either a Tracor 560 or Perkin Elmer 900, both equipped with

nitrogen-phosphorus detectors. Columns (2 mm i.d. x 1.8 m)
containing 3% OV-17 on Chromosorb W-HP (80/100 mesh) were
operated at 200°C for analysis of fenitrothion and AF. MNP was
chromatographed on a column of 1% SP-1240 DA on Supelcoport
100/120 mesh at 190°C.

HPLC separations were carried out with a reverse-phase
column (μBondapak C-18) using methanol-water (45:55) at 1.8
mL/min for 13.5 min followed by methanol-water (60:40) for 20
min.   A Waters 6000A pump, Model 440 UV absorption detector and
a fraction collector (LKB Multirac) were used. Fractions eluting
from the column were collected and assayed by LSC. Retention
times of fenitrothion, AF, and MNP under these conditions were
27.0, 11.0, and 7.5 minutes, respectively.

TLC separations were performed on silica-gel plates using
two solvent systems: I.   Toluene:ethyl formate:formic acid
(5:7:1)(10) and II. CCl$_4$:DCM:methanol (5:7:1). Autoradiography
was carried out by exposing TLC plates to X-ray film (Kodak
NS-2T) for up to one month. Radioactive spots were scraped and
extracted with methanol to establish the quantity of each
degradation product. R_f's (fenitrothion = 1.0) of AF, MNP, FO
and SMF were 0.22, 0.76, 0.53 and 0.73 on System I and 0.83,
0.66, 0.77 and 0.60 on System II.

Results and Discussion

Water. Fenitrothion disappeared rapidly from unshaded ponds
decreasing to <0.01 μg/L from an initial level of 70 μg/L within
10 to 13 days each year (Fig. 1). In shaded water fenitrothion
levels decreased more slowly reaching 0.01 to 0.02 μg/L by about
17 days each year (Fig. 2). Half-lives of fenitrothion
calculated from first-order decay curves (ln concentration vs
time (days)) were significantly greater in shaded treatments each
year (Table 2). The half-lives observed were within the range
found elsewhere in field studies in ponds and small lakes (1).

The cover over the shaded pond was removed at 17 days
post-treatment in the first year of the study due to damage from
a rain storm. Removal coincided with an unexplained increase in
fenitrothion concentrations (Fig. 2). This increase was not
observed in Year 2 when the shade was removed at the same time
(Fig. 2). It is possible that disturbance of the water and sides
of the ponds may have released sediment and plant-associated
fenitrothion back into the water column, however, levels of
degradation products did not increase proportionally.

MNP was the major degradation product identified in water
extracts in the unshaded ponds representing 47% of extractable
[14]C at 21 days post-treatment. MNP was also a major residue
under shaded conditions during the first 13 days each year but
declined to less than 20% of extractable ^{14}C by 21 days (Fig.
2). Amino-fenitrothion was also detected along with four other
products which could not be identified. Two of the unknowns were

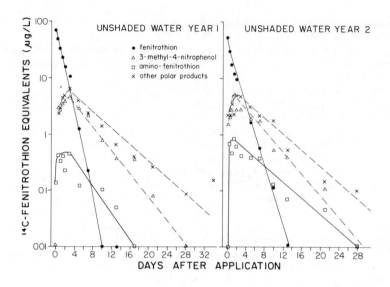

Figure 1. Disappearance of fenitrothion and degradation products in unshaded pond water following addition of the insecticide each year.

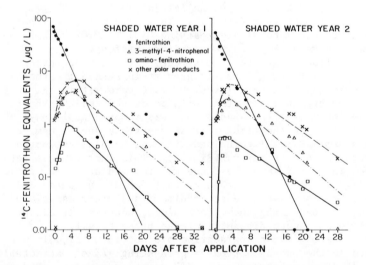

Figure 2. Disappearance of fenitrothion and degradation products in shaded pond water following addition of the insecticide each year.

major products having R_fs of 0.44 and 0.40 (relative to
fenitrothion) in System I. In System II one major unidentified
spot (R_f = 0.37) was observed along with radioactivity at the
origin. The relatively low concentrations of the unknowns (<10
μg/L) prevented further identification. They did not have the
R_f of fenitrooxon or S-methyl fenitrothion, however, their TLC
mobility in System I was similar to carboxyfenitrothion and
desmethyl fenitrothion (10). Both compounds have been previously
identified in natural waters (4). The radioactivity which was
immobile in System II may have consisted of desmethyl
fenitrothion which is immobile in non-acidic TLC solvent systems
(10) as well as other polar products such as
desmethylaminofenitrothion. The concentrations of all of the
unidentified products were summed and plotted in Fig. 1 and 2 as
"other products". These products represented about 75% of the
extractable radioactivity in extracts of 21 day water samples in
the covered pond and about 53% in the uncovered pond.

AF and "other products" disappeared more rapidly in unshaded
than shaded water each year (Table II) while MNP showed no

Table II. Half-lives (t 1/2) of fenitrothion and degradation
products in pond water - Year 1 and 2.

Compound	Condition	Time interval (days) Year 1	Year 2	t 1/2 (days) ±CL Year 1	Year 2
Fenitro-thion	S	0-17	0-18	1.56±0.12	1.70±0.14
	U	0-10	0-17	0.79±0.05*	1.22±0.08*©
MNP	S	3-28	3-28	2.93±0.75	3.51±0.54©
	U	3-28	1.5-21	2.94±0.24	3.69±0.32©
AF	S	3-28	3-28	3.80±0.25	6.54±0.91©
	U	3-17	1.5-28	3.62±2.68	4.42±0.49*
Other products	S	3-28	3-35	4.97±0.59	5.42±0.38©
	U	3-28	2-35	4.13±0.32*	4.98±0.66*©
Total ^{14}C	S	0-28	0-35	4.44±0.48	4.03±0.15©
	U	0-28	0-35	2.97±0.26*	3.64±0.37*©

*indicates significant differences between first order rate
 constants (0.05 level of significance) in shaded and unshaded
 ponds using the t-test.
©indicates significant differences (P = 0.05) between rate
 constants observed each year within treatments (shaded or
 unshaded) using the t-test.
"other products" refers to all unidentified spots on TLC plates.

significant differences although it decreased more rapidly in the
first year of the study. Maximum concentrations of MNP and
"other products" were observed at 2-3 days post-treatment each
year and were higher in unshaded water. However, degradation of
MNP and "other products" was slower in shaded ponds so that by 17
days higher levels of these products were present in shaded
water.

Much of the radioactivity in the water samples (Table III)
was unextractable with DCM (at pH 2) within 48 hours after
treatment (23%, shaded; 41%, unshaded). Unextractable
radioactivity increased to 71.5% (shaded) and 94% (unshaded) by
21 days. The identity of this unextractable material was not
investigated since levels were <10 μg/L. Weinberger et al (4)
have reported similar high proportions of unextractable ^{14}C
(about 70% at 20 days) in lake water following fenitrothion
treatments and identified carboxyaminofenitrothion in the "polar"
fraction. Desmethylfenitrothion and desmethylaminofenitrothion
are also possible components of the aqueous phase since like
other phosphate diesters they are not efficiently extracted into
organic solvents at acid pH (11).

The longer half-lives of fenitrothion and degradation
products under shaded conditions indicates the importance of
photolysis in the disappearance of the insecticide from shallow
water bodies (1). However, the differences in half-lives were
less than 2-fold compared to about 30-fold greater light
intensity (in the visible range) under unshaded conditions (2 cm
depth, Table I).

Sediment. (^{14}C)-fenitrothion reached maximum concentrations in
sediment within 5 days post-treatment. After 77 days levels had
declined to about 30% and 60% of the maximum in shaded and
unshaded ponds, respectively, during the first year. The decline
in radioactivity in sediment was much more rapid during Year 2;
after 35 days levels were similar to those observed in
pre-treatment samples (Table III). Levels of radioactivity were
consistently higher in sediment of unshaded pools. The greater
productivity under unshaded conditions which was evident from
larger duckweed biomass, higher suspended solids, chlorophyll and
suspended carbon (Table I), may have resulted in the deposition
of more (^{14}C)-fenitrothion on the bottom of the unshaded pond in
falling detritus during the first 17 days. Higher levels of
radioactivity were observed at 350 days post-treatment
(Pre-treatment Year 2, Table III)(in both ponds) than at 77 days
due to deposition of duckweed and other plants from the previous
summer. Sedimentation has been demonstrated to be an important
mode of loss of hydrophobic compounds from the water column in
aquatic systems (12). However in the present study the exact
quantity of deposition was not measured.

AF was the major degradation product in sediment
representing 64% and 62% of extractable radioactivity in shaded

Table III. Total radioactivity[a] expressed as fenitrothion equivalents
(μg/kg) in various compartments of each pond during a two year study.

Time/year	Pond	Total fenitrothion concentrations (μg/kg)[b]						
		water	sediment	duckweed	cattails	fish	algae	air[c]
Year 1								
Pre-treat	S	<0.01	<0.5	<100	<10	<10	–	<0.001
	U	<0.01	<0.5	<100	<10	<10	–	<0.001
1 hour	S	70.3	–					
	U	72.0	–					
12 hours	S	54.3	–					
	U	44.4	–					
24 hours	S	46.7	34.0	17471	578	3320	–	0.098
	U	40.5	131.6	12343	355	4919	–	0.020
2 days	S	35.9	37.6	17171	360	3113	–	0.028
	U	24.7	74.1	19886	820	2166	–	0.004
5 days	S	16.5	66.2	17800	454	1517	–	0.010
	U	7.36	128.6	23486	498	690	–	0.009
10 days	S	6.01	40.0	n.s.	1783	491	–	0.002
	U	2.28	98.8	17200	2188	340	–	0.001
21 days	S	2.62	39.4	13829	773	176	–	<0.001
	U	0.36	82.0	8657	804	363	–	<0.001
35 days	S	1.72	33.0	2971	208	178	–	–
	U	0.16	83.4	5000	1104	264	–	–
77 days	S	0.01	19.6	2429	96	224	–	–
	U	<0.01	80.0	1900	77	263	–	–
Year 2								
Pre-treat	S	<0.01	81.8	<100	213	<10	<10	<0.001
	U	<0.01	146.4	<100	213	<10	<10	<0.001
1 hour	S	58.4	–	–	–			
	U	60.3	–					
12 hours	S	48.1	–	–	–	1827		
	U	41.0	–	–	–	3053		
24 hours	S	37.0	192.4	14243	2334	1198	–	0.048
	U	36.5	321.8	5757	1417	931	–	0.049
2 days	S	32.3	96.2	11600	3367	1536	–	0.028
	U	30.4	271.2	9229	320	1176	–	0.014
5 days	S	22.7	131.4	17129	511	796	–	0.004
	U	19.1	347.2	13143	658	569	–	0.009
10 days	S	15.6	166.6	21529	2122	692	–	0.001
	U	9.40	263.6	12686	833	336	–	<0.001
21 days	S	3.68	113.0	6600	692	366	–	0.001
	U	0.36	255.4	7114	272	432	8236	0.001
35 days	S	0.10	85.4	1900	1202	148	–	–
	U	0.08	141.6	2657	77	482	4427	–
77 days	S	<0.01	87.4	686	24	229	–	–
	U	<0.01	143.2	n.s.	85	240	–	–

a – Determined by combustion of sediment, duckweed, cattail, fish and algae
    sub-samples and by direct assay of water samples using LSC. Average of
    duplicates (water or triplicate analyses (all others except air).
b – All results are expressed on a dry weight basis except fish (fresh wt
    whole fish). Water content: Sediment (50%), duckweed (93%), Cattails
    (75-90%).
c – Air results as μg/m^3 averages at 10 cm height over time interval.

and unshaded ponds, respectively, after 5 days (Table IV). After 21 days unidentified polar products (eluting in the solvent front on HPLC analysis) represented a large portion of the extractable radioactivity. More radioactivity was unextractable from sediment in unshaded ponds especially in the 10–50 day post-treatment period. Fenitrothion yielded about 22% unextractable residue when incubated with silt loam soils under submerged conditions for 30–60 days (10) and a similar portion of the radioactivity was unextractable in the shaded pond sediment.

Table IV. Concentration of fenitrothion and major degradation products in sediment extracts – Year 2 determined by HPLC analysis.

Time (days)	Extractable[a] (%)	μg/kg (dry wt) as fenitrothion equivalents			
		Fenitro	AF	MNP	polar pdts[b]
Shaded					
Pre-	47.7 (86.8)	–	–	–	–
1	65.4 (74.0)	8.0	82.0	7.4	28.0
2	76.9	7.6	49.6	3.8	13.0
3	61.1 (75.0)	–	–	–	–
5	70.1	4.2	59.0	6.4	22.2 ,
10	54.7 (65.7)	4.2	28.4	4.8	54.0
13	64.2	9.0	26.8	4.2	40.2
21	58.4 (69.0)	<0.5	32.0	4.4	29.6
50	56.8 (72.7)	<0.5	36.8	<0.5	13.4
Unshaded					
Pre-	23.2 (41.0)	–	–	–	–
1	68.9 (74.0)	32.4	100.8	28.0	60.0
3	59.6 (76.3)	–	–	–	–
5	54.8	9.4	118.2	17.0	37.2
10	47.0 (54.3)	<0.5	49.2	8.0	67.0
13	37.6	13.2	38.6	14.6	63.0
21	23.5 (29.4)	1.6	25.2	<0.5	33.4
50	30.1 (38.2)	–	–	–	–

a – extractable with a single 17 hour acetonitrile-water reflux.
   Results in parentheses indicate % extractable from the
   sediment residuum after additional extraction with 1N HCl.
b – other polar products which eluted (as radioactive peaks) in
   the solvent front under the conditions used in HPLC analysis.

The greater proportion of unextractable residues in the unshaded system may reflect formation of degradation products in the water column which are subsequently irreversibly bound to sediments or sedimented detritus. Phosphate diesters, in particular, are difficult to extract from sediments as well as water (13) and may account much of this unextractable residue.

The predominance of AF in sediments may account for its appearance in the water column at low levels during the first 21 days post-treatment. AF is more polar than fenitrothion and would be expected to partition more readily back into the water column. AF has frequently been reported as a major degradation product of fenitrothion in stagnant pools (2)(5) and in flooded soils (10).

Aquatic plants and fish. Duckweed rapidly accumulated (^{14}C)-fenitrothion from the water column and maximum concentrations were observed after 5 to 10 days post-treatment in both years (Table III). The levels observed at 5 days represented concentration factors (BCFs) of 754 and 688 in shaded and unshaded exposures, respectively (Year 2), based on total radioactivity in water and plants. Concentrations in duckweed decreased to <10% of the maximum by 35 days each year. Levels of radioactivity in the plants were not significantly different in shaded and unshaded conditions. This differs from results of Weinberger et al (4) who observed 3-fold greater concentrations of (^{14}C)-fenitrothion in **Elodea densa** in field microcosms under lighted compared to darkened conditions. Duckweed did not grow well under shaded conditions and by 17 days the density of the plant was about 10% of that in the unshaded pond.

Radioactivity was poorly extracted from duckweed suggesting transformation to polar products which were conjugated, irreversibly bound to plant tissue or incorporated into natural components. Fenitrothion, AF and MNP were identified in duckweed extracts (Table V). The proportion of each compound was similar to that observed in water at the same sampling time suggesting that the MNP and AF may have been accumulated from water rather than formed in the plant. BCFs calculated with actual water and plant concentrations of fenitrothion were 108 and 140 in shaded and unshaded ponds, respectively, at 3 days post-treatment (Table 5). These BCFs are similar to results obtained in laboratory studies with fenitrothion (14) where equilibrium BCFs of 280 were observed during 5 day exposures, and are higher than BCFs observed in field monitoring following aerial spraying (5).

Cattails contained 10 to 20 fold lower levels of (^{14}C)-fenitrothion than duckweed throughout the study. This difference probably reflects the greater surface area to volume ratio of the duckweeds. No differences between shaded and unshaded plants could be discerned. The large variability in the results compared to duckweed may be attributable to the difficulty in obtaining representative samples from the large plants. Radioactivity was detected in cattails in pre-treatment samples (350 days post-treatment Year 1)(Table III) although levels of radioactivity in water and duckweed were below detection limits. The plants appeared to be accumulating radioactivity from sediments, the major sink for radioactivity at 350 days, and translocating it to the emergent portion of the plant. The low extraction efficiency of the radioactivity in sediment at 350 days and the rapid degradation of fenitrothion (Table IV) suggests that cattails were accumulating polar degradation products from sediment.

Table V. Concentrations of fenitrothion or degradation products in duckweed extracts - Year 2.

Time	Extractable	$\mu g/kg$ (dry wt) fenitrothion equivalents[a]				
(days)	(%)	Fenitro	phenol	AF	polar pdts[b]	BCF[c]
Shaded						
3	45.2	1086	871	129	3285	108
7	20.3	571	1300	43	2472	204
13	25.8	243	2486	671	714	810
Unshaded						
3	40.9	629	1986	57	2699	140
7	35.7	186	1143	129	3071	310
13	17.8	243	1029	14	1214	24300

a - determined by assay of radioactive spots on TLC plates (System I) and confirmed by HPLC.
b - polar products refers to unidentified radioactive spots on TLC plates having short Rf values on System I and radioactivity not partitioned into dichloromethane.
c - BCF calculated with actual concentrations of fenitrothion in water (Fig. 1 and 2) and duckweed.

Recovery of radioactivity from cattail tissue by blending with methanol averaged only 23.7% in samples from 3, 7 and 14 days post-treatment indicating extensive breakdown of fenitrothion by the plant. The identity of the radioactivity was not determined.

Filamentous green algae absorbed relatively high levels of radioactivity from water with a concentration factor of 846

(based on total ^{14}C in water) at 10 days post-treatment. The
algal bloom occurred only in the unshaded pond in Year 2 between
10 and 35 days post-treatment. Algal blooms are commonly
observed following insecticide addition to ponds due to reduction
in grazing crustacean zooplankton by the insecticide (15).
Similar concentration factors for fenitrothion in two species of
autotrophic algae were observed by Weinberger et al (4).
    Maximum concentrations of (^{14}C)-fenitrothion in fathead
minnows were observed at the initial sampling time each year
(Table III). Levels in fish were similar in unshaded and shaded
ponds reflecting the fact that during the first 24 hours
post-treatment intact fenitrothion was the major form of
radioactivity in water in both ponds. Fenitrothion is likely to
be more rapidly accumulated from water than its more polar
degradation products. Concentration factors of 42 and 54
(calculated with actual fenitrothion concentrations in water)
were observed in minnows at 24 hours post-treatment (Year 2).
These BCFs were about 3-fold lower than equilibrium BCFs
calculated from laboratory studies with rainbow trout but are
within the range predicted for fenitrothion based on its
octanol-water partition coefficient or water solubility (14).
Radioactivity in fish decreased to less than 50% of the initial
concentrations by 10 days post-treatment but low levels persisted
in fish during the remaining sampling period. The persistence of
radioactivity may be due to ingestion of contaminated detritus by
the minnows as well as to utilization of some of the
^{14}C-ring-label by the fish in natural products.

Air. Concentrations of fenitrothion in air sampled 10 cm above
treated ponds were highest in the first 24 hours post-treatment
(Table III). GLC analysis of the extracts from polyurethane foam
traps indicated that only fenitrothion was present. The levels
of fenitrothion were generally higher above shaded ponds. This
was expected because the polyethylene shelter reduced wind
movement over the water surface which would dilute the observed
concentrations. Recently Mallet and Volpe (7) reported the
detection of ng/L levels of AF as well as fenitrothion in air
samples collected near treated areas in New Brunswick (Canada)
however, the source of AF was not clear from their study.
    During Year 2 a concentration gradient was observed in
samples taken 2, 5 and 10 cm above the water surface (Table VI).
The concentration gradient ($\mu g/m^3$) was converted to a flux ($\mu g/m^2$
hr) by use of the aerodynamic equation (16) which incorporated
wind speed and temperature gradient data obtained at a nearby
monitoring site. Only daily averages of wind speed and
temperature could be used since air samplers were changed on a 24
hour basis during the first 3 days post-treatment. Therefore the
calculations can only roughly approximate the actual
volatilization of the compound from the unshaded pond. Actual
wind speeds over the shaded pond were not measured so in order to

estimate a flux the wind gradient was assumed to be 10% of that
in unsheltered conditions.

Flux of fenitrothion from the pond surface was also
estimated by use of the Fick's Law relationship:

$$Flux = (K_{01})(Ci)$$

where K_{01} is the overall volatilization rate constant (m/hr)
calculated using the procedure of Smith et al. ([17]) and Ci is the
concentration gradient between the water and air (approximately
equal to the water concentration) over the time interval. To
obtain K_{01} values mass transfer coefficients for oxygen from
water of 1.8 cm/hr and the gas mass transfer coefficent of water
of 2100 cm/hr were used. These values are typical of ponds and
lakes 100 to 1000-fold larger in surface area than those in the
present study so they may over estimate actual volatilization
rates. The value of K_{01} obtained was 2.18×10^{-4} m/hr which
suggests a half-life of fenitrothion of 66 days for a 0.5 m depth
([18]). Similar half-lives have been observed in laboratory
studies ([2]). The flux of fenitrothion predicted from the Fick's
Law relationship was 2 to 3-fold greater than that calculated by
use of the aerodynamic equation (Table VI). Although the
concentrations of fenitrothion were high enough to be readily
detected up to 10 cm above the water in windy conditions the loss
of fenitrothion is small since mg/m^3 quantities were present in
the water column. A higher predicted than calculated flux is
consistent with observations that fulvic acids in water reduce
the volatilization rate of fenitrothion ([2]).

Mass balance. Greater than 90% of the radioactivity added to the
ponds could be accounted for during the first 2 days
post-treatment in Year 2 (Table VII) by multiplying the
concentrations of total ^{14}C observed by the weight of each
compartment. The weights of the water and sediment (0-3 cm
depth) compartments were thought to be within 10% since the
dimensions of the ponds were known. Weights of aquatic plants
were estimated by multiplying their area by plant density and are
therefore subject to considerable error. Water was the major
compartment for (^{14}C)-fenitrothion for the 1 to 5 day period but
by 21 days most of the remaining radioactivity was in sediments
expecially in the unshaded pond. Aquatic plants, fish and air
were minor compartments of radioactivity throughout the study.
The accountibility of (^{14}C)-fenitrothion was considerably reduced
by 21 days. In Year 1 estimates of total fenitrothion in water
were obtained by use of extractable radioactivity which was low
by Day 5 resulting in low estimates of the total fenitrothion in
water. Another source of error could be greater deposition of
fenitrothion on sediments on the sides of the ponds which is not
taken into account by sampling the pond bottom. This has been
observed with pyrethroid insecticides in similar outdoor ponds

Table VI.   Calculated[a] and predicted[b] flux of fenitrothion from treated ponds.

Time interval (days)	Temp.[c] T2-T1 (deg K)	Wind[c] U2-U1 (m/sec)	Concentration C2-C1 ($\mu g/m^3$) S	U	Flux ($\mu g/m^2$ hr) S	U	predicted
0 - 1	0.75	0.45	0.151	0.113	0.127	5.52	14.4
1 - 2	1.75	0.60	0.084	0.060	0.079	3.80	5.6
2 - 3	0.25	0.10	0.020	0.004	0.011	0.03	3.0
5 - 7	1.75	0.10	0.004	0.0017	<0.001	0.005	0.5

a - calculated by use of the aerodynamic method (16).
b - predicted by use of the equation: Flux = $K_{01}(C_i)(17)$, K_{01} = volatilization rate in a 0.5 m depth system, C_i = average concentration of fenitrothion in water over the time interval. $K_{01} = [1/K_w + RT/HK_g]^{-1}$ for 1 m depth. H = Henry's constant (atm m^3/mol) and K_w and K_g are liquid and gas phase mass transfer coefficients for fenitrothion in ponds calculated from k_w and k_g values for oxygen and water respectively as described by Smith et al. (17).
c - temperature gradients (T2 at 10 cm and T1 at 2 cm) are average values for the time interval. Wind speed gradients were estimated for a graph of ln height vs average speed (m/sec)(U2 = 10 cm, U1 = 2 cm) for the unshaded pond. Wind speeds in the shaded pond were estimated to be 10% of those in the unshaded treatment.

Table VII. Percent[a] of added ^{14}C-fenitrothion in each compartment.

Time (days)	Water S	Water U	Sediment S	Sediment U	plants S	plants U	fish S	fish U	air S	air U	total S	total U
Year 1												
0.5	109.2	90.60	–	–	–	–	–	–	–	–	–	–
1	93.9	82.6	5.1	20.8	2.8	3.7	1.1	1.7	–	–	102.9	108.8
2	72.2	50.4	5.4	11.7	2.6	6.1	1.1	0.7	–	–	81.5	68.9
5	32.2	15.0	9.9	20.3	0.8	7.0	0.5	0.2	–	–	43.4	42.5
21	5.2	0.7	5.9	13.0	0.4	2.5	0.3	0.3	–	–	11.8	16.5
Year 2												
0.5	103.7	89.6	–	–	–	–	–	–	–	–	–	–
1	79.8	79.8	17.8	29.7	3.2	2.3	0.7	0.7	<0.1	0.6	101.5	113.1
2	69.6	66.4	17.0	21.2	3.4	2.7	1.1	0.1	<0.1	1.0	91.1	91.4
5	48.9	41.7	8.0	34.0	0.7	4.1	0.2	0.2	<0.1	1.0	57.8	81.0
21	7.9	0.8	5.0	18.5	0.2	0.2	0.3	0.1	<0.1	1.0	13.4	22.6

a – estimated using the following compartment sizes: water = 3.55 m^3 shaded, 3.6 m^3 unshaded; sediment = 264.4 kg dry wt shaded, 279.2 kg dry wt unshaded; duckweed, 0.5 kg dry wt (unshaded), 0.05 kg shaded at 5 and 21 days; cattails 1 kg dry wt; fish 0.6 kg. Air losses by use of the aerodynamic equation results.

and appears to be due to initial stratification of the formulation in the warm upper 10 cm of water layer which is observed in the ponds during the day (19). Movement of water soluble products below the 3 cm sampling depth may also have occurred. Breakdown of degradation products in the water column via microbial activity to yield $^{14}CO_2$ or other volatile carbon fragments is another possible pathway of loss.

Volatilization of AF or MNP is unlikely however since they have smaller K_{01} values than fenitrothion.

Conclusions

The effect of shading an outdoor pond for the first 17 days after addition of fenitrothion was to increase the half-life of the insecticide by about 50%. Despite a 30-fold reduction in light intensity, however, the decline in insecticide residues in water was rapid dropping from 70 µg/L to about 0.01 µg/L by 17 days. Shaded conditions decreased the quantities of other products and MNP (but not AF) that were formed however no major products unique to shaded or unshaded conditions were identified.

A large portion of radioactivity in water, sediment and plants was unextractable with conventional techniques especially in samples taken after 10 days post-treatment. Fenitrothion and MNP were not major components in these compartments in shaded or unshaded conditions after this time. It appears that most of the radioactivity was in the form of products difficult to partition from water to organic solvents such as those with amphoteric characteristics (aminocresols) or phosphoric acid esters. Other field studies with (^{14}C)-fenitrothion have observed a similar proportion of unextractable material (4). Further studies on the fate of fenitrothion may need to overcome analytical difficulties posed by these products. The biological significance of this highly polar material needs to be assessed. Results at 350 days post-treatment were interesting from the viewpoint of long-term persistence of the ^{14}C-ring label. Most of the radioactivity in the ponds was present in sediment (likely from sedimentation of plant material from the previous year) and 77% was unextractable with methanol indicating that it was not in the form of fenitrothion. Cattails appeared to be accumulating this radioactivity from sediment and translocating it to the growing portion of the plant.

Predicted and calculated flux of fenitrothion from water were similar although values were arrived at independently. Both results suggest that volatilization from water is slow compared to other paths of degradation of the insecticide which confirms predictions of the two-film theory of volatilization (17)(18). Losses of fenitrothion from surface films have been shown to be very rapid (2) but a surface film was not formed in the present work because the insecticide was mixed into the upper 10 cm of the water column.

The radioactivity added to the ponds was only accounted for successfully during the first 5 days post-treatment despite knowledge of the size of the major compartments and the use of direct assays such as combustion to $14CO_2$. Loss of radioactivity due to penetration to lower depths in sediment and degradation of the ring label to volatile carbon fragments and $14CO_2$ in the water column may have occurred but are unlikely to total all of the 70 to 80% unaccounted for. The ultimate fate of the radiolabelled material in aquatic systems under field conditions is in need of further study.

Acknowledgments

We thank R. Greenhalgh and W.L. Lockhart for providing advice on the design of the study and Y. Sato (Sumitomo Chemicals) for providing the radiolabelled fenitrothion.

Literature Cited

1. Symons, P.E.K. Residue Rev. 1977, 68, 1-36.
2. Maguire, R.J.; Hale, E.J. J. Agric. Food Chem. 1980, 28, 372-378.
3. Weinberger, P.; Greenhalgh, R.; Sher, D.; Ouellette, M. Bull. Environ. Contom. Toxicol. 1982, 28, 484-489.
4. Weinberger, P.; Greenhalgh, R.; Moody, R.P.; Boulton, B. Environ. Sci. Technol. 1982, 16, 470-473.
5. Moody, R.P.; Greenhalgh, R.; Lockhart, L.; Weinberger, P. Bull. Environ. Contam. Toxicol. 1978, 19, 8-14.
6. Metcalfe, C.D.; McLeese, D.W.; Zitko, V. Chemosphere, 1980, 9, 151-155.
7. Mallet, V.N.; Volpe, G. J. Environ. Sci. Hlth. 1982, B17, 715-736.
8. Muir, D.C.G.; Grift, N.P.; Blouw, A.P.; Lockhart, W.L. J. Environ. Qual. 1980, 9, 151-156.
9. Grover, R.; Kerr, L.A. J. Environ. Sci. Hlth. 1981, B16, 59-66.
10. Takimoto, Y.; Hiroto, M.; Inui, H.; Miyamoto, J. J. Pestic. Sci. 1976, 1, 131-143.
11. Greenhalgh, R. Presented at the 6th Annual Spring Workshop of the Assoc. Offic. Anal. Chem., Ottawa, May 1981.
12. Hamelink, J.L.; Waybrant, R.C. Trans. Amer. Fish. Soc. 1976, 105, 124-134.
13. Muir, D.C.G.; Grift, N.P. J. Assoc. Offic. Anal. Chem. 1983, 66, 684-690.
14. Lockhart, W.L.; Metner, D.A.; Billeck, B.G.; Muir, D.C.G. Presented at the Symposium on Implications of Chemical and Biological Control Agents in Forestry, Seattle, March 1983.
15. Hurlbert, S.H. Residue Rev. 1975, 57, 81-148.
16. Parmele, L.H.; Lemon, E.R.; Taylor, A.W. Water, Soil, Air Pollut. 1972, 1, 433-451.

17. Smith, J.H.; Bomberger, D.C. Jr.; Haynes, D.L. Chemosphere,
     1981, 10, 281–289.
18. Mackay, D.; Leinonen, P.J. Environ. Sci. Technol.   1975, 9,
     1178–1180.
19. Rawn, G.P.; Grift, N.P.; Townsend, B.E.; Muir, D.C.G.
     Preliminary report on the Fate of Deltamethrin in small
     ponds. Freshwater Institute, Winnipeg, Canada, 1983.

RECEIVED September 28, 1983

Bioaccumulation of Some Forestry Pesticides in Fish and Aquatic Plants

W. L. LOCKHART, D. A. METNER, B. N. BILLECK, G. P. RAWN, and D. C. G. MUIR

Department of Fisheries and Oceans, Freshwater Institute, 501 University Crescent, Winnipeg, Manitoba, R3T 2N6, Canada

Bioaccumulation of some pesticides (fenitrothion, aminocarb, permethrin) with real or potential application in forestry in Canada has been examined in laboratory experiments using larval rainbow trout and common duckweed. Bioaccumulation of an aromatic hydrocarbon, fluorene, has also been examined since some commercial formulations employ hydrocarbon solvents. Laboratory exposures of fish or plants were carried out by placing the organisms in dilute aqueous solutions of ^{14}C labelled pesticide or hydrocarbon, and by measuring transfer of radioactivity from water to fish or plants. After transfer of fish or plants to untreated water, loss of radioactivity was measured similarly. These measures allowed calculation of uptake and depuration rate constants which were used to predict residue accumulations under various exposure conditions. Predicted residue accumulations agreed substantially with other predictive equations in the literature and with reported field observations.

Bioaccumulation of pesticides in aquatic organisms following aerial applications in forest spraying, agricultural spraying, and public health spraying remains a topic of public concern in Canada. People frequently ask whether fish may become contaminated after spraying operations, and if so, what time period must elapse before pre-spray conditions are reestablished. Significant progress has been made in efforts to predict the tendency for residues to accumulate in fish since publication of the proposal that exchange equilibria control degrees of bioconcentration of organochlorine compounds (1). Several authors have developed regression equations relating equilibrium bioconcentration factors for non-polar organic compounds to physical properties like water solubility or octanol/water partition coefficient (2-6). Some authors have

0097-6156/84/0238-0297$06.00/0
Published 1984 American Chemical Society

resolved bioconcentration into its component balance of uptake
and depuration rates (7-12) and it seems likely that future
effort will improve definition of these rate constants (13).
    Relatively little attention has been given to aquatic
organisms other than fish, and predictive equations for fish do
not necessarily hold for other organisms. For example, Kenaga
and Goring (5) compared bioconcentration by Daphnia with
bioconcentration by several species of fish and found that
although values were not the same there was at least a
statistically significant relationship between them. This was
described by the equation:

    log Daphnia BCF = 0.987 + 0.679 (log fish BCF).

    There is virtually no literature describing bioconcentration
of organic compounds by wild aquatic macrophytes in spite of the
facts that these plants are often the major primary producers in
shallow inland waters, and are essential habitat components for
both aquatic and terrestrial animals. Lockhart et al. (14)
provided a regression equation describing uptake curves for a
variety of organic compounds by duckweed (Lemna minor) cultures
in laboratory exposures. Predictions from the regression
equation agreed quite well with field observations on
bioconcentration of permethrin in outdoor ponds (15).
    The intent of this study was to derive rate constants
describing uptake and depuration of some forest pesticides using
fish (rainbow trout, Salmo gairdneri) and an aquatic macrophyte
(duckweed, Lemna minor) in laboratory tests. Since some
formulations of forest pesticides also contain solvents of
petroleum distillates, experiments were also carried out with a
hydrocarbon, fluorene, which is a component of fuel oil (16).
Rate constants were derived and used to calculate expected
bioconcentration factors for comparison with other estimates and
with field observations.

Materials and methods

Biological materials. Rainbow trout were obtained as "eyed" eggs
from a disease-free hatchery, Spring Valley Trout Farm,
Petersburg, Ontario. Eggs and larvae hatching from them were
kept at 10°C in flowing dechlorinated City of Winnipeg tap
water. When fish were taken from rearing to experimental rooms,
temperature and water quality remained unchanged. Larval fish
were fed commercially prepared trout starter food (Martin Feed
Mills) at recommended rates at all times except during exposures
to chemicals.
    Clones of duckweed plants were grown axenically in Stewart's
growth medium (17) with asparagine at 132.1 mg/L as nitrogen
source. Cultures were maintained in 250-mL Erlenmeyer flasks
with 100 mL of medium per flask in controlled environment rooms

at 25°C. Light was supplied by General Electric Gro & Sho lights at about 60 uE/m^2/sec with a photoperiod of 16 hr light and 8 hr dark.

Chemical materials. Ring-labelled ^{14}C fenitrothion was supplied by the Sumitomo Chemical Co., Osaka, Japan (20.23 uCi/uM). Aminocarb was obtained from Mobay Chemical Co., Kansas City, Mo., USA, as ring-labelled ^{14}C material (11.7 uCi/uM). Cis- and trans- permethrin were synthesized as methylene-^{14}C compounds (59.7 uCi/uM), or as cyclopropyl-^{14}C compounds (50 uCi/uM) by ICI Ltd., Jealotts Hill, UK. Fluorene was purchased as 9-^{14}C material from California Bionuclear Corp. (2.61 uCi/uM).

After exposures to radioactive compounds in water, fish and plants were burned in a Packard 306 oxidizer and ^{14}C-carbon dioxide was measured with a Beckmen LS-7500 liquid scintillation counter using PCS (Amersham):xylene (2:1) as counting solution with ^{14}C toluene (Amersham) as standard.

Exposures of fish. Fifty rainbow trout larvae (ca 250 mg) were added to 4 liters of dechlorinated Winnipeg water in glass aquaria at 10°C. Fish were allowed to acclimate for one day and then radioactive compounds were added to the water using acetone as a carrier. Concentrations in water at the start of exposures were: fenitrothion, 4.68 µg/L; aminocarb, 6.08 µg/L; cis-permethrin, 0.58 µg/L (cyclopropyl label); trans-permethrin, 0.87 µg/L (cyclopropyl label); fluorene, 19.1 µg/L. At time intervals generally of 1, 3, 6, and 24 hours after addition of a compound, five fish were removed per aquarium; duplicate 1-mL water samples were also taken when fish were sampled. Fish were rinsed with water, weighed, and then burned for determination of radioactivity. At the end of the 24-hr uptake phase the remaining fish were transferred to clean flowing water and sampling was continued.

Exposures of plants. Duckweed fronds were exposed to the labelled compounds in 125-mL Erlenmeyer flasks. Stewart's medium was prepared and 50 mL were added to each flask; then the flasks were autoclaved. After cooling the ^{14}C compound was added to each flask along with 30 fronds from stock cultures. Average starting concentrations in media were: fenitrothion, 3.89 µg/L; aminocarb, 6.26 µg/L; cis-permethrin, 2.29 µg/L (methylene label); trans-permethrin, 2.95 µg/L (methylene label); fluorene, 23.6 µg/L. After exposure for 2, 4, 24, 48, 96, and 120 hours, flasks were removed and fronds were counted, blotted dry, weighed and burned for radioactivity measurement. Water samples were taken at the start of each exposure and at the same time as plants were collected. At the end of the uptake phase (120 hours) the remaining flasks were drained and fresh medium containing no labelled material was added. Periodically during this depuration phase plants were collected for determination of radioactivity as described above.

Results and discussion

Uptake and depuration curves for rainbow trout have been
plotted in Fig. 1, and data were used to calculate rate constants
shown in Table I. All uptake curves showed the typical curvature
tending toward an upper limit on the quantity of material
accumulated. In principle the curves should reflect
establishment of a steady state condition during which the uptake
rate is equal to the depuration rate so that there is no net
change in the quantity of material in the fish. In these static
experiments another contributing reason for the tendency to reach
an upper limit may be the loss of material from the exposure
water. For example, during the 24-hr exposure periods
concentrations in water declined by the following amounts:
fenitrothion, 17%; aminocarb, 1%; trans-permethrin, 66%;
cis-permethrin, 40%; fluorene 65%. The procedure given by Zitko
(10) was used to calculate valid rate constants in spite of
falling water concentrations typical of static exposures. The
drop in each exposure concentrations was described with a linear
regression equation:

$$Ln\ Cw = Ln\ A - BT$$

where Cw is the concentration of compound in exposure water, T is
exposure time, and A and B are regression constants. Values for
A and B were used, together with the depuration rate constants,
K2, to calculate the uptake rate constant. Falling exposure
concentrations of this type are typically reported from studies
monitoring pesticides in water after forest spraying.

The depuration curves generally show deviations from the
straight line logarithmic plots expected on the basis of first
order depuration, dependent only on the content of material in
the fish at any instant. For calculation
of depuration rate constants, a minimum of the first three points
were included in a linear regression equation, and subsequent
points were included only if inclusion resulted in an increase in
the coefficient of determination R^2. The slope of this linear
equation was taken as the depuration rate constant, K2, and was
used together with the constants A and B describing the loss of
material from water during the uptake phase to calculate the
uptake rate constant K1 from Zitko's expression:

$$K1 = \frac{C_f\ max\ K2}{A\ \ e^{-BT}max}$$

where $C_f$max is the maximum concentration of compound observed
in the organism and Tmax is the time at which $C_f$max was
observed.

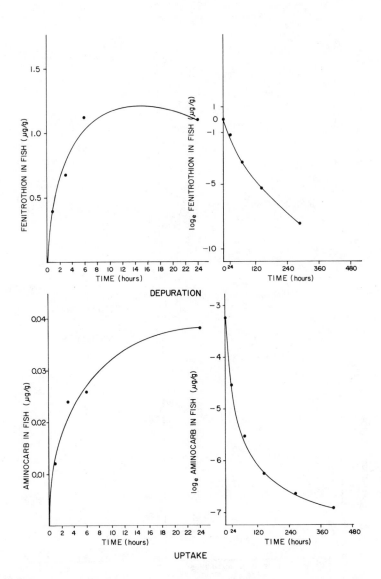

Figure 1a. Uptake and depuration curves for fenitrothion and aminocarb in laboratory studies with larval rainbow trout.

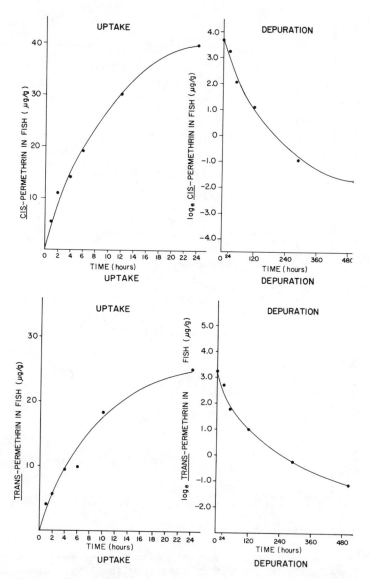

Figure 1b.   Uptake and depuration curves for cis- and trans-permethrin in laboratory studies with larval rainbow trout.

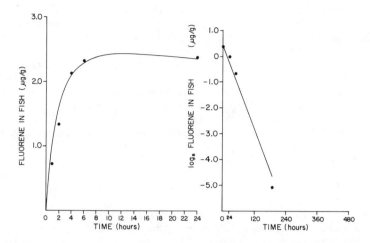

Figure 1c. Uptake and depuration cuves for fluorene in laboratory studies with larval rainbow trout.

Table I. Bioconcentration factors (BCF) for rainbow trout in laboratory exposures to several pesticides and a hydrocarbon. The calculated bioconcentration factors were taken as the ratio (K1/K2) of uptake rate constants (K1) to depuration rate constants (K2). The measured bioconcentration factors were taken as the ratio of measured radioactivity in fish to that in exposure water after 24 hours exposure.

Compound	Uptake rate Constant (hr^{-1}) (K1)	Depuration rate Constant (hr^{-1}) (K2)	Calculated BCF (K1/K2)	Measured BCF
fenitrothion	5.575	0.0382	146	116
aminocarb	0.221	0.0299	7	7
t-permethrin	1.156	0.0082	141	84
c-permethrin	2.027	0.0155	131	113
fluorene	13.094	0.0310	422	512

The ratio of K1/K2 provides an estimate of the steady state bioconcentration for each compound, and these have been tabulated for rainbow trout in Table I along with measured values taken simply as the ratio of radioactivity per gram of fish to that in water at the 24-hour sampling time. Generally these two values agree well and it is clear that the kinetic approach gives a good description of bioconcentration in these experiments, even though true steady state conditions may not have been established. For comparison of these results with other predictions of steady state bioconcentration, results using several published equations are presented in Table II, and our results generally fall within the range of expected values based on those equations. For both isomers of permethrin, however, the bioconcentration calculated from the rate constants is lower than that expected by the earlier calculations.

By comparison with many predictions, the pond data (18) indicate relatively low bioconcentration of cyclopropyl-^{14}C permethrin by fathead minnows. The range of bioconcentration factors was reported to be from 24 to 151, which overlaps with our predicted bioconcentration factors for permethrins (Table I). Rawn et al. (18) also reported bioconcentration factors for methylene-^{14}C permethrin, and these were notably higher with a range from 174 to 1433.

Residues of fenitrothion in fathead minnows were reported by Malis and Muir (19) following treatment of small ponds. Bioconcentration factors were 42 and 54 at 24 hours post treatment, as compared with predicted steady state bioconcentration factors of 146 (Table I). Following actual forest spraying Lockhart et al. (20) reported 13.7 µg fenitrothion per gram in fish taken from a stagnant pond in the spray zone. The peak water concentration observed was 75.5 µg/L, and so the bioconcentration factor was at least 180. Similarly, Lockhart et al. (21) found maximum fish residues of 4.28 µg/g from the same area sprayed two years later, and in this case the peak water concentration was 22.8 µg/L, with a calculated bioconcentration factor of 190.

Residue accumulations of aminocarb in fish are expected to be relatively low (Tables I and II) based on experimental calculations. This generally appears to be the case with field observations also (22), although relatively few such observations allow calculation of a bioconcentration factor. Coady (23) found that only 2 of 26 fish captured 2 days after spraying contained measurable aminocarb at 0.2 and 0.4 µg/g. Water samples from the stream ranged from 24 µg/L down to <1 µg/L. If an "average" exposure of 10 µg/L were assumed, then the two most extreme fish, would have bioconcentration factors of 20 and 40. Holmes and Kingsbury (24) reported bioconcentration factors smaller than 1 for fish caged in a stream receiving experimental sprays with several aminocarb formulations. An experimental study by Lamb

Table II. Some calculated steady state bioconcentration factors for fish.

Equation used	Fenitrothion	Aminocarb	Permethrin	Fluorene
A	90	13	910	245
B	293	24	3620	731
C	46	2	2490	259
D	114	9	1530	421
E	149	7	5570	714
F	12	1	428	58
	---	---	----	----
Mean	117	9	2420	405

A Log BCF = 0.542 log Kow + 0.124.   Neely et al. ($\underline{2}$)
B log BCF = 3.41 - 0.508 log Solubility.   Chiou et al. ($\underline{3}$)
C Log BCF = 0.935 log Kow - 1.495.   Kenaga and Goring ($\underline{5}$)
D Log BCF = 2.791 - 0.564 log Solubility. Kenaga and Goring ($\underline{5}$)
E Log BCF = 0.850 log Kow - 0.70. Veith et al. ($\underline{4}$)
F Log BCF = 0.830 log Kow - 1.71. Ellgehausen et al. ($\underline{6}$)

and Roney (25) was reported by the National Research Council of
Canada (22) in which channel catfish were exposed to
radioactively labelled aminocarb, and a bioconcentration factor
of about 6 was observed. This study also included the depuration
phase and a biological half-life of about one week was indicated,
based on radioactivity content.

Accumulations of fluorene in fish were found to be higher
than any of the pesticides (Table I). We are not aware of any
field study which may have reported the bioconcentration of this
particular hydrocarbon, and the results presented here may serve
to emphasize the argument that formulation materials are often as
desirable research subjects as are the active components.

Bioconcentration of organic compounds by aquatic plants has
received relatively little research attention. Curves showing
uptake and loss of radioactivity by duckweed plants exposed to
labelled compounds in axenic cultures are shown in Fig. 2. Rate
constants and calculated equilibrium bioconcentration factors are
shown in Table III. By comparison with fish data shown in Table
I, the plants concentrated fenitrothion and fluorene rather
poorly, and aminocarb surprisingly well. Lockhart et al. (14)
presented a regression equation based on data from uptake curves:

$$
\begin{aligned}
\text{Log plant conc (pg/g)} \ =\ & 0.061\ (\log Kow)^2 \\
& + 0.178\ (\log \text{water conc, pg/mL})^2 \\
& - 0.256\ (\text{water type, lab=1, river=2}) \\
& + 0.00074\ (\text{exposure time, hr}) \times (\log Kow) \\
& + 1.982.
\end{aligned}
$$

Calculation of expected bioconcentration factors for this
equation using compounds and concentrations reported here yields
values shown in Table IV. It is apparent that the kinetic and
regression methods agree well except for aminocarb, in which case
the slow rate of loss of radioactivity (Fig. 2) has resulted in a
very small depuration rate constant, K_2, with the consequent high
value for the equilibrium bioconcentration factor. Inspection of
the aminocarb depuration curve (Fig. 2) reveals somewhat erratic
points; the correlation coefficient was greatest when all seven
points were used, but it was only -0.738, the smallest among the
five compounds. Ellgehausen et al. (6) included a green alga in
their tests, and they derived the equation below:

$$\text{Log BCF} = 0.70 \log Kow - 0.26$$

Predicted bioconcentration factors using this equation are also
shown in Table IV, and these are generally higher than
predictions derived with duckweed plants.

Comparisons among laboratory and field observations are
understandably less readily available for aquatic plants than for
fish, but some field work has been done with duckweed. The data
from pond studies by Rawn et al. (15) with permethrin allow some

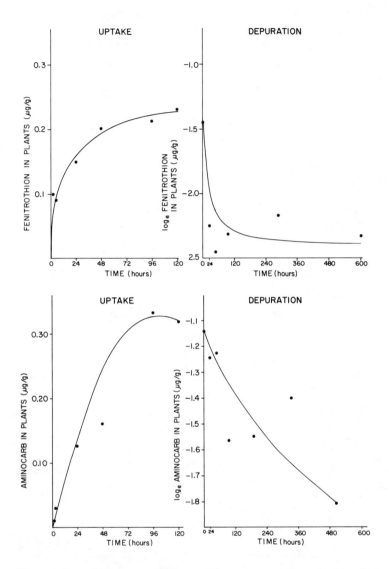

Figure 2a. Uptake and depuration curves for fenitrothion and aminocarb in laboratory studies with axenic clutures of duckweed.

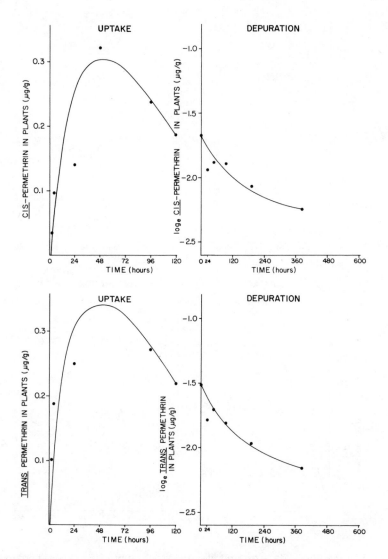

Figure 2b. Uptake and depuration curves for cis- and
trans-permethrin in laboratory studies with axenic cultures
of duckweed.

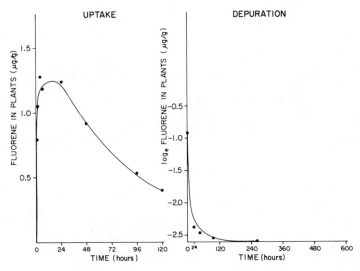

Figure 2c. Uptake and depuration curves for fluorene in laboratory studies with axenic cultures of duckweed.

Table III. Bioconcentration factors (BCF) for Lemna plants in laboratory exposures to several pesticides and a hydrocarbon. The calculated bioconcentration factors were taken as the ratio (K1/K2) of uptake rate constants (K1) to depuration rate constants (K2). The measured bioconcentration factors were taken as the ratio of measured radioactivity in plants to that in exposure water after 120 hours exposure.

Compound	Uptake rate Constant (hr^{-1}) (K1)	Depuration rate Constant (hr^{-1}) (K2)	Calculated BCF (K1/K2)	Measured BCF
fenitrothion	0.550	0.0229	24	20
aminocarb	0.0775	0.0012	65	56
t-permethrin	0.4700	0.0017	276	202
c-permethrin	0.4814	0.0015	321	151
fluorene	3.292	0.0372	88	105

Table IV. Comparison of three estimates of bioconcentration factors for aquatic plants in laboratory tests. Values for duckweed were calculated from the rate constants shown in Table III, and from the regression equation of Lockhart et al. (14), using a value of 120 hours for exposure time. Values for green algae were calculated from the equation of Ellgehausen et al. (6).

Compound and Log Kow	Bioconcentration factor		
	Duckweed rate constants	Duckweed regression equation	Green algae regression equation
Fenitrothion 3.38	24	40	128
Aminocarb 1.85	65	7	11
t-permethrin 5.23	276	315	2520
c-permethrin 5.23	321	311	2520
fluorene 4.18	88	119	464

Equations of Lockhart et al. (14) and Ellgehausen et al. (6) are given in the text.

comparison. For example, a surface water concentration of 15.5 μg/L as reported 2 hours after pond treatment, but this declined to only 1.4 μg/L after 24 hours, at which time duckweed were found to contain 30 μg/g on a dry weight basis. If an average exposure concentration of 8.5 μg/L were assumed, than the observed biconcentration factor would be about 3500. Our predicted values for steady state conditions ranged from 276 to 321 on a wet weight basis. Plants in our cultures are only 6.3% dry matter, and so our predictd bioconcentration factors can be increased by as much as 15.9 times (100/6.3) on the assumption that all the radioactivity is associated with the dry matter. This would yield predicted values from about 4400 to 5100, in relatively good agreement with the pond observation.

Moody et al. (26) reported concentrations of fenitrothion in duckweed from a high of 4.19 μg/g at 10 hr following forest spraying, falling to 0.032 μg/g 192 hr after spraying. Surface water samples from the site fell from 44 to 0.67 μg/L during the same period. Bioconcentration factors calculated from plant and water concentrations at the same time range from about 10 to about 90, as compared with a predicted value of about 20 for steady state conditions. Moody et al. (26) used a centrifugation step to fractionate homogenized duckweed plants, and they reported that about 85% of fenitrothion was associated with the insoluble residue. Under actual forest spraying conditions we might expect the surface layer of water and any neuston organisms to be exposed to particularly high concentrations for a short period before any spray deposit had mixed. Duckweed might be expected to concentrate material from the water, and also by direct physical contact with falling droplets. For example, a spray of 280 g/ha (4 oz/acre) might deposit as much as 2.8 μg/cm^2. A layer of one gram of duckweed only 1 plant in thickness would cover several cm^2. Moody et al. (26) observed a very high surface layer concentration of 701 μg/L of fenitrothion 1 hour after spraying, but duckweed plants collected at that time contained only 1.7 μg/g, a bioconcentration factor of less than 3. Evidently the short-term high exposure did not result in a correspondingly high bioconcentration by the plants.

Malis and Muir (19) treated an experimental pond with ^{14}C fenitrothion and observed that fenitrothion levels in duckweed changed relatively little from 1 to 10 days after treatment. The averages of radioactivity (as fenitrothion) in the plants over that interval were 17480 and 18229 μg/kg in shaded and sunlit ponds respectively, on a dry weight basis. During the period after treatment water content of radioactivity declined continuously, but "average" values taken as the means of initial and 10-day samples were 43 and 37 μg/L for the same ponds. Calculated bioconcentration factors were therefore 406 and 492 fold for the shaded and sunlit ponds. The rate constant ratio (Table III) indicates a steady state prediction of 24 on a wet

weight basis. and this can be converted to dry weight using a
factor of (100/6.3) to give a dry weight prediction of 381.

With aminocarb, field data for duckweed do not seem to be
available. An unanticipated feature of the laboratory exposures
was the low value for K2 (Table III). Recent literature has
shown a significant negative correlation between Kow and K2 (13)
and we might have expected aminocarb with the smallest Kow to
have had the largest K2. Biological half lives are calculated
from K2 values as (Ln2/K2), and these are shown in Table V.
Half-lives for aminocarb in a number of environmental
compartments were tabulated by the National Research Council (22)
and the longest was 11 days. Our value of 600 hr (25 days) may
well represent ^{14}C label retained by the plants in forms other
than aminocarb. The National Research Council report also cited
work by Prasad in which duckweed were observed to accumulate ^{14}C
aminocarb and to form several metabolic products with different
retention times on thin layer chromatograms.

Similar to the case with fish, we are not aware of field
studies with fluorene in plants. Figure 2 shows the very rapid
depuration of label from duckweed in culture, resulting in the
high K2 (Table III) and the short half-life (Table V). In view
of the volatility of fluorene, and its short half-life it would
not be expected to persist long in plants after a spray with a
solvent containing fluorene. McLeese et al. (27) examined the
uptake and depuration of "585 oil" by mussels and found a similar
result. The steady state bioconcentration factor was 160 but the
half-life was only 0.3 days.

For the types of comparisons reported here it has generally
been convenient to use steady state assumptions, but these
clearly do not apply to conditions after forest spraying.
Monitoring studies typically report rapid penetration of
pesticides to forest streams followed by rapid dissipation of
residues by a number of processes. Most published
bioconcentration equations do not contain a time term and so they
cannot readily be applied to short intervals when only a small
fraction of the time to reach equilibrium would apply. The rate
constants and other descriptive equations offer the possibility
of predicting bioconcentration under non-equilibrium conditions.

In principle the concentration in an animal or plant (Cf)
can be described at any time if the organism is considered a
single compartment and if one knows the rate constants (K1, K2)
and the exposure concentration in the water (Cw) using the
expression below (4).

$$C_f = (K1/K2)C_w(1-e^{-K2T})$$

The concentration in the water is assumed to be constant over the
time interval T, but several options are available to avoid that
limitation.

Table V. Biological half lives (hours) of compounds in rainbow trout and duckweed plants under laboratory conditions. Estimates are based on content of radioactivity and should be considered maximum values.

Compound	half life in trout (hr)	half life in plants (hr)
fenitrothion	18	30
aminocarb	23	600
t-permethrin	85	400
c-permethrin	45	460
fluorene	22	19

In spite of the limitations on values produced by simple laboratory experiments reported here (use of radioactivity to indicate a compound, single exposure concentrations, steady state assumptions, lack of allowance for growth dilution, first order depuration kinetics), the rate constants derived have given a surprisingly good estimate both of some published field biconcentration measurements and of other predictions based on larger amounts of data.

Acknowledgments

We wish to acknowledge the assistance of Mr. R.W. Danell, Mr. D.A.J. Murray and Mrs. G. Decterow.

Literature Cited

1. Hamelink, J.L.; Waybrant, R.C.; Hall R.C. Trans. Am. Fish. Soc. 1971. 100, 207.
2. Neely, W.B.; Branson, D.R.; Blau, G.E. Environ. Sci. Technol. 1974. 8, 1113.
3. Chiou, C.T.; Freed V.H.; Schmedding, D.W.; Kohnert, R.L. Environ. Sci. Technol. 1977. 11, 475.
4. Veith, G.D.; DeFoe, D.L.; Bergstedt, B.V. J. Fish. Res. Board Can. 1979. 36, 1040.
5. Kenaga, E.E.; Goring, C.A.I. in "Aquatic Toxicology"; Eaton, J.G.; Parrish, P.R.; Hendricks, A.C., Eds.; American Society for Testing and Materials. 1980. ASTM STP 707, 78.
6. Ellgehausen, H.; Guth, J.H.; Esser, H.O. Ecotoxicol. Environ. Safety. 1980. 4, 134.
7. Krzeminski, S.F.; Gilbert, J.T.; Ritts, J.A. Arch. Environ. Contam. Toxicol. 1977. 5, 157.
8. Branson, D.R. in "Estimating the Hazard of Chemical Substances to Aquatic Life"; Cairns, J. Jr.; Dickson, K.L.; Maki, A.W., Eds.; American Society for Testing and Materials. 1978. ASTM STP 657, 55.
9. Spacie, A.; Hamelink, J.L. Environ. Sci. Technol. 1979. 13: 817.
10. Zitko, V.; in Klaverkamp, J.F.; Leonhard, S.L.; Marshall, K.E., Eds.; Can. Tech. Rep. Fish. Aquat. Sci. 1980. 975, 243.
11. Bruggeman, W.A.; Martron, L.B.J.M.; Kooiman, D.; Hutzinger, O. Chemosphere. 1981. 10, 811.
12. Galassi, S.; Calamari, D.; Setti, F. Ecotoxicol. Environ. Safety. 1982. 6, 439.
13. Spacie, A.; Hamelink, J.L. Environ. Toxicol. Chem. 1982. 1, 309.
14. Lockhart, W.L.; Billeck, B.N.; deMarch, B.G.E.; Muir, D.C.G. in "Aquatic Toxicology amd Hazard Assessment: 6th Symposium"; Bishop, W.E.; Cardwell, R.D.; Heidolph, B.B.,

Eds.; American Society for Testing and Materials. 1983.
ASTM STP 802, 460.
15. Rawn, G.P.; Webster, G.R.B.; Muir, D.C.G. J. Environ.
Sci. Health. 1982. B17, 463.
16. Anderson, J.W.; Neff, J.M.; Cox, B.A.; Tatem, H.E.;
Hightower G.M. Mar. Biol. 1974. 27, 75.
17. Stewart, G.R. J. Exp. Bot. 1972. 23, 171.
18. Rawn, G.P.; Webster, G.R.B.; Muir, D.C.G. Proc. 15th
Annual Workshop for Pesticide Residue Analysts. 1980, 25.
19. Malis, G.P.; Muir, D.C.G. 1983. In this book.
20. Lockhart, W.L.; Metner, D.A.; Grift, N. Manit. Entomol.
1973. 7, 26.
21. Lockhart, W.L.; Flannagan, J.F.; Moody, R.P.; Weinberger,
P.; Greenhalgh, R. Proc. Symp. on Fenitrothion, the
Long-Term Effects of its use in Forest Ecosystems.
National Research Council of Canada. 1977. NRCC 16073,
233.
22. National Research Council of Canada. "Aminocarb: the
Effects of its Use on the Forest and the Human
Environment". 1982. NRCC 18979.
23. Coady, L.W. Environment Canada, Atlantic Surveillance
Report. 1978. EPS 5-AR-78-1.
24. Holmes, S.B.; Kingsbury, P.D. Forest Pest Management
Institute, Canadian Forstry Service. 1982. FPM-X-55.
25. Lamb, D.W.; Roney, D.J. Mobay Chemical Corp. 1976.
Report 49309 (confidential).
26. Moody, R.P.; Greenhalgh, R.; Lockhart, L.; Weinberger, P.
Bull. Environ. Contam. Toxicol. 1978. 19, 8.
27. McLeese, D.W.; Sergeant, D.B.; Metcalf, C.D., Zitko, V.,
Burridge, L.E. Bull. Environ. Contam. Toxicol. 1980. 24,
575.

RECEIVED September 9, 1983

ECOTOXICOLOGY AND HAZARD ASSESSMENT

Monitoring Human Exposure During Pesticide Application in the Forest

T. L. LAVY and J. D. MATTICE

Altheimer Laboratory, Agronomy Department, University of Arkansas, Fayetteville, AR 72701

The extent to which exposure to pesticides may be hazardous to applicators depends upon exposure levels and the toxicity of the compounds. The phenoxy herbicides have been used for nearly 40 years, and no injury to workers properly using these herbicides has been clearly established.

In spite of their record of producing no detectable harm to humans, the phenoxy herbicides 2,4-dichlorophenoxy acetic acid (2,4-D) and 2,4,5-trichlorophenoxy acetic acid (2,4,5-T) have acquired a less than desirable reputation. This reputation has been the result of their association with low levels of impurities. They have commonly been used as a mixture, which contains trace amounts of highly toxic 2,3,7,8-tetrachlorodibenzo-p-dioxin, a minor product in the manufacturing of 2,4,5-T. In early production of 2,4,5-T a low level of dioxin was retained. Today's manufacturing process produces 2,4,5-T with no more than 0.1 ppm of the 2,3,7,8 tetrachlorodibenzo-p-dioxin. This association with toxic dioxin and confusion of the public and the media regarding these issues have led to public distrust in the safety of using phenoxys and to the need to establish clearly the extent of human exposure to these compounds as well as the resulting effects of this exposure.

The phenoxys have become a major tool in silviculture. They have allowed the forest industries to eliminate more economically the competing vegetation which impedes the rapid growth and harvest of conifer forests.

Until recently little data had been gathered on human exposure to these compounds. To evaluate their safety, the exposure received and dose absorbed must be considered in relation to their toxicity. Since restrictions were placed on the use of 2,4,5-T by the EPA in 1978, several exposure studies have been conducted with 2,4,5-T and also with 2,4-D and other compounds used in forest operations. Recent interest in evaluating human

exposure to pesticides in forestry has paralleled these interests
in agronomic and horticultural crop production. However,
numerous studies in these other areas preceded most of the forest
work. Since the 1970's several studies have specifically dealt
with forest applications of phenoxys and other pesticides. Since
different pesticides as well as different experimental designs
and methods have been used in the evaluations, it is not always
simple to make accurate comparisons among studies. However, some
comparisons can be made and each study has contributed to the
studies of today. The review of studies on 2,4,5-T by Leng et
al. (1980) suggests the kinds of differences as well as the comparisons that can be made among exposure studies.

Tarrant and Allard (1972) tested forestry workers in the
early 1970's to determine dose absorbed from the application of
cacodylic acid by analyzing the urine for arsenic. Analysis of
urine has come to be regarded as the best method for determining
dosage for the phenoxys. Exposure studies on 2,4-D and 2,4,5-T
in recent years have included those by Sauerhoff et al. (1977).
Kolmodin-Hedman et al. (1979) in Sweden compared plasma and urine
levels for 2,4-D and 2,4,5-T in a four-man forestry study. They
speculated that uptake was both by inhalation and dermal exposure
and that elimination through urine was rapid. They concluded
that the highest levels of phenoxy acids were found in the urine.
Draper and Street (1982) monitored two groups performing ground
applications of a 1:1 mixture of the dimethylamine salt of 2,4-D
and dicamba. One group sprayed once for 5.5 hours; the other
continued daily spraying. First void urine samples were used
each morning of the experiment. Ethanol hand rinses removed considerable 2,4-D and dicamba from the hands. The effect of
rinsing in this way on the amount absorbed and later excreted is
not known. Removing the herbicide should mean that the internal
dose would be reduced since dermal exposure to the hands would be
reduced. However, the possibility exists that the herbicide
dissolved in the solvent may more readily penetrate the skin,
increasing the internal dose. Maximum urinary excretion occurred
after 48 hours. Higher concentrations of 2,4-D were excreted
than dicamba or its isomer. They also concluded that respiratory
exposure was minor compared to dermal exposure.

Our evaluations using 2,4,5-T and 2,4-D have been conducted
over the past 5 years in forests in Arkansas, Oregon and
Washington. Objectives were to measure external exposure and
internal doseage as determined by the total amount of the herbicide excreted in the urine and also to develop the best
possible techniques for assessing exposure and dose absorbed.
Exposure levels were related to job responsibilities and to protective techniques designed to limit exposure.

The data collected from exposure studies can be used with
toxicological data to assess the safety of applying the pesticides in forest operations.

Experimental Procedures

Field crews that normally apply pesticides were monitored during their routine working day with as little interruption as possible to their customary work procedures or habits. When human error or mechanical irregularities occurred, the study was continued, and the irregularity was incorporated into the analysis of data. In this way we could monitor exposure that would include unexpected difficulties and spontaneous or habitual human reactions under actual "real-life" conditions.

Measurements were made of the concentration of pesticide in the breathing zone of the workers, on patches attached to the workers' clothing, and in the urine of crew members. In the 2,4-D tests, comparisons were made between amounts found under normal spray operations and amounts found when techniques for limiting exposure were used including special instructions and the use of protective clothing consisting of hat, boots, gloves, and Tyvek coveralls.

The dermal exposure patches were made of 9-ply gauze (2,4,5-T study) or denim (2,4-D study) and were attached with safety pins to workers' clothing by research team members wearing clean gloves. Following the spray activities, the patches were placed in individual specimen bottles and transported to the laboratory for analysis. In the 2,4,5-T study, all six patches from each individual were pooled before analyses were made; in the 2,4-D studies the patches were kept separate and analyzed individually. Using a photograph of the worker in his spray attire and the amounts of pesticide found on the patches, we estimated total dermal exposure for each worker (Durham and Wolfe, 1962).

Pesticide vapors and airborne particles in a worker's breathing zone were pulled through a trapping medium by a battery-powered air pump attached to his belt. Cassettes containing the trapping medium were removed at the conclusion of the test and transported to the laboratory where they were analyzed. Collection of the total urine voided began 1 (2,4,5-T) or 2 (2,4-D) days prior to each spray operation and continued for at least 4 days afterward. Samples were collected in 12-hour intervals. These specimens were kept in a cool location and transported to a central storage facility at 2-day intervals. To ensure integrity throughout the analytical determination, blind-fortified specimens containing known levels of the pesticide were intermingled with the actual field specimens.

2,4,5-T Study

Twenty-one crew members participated in a 2,4,5-T forestry study which was repeated after an interval of one or two weeks.

Exposure was measured for four crews in Arkansas using three methods of pesticide application: backpack, tractor-drawn mist blower, and helicopter (two crews). Comparisons of exposure levels were made between crews and within crews in relation to work duties.

The backpack team was composed of seven crew members, including a mixer-supervisor and six applicators. The tractor-mounted mist blower operation included a supervisor, two tractor drivers, and a mixer. Each of the helicopter crews had a pilot, a mixer, a supervisor, and two flagmen. All workers, except two backpack applicators, were men. Prior to this spray program, each worker filled out a form which provided personal information regarding the worker's vital statistics and history of any previous involvements with 2,4,5-T use. Workers indicated that they had not worked with the test compound for two weeks prior to the study. The typical attire for members of the spray crews included long trousers, shirt (long or short sleeves), and cloth sneakers, leather shoes, or field boots. Most crew members did not wear gloves or other protective clothing, but all wore hats except four members of the backpack crew.

The air pump worn by each worker in the 2,4,5-T study contained an Amberlite XAD-II resin. Air from the breathing zone was drawn across the resin at an approximate rate of 0.1 to 0.15 litres/min. The resin was retrieved after each operation and analyzed for 2,4,5-T.

Patches to collect measurements of dermal exposure were attached to clothing on the chest, back, thighs and forearms of each individual. To calculate total dermal exposure, the concentration of 2,4,5-T detected on the patch area was multiplied by the total skin area exposed (Lavy, 1978).

2,4-D Study

The 2,4-D study was similar to the 2,4,5-T study which included analyses of air, patches and total urine. In this study three helicopter crews were monitored during their routine forest spray operations in Washington and Oregon. An additional objective in this study was to compare exposure from the routine operation (T_1) with that received when workers wore protective clothing and followed added precautions designed to limit exposure (T_2). The T_1 and T_2 operations were conducted with the same individuals in each crew with a 1-week interval between spray operations. Each crew included a pilot, a batchman, a mechanic, a supervisor, and two observers. The observers were located from 67 to 168 m away from the spray operator. Their role was to represent persons who might be in the area, but who were not directly associated with the spray operation. Protective clothing worn in the T_2 operation included Tyvek coveralls, clean hats, rubber gloves, rubber boots, and goggles.

The collection and handling techniques for monitoring 2,4-D exposure levels in the breathing zone, on patches to measure dermal exposure, and in urine were similar to the procedures carried out in the 2,4,5-T tests. One difference was in the type and location of patches used. Denim strips were attached to workers' clothing near bare skin areas. A 2.5 by 40-cm strip was attached to the workers' collar, a 2.5 by 48-cm strip to the hatband, and two 2.5 by 15-cm strips around the wrists to the cuff.

Results and Discussion

Determining Acceptable Parameters for Field Measurement

Patches attached to clothing commonly have been used to obtain predictions of the amount of dermal pesticide exposure a field worker using pesticides would receive. The ease of patch construction, simplicity of attaching to clothing, and the fact that conceivably an exposure study could be completed during one application day make the use of patches highly attractive. By analyzing the amount of spray material deposited on the patches and evaluating the area of bare skin exposed for each worker via photographs, one can theoretically obtain a good estimate of the amount of pesticide contacting the exposed dermal area of the worker.

Pharmacokinetic studies with 2,4-D in rats (Sauerhoff et al., 1977) have shown that orally ingested or intravenously administered 2,4-D is excreted primarily in the urine by a first order process with a half-life of approximately 2 hours. Thus, the rapid and efficient urinary excretion of 2,4-D appears to be essentially independent of the route of administration. Further studies (Wolfe et al., 1972) have shown that the propylene glycol butyl ether esters of 2,4-D applied to the skin of rats are absorbed through the skin at a first order rate with a half-life of about 20 hours, and are then rapidly excreted as 2,4-D acid in the urine. In human volunteers (Gehring et al., 1973) given an oral dose of 5 mg 2,4-D per kg body weight, virtually the entire dose (greater than 95%) was excreted in the urine as 2,4-D and 2,4-D conjugates by a first order process with an average half-life of approximately 11 hours.

Since analysis of urine is an acceptable means of assessing the absorbed dose, it appears to be a relatively simple matter of collecting a urine sample at a pre-specified time and analyzing it for the pesticide. From our studies (Lavy, 1978) when consecutive 12-hour samples were collected, diurnal fluctuations in pesticide excretion were common among the different crewmembers.

When a specimen is collected at one specific time of day, one person may be excreting at his maximum concentration and another person at his minimum concentration. For example, one day a person excreted 6300 ml of urine while one of his colleagues employed in a similar duty excreted 606 ml. Assuming both had absorbed the same amount of pesticide, we would expect similar amounts to be excreted. If only a partial urine sample was collected and analyzed, a tenfold error would be made due to dilution. Consequently, all of the urine excreted daily must be collected and the volume recorded before an aliquot is taken for analysis.

Of primary concern in exposure studies is the amount of compound actually entering the body via ingestion, inhalation, or dermal absorption. In order to evaluate the effectiveness of patches in predicting the absorbed dose, during two studies we attached patches to the clothing at strategic locations in addition to collecting total urine samples. As an example of the fluctuation in 2,4,5-T exposure from one patch to another, Table 1 provides information derived from individual patch analyses from four mist blower crewmembers.

Table I. Micrograms 2,4,5-T detected on 100 cm^2 gauze patches of individual mist blower crewmembers.

	Chest	Back	Left arm	Right arm	Left thigh	Right thigh	Total on patches
			(μg)				
Driver I	31	102	44	57	17	101	352
Driver II	58	111	156	66	58	77	526
Mixer	74	8	2	449	108	876	1517
Supervisor	27	38	52	47	64	130	358

Although EPA estimates that 10% of the pesticide contacting dermal surfaces will be absorbed, this value will probably vary depending on compound, carrier type, formulation, the amount of moisture on the skin, which area of the body is contacted, and several other factors. In addition to analyzing for the amount of 2,4,5-T on the patches, the size of the crewmember and the amount of bare skin exposed must also be known and appropriate calculations made. Results obtained from correlating exposure information (patch vs. urine) for 57 forest workers indicate that the values were not highly correlated (Lavy, 1978; Lavy, 1980).

Table II lists the potential exposure via inhalation and dermal absorption and the amount of 2,4,5-T excreted for four of the more highly exposed 2,4,5-T crewmembers.

Table II. Levels of 2,4,5-T detected in air, patch, and urine samples for four of the more highly exposed forestry crewmembers.

Duty	Ex-posure	Potential exposure		Actual excretion (urine)
		Air (resin)	Skin (patch)	
		(mg/kg)		
Backpack sprayer	1	0.00058	0.711	0.069
	2	0.00089	0.807	0.074
Mist blower driver	1	0.00019	0.179	0.042
	2	0.00040	2.987	0.032
Helicopter pilot	1	nd	nd	0.031
	2	nd	nd	0.039
Helicopter mixer	1	nd	0.085	0.071
	2	nd	nd	0.138

Exposure and Work Duty

No significant difference in exposure level occurred between work crews. Data indicate that backpack and mist blower crews received more exposure; however, this exposure was not significantly different from that of the aerial crew (Table III). Each spray operation had one mixer whose exposure level was relatively high. If he had not been included in the calculations there would have been statistical differences in the means.

Table III. Mean exposures of 2,4,5-T received as determined by urine analysis: classified by spray operation and duty of crewmember. (Modified from Lavy et al., 1980.)

Spray operation	Mean[a] (µg/kg)	Duty		Mean (µg/kg)
Backpack (7)[b]	55 a	Mixer	(4)	62 a
Mist blower (4)	44 a	Backpack sprayer	(6)	47 a
Aerial (10)	22 a	Mist blower driver	(2)	35 ab
		Helicopter pilot	(2)	22 ab
		Supervisor	(4)	11 b
		Helicopter flag- man	(4)	1 b

[a]Means within a group followed by the same letter are not different at the 0.05 significance level as determined by Duncan's multiple range test.
[b]Number of workers in the group.

Differences did, however, occur in relation to work duties within crews (Table III). Totals per exposure ranged from a high of 0.096 mg/kg (mixer) to a low of 0.001 mg/kg (flagmen). With one exception the mixer in each of the four crews showed higher exposure levels than any of his fellow crew members. These three mixers also had higher 2,4,5-T excretion values on day 0 than others in their crew probably because they mixed the 2,4,5-T the day before the actual spray occurred. Optimum preexposure data would have required the mixers to begin urine collection at least 1 day earlier. The fact that the one exceptional mixer endorsed cautious work habits and wore gloves may account for the comparatively low level of 2,4,5-T measured in his urine.

     Categorized by work duties, mixers (those handling concentrate) received the highest internal dose of 2,4,5-T, followed in order by backpack sprayers, mist blower drivers, helicopter pilots, supervisors, and flagmen for the helicopter operation. One helicopter pilot excreted considerably less 2,4,5-T in his urine than did the other pilot. This difference appeared to be related to the fact that the second pilot routinely checked and unplugged nozzles at each fill-up time. In addition, he helped change the spray boom on the helicopter before and after each spray period.

2,4-D Study

Although none of the 2,4,5-T crewmembers received doses approaching health endangering levels, some of the crewmembers received considerably more exposure than others. The study using 2,4-D was designed to give us additional data on exposure under routine operations (T_1) and to see if the use of protective clothing and special precautions (T_2) could be employed to decrease exposure.

Even in the T_1 study, levels were so low that there was hardly a possibility of noting significantly reduced exposure in the T_2 test where protective measures were taken. In spite of the low levels of exposure, there was still a relationship between exposure and workers duties as had been evident in the 2,4,5-T study.

Less than 30% of the 524 urine samples analyzed contained levels of 2,4-D above the 0.04-ppm detection limit. Table IV reveals that most of the positive samples were from the crew members most closely involved with the actual spraying (batchman-loaders, pilots, and mechanics). Except for one pilot who had assisted in cleaning spray nozzles, batchman-loaders and mechanics showed the highest levels of 2,4-D in the urine, while observers received the lowest levels. Urine samples from observers standing near the heliport rarely contained any 2,4-D and then in only negligible amounts approaching the limit of detection. The only supervisor excreting 2,4-D was probably exposed when the automatic transfer system for moving the concentrate from the barrels to the mix truck failed and he helped manually transfer the chemical with buckets during the T_1 application. Similar exposure did not occur during T_2, and no 2,4-D was detected in his urine in T_2 (Table IV).

Nash et al. (1982) studying the exposure of ground applicators to 2,4-D found maximum mean one-day 2,4-D urinary excretion of 0.002, 0.003, and 0.004 mg/kg body weight, respectively, for applicators, mixer/loaders, and mixer/loader/applicators from a one-time exposure. When aerial application was used they found from 0.006 mg/kg body weight for pilots to 0.02 mg/kg body weight for mixer/loaders. The Nash study was conducted with applicators of 2,4-D in wheat fields. They found levels similar to those exposure levels found in forest operations in Arkansas, Washington, and Oregon (Lavy et al. 1980, Lavy et al. 1982). Newton and Norris (1981) pursued additional studies on dose absorbed by applying known quantities of 2,4,5-T to human skin. They found 2,4,5-T excretion rates which were similar to those we found in the field studies.

Table IV. Comparisons of total dose 2,4-D received by workers during normal operations (T_1) and "protective clothing" operations (T_2). (Modified from Lavy et al., 1982.)

Worker duty	Dose mg/kg[a] + SD	
	T_1	T_2
Pilots (3)[b]	0.0198 + 0.310	0.00854 + 0.01316
Mechanics (3)	0.00545 + 0.00712	0.00301 + 0.00269
Batchmen (3)	0.0196 + 0.0018	0.0140 + 0.0117
Supervisors (3)	0.00231 + 0.00400	0.000013 + 0.00022
Observers (6)	0.00049 + 0.00059	0.00009 + 0.00023
Total dose	0.00802	0.00429

[a]Values include 2,4-D excreted on the spray day plus 5 days following.
[b]Number in parenthesis represents the number of workers in the group.

This study found that some crew members involved in the aerial application of 2,4-D for forestry purposes absorbed low levels of 2,4-D, but the doses as indicated by urine analyses were several orders of magnitude below the 24 mg/kg no-observable-effect-level determined in toxicology studies. These results are in agreement with those of Nash et al. (1982). The doses were comparable to those found in an earlier test involving aerial application of 2,4,5-T but were substantially lower than those found for ground application of that herbicide (Lavy et al., 1980).

The absorbed dose measured in this study, as shown by the urine analyses, were too low and the replications too limited to allow accurate statistical comparisons for each worker duty. However, the total dose absorbed by workers in T_1 was nearly double that of workers wearing the protective clothing in T_2.

If one assumes a no-observable-effect-level of 24 mg/kg of body weight, as determined from toxicology tests with laboratory animals, then safety factors for the categories of workers involved in this test are substantial (Hall, 1980). They ranged from 1212 for the pilots and batchmen in T_1 to 266,667 for the observers in T_2.

The literature contains reports of many exposure studies. To conduct a good exposure study requires considerable forethought, an in-depth literature search, detailed protocol development, and extensive planning. Even then loopholes may exist. Findings from our studies reveal shortcoming in the following areas:

1. Inadequate pre-exposure information. Although workers fill out questionaires indicating that they have not used phenoxy herbicides during the previous two weeks, sometimes these workers come into the study with positive background levels of phenoxy in their urine.

2. Lack of ensuring that there is no post-application exposure. Excretion curves for several workers in our studies indicate that occasionally some avenue of re-exposure occurs after the actual spray day.

The source of the exposure either before or after the actual spray date appears to be related to some contact with the phenoxys of which the crewmember was not aware. Possible avenues of re-exposure include wearing phenoxy contaminated clothing on days other than the planned spray day, i.e., gloves, boots, pants, shirts, or chaps. Workers may also have received some exposure from their phenoxy application equipment. This may occur if a worker has a spray operation scheduled and wants to clean or check his equipment in advance. Another potential source of exposure is the vehicles in which the workers ride. Often workers, pesticide concentrate, empty containers, and equipment are hauled in the same pick-up truck or van.

Due to our awareness that extraneous exposure can occur, we have taken measures to limit these types of pre-exposure in our most recent studies. The data we have collected supply adequate evidence that extraneous means of exposure are common. If it occurs in these phenoxy studies, it is likely that it occurs for workers applying more toxic pesticides.

Including this extraneous exposure, the degree of safety that we calculated for forest workers using phenoxy herbicides was such that even the most highly exposed crewmembers received exposure which was several orders of magnitude below the no-observable-effect-level. Decreases in the level of exposure with the use of protective measures, however, may be of real consequence to workers applying more toxic materials.

We suggest that exposure to any pesticide may be decreased with the following precautions:

1. Wear clean clothing
2. Wash or shower soon after application
3. Launder clothes properly

4. Do not use tobacco while working
5. Wear gloves impervious to chemicals
6. Cover bare skin areas
7. Know factors contributing to exposure

Acknowledgment

The authors appreciate the assistance of Martha Davis in preparing this paper.

Literature Cited

Draper, W. H. and Street, J. C. 1982. _J. Environ. Sci. Health_ B17(4)321-339.
Durham, W. F. and Wolfe, H. R. 1962. _Bull. WHO_ 26: 75-91.
Gehring, P. J.; Kramer, C. G.; Schwetz, B. A.; Rose, J. Q.; and Rowe, V. K. 1973. _Toxicol. Appl. Pharmacol._ 26: 352.
Hall, J. F. 1980. Preface letter in Lavy, T. L., Ed. Project Completion Report submitted to National Forest Products Association; Washington, D.C., 1980. pp. 1-6.
Kolmodin-Hedman, B.; Erne, K.; Hakansson, M.; and Engquist, A. 1979. Arbete och halsa, Vetenskaplig Skrift Serie No. 17.
Lavy, T. L. 1978. Measurement of 2,4,5-T exposure workers. Project Completion Report submitted to National Forest Products Association; Washington, D.C. 1978.
Lavy, T. L. 1980. Determination of 2,4-D exposure received by forestry applicators. Project Completion Report submitted to National Forest Products Association; Washington, D.C. 1980.
Lavy, T. L.; Shepard, J. S.; and Mattice, J. D. 1980. _J. Agric. Food Chem._ 28: 626-630.
Lavy, T. L.; Walstad, J. D.; Flynn, R. R.; and Mattice, J. D. 1982. _J. Agric. Food Chem._ 30: 375-381.
Leng, M. L.; Ramsey, J. C.; Braun, W. H. and Lavy, T. L. 1980. Chapter II in Pesticide Residues and Exposure, American Chemical Society Symposium Series 182.
Nash, R. G.; Kearney, P. C.; Maitlen, S. C.; Soll, C. R.; and Fertig, S. N. 1982. Chapter 10 in Pesticide Residues and Exposure, American Chemical Society Symposium Series 182.
Newton, M. and Norris, L. A. 1981. _Fund. Appl. Toxicol._ 1: 339-346.
Sauerhoff, M. W.; Brun, W. H.; Blau, G. E.; and Gehring, P. J. 1977. _Toxicology_ 8: 3-11.
Tarrant, R. F. and Allard, J. 1972. _Arch. Environ. Health_ 24(4): 277-280.

RECEIVED September 9, 1983

Pesticide Drift: Toxicological and Social Consequences

JAMES M. WITT

Department of Agricultural Chemistry, Oregon State University, Corvallis, OR 97331

The drift of pesticides in the forestry
environment has the potential for greater
environmental impact than in an agricultural
environment and results in a greater social
concern for their impact on human health. The
factors affecting drift transfer of pesticide,
especially herbicides, will be examined, the
probable deposit and exposure level identified,
and the risk of probability of injury to human
health calculated.

The role of an Extension Specialist in chemistry is somewhat
different than that of a research chemist. A research chemist
produces data; an Extension chemist utilizes this data,
interpreting it, applying it to specific problems, and
presenting the conclusion to the public. The research data you
have presented here and elsewhere, to ultimately be of value,
must contribute to making social decisions, such as, to use a
pesticide or disdain its use. When such decisions are made in
the social, political, or even jurisprudical arena, the research
data must be simplified--often to the point that it will not be
easily recognizable even by its originators. It must, however,
continue to be correct and never be simplified to the point
where it will support misleading conclusions.

As research chemists, you may be interested in how your
data are sometimes used and how they are presented to the
concerned public. Conclusions or simplified research data may
be presented by public agencies--such as state or federal
departments of agriculture, forestry, public health, or
occasionally the EPA or a Department of Environmental Quality,
and by citizens or public interest groups (especially by those
groups which are opposed to the use of pesticides in general),
and also by university research, teaching, or extension faculty.

I represent the extension faculty in Oregon. I frequently
must discuss the risk to human health from pesticide spray

0097-6156/84/0238-0331$06.00/0

drift. This information is most often presented in situations
where confrontation, and even antagonism, exists; where one
group is pitted against another regarding the issue of whether a
particular pesticide should be used in a pest control program,
or whether such a program should even proceed at all. In this
atmosphere it is often difficult for the persons involved to
direct their attention to a thorough examination of the research
available and make a careful assessment of the risk.

I shall present a perception of the public concerns and a
little of how I evaluate and how I present the risks. I will
present information on pesticide use, public concerns as they
are expressed in the news, allegations of harm, toxicity of a
forest pesticide--2,4-D, human exposure to drift of this
pesticide, and the margins of safety which exist when this
exposure occurs.

It is interesting to compare the concerns expressed about
pesticide use with the actual types, locations, and pesticide
use levels. Table I shows pesticide use in Oregon. These data
are the result of a pesticide use survey, or census, carried out
in Oregon for 1981 and shows the ten pesticides used in largest
amounts in Oregon. Some surprises are revealed by this survey.

Table I.   Oregon Pesticide Use Estimates, 1981

Rank	Pesticide	Pounds
	A. THE TOP TEN	
1	Creosote	15,000,000
2	Dichloropropane/dichloropene (D-D, Telone)	2,938,000
3	Pentachlorophenol (Penta)	1,590,000
4	2,4-D	1,169,050
5	Spray oil	1,065,700
6	Chromated copper arsenate	1,000,000
7	Diuron (Karmex)	520,000
8	Metam-sodium (Vapam)	440,000
9	Dinoseb (Dow General)	423,000
10	EPTC (Eptam)	395,000
	B. AGRICULTURAL AND FORESTRY USE	
1	Dichloropropane/dichloropropene (D-D, Telone)	2,938,000
2	2,4-D	1,169,050
3	Diuron (Karmex)	520,300
4	Metam-sodium (Vapam)	440,000
5	Dinoseb (Dow General)	423,400
6	EPTC (Eptam)	395,500
7	Sulfur	360,500
8	Captan	320,000
9	Bromoxynil (Brominal, Buctril)	308,400
10	Carbaryl (Sevin)	305,000

The most commonly used pesticide is not one we normally call to mind when we consider pesticide use to control insects, weeds and plant diseases in agriculture and forestry. It is creosote, a wood preservative. Its use exceeds that of all other pesticides combined, being used in an amount of approximately 15 million pounds per year. Other wood preservatives in the top ten are pentachlorophenol and chromated copper arsenate, the third and sixth most used pesticides, respectively. The second most commonly used pesticide is a soil fumigant, DD or telone, used at about 3 million pounds per year.

Finally, in fourth place we find 2,4-D, which is used at a little over 1 million pounds per year. This is the first pesticide which we might normally think of when considering the most common pesticides. This is followed in 7th-10th positions by four other herbicides, Diuron, Vapam, Dinoseb, and Eptam.

Table II shows pesticides used by the US Forest Service and the amounts used in 1980. On this list 2,4-D is in first place, being used at in an amount of 215,000 pounds per year. In 1980 the second most commonly used pesticide by the USFS was the insecticide malathion at in an amount of 102,000 pounds. There are only three insecticides on this list of the nine most commonly used pesticides in the USFS. The insecticide use rate will vary considerably from year to year as its use is dependent on insect outbreaks, whereas herbicides are used at a more constant rate because the appearance of weeds and brush, as they affect forest management, do not occur as periodic outbreaks.

Table II. Oregon Pesticide Use Estimate

Pesticide	Pounds.
A. PESTICIDE USE BY THE USFS, 1980	
2,4-D	215,000
Malathion	102,000
Picloram	40,000
Atrazine	30,000
Carbaryl	30,000
Azinophos Methyl	18,000
Glyphosate	10,000
Dalapon	9,000
Fosamine	8,000

Continued on next page

Table II. Continued

Pesticide	Pounds
B. USE ON OREGON FORESTLAND, 1981 (25,000,000 acres)	
2,4-D	130,000
Glyphosate (Roundup)	37,000
Atrazine (Aatrex)	22,000
Fosamine ammonium (Krenite)	21,000
Hexazinone (Velpar)	20,000
Picloram (Tordon)	16,000
2,4-DP	16,000
Dicamba (Banvel)	6,400

Pesticide use in private forestry will more-or-less parallel that in the USFS, with one exception. They will not use malathion, carbaryl, or azinophos-methyl, the insecticides shown in Table II, because nearly all insect outbreaks are managed by either a federal or other public agency rather than by private forestry. Although 2,4-D is the principal pesticide used in forest management, Table III shows that its use in Oregon for 1979 in forestry is only about 10 percent of the total use in the State. The principal use is in wheat and other grains, which utilized nearly 3/4 of a million pounds, while forestry used 147,000 pounds.

Table III. 2,4-D Use in Oregon, 1979

Crop	1979
Cereal grains	731,000
Range and pasture	185,000
Forestry	147,000
Grass Seed	97,000
Home and garden	70,000
Rights-of-way	43,000
Miscellaneous	13,000
TOTAL	1,287,000

If we combine the use on grass grown for seed with home and garden use, both of which are principally in the Willamette Valley, we find that the total used in the Valley, 167 thousand pounds, exceeds the amount used in forestry by a small margin. Nevertheless, we find the principal public concern about 2,4-D use does not focus on its Willamette Valley use, the region of

highest population density in Oregon, nor its use in wheat and
cereal grains, which is the principal use of 2,4-D, but is used
in eastern Oregon where there are far fewer people, but with few
exceptions focuses almost solely on its use in forestry.

Public concern over 2,4-D use is reflected by a constant
parade of newspaper articles and headlines, such as "200 Fleeing
Herbicide Spraying", and expressions of concern in these
articles, such as "I am nursing a five-month-old baby this time
and I am even more scared. There is no way they can tell me it
is not dangerous to babies," or, "The last time the Forest
Service sprayed here, they didn't tell us, and our children
immediately contracted extreme nausea." The newspaper stories
are not confined to quotations from concerned citizens, but
sometimes involve agency officials, such as the following
quotation from the recent head of the EPA Office of Toxic
Substances, Steve Jellenik, who stated, "Now we have a lot of
dead bodies, a lot of dead fetuses in Alsea." It is small
wonder that a very large segment of the public are very
concerned and very fearful of 2,4-D use when all they know is
what they have read in the newspapers. This is a good example
of the kind of information they most frequently receive.

We frequently find that newswriters add to the confusion
concerning the possible effects of pesticides. For example, in
newspaper discussions of the EPA "Alsea II" study, articles
frequently leaped from a discussion of 2,4,5-T, which was the
pesticide at issue, to all "phenoxy herbicides" and from there
to simply "herbicides".

The news headlines show varying stories of 2,4-D
controversy outcomes, such as "BLM Ordered to Halt Herbicide
Spraying Effort", "Environmentalists Fail in Attempt to Stop
Spraying of 2,4-D", and "Ozark Forest Spraying Stopped".
Sometimes the stories carry humorous headlines, such as "Spray
Protestors Didn't Run Naked in Woods, Leader Says". Sometimes
stories are of a more grave nature, "No Cause for Civil
Disobedience." The result of many persons concerns have ranged
from civil disobedience to violence, much of it with grave
overtones. These vary from sitting or standing in spray areas
to prevent the spraying from proceeding, attempting to
physically block the spraying, threatening personnel involved,
armed confrontations, burning and destruction of spray
helicopters, and firing shots at low-flying spray aircraft.

The technical basis for this high, even agitated, level of
concern over herbicide use, can be well expressed by a news
story quotation of an attorney representing plaintiffs in a suit
against BLM herbicide use in the forests, "There are good
studies on the other side of that question that suggest <u>there is</u>
<u>no safe exposure level to any of the herbicides</u>. And, if you
take those studies and combine them with the <u>20-mile spray</u>
<u>drifts and the mutagenic and carcinogenic properties of the</u>
<u>chemicals</u>, ..." It is this perception and these fears which

provide the basis for public concerns reflected in the news stories quoted above.

There are many episodes or allegations of harm from pesticide use. The roster is a litany of place names: Alsea, Ashford, Broken Bow, Lincoln City, Orleans, Rose Lodge, Roseburg, Swan Valley. The list could go on and on. Although much of this concern has been expressed in Northern California, Oregon and Washington, it ranges from the Pacific states through Montana, Arkansas, and all the way to Newfoundland. All over the United States and Canada there are many citizen groups who fear herbicide use and actively oppose their use through the courts, and hearings of governmental bodies from school boards to county commissioners, on county and statewide ballots, and, as indicated, through confrontation and violence.

The allegations of harm are not so very different than those effects we know can be caused by the herbicide 2,4-D. The allegations of acute effects include headaches, shortness of breath, substernal pain, gastrointestinal distress, nausea, bloody diarrhea, skin rash, parathesis of the extremities, and hysterical anxiety or tachycardia. Parathesis of the extremities is generally exhibited as a numbness or tingling in the fingers and has been observed in cases of extreme or high-level exposures to 2,4-D. Hysterical anxiety is not a comment, but a medical condition which is associated with tachycardia.

The allegations of chronic effects include spontaneous abortion, birth defects, cancer, mutation, and peripheral neuropathy. Peripheral neuropathy is a chronic condition which is a sequela of the acute effect of parathesis of the extremities. Some allegations are categorized as "bizarre" and these are burning and blisters in the mouth, first and second degree skin burns, and coughing of blood. These effects are categorized as bizarre on the basis that when the patient presents himself or herself to a physician's office complaining of these effects, they cannot be detected by the examining physician even though these should be objective, easily identifiable clinical effects. For example, the person will insist they have blisters in their mouth, yet none are present. They may insist they had them yesterday, and they must be gone now. If this were so, there would be evidence of recent mouth blisters. And so on for the other effects.

Many of the concerns are not expressed as allegations of harm to health, but as philosophical positions. Some of these are that there is not a "no-effect level" or such a thing as a safe exposure level. There is a strong philosophical position which states that a person wishes to experience "zero risk". This will take the form of "I don't care if you just proved that this herbicide will not harm us, we don't want to be exposed to any. We want zero risk."

This also takes the form of objection to "chemical trespass". It is, of course, not an unreasonable position to hold that people and things should be prevented from trespassing upon your private property. But when one deals with the concept of chemicals being carried by the air over your property, whether they be herbicides, automobile exhaust, or chemicals emitted by trees in the forest, the concept of zero chemical trespass is difficult to encompass. It might be more useful to determine how much chemical is trespassing, whether there is enough chemical present to cause any biological or biochemical effect, and whether these effects are adverse, rather than holding the concept of zero trespass and zero risk. These philosophies often culminate in a distrust of institutions, whether these be chemical companies, universities, or regulatory agencies, such as the EPA.

The outcome of these concerns and philosophies is that pesticides are no longer being regulated on a national basis by a single agency--the EPA. They are being regulated at all political levels by a great many institutions--from court appeals to county government, from park boards to school boards, from state agencies to congressional committees. These bodies or institutions often usurp the role of EPA in regulation and evaluation of the toxicology of a pesticide and determination of the risk associated with a particular use pattern. At each of these political jurisdiction levels, it is expected by the public that the political body, be it a judge in the courtroom or a park board, have the expertise, the chemical knowledge, and the toxicological knowledge to make or assess a pesticide hazard evaluation which will result in imposing restrictions intended to result in public safety.

I believe that much of this concern has its genesis in the fact that many persons in the public have difficulty in distinguishing between and properly utilizing the concepts of toxicity, hazard, and safety.

Toxicity is the inherent ability of a chemical to cause injury. It is a property of the molecule and does not change. Hazard, on the other hand, involves toxicity but also involves exposure. And exposure involves many factors, some of them difficult to quantify. However, it can be said that hazard is the probability that a chemical will cause injury. The distinction between toxicity and hazard is often omitted in public discussions of risk from the use of herbicides in the forest.

Many people will correctly identify the toxicity or toxic effects which can be elicited from a particular chemical, and leap to the conclusion that there is a hazard without any intervening attempt to identify the exposure levels, and thus the likelihood that enumerated effects will in fact occur. Toxic effects are often hung out like a laundry list, eliciting

concern on the part of the public with no attempt to relate
toxic effect to dose or exposure levels.

Safety is a difficult concept to deal with and absolute
safety is probably impossible to prove. We define safety as the
practical certainty that a chemical will not cause injury. We
cannot absolutely demonstrate that safety exists, because in a
sense it is a negative entity. You can demonstrate through many
laboratory experiments that toxicity exists. But, you cannot
demonstrate that one further experiment will not reveal an
unexpected toxic effect, and therefore you cannot demonstrate
that safety is absolute.

Undergirding this confusion is that the first and simplest
law of toxicology, that there is such a thing as a dose-response
relationship, seems to be a most difficult concept to present to
the public. That an increasing exposure or increasing dose will
result in increasing severity and frequency of effects, and that
conversely decreasing the dose level will result in a decreasing
frequency and severity of effects and that there is a dose level
below which no effects will occur has been demonstrated so often
that it is routinely taken by granted by all of us working in
the field.

However, many of the public are not comfortable with this
as a concept and do not use it in their evaluation of pesticide
risk. Part of the difficulty in their acceptance of the
dose-response relationship and threshold concepts in toxicology
has to do with the fact that there is, of course, a debate in
toxicology as to whether there is a threshold for chemical
injury in the self-replicating diseases such as cancer and
mutagenesis. This has been rapidly extended in the minds of
many people to include all chemical injury and not just
restricted to self-replicating disease. That we can assume
there is no threshold with regard to chemical carcinogenesis,
and still calculate a safe dose level, is not a concept easily
accepted by many of the public. The knowledge that
carcinogenesis follows a dose-response relationship, with or
without a threshold, and that the result of this is that lower
and lower doses result in fewer tumors per individual, a lower
frequency amongst individuals, and, perhaps most importantly, a
longer time to tumor, is not well understood. This results in
the possibility of determining a dose level of a carcinogen
which will not result in the onset of a tumor within the
lifetime of an exposed individual.

A brief summary of the toxicity of the forest herbicide
2,4-D can be presented as follows. Table IV shows the acute
LD-50 values of most of the phenoxy herbicices. These range
from 300 mg/kg for 2,4,5-T and 375 mg/kg for 2,4-D up to 6400
mg/kg for Bifenox. It is useful to set the acute oral toxicity
for 2,4-D in the context of other phenoxy herbicides and in
relation to other pesticides so the public can gain a perception
of where 2,4-D fits on a scale of relative values with regard to

the onset of acute toxicity symptoms and to show that all
phenoxies are not identical in their acute toxicity but cover a
wide range of toxicities.

Table IV. Acute Oral LD_{50} Values (mg/kg)

PHENOXY HERBICIDES

Herbicide	Value	Herbicide	Value
2,4,5-T	300	MCPA	700
2,4-D	375	MCPB	680
2,4,5-TP	375	MCPP	930
2,4-DB	500	Bifenox	6,400

The acute toxicity values for 2,4-D are expanded to cover a
number of species in Table V and show that the 375 mg/kg we
commonly use is the acute oral toxicity for the mouse. The
chemical is not that toxic to nearly all other species, from the
rat, to the rabbit, to the guinea pig. The one exception to
this is 2,4-D toxicity to the dog, which is greater than to the
mouse, having a toxicity of 100 mg/kg. It is considered that
this is because dogs, as a species, do not excrete aryl acids as
do the rodents--the mouse, rat, and rabbit-- nor do they excrete
these acids as readily as does man. Sometimes we find that
pesticide users are resistant to accepting the knowledge that a
herbicide such as 2,4-D is a toxic chemical and that it can kill
animal organisms as well as plants. It should be obvious that
any chemical which has an LD-50 (for any laboratory test
animal), is capable of causing death to animals.

Table V. Median Lethal Doses of 2,4-D

Mouse	375 mg/kg
Rat	666 mg/kg
Rabbit	800 mg/kg
Guinea Pig	1,000 mg/kg
Dog	100 mg/kg
Monkey	ca. 400 mg/kg
Chicken	ca. 900 mg/kg

Table VI shows that the toxicity of 2,4-D is not restricted
to mammals which are commonly used as test organisms in the
laboratory, but is also capable of being lethal to birds, fish,
aquatic insects, and aquatic crustaceans. This point must
sometimes be made quite strongly to this chemical's users so

that they will want to use safeguards in its application to
prevent injury to these organisms.

Table VI. 2,4-D Toxicity to Environmental Organisms

Species	Toxicity
Mammals	375 - 1,000 mg/kg
Birds	540 - 2,000 mg/kg
Fish	1 - 435 ppm--48 hr
Aquatic Insects	2 - ppm--96 hr
Crustacean	60 - ppm--48 hr

It is interesting to consider the symptoms which are known
to occur in humans and have been demonstrated in cases of
overexposure, particularly in cases of deliberate ingestion of
2,4-D, and have been demonstrated with laboratory animals.
These symptoms are irritation at the point of contact: the
skin, respiratory tract and the gastrointestinal tract. 2,4-D
can also cause nausea, vomiting, muscle twitching and pain,
muscle stiffness (myotonia), fatigue, and nerve damage. It is
important to realize these symptoms occur usually at only high
doses; that is, high in relation to the LD-50 values. The onset
of symptoms is usually at or over 100 mg/kg for 2,4-D, or
approximately 1/3 of the LD-50 value. This is a rather high
exposure value.
     However, most public concern does not center around death
or other acute intoxication symptoms, but rather those chronic
injuries which we term as irreversible. These are
carcinogenesis (cancer), teratogenesis (birth defects), or
mutagenesis (genetic defects). There have been three good
studies involving the ability of 2,4-D to cause cancer. The
conclusion by the authors of these three studies is that there
is no evidence that 2,4-D causes cancer. However, the study
design was such that they were not adequate to prove that 2,4-D
could not cause cancer, and as a result, further cancer studies
were required by the EPA which should provide a definitive
answer.
     Since the discovery by Dr. Bruce Ames of the Ames test for
mutagenesis of chemicals, there has been a proliferation of a
great many types of laboratory tests to discover whether a
chemical is mutagenic. Examination of 2,4-D mutagenicity tests,
reveal that of 18 tests, 15 were negative and 3 were positive.
This places 2,4-D in the category of being a weak mutagen and it
has an insufficient number of positive responses to trigger
action against it on the basis of its being a mutagenic
chemical.

There is in the public mind a misperception as to the implication of a chemical being determined to be a mutagenic chemical. This term raises fear of a production of monsters arising from mutation or the production of a new genetic or biochemical disease such as Tay-Sachs disease or Sickle-cell anemia. To reach such a conclusion is a long leap from a positive mutagenic assay. The principle piece of information gained from a mutagenic assay is the probability that the chemical will be a carcinogen and should be thoroughly tested for carcinogenicity. But, our knowledge of this field is insufficient to reach firm conclusions about the possibility or probability of an increasing rate of mutations.

An important and recurrent concern on the part of the public is that of birth defects and miscarriages and whether they can be caused by herbicides such as 2,4-D. 2,4-D most certainly can cause birth defects, and has in tests with laboratory animals. It is a teratogenic chemical and the onset of teratogenic effects will occur at a dose level of about 75 mg/kg, repeated daily, in rats from the 6th to the 15th day of pregnancy. The corresponding human dose time would be the 15th through the 60th day of pregnancy. At a dose level of 20 mg/kg, there is no teratogenic effect, and this is considered to be the no-observable- effect level, NOEL, for 2,4-D. This is the most sensitive NOEL. We use this NOEL in all of our risk calculations and believe that it pertains to birth defects, spontaneous abortions, and miscarriages, even though it only applies to only a small portion of the population: those persons who are pregnant and in their 15th to 60th day of pregnancy. There is no argument in the field of toxicology as to whether there is a threshold for the onset of teratogenesis.

The principle public concern with regard to risk from herbicide application in the forest is not the overt, or occupational, exposure to pesticide applicators or to persons who might be in the spray zone. It is the possible injury from pesticide drift at a distance of a few hundred yards or a quarter of a mile, up to 5 to 20 miles. All aerially-applied pesticides will drift for some distance, whether they be applied by fixed-wing craft or helicopter.

It is sometimes difficult for pesticide applicators to realize that chemical spray will drift farther than it appears to be drifting from observation of the spray. One might observe a spray drifting for a few tens or hundreds of feet at most, but chemical analysis can reveal that some small amount of the spray, unobserved by the eye, can continue to drift for long distances. This distance has often been measured to be up to a mile, and in many cases, several miles. The question is not how far the chemical drifts, but how much drifts and what is the effect of the amount that drifts a given distance.

There are many variables affecting deposit from drift of pesticide spray and these variables will seldom be quantified or

known in advance at a given spray site. This makes it difficult
to predict exactly the amount of exposure to expect from a
proposed treatment. One can, at the minimum, show a range of
deposit or exposure levels arrived at in different
circumstances. Table VII presents three types of results:
drift levels from a single experiment in Oregon under high wind
conditions, an average of a number of experiments with coarse
sprays under typical agricultural spray conditions, and the
average of a few (four) trials under forest conditions on steep
slopes with a five (insecticide) spray application.

Table VII. Drift Deposit

Distance Downwind	Single Trial Flat Land Medium Spray High Wind Small Target		Multiple Trials Flat Land Coarse Spray Small Target		Multiple Trials Steep Land Fine Spray Large Target	
	% of Dep.	ng/ft^2	%	ng/ft^2	%	ng/ft^2
1/4 mi.	0.01	1	0.001	100	2	200
1/2 mi.	0	0	0.0005	20	0.5	50
1 mi.	0.0	0	0.0001	10	0.15	15

The first column of drift data is from the medium spray
(300-400μ) experiment conducted mainly under wind conditions of
10 to 15 mph, or high wind conditions in Dallas, Oregon by
Phipps, Montgomery and Witt. (1). The drift in the first 50
feet downwind is 250 millipounds per acre, or 25% of amount
deposited on target. The level of deposit drops off rapidly and
is about 10% of that value at 165 feet (20 millipounds). As
shown in Table VII, the deposit at 1/4 mi. is 0.1
millipounds/acre or 1 μg/square foot and decreases to zero, or
less than 1 μg/square foot at 1/2 mile and beyond. This
experiment shows less drift for the longer distances than
expected, and is probably because of the high wind. Although a
high wind velocity will cause more drift, it may result in less
deposit from drift (beyond the first 200 feet or so) because the
short transit time over a given point results in less time of
exposure to the drift cloud.
    For the purpose of attempting to predict the amount of
drift one might expect in general from a spray operation, it is
more useful to composite the data from a number of drift
experiments into a generalized curve and extrapolate from that
to the operation being considered. Table VII shows such data
developed by Dr. Norman Akesson from the University of
California, Davis. (2,3,4). This data is for a coarse spray

with a diameter of 900 microns used on agricultural, or level, crop lands.

The expected levels of drift deposit are from 10 ng/square foot at 1/4 mile to 1 ng/square foot at 1 mile. In utilizing averaged data it must be understood that variations in drop size, application methods, meteorological conditions, or terrain can increase or decrease the drift deposition by 10 fold or one can imagine, in oder to be ultra conservative, even as much as 1,000 fold.

Another factor that will increase the drift is the target size or number of spray swaths. If the spray block is more than about 200 yards wide, then the expected deposit amount could increase by a factor of 2- to 10-fold. There is a need for a great deal more drift data and for it to be summarized into generalized drift curves with some limitations placed on them as to the upper and lower limits of expected spray drift amounts under a variety of conditions so that they can be applied to various spray situations. There is not a great deal of drift data specific to forest spraying.

One set of good spray experiments was also conducted by Dr. Norm Akesson and reported in 1979 and 1982. (5,6). Table VII shows the deposit levels for the mean drift values in a set of experiments in forest land conducted by him with a fine spray of 75-150 microns median diameter on steep terrain which had a slope of 700 to 1000 feet per mile. These data result from spraying very large tracts, up to three miles in diameter, and apply to insecticide sprays, rather than herbicide sprays.

It is important for the public to recognize that there is no fixed distance or buffer zone for a safe distance to provide protection from spray drift. This will be a function of the pesticide being used, its toxicity and environmental behavior such as bioaccumulation, the nature and sensitivity of the downwind sites, and the nature of the application method, meteorological conditions, and so on.

The interpretation of the effects of such drift, particularly its potential for adverse effects on human health, is dependent on some of the parameters of environmental behavior shown on Table VIII. The dose is given at 2 lbs/acre and translated into a deposit level of 20 mg/square foot, which is more useful in the interpretation of exposure data. The figures given for the deposit amount from spray drift at 100 yards and 1/2 mile are the figures for drift from a coarse spray on flat land for small target areas and are average drift amounts. The figure of 20 mg/kg is the NOEL for 2,4-D.

Table VIII. Environmental Behavior

Dose	–		20 mg/square foot
Deposit	–	10–100 ppm	
T-1/2	–	plants, litter, soil	2 weeks–2 months
		water	1 week
		mammals	1 day
Drift	–	total	0.25 – 4.0%
		100 yards (avg.)	1 μg/square foot
		1/2 mile (avg.)	20 ng/square foot
NOEL	–		20 mg/kg/day

The exposure for a person standing directly under a spray plane with 50% of their skin area exposed is shown in Table IX. This results in a risk calculation giving a margin of safety of 100. Or, more exactly, 100 per day if repeated daily, because the margin of safety assumes a daily exposure for a given period of time during the pregnancy. This calculation does not include exposure from inhalation of drift particles because, as shown by Akesson, this is a negligible amount in drift exposures. Exposure from inhalation in occupational exposure by a sprayman handling a spray nozzle may be as high as 1-3% of his dermal exposure, but generally is well below that from inhalation from drift exposures.

Table IX. 2,4-D Risk of Birth Defects or SAB

Direct Deposit - under a spray plane

Assumptions   – 2 lb/acre (20 mg/ft^2)
              female, enceinte, 15–60th day
              50% of skin exposed (10 ft^2)
              weight, 110 lb (50 kg)

Calculations – 20 mg/ft^2 x 10 ft^2 ÷ 50 kg = 4 mg/kg
              Dermal penetration = 5%;
                0.05 x 4 mg/kg = 0.2 mg/kg

              NOEL for 2,4-D = 20 mg/kg

$$\text{Margin of Safety} = \frac{\text{NOEL}}{\text{Dose}} = \frac{20 \text{ mg/kg}}{0.2 \text{ mg/kg}} = 100/\text{day}$$

Exposure from deposit directly under a spray plane would have to be considered an unusual exposure situation. A more common situation would be that resulting from drift. Table X shows a summary of a similar risk calculation resulting from the subject being 1/2 mile downwind. That results in a margin of safety of 100,000,000. Again, one should caution the reader that you can make different assumptions about the deposit of drift than those made herein and arrive at deposits from drift being 20 to 1000 times greater, which would result in a margin of safety of only 100,000.

Table X. 2,4-D Risk -- Drift

Deposit   - 2 lb/acre = 20 mg/ft^2 VDM =$_2$900 μ
Distance - 1/2 mile Downwind = 20 ng/ft^2
Subject   - female, pregnant, 15-60th day,
             50 kg, 10 ft^2 dermal surface
Dose   - 10 x 200 x 0.05 x 1/50 = 0.2 ng/ft^2

Margin of Safety = $\dfrac{\text{NOEL}}{\text{Dose}}$ $\dfrac{20 \text{ mg/kg/day}}{0.2 \text{ mg/kg}}$

An area of concern with regard to 2,4-D which is commonly encountered, is the drift of 2,4-D into surface water to be used for drinking water. Table XI shows a calculation of risk involving drinking water which has been subject to direct spray from aircraft at the rate of 20 mg/ft^2 and, given the assumptions shown, results in a margin of safety of about 700. The same water exposed to drift with a 200 foot buffer zone would have a margin of safety of 7,000,000. It should be pointed out that these are maximum concentrations that would exist in a plug of water that would pass by a given water-intake point within 10 minutes. The possibility of using that water, contaminated at those levels over a period of time sufficient to replicate the chronic exposure experiments on which the NOEL is based would be very slight to non-existent.

Table XI. 2,4-D Risk -- Water

Direct Spray   -   Overflight, 1/2 mile of stream

Stream   -   1 foot deep, velocity 3 mph
Deposit   -   20 mg/ft^2 = 700 ppb = 0.7 ppm
Consume   -   2 qt/day, 50 kg = 0.028 mg/kg

$$\text{Margin of Safety} = \frac{\text{NOEL}}{\text{Dose}} = \frac{230 \text{ mg/kg/day}}{0.028 \text{ mg/kg}} = 714$$

DWS = 0.1 ppm = 100 ppb, MOS = 5,000
                 Drift 200' downwind
                 DG, JB and Visc. Ag.
Deposit 2 μg/ft^2 = 0.07 ppb
Margin of Safety = 7,140,000

We have shown in three scenarios that the margin of safety
for 2,4-D exposure could range from 100 to 10,000,000, and yet
we have not related the magnitude of these values to other
common margins of safety which people might encounter in their
daily life.

Table XII shows some margins of safety calculated by Dr.
Sheldon Wagner of Oregon State University, for a set of common
prescription medicines. These include caffeine when prescribed
at the dose level for which it is prescribed as a medicine,
antibiotics, tranquilizers, vitamins, and other drugs. Notice
that the margins of safety range from 1/2 through 100, 200, and
up to 1000.

Table XII. Comparative Margin of Safety

Chemical	Teratogenic Dose		Clinical Dose		MOS by Dose
Caffeine	75	mg/kg	2.5	mg/kg	30
Chlorotetracycline	10	mg/kg	20	mg/kg	0.5
Diazepam	200	mg/kg	0.8	mg/kg	250
Phenytoin	75	mg/kg	6	mg/kg	12.5
Vitamin A	35,000	I.U.	8,000	I.U.	1,000*
Prednisolone	2.5	mg/kg	0.2	mg/kg	125
Reserpine	1.5	mg/kg	0.02	mg/kg	75
Tetracycline	40	mg/kg	20	mg/kg	2
Salicylate	300	mg/kg	50	mg/kg	6

*Adjusted to I.U./kg

When one compares the risk of caffeine as taken in one cup of
coffee to that from the forest herbicide, 2,4-D, one finds that
the margin of safety for teratogenesis or birth defects ranges
from 5 to 16 (Table XIII).

Table XIII. Comparative Risk -- Coffee

Caffeine is a teratogen
  MDL = 75 mg/kg   (2,4-D = 75 mg/kg)
  NOEL = 25 mg/kg   (2,4-D = 20 mg/kg)
  Dose = one cup of coffee
         Bertrand 25 mg/kg/liter = 5 mg/kg/cup

Margin of Safety $= \dfrac{25}{1.5 - 5} = 5 - 16$

Many persons consider such comparisons invidious because they
feel that they have a choice as to whether or not to drink a cup
of coffee, but not as to whether they will be exposed to a
herbicide spray drift. The point is not to enter a discussion
of that philosophy, but to compare a commonly encountered
phenomena by carrying out the same type of analysis as we do for
pesticides, and thereby obtain comparable Margin of Safety
values, independent of philosophical differences. Philosophy
does not change toxic action, or the lack of it.
     The value of 100 is generally considered a good margin of
safety. This value may be increased depending on the quality of
data undergirding the risk evaluation, or the type of injury
sustained from exposure to the chemical. A socially acceptable
margin of safety may be increased for unwilling exposure over
the margin of safety acceptable for occupational exposure.
However, a comparison of the margin of safety from drinking one
cup of coffee or any other common activity allows the public to
compare what may be an unusual exposure to them, herbicide
drift, to a common phenomenon in our society.
     One can also compare the margin of safety of a herbicide
such as exposure to 2,4-D from direct spray at 2 lbs/acre to
another common experience, taking aspirin according to the label
directions, 2 tablets every 4 hours. Table XIV shows that the
margins of safety for aspirin taken at this rate are
considerably smaller than the margins of safety for direct spray
exposure to 2,4-D. These comparisons of MOS should assist the
public in developing a frame of reference for what constitutes a
large or small Margin of Safety.

Table XIV. Comparative Margins of Safety

Chemical	Exposure	Margin of Safety	
		Death	Birth Defects
Aspirin	2 tab./4 hours	3.5	1.3-6.8
2,4-D	direct spray	625	100
2,4-D/Aspirin	RATIO	178:1	15:1

Identification of risk levels and margins of safety in comparisons with other commonly encountered chemicals do not finally solve the problem whether a particular chemical risk constitutes a socially acceptable risk. This must finally be determined in the social institutions mentioned earlier at the various political jurisdictions. Whether a risk will be socially acceptable depends not only on the level of risk, which we have dealt with here, but on the nature of the risk, on who assumes the risk, who receives the benefit, and one's personal philosophy of accepting any risk versus zero risk.

Perhaps the dilemma is best summed up and its timeliness underscored by an editorial which appeared in this city on the first day of this symposium in which the mayor of Seattle, in relation to a local controversy regarding the spraying of carbaryl (Sevin) for gypsy moth eradication, was quoted as saying, "Carbaryl poses no significant public health hazard--even to children, the elderly, or the pregnant." Nonetheless, he opposed aerial spraying of carbaryl, stating in effect, "It is harmless, but lets not use it." The editorial continued, "In politics, perception, not reality, is everything."

The lesson for scientists involved in these issues is that we must present what we learn here in a clear enough way so that public perceptions of pesticide application, toxicity, and risk are congruent with reality. The public's social decisions regarding pesticide use will then be based on a careful appraisal of the risk or margin of safety, and not on fear and fear alone.

Literature Cited

1. Phipps, Frank, in "A Study of Drift of Aqueous and Propylene Glycol 2,4-D Amine Formulation from Aerial Application"; Montgomery, M.M.; Witt, J.M.; Oregon State University, Dept. of Agricultural Chemistry, 1981; Unpublished data.

2. Akesson, N.B., in "What's Happening in Aerial Application
    Research"; Yates, W.E.; Cowden, personal communication.
3. Wilce, S.E., in "Drop Size Control and Aircraft Spray
    Equipment"; Akesson, N.B.; Yates, W.E.; Christensen, P.;
    Cowden, R.E.; Hudson, D.C.; Weigt, G.I.; Agricultural
    Aviation, 1974; Vol. 16 (1), p. 7-16.
4. "A Study of the Efficiency of the Use of Pesticides in
    Agriculture", Von Rumker, R.; Kelso, G.L.; 1975,
    EPA-540/9-75-025.
5. Yates, W.E., in "Atmospheric Transport of Sprays from
    Helicopter Applications in Mountainous Terrain";
    Akesson, N.B.; Cowden, R.E.; Am. Soc. Agric. Engineers,
    1978; p. 78-1504.
6. Gharserni, M., in "Estimating Drift and Exposure Due to
    Aerial Application of Insecticides in Forests"; Painter,
    P.; Powers, M.; Akesson, N.B.; DeLarco, M.; Env. Sci. &
    Tech., 1982; Vol. 16 (8), p. 510.

RECEIVED October 3, 1983

Ecotoxicity of Adjuvants Used in Aerial Spraying

PEARL WEINBERGER
Department of Biology, University of Ottawa, Ottawa, K1N 6N5, Canada

R. GREENHALGH
Chemistry and Biology Institute, Agriculture Canada, Ottawa, K1A 0C6, Canada

The effects of the adjuvants in the fenitrothion and
aminocarb formulations used in the Spruce Budworm
Spray Programme in Canada were determined in terms
of degradation of the parent pesticides, bioaccumulation and perturbation of biomass, development,
photosynthesis or ultrastructural integrity of some
aquatic and terrestrial non-target phytobiota. The
persistence and degradation of fenitrothion and
aminocarb was altered by the adjuvants. A toxicity
rating indicated nonylphenol > Cyclosol 63 = Aerotex
3470 > Atlox 3409 in the range of 1.0, 5.0 and 40
$\mu g/ml$ respectively. No acute physiological effects
were observed following treatments with the pesticides alone (>40 $\mu g/ml$). Apart from Dowanol $1X10^{-3}$
$\mu g/ml$, the adjuvants perturbed all the physiological functions monitored and led to gross ultrastructural damage.

Pesticides are the "active" chemicals used by forest pest managers
to contain and reduce tree loss from pest predation. They are
usually marketed in formulations which also contain adjuvants.
The adjuvants ("inerts") are added to the active compounds to
impart storage stability and enhance performance characteristics
so that the dilution of the formulation into the final spray mix
is facilitated, evaporation and surface tension is reduced and
the permeation of the active ingredient through intervening
biotic membranes is enhanced (1).
    Field observations during aerial spray applications have
demonstrated that anywhere from 15-75% of the pesticide mix ad-
mitted from the aircraft reaches the forest canopy (2). In some
cases under unstable conditions, "on-target" deposit was less
than 2% of the total emitted material. The portion of the spray
deposit that does not land "on-target" (i.e. on conifer foliage)
may be transported to aquatic and other non-target habitats.
Overall, the amount of adjuvants in the mixes that deposits onto

0097–6156/84/0238–0351$06.00/0
© 1984 American Chemical Society

plant foliage represents about 6% of the formulated pesticides
(2). It has been estimated that in 1966, in the U.S. alone, this
amounts to about 2.7×10^7 Kg of adjuvants (1). These adjuvants,
which are detergents and solvents are surface active agents which
are chemically similar insofar as they both have groups which are
strongly lipophilic or lipophobic, and may have other groups
which are less strongly non-polar or polar. The less complex
surface active agents are classified as anionic, cationic, ampho-
lytic, or non-ionic depending on the nature of the ionic charge,
or lack of ionization on the hydrophilic end of the molecule.

There are thousands of surfactants and solvents in use; some
of these are single chemical compounds, many more consist of
mixes of similar chemicals, while the composition of others,
particularly oil distillates which may contain unknown impurities,
vary with the source and batch used.

The containment of infestations of the spruce budworm is the
major concern of Canadian forest spray programs (3). By 1976,
the total area of severe budworm infestations in Canada exceeded
30 million ha, of which about 5 million ha were in New Brunswick,
12 million ha in Quebec and over 13 million ha in Ontario. Smaller infestations (less than 1 million ha) occurred in Nova
Scotia, Prince Edward Island and Newfoundland (4). The vast area
involved has necessitated the use of aircraft for insecticide dispersal. Direct contamination of aquatic habitats situated within
the spray region has been reported following aerial deposition of
fenitrothion, the favored pesticide, while indirect contamination
may have resulted from spray drift or from surface run-off following rainfall (5, 6).

Two pesticides have been registered for use in this program,
namely fenitrothion (0,0-dimethyl-0- (4-nitro-m-totyl phospho-
rothiote) and aminocarb (4-dimethyl amino-m-totyl methylcarbamate).

Fenitrothion is applied either in a water emulsion or as an
oil solution. The most frequently used fenitrothion formulation
is composed of the "active" material mixed with the adjuvants
Atlox and Aerotex in the ratio of 11.5:1.5:1.5 w/v/v respectively.
Aerotex is added to dissolve fenitrothion. Atlox, a detergent, is
added to emulsify the Aerotex-fenitrothion solution in water.
Since 1980, Aerotex has been replaced by Dowanol in fenitrothion
formulations for experimental use.

The aminocarb formulation presently in use, Matacil 1.8D OSC
contains the adjuvants nonylphenol, a surfactant and "585" oil as
diluent. In 1981, a new aminocarb "flowable" formulation which
does not contain nonylphenol was introduced for experimentation.

When diluted for spraying a single swathe coverage would give
concentrations of adjuvant ranging from 0.5 to 1.0 mg/L at ground
level if unimpeded by forest canopy. Multiple coverage has been
reported over bodies of water used as boundary markers for spray
blocks (3, 4). Surface tension, salinity, pH, localized climatic
and topographic effects may well modify these values (2).

Extensive testing of pesticides and their formulations is required before they are granted registration in Canada. However, no data is presently obtained on the chemical or biological effects of the final spray mix which contain more adjuvant. This is surprising as in some mixes, such as the Matacil 1.8D OSC, the final adjuvant content is greater than that of the pesticide. This lack of concern is underlined by the fact that there is little data on the total amounts of adjuvants released into the environment even though it has been estimated that between 1965-1969 between $4X10^8$ and $9X10^8$ L of surfactants had been used in pesticide spray operations alone (7). Concern that bodies of water, aquifers and forested areas may be perturbed by some adjuvants led to the present ongoing research program which has focused solely on some typical non-target phytobiota likely to be found in many of these habitats. The aquatic non-target test organisms included the aquatic alga Chlorella pyrenoidosa Chick, Chlamydomonas reinhardtii Dang and Scenedesmus obtususculus Chod. These organisms, because of their small size, have a high surface to volume ratio and relatively large amounts of lipids in their membranes and are thus sensitive to modification. The aquatic macrophytes Lemna minor L, Ceratophyllum demersum L, Elodea canadensis L, Valisneria spp and Myriophyllum spps, are all ubiquitous in spray regions either surface dwelling or occupying the epilimneon and so are vulnerable to the higher concentration of surfactants at interfaces. Jack pine (Pinus banksiana Lamb) and paper birch (Betula alleghaniensis Marsh) seeds were chosen as the representative non-target tree seeds as they are commonly found in the conifer and mixed forest regions subject to budworm infestation.

Adjuvants: Aerotex 3470 manufactured by Texaco Chem. Co. and Cyclosol 63, a product of Shell Canada, are high boiling point aromatic solvent distillates obtained as a by-product of refining crude oil. They contain a mix of over 100 components including alkylated naphthalenes, benzenes, fluorenes and phenantharenes as well as some of the parent hydrocarbons, (8). Naphthalene has been shown to be highly interactive with marine and fresh water aquatic life (9, 10), and to inhibit the growth, photosynthesis and ATP synthesis of algae (10, 11).

Atlox 3470, a product of ICI Ltd. is classed as an anionic/non-ionic surfactant comprised mainly of dodecyl benzene sulfonate (anionic) and a nonylphenol ethoxylate of polyethylene glycol (non-ionic emulsifyer). Recent evidence strongly suggests that the active agent in the viral enhancement coincident with Reye's syndrome is a polyethylene glycol derived from the polyethylene moiety of the parent emulsifyer when the number of repeating ethoxy units in the polymer approaches 9 or 10 (12).

Dowanol, manufactured by Dow Chemicals, is a single-component solvent, tripropyleneglycol methylether, of relatively high purity.

Nonylphenol, a product of Union Carbide, Canada Ltd., consists
of a mix of p-substituted monoalkyl nonyphenols, (randomly
branched), with approximately 3% of the o-isomer and 4% dinonyl-
phenol also represent. Apart from Dowanol, all the adjuvants
mentioned contain minor variable amounts of undefined contaminants
which are a function of the well head source and batch from which
they were distilled (Aerotex, Cyclosol) or the method of synthesis (Atlox and nonylphenol). These chemicals and related compounds are also widely used in a wide range of household products
including detergents, cleaners, shampoos, foods and other consu-
mer and commercial products.

Diluent oil 585, marketed by Shell Canada Ltd., is a 585°F
distillation product of crude oil. At this distillation temperature the polynuclear aromatics such as the naphthalenes are not
carried over into the end product. This distillation temperature
also reduces the formation of double bonds, thereby reducing
biotic toxicity.

Chemical Interactions: The time to half degradation ($t\frac{1}{2}$) of
fenitrothion and aminocarb varies from several hours (13, 14) to
weeks (15, 16) depending upon the intensity of sunlight (photolysis), pH, and turbulence of the medium (16). These values are
modified by the formulation adjuvants, such that under controlled
environmental conditions the persistence of the pesticides was
increased at least 2-fold. The $t\frac{1}{2}$ for fenitrothion increased
from 1.7 d to 3.8 d in the Aerotex formulation and >7 d in the
Dowanol mix, and the aminocarb $t\frac{1}{2}$ was increased from 3.8 d to 7 d
(17). The fate of these chemicals in the presence of adjuvants
and plants is also changed such that the ratio of their non-polar
(NP) ethyl acetate soluble fractions to polar (P) (ethyl acetate
insoluble) fractions is substantially modified during degradation
in water (17). In the presence of Aerotex, the fenitrothion NP:P
fractions were as 3.5:1.0; with Dowanol substituted in the mix,
the ratio was 1.5:1.0. Nonylphenol modified aminocarb degradation
the NP fraction was 3-4-fold higher when the formulated Matacil
1.8D OSC mix was used as compared to systems containing aminocarb
alone; see Figure 1.

Bioaccumulation: All classes of surfactant are active surface
tension depressants. At the critical micelle concentration (CMC)
abrupt changes occur in the characteristic properties of surfactants such that surface and interfacial tensions in an aqueous
system are at their minimum while osmotic pressure and surface
detergent properties are significantly increased. The CMC for
most surfactants is reached around 0.01% (18, 19). These effects
have an impact on the potential for bioaccumulation of the pesticide, and in the organisms monitored the presence of Dowanol and
nonylphenol increased the accumulation of fenitrothion and
aminocarb at least 20-300% respectively, over the accumulation
obtained in their absence (20). In effect, these adjuvants

increased the partition coefficients of the pesticides in the algal membrane lipids by reducing the surface tension around the bounding membranes. Only 30% of the accumulated pesticide was desorbed when the algae were placed in clean media (20). The retained 60-70% of the accumulated pesticide was only degraded following senescence of the organism, or via its metabolism in phytophagous organisms. Thus, phytophagous and bottom feeding fish may be at greater risk than would have been evaluated from purely chemical considerations.

Biomass: A range of phytotoxic and growth inhibitory effects have been attributed to surfactants (1). Increased lag phase growth was observed in Chlamydomonas and Chlorella attributable to > 1 µg/ml nonylphenol (20), 5 µg/ml Aerotex (10) > 7.5 µg/ml Cyclosol (17). No population growth effects were observed with Atlox or 585 oil < 30 µg/ml, or Dowanol < 1000 µg/ml. Both in the algal cells and in a range of aquatic plants initially exposed to surfactants and observed over a period of 21 days, a depressed biomass was coincident with increasing adjuvant concentrations. In all the aquatic plants, treatment with 6.25 g/ml nonylphenol led to complete bleaching. In Lemna, root friability and an 80% reduction in frond production appeared within 24 hours of exposure (21).

The onset of germination of the tree seeds was unaffected by treatments of up to 50 µg/ml of nonylphenol, but subsequent seedling growth was greatly impaired. The birch seed embryos were markedly affected by 5 µg/ml nonylphenol or 20 µg/ml Cyclosol, Figure 2. The earliest effects were seen in the emergent roots. Apart from Dowanol, the other adjuvants produced less marked dwarfism at a threshold of 50 µg/ml. Dowanol at concentrations below 100 µg/ml had no effect. Higher concentrations were not tested (17). Endo et al (22) and Parr (1) also noted that roots are early indicators of surfactant phytotoxicity.

ATP: The total ATP Content of an organism is a measure of its metabolic status (23). Comparatively low values indicate a loss of vigor.

At field relevant concentrations of adjuvants there were only minor effects in the aquatic and terrestrial test organisms. Reduced growth of these phytobiota was observed at higher concentrations and within 1 hr of exposure to the more toxic adjuvants this was reflected in abnormal levels of in vivo, ATP. In these, Aerotex (2 µg/ml), nonylphenol (2.5 µg/ml) and Matacil 1.8D (2.50 µg/ml nonylphenol) led to a 20% reduction in the ATP content of the aquatics and disruption of the normal sequence of ATP production in the tree seeds (17). Dowanol alone did not perturb the system at concentrations less than 100 µg/ml; higher concentrations were not tested.

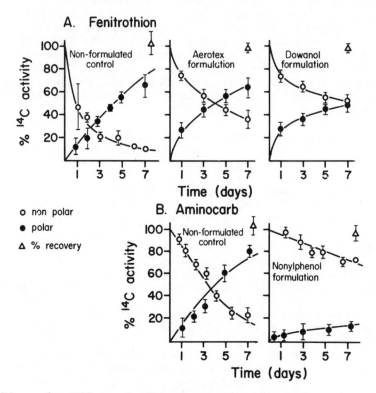

Figure 1. Effect of adjuvants on the degradation of
fenitrothion and aminocarb (17).

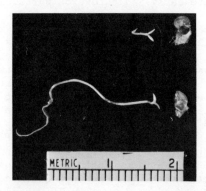

Figure 2. Control and treated seedlings of paper birch
(Betula alleghaniensis Marsh.) dwarfed following exposure
to 5 µg/ml nonylphenol or 20 µg/ml Cyclosol.

Conductivity and Ion Leakage: The effects of the surfactants on ion leakage is an early indicator of membrane perturbation. St. John et al (24) used isolated higher plant cells to study surfactant-permeability interactions. No relationship to the ionic type of the surfactant was obtained but a correlation was observed between changes in ion leakage and phytotoxicity. Tree seedlings of Jack pine were unaffected by exposure to 10 µg/ml Atlox or 50 µg/ml aminocarb or fenitrothion, Aerotex (5-10 µg/ml) enhanced leakage 30%, other treatments depressed ion leakage. By contrast, Paper birch seedlings exposed to aminocarb (50 µg/ml) showed a 50% increase in ion leakage; when treated with aminocarb as a component in the Matacil 1.8D mix, depressed leakage was observed, and this effect was mainly attributable to the nonylphenol, in the formulation (17).

The potassium membrane pump mediates transport both intracellularly and between the root/soil water interface. Changes in the leakage of this ion is indicative of cellular perturbation. Nonylphenol (15 µg/ml) and Atlox (10 µg/ml) increased K^+ ion leakage 2 to 3-fold over control roots. The Atlox effect was possibly due to the non-ionic nonylphenol ethoxylate of the polyethylene glycol component. Ion leakage of this order of magnitude was also obtained with Cyclosol 20 µg/ml and Atlox 10 µg/ml. Other non-ionic surfactants have been shown to effect electrolyte leakage from roots (25, 26). Atlox has also been implicated in causing fluid loss and electrolyte imbalance in animal cells (12). Changes in the permeability and integrity of cellular membranes following nonylphenol treatment has also been noted in shrimp, clams and salmon (27). Hutchinson et al (27) obtained a positive correlation between the lipophilicity of test hydrocarbons and their ability to induce leakage. Mg^{++} ion leakage was not affected by exposure to the range of surfactants (17). Although there are exceptions, anionic surfactants are generally less phytotoxic and more species specific (1, 28).

Photosynthesis: Surfactants that alter membrane permeability are likely to affect not only the plasmalemma of bounding cells, but may penetrate the cytosol and affect membrane bound organelles such as the chloroplast and its thyllakoid membranes. A rapid and sensitive method for monitoring the integrity and functional ability of cells to photosynthesize utilizes a miniaturized fluorometer, which can monitor changes in the intensity of chlorophylla fluorescence (29). Fluorescence transients (changes in fluorescence intensity over time) are sensitive indicators of photosynthesis and have helped unravel some of the light reactions in photosynthesis (30). Although fluorometric analysis of algal photosynthesis has been well documented (29, 31), the application of the method to assess the relative algicidal activity of environmental pollutants was first successfully employed by Moody et al (32). Complete suppression of photosynthesis was obtained with parent pesticides and adjuvants. Nonylphenol 0.5 to 0.75 µg/ml

1 h exposure caused total cessation of photosynthesis in the algae Chlamydomonas. The benzene and naphthalene constituents of Aerotex also suppressed fluorescence and a relationship between the concentrations required to do this and their octanol-water partition coefficients were obtained (32), Figure 3. Inhibition of photosynthetic activity by surfactants was also reported by St. John (24).

Transmission Electron Microscopy: The primary site of surfactant activity appears to be the cell membrane (25, 32). Other effects have been reported such as the denaturation of proteins, inactivation of enzymes and inhibition of mitosis.

Membrane integrity was lost and mitochondrial identity difficult to delineate when algal cells were exposed to 1.0-1.5 μg/ml nonylphenol, alone, or at this concentration in the Matacil 1.8D OSC mix, 5 μg/ml Cyclosol or Aerotex, 40 μg/ml Atlox or 585 oil, 50-60 μg/ml aminocarb or fenitrothion (17).

Typically, at these concentrations some membrane damage was found and in some cases it was widespread. Following exposure to 1.0 to 1.5 μg/ml nonylphenol, more than 20% of the cells manifested an unusual ultrastructural deformation of their flagellae indicative of microtubular damage, Figure 4a and b. Similar effects were also observed when C. angulosa was exposed to naphthalene or crude oil (34, 35). Membrane perturbations of this type has been related to their lipophilia, as they are sorbed, so the membranes expand thereby impairing their function (8).

The mechanism of mitochondrial swelling in animal cells has been examined intensively (36). This phenomenon is less well documented for algal cells.

General Comments: The species of Chlamydomonas and Chlorella used in this study have a high lipid and protein content in their cell walls and little cellulose (28). The lipid content facilitates the penetration of hydrophobic surface active agents, and the proteins contribute to the destruction of wall integrity as they tend to unfold under adjuvant stress with consequent destruction of structural and metabolically active protein sites. The cell wall proteins with metabolic (enzyme or channel gating) properties are particularly vulnerable to the action of ionic surface active agents which have strong surface tnesion and electrostatic properties. However, Ernst et al, (37) were not able to demonstrate a positive correlation between phytotoxicity and the surface tension (S.T.) reducing properties of the surfactants they surveyed.

Algal and plant pesticide toxicity studies are important as any perturbance of primary productivity affects the total energy budget of the system, and could ultimately affect phytophagous organisms, diversity within a community, and impinge on natural reforestation and biotic vigor. There is a wide variability in species susceptibility to adjuvants. Population dynamic changes

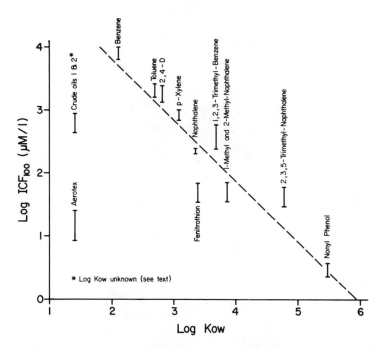

Figure 3. Plot of concentration, log ICF_{100} μM/1, of test chemical required to suppress the fluorometer (P-T) transient for <u>Chlamydomonas</u> vs, octanol-water partition coefficient log K_{ow} (<u>32</u>).

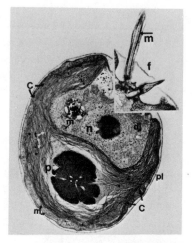

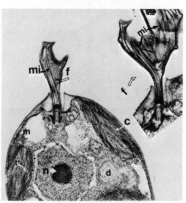

Figure 4.   Electron micrograph of longitudinal sections of
Chlamydomonas reinhardtii Dang. A. Control cell; B. Cell
treated 1 h with 1.0-1.5 g/ml nonylphenol; C. Chloroplast;
d. dichtyosome; f. flagella; m. mitochondrion; mi.
microtubules; n. nucleus; p. pyrenoid; pl. plasmalemma.

may not become apparent if total productivity is used as an indicator of habitat stability but altered species composition may occur (38, 39).

The autotrophic microphytes in the soil and aquatic forest systems, and the aquatic macrophytes in the ponds, rivers and streams provide the habitat and food resource for many phytophagous organisms.

The effects of the nonylphenol in the Matacil 1.8D OSC formulation give greatest cause for concern. At a concentration of 1.1 µg/ml that has been found in the field (40), nonylphenol can significantly delay the growth of a population of Chlorella pyrenoidosa, where swathe overspray occurs, concentrations may be obtained that could kill the whole population of exposed cells (20). Delays in population growth in Chlamydomonas reinhardtii and Chlorella vulgaris was also observed after treatment with Aerotex (10).

The evidence, to date, clearly indicates that surface active agents added to formulations can modify chemical changes of the parent pesticide so that fate-transport studies undertaken in their absence, may not be fully indicative of the real degradative processes taking place. Further, far from being inert, the adjuncts have the capacity to perturb membranes and thus alter photosynthesis, and transport mechanisms directly, and indirectly by membrane charge changes due to ion leakage. The least perturbant adjunct was Dowanol. Organisms exposed to many of these surfactants are put under stress such that their total ATP is depleted and their elastic response to "normal" stressors may be so limited as to endanger species response.

Nonylphenol is not only used as a surfactant and solvent in the Matacil 1.8D formulation, but is also a widely used constituent of paints, inks and shampoos. The fact that it is lethal to some algae and reduces the growth of paper birch seedlings does not mean that it may be toxic to higher organisms. However, it should signal the fact that neither this adjuvant, nor others should, a priori, be regarded as biologically inert. Concern that nonylphenol is showing up in sewage effluents in concentrations ranging from 36 to 202 µg/L (41) should underline a sense of urgency for getting registration procedures "in place" for all major adjuvants.

Acknowledgments: The authors wish to express their appreciation for the NSERC funding (grants A1737 and GO 240) which partially supported the research emanating from the University of Ottawa, Dept. Biology, and the graduate students S. Iyengar, R.P. Moody, M.S. Rea and R. Vladut whose studies provided an intrinsic part of this review.

Literature Cited

1. Parr, J.F. "adjuvants for Pesticides", 1982; p. 93-114.
2. Armstrong, J.A.; Randall, A.P. Proc. 4th Intl. Agric. Aviat.
    Congr. Kingston, Canada, 1969, 196-202.
3. Varty, I.N. "Environmental Surveillance in New Brunswick"
    1978-1979. Univ. New Brunswick Press; p. 76.
4. Symons, P.E.K. Residue Rev. 1977, 65, 1-36.
5. Eidt, D.C. Can. Entomol. 1975, 107, 743-760.
6. Eidt, D.C.; Sundaram, K.M.S. Can. Entomol. 1975, 107, 735-742
7. Kay, K. Environ. Res. 1974, 7, 243-271
8. Safe, S.; Plugge, H.; Crocker, J.F.S. Chemosphere 1977, 10,
    641-651.
9. Lee, W.Y.; Winters, K.; Nicol, J.A.C. Environ. Pollut. 15,
    167-183.
10. Moody, R.P.; Weinberger, P.; Greenhalgh, R.; Massalski, A.
    Can. J. Botany, 1981, 59, 1003-1013.
11. Vandermeulen, J.H.; Ahern, T.P. "Effects of Pollutants on
    Aquatic Organisms", Ed. A.P.M. Lockwood, 1976, Cambridge
    Univ. Press, p. 107.
12. Spitzer, W.O. "New Brunswick Task Force Rept on the Environ-
    ment and Reye's Syndrome" N.B. Fredericton, 1982.
13. Greenhalgh, R.; Dhawan, K.I.; Weinberger, P. J. Agric. Food
    Chem., 1980, 28, 102-105.
14. MacKay, D.; Leionen, P.J. Environ. Sci. Technol. 1975, 9,
    1178-1180.
15. Truchlik, S.; Drabek, I.; Dovac, I.; Gager, S. 1972, Proc.
    3rd Cont. NTIS JPRS 57825, U.S. Dept. Commerce, p. 129.
16. Smith, J.H.; Bomberger, D.C.; Haynes, D.L. Environ. Sci.
    Technol. 1980, 14, 1332-1337é
17. Weinberger, P.; Greenhalgh, R. Environ. Toxicol. Chem., 1983.
    In press.
18. Jansen, L.L. Weeds, 1965, 13, 117-120.
19. Wayman, C.E.; Robertson, J.B.; Page, H.G. Geol. Surv. Res.
    D., 1962, 190-192.
20. Weinberger, P.; Rea, M.S. Environ. Exptl. Botany, 1982, 22,
    491-495.
21. Weinberger, P.; Iyengar, S. personal communication.
22. Endo, R.M.; Letey, J.; Valokas, N.; Osborne, J.F. Agron. J.
    1969, 61, 850-854.
23. Patterson, J.W.; Brezonick, P.L.; Putnam, H.D. Environ. Sci.
    Technol. 1970, 4, 569-575.
24. St. John, J.B.; Bartels, P.G.; Hilton, J.L. Weed Sci., 1974
    22, 233-238.
25. Parr, J.F.; Norman, A.G. Plant Physiol. 1964, 39, 502-507.
26. Parr, J.F.; Norman, A.G. Bot. Gaz. 1965, 126, 86-96.
27. McLeese, D.W.; Zitko, V.; Metcalfe, C.D.; Sergeant, D.B.
    Chromosphere, 1980, 9, 79-82.
28. Ukeles, R. J. Phycol. 1965, 1, 102-110.

29. Papageorgiou, G. "Bioenergetics of Photosynthesis", Academic Press New York, N.Y., 1975, p. 320.
30. Schreiber, U.; Vidaver, W.; Runeckles, V.C.; Rosen, P. Plant Physiol. 1978, 61, 80-84.
31. Mohanty, P.; Papageorgiou, G.; Govinjee, G. Photochem. Photobiol. 1971, 14, 667-669.
32. Moody, R.P.M. "Algicidal Activity of Formulated Fenitrothion", 1982, Ph.D. Dissertation, University of Ottawa, Ont., Canada.
33. Helenius A.; Simons, K. Biochem. Biophys. Acta. 1975, 415, 29-79.
34. Soto, C.; Hutchinson, T.C.; Sheath, R.G. Can. J. Bot. 1979, 57, 2729-2739.
35. Soto, C.; Hutchinson, T.C.; Hellebust, J.A.; Sheath, R.G. Can. J. Bot. 1979, 57, 2717-2728.
36. Blondind, G.A.; Green, D.E. Proc. Nat. Acad. Sci. 1967, 58, 642-648.
37. Ernst, R.J.; Ardetti, J.A.; Healy, P.L. New Phytol. 1971, 70, 457-459.
38. Mosser, J.L.; Fisher, N.S.; Wurster, F. Science 1972, 176, 533-537.
39. Taub, E.D. Intern. J. Environ. Studies 1976, 10, 457-459.
40. Sundaram, K.M.S.; Szeto, S.; Hindle, R.; MacTavish, D. J. Environ. Sci. Health 1980, B15, 403-419.
41. Stephanou, E.; Giger, W. Environ. Sci. Technol. 1982, 16, 800-805.

RECEIVED September 28, 1983

Environmental Impact Assessment of Insecticides Used in Canadian Forests

P. D. KINGSBURY

Forest Pest Management Institute, Canadian Forestry Service, Environment Canada, 1219 Queen Street East, Sault Ste. Marie, Ontario, P6A 5M7, Canada

Increased environmental awareness and the implementation of more rigorous registration protocols have led to the conducting of extensive field studies to document the environmental impact of insecticides currently used or proposed for use in controlling insect pests of Canadian forests. Methods used to study effects on fish, aquatic invertebrates, forest songbirds, small mammals, and non-target insects present in forest environments are outlined. Studies conducted during pre-registration evaluations and during monitoring of operational pest control programs are described, and results pertaining to the effects of a number of organophosphate, carbamate and pyrethroid insecticides on these various groups are summarized.

The program of the Forest Pest Management Institute of the Canadian Forestry Service is devoted exclusively to the development of new and/or improved pest control products and strategies for their use, which will assist forest managers in achieving forest protection objectives without jeopardizing public health or causing unacceptable disturbances of environmental quality. In order to fulfill this mandate, extensive field programs have been carried out to generate data on the impacts of chemical and biological insecticides on various non-target organisms present in treated forest areas. These data are used by federal and provincial pesticide regulatory agencies in hazard evaluation and decision making regarding the registration and use of forest insecticides, and by forest managers planning actual control programs.

The environmental impact programs carried out over the past decade have primarily been concerned with evaluating impacts on forest songbirds, small mammals, fish, aquatic invertebrates, honeybees, and non-target insects of various formulations of

0097-6156/84/0238-0365$06.00/0
© 1984 American Chemical Society

chemical and biological insecticides in operational use or being evaluated for use against the eastern spruce budworm, *Choristoneura fumiferana* Clem. Field programs have been conducted in forest plots receiving experimental aerial applications of acephate, aminocarb, azamethiphos, *Bacillus thuringiensis,* carbaryl, chlorpyrifos-methyl, diflubenzuron and other insect growth regulators, fenitrothion, juvenile hormone analogue, permethrin, phosphamidon, and several insect viruses. Many of these and other materials have also been evaluated during provincial pest control programs in British Columbia, Manitoba, Ontario, Quebec, New Brunswick and Newfoundland. Methods employed in these studies, and some of the results pertaining to the effects of a number of organophosphate carbamate and pyrethroid insecticides, are discussed in this paper.

Environmental Impact Testing of Candidate Insecticides

The environmental impact of a candidate insecticide is evaluated in a progressive fashion in concert with evaluations of its efficacy toward important forest pests. The initial selection of candidate materials places considerable emphasis on their potential safety towards non-target organisms. Toxicology and impact data available from the insecticide developer, or experiences with use of the material in other areas (e.g., agriculture, biting fly control), are screened to identify potential strengths and weaknesses of the material. Known effects of similar insecticides and hazard assessments made on the basis of chemical structure, mode of action, and potential exposure of different organisms caused by such properties as water solubility and volatility can provide valuable indications of potential impacts. The field testing program for each compound is oriented toward potential problem areas, with the timing and scale of the studies proportional to the potential hazard. For example, extensive field testing to determine the impact of synthetic pyrethroids on aquatic systems was carried out early in the evaluation of the efficacy of these materials towards spruce budworm because available lab toxicity data suggested that adverse aquatic impacts might severely limit the dosage or use of these insecticides in forestry situations. Impact studies may progress from laboratory to ground, small plot aerial, and operational scale applications done under experimental research permits prior to registration.

Impact Assessment Methodologies

Forest songbirds. Forest songbirds are censused by a singing male territorial mapping technique similar to that described by Kendeigh (1, 2). Size and shape of areas censused include plots up to 8 ha (20 acres) in size, transects up to 0.8 km (0.5 mile) long, the area surrounding an individual point, or a combination of these depending upon the size and accessibility of the treated block, the homogeneity of the forest cover and the objectives of the study. Impact assessments are usually based on five immediate pre-spray and five immediate post-spray censuses taken daily within the period of peak songbird activity immediately after dawn. Censuses are not made or included in assessments if adverse weather conditions (high winds or heavy rain) depressed bird activity. Data collected on treated plots are always compared directly with data collected on the same dates in nearby untreated areas with similar forest type and songbird populations. Plot searches are conducted following treatments to look for birds exhibiting poisoning symptoms. In some cases, mist-netting is carried out within the census plots at the end of the program in order to evaluate the numbers, species composition and growth of juvenile birds fledging from nests in the area.

Small Mammals. Insecticide impact studies have concentrated on shrews, mice and voles as indicators of effects on forest mammals because their relatively high population densities make them easier to study than larger mammals. Their small size, high metabolic rates, population cycles, and in some cases insectivorous habits, also tend to make them relatively sensitive to insecticide impacts. Populations of these small mammals are at a yearly low in late spring when spruce budworm spraying occurs due to natural mortality and predation over the winter. Impact assessment is based on trapping censuses carried out 6 to 8 weeks after spraying when young-of-the-year, present as embryos or nestlings at the time of spraying, have become active enough to be caught in snapback or pit-fall traps. The population structure and reproductive status of mature individuals in treated and untreated control areas are compared in order to look for impacts on either reproduction or juveniles. Comparable numbers of juveniles and females which are either pregnant or bearing recent placental scars in treated and untreated areas are taken as evidence of a lack of impact on small mammal populations.

Fish. The aquatic ecosystems at greatest potential risk to insecticide applications to forests are headwater stream systems which serve as primary nursery and rearing areas for salmon and trout. Impact studies focus on these species, particularly Atlantic salmon, *Salmo salar* L., and brook trout, *Salvelinus fontinalis* Mitchill, but sometimes also consider cohabiting forage fish such as the slimy sculpin, *Cottus cognatus* Richardson. Various study methods are employed depending on available treated sites, their resident fish populations and program objectives. Caging studies of various life-stages are used to look for lethal or sub-lethal effects and to document insecticide residue accumulation by fish. Native fish population densities are assessed before and after insecticide treatments using electroshocking equipment within areas temporarily isolated by nets from the rest of the stream. Captured fish provide data on size, growth and condition as well as

population structure and density. Native fish are also sampled
for stomach content analysis to look for changes in diet resulting
from impacts on fish food organisms.

Aquatic Invertebrates. The initial impact of insecticides on most
benthic invertebrates in streams is the inability to maintain
their position on the streambed resulting in increased numbers
being carried downstream in what is termed drift. Invertebrate
drift in treated streams is easily sampled by holding a net in the
current. Post-spray catches can be compared to both pre-spray
diurnal patterns and catches at an untreated upstream station or
in an untreated control stream. This method also can be used to
document knockdown of streamside foliage-dwelling or arboreal insects if the net is set so as to sample the stream's surface.
Impacts on stream invertebrates can also be determined by caging
studies and by pre- and post-spray bottom fauna population assessments which either sample the numbers within a given area of natural streambed (e.g., Surber sampler) or on artificial substrates
intentionally set in the stream before treatment to be colonized
by resident populations.

Honeybees. Honeybee colonies have been used both to look at the
impact of forest insecticides on apicultural activities within
treated areas, and as indicators of impacts on other non-target
insects including wild pollinators. Honeybee colonies are only
studied within insecticide treated blocks of sufficient area to
cover most of the bees' potential foraging range. Colonies are
moved early enough before treatment to allow the bees to become
oriented to their new surroundings prior to treatment, otherwise
their foraging behavior may be too limited to give a true indication of the impact of the insecticide applied. Colonies are
equipped with a dead bee box, a pollen trap and an electronic
activity counter activated by bees crossing over photocells at the
entrance to the hive. Mortality at the hive, pollen collection,
and activity at the hive entrance are compared to comparable
measurements taken from colonies in similar untreated areas.
Hives can also be opened to examine brood production and development and honey production. Samples of bees, pollen, nectar or wax
can be taken from colonies for analysis of insecticide residues
picked up by foraging bees as they move about within treated
forests.

Other Non-target Insects. Insecticide effects on foliage dwelling
and arboreal arthropods are documented by measuring knockdown into
tubs or drop sheets set out beneath selected trees and shrubs.
Numbers of wild pollinators visiting native blossom in treated and
control areas are compared, and sometimes large pollinating insects such as bumblebees are exposed to sprays in cages to look
for lethal impacts. The effects of insecticides on fruit set of
certain insect pollinated plants blooming around the period of

spray application can be studied by tagging individual flowers opening at the time of treatment, and later collecting tagged fruits and comparing proportions of fertilized to unfertilized ovules in treated and untreated control areas. Impacts on ground insect populations can be measured by pit-fall trapping in treated and untreated control areas to measure pre- and post-spray populations.

Results of Environmental Impact Assessments

The following results summarize the findings of studies carried out by the Forest Pest Management Institute's environmental impact section on a number of chemical insecticides. Significant results from studies conducted by other agencies are referred to in some instances, but no attempt has been made to include exhaustive reviews of all field studies done on each material, as this is well beyond the scope of this paper.

Organophosphate insecticides

Fenitrothion. The organophosphate fenitrothion has been the insecticide used most extensively in Canadian forests over the past decade; its impacts on many non-target organisms have been extensively studied and reviewed (3, 4). Breeding songbird or small mammal populations do not appear to be disrupted by single applications of fenitrothion up to dosages of 280 g/ha, the registered limit for spruce budworm control (5, 6). Some forest songbird mortality and disruption of songbird and small mammal reproductive success has been found when application rates reach or exceed 420 g/ha (7, 8). Applications of 280 g/ha appear to consistently depress brain cholinesterase activity in songbirds within treated areas without inducing noticeable abnormal avian behavior (9).
Conventional applications of fenitrothion at 210-280 g/ha have been found to sometimes induce short-lived increases in invertebrate drift and opportunistic feeding by native fish on aquatic and terrestrial invertebrates drifting in streams following spraying, but do not appear to cause significant depletion of stream bottom fauna (10, 11). Applications of dosages up to 420 g/ha fenitrothion have been found to have limited impacts on lake fauna aside from occasional short term suppression of zooplankton populations (10, 12, 13).
Fenitrothion applied to forest areas at 210-280 g/ha has been shown to sometimes cause moderate mortality among foraging honeybees, but not to significantly impact on the overall vitality of colonies set out in treated areas (7, 14, 15). Applications of 210 g/ha fenitrothion appear to have a more substantial impact on wild pollinators causing heavy mortality of caged bumble bees, solitary bees and vespid wasps, reducing bumble bee densities and reducing pollination activity in sprayed areas (16-18). Fenitrothion sprays produce some mortality of some non-target terrestrial

arthropods, but populations recover rapidly and predation and parasitism processes do not appear to be affected, even with the occurrence of repeated annual treatments (19).

Phosphamidon. Phosphamidon was introduced into Canadian spruce budworm control programs in the mid-60s to reduce the adverse effects on aquatic organisms, particularly Atlantic salmon stocks, which had accompanied the use of DDT in previous programs. Its relatively low toxicity to fish led to the application of phosphamidon within buffer strips along streams and rivers inside large DDT spray blocks. These protective measures greatly reduced fish losses within DDT treated areas (20). Phosphamidon has also been shown to have only limited effects on aquatic insects (21, 22).

Unfortunately, phosphamidon's low toxicity to aquatic organisms is accompanied by high toxicity to birds. Phosphamidon applied as a spruce budworm larvicide at dosage rates in excess of 140 g/ha has repeatedly been shown to cause substantial mortality among the small forest songbird populations (15, 23, 24). Single or multiple experimental applications of phosphamidon at 70 g/ha for adult spruce budworm population suppression have been shown to have a much less harmful effect on forest songbirds (25). Phosphamidon use in control programs in the 1970s was first severely limited and later entirely eliminated because dosage rates marginally tolerated by birds did not provide acceptable control of insect damage.

Acephate. Acephate is a highly water soluble organophosphate with low fish toxicity (26) and very limited impact on aquatic organisms when used in forest spraying (27). Studies on the effects of applications of acephate of between 0.28 and 1.40 kg/ha in eastern and western Canada on forest songbirds have not revealed statistically significant population declines after treatments, although some nonstatistical decreases among some species have been noted at higher dosages and a marked one-day decline in singing activity was documented on one of several plots studied in 1.12 kg/ha application blocks (24, 28, 29). Similar non-statistical declines have been noted among songbird populations in western U.S. areas treated with acephate at 1.12 or 2.24 kg/ha. Several birds were found exhibiting poisoning symptoms and extensive brain cholinesterase depression was documented among large portions of the bird populations within these treated areas (30). Acephate applied at 0.56 kg/ha caused considerable mortality of honeybees for several days after application to an eastern Canada forest block, but did not severely affect overall colony vigor over the summer (28). Acephate applications of 1.12 and 2.24 kg/ha to western U.S. forests have severely affected honeybee colonies by permanently breaking brood cycles resulting in colonies being technically dead within 48 hours of treatment (31).

Chlorpyrifos-methyl.   Two applications six days apart of 0.007 kg chlorpyrifos-methyl/ha to a forest block had no noticeable effect on breeding songbird populations and induced only limited drift increases of aquatic invertebrates without significantly altering benthos populations or native fish diets (32).   Applications of 0.72-0.86 kg chlorpyrifos-methyl/ha to streams caused severe disturbances of aquatic invertebrates and substantial depressions of benthos populations for several months (33).   Diets of native fish were significantly altered due to effects on fish food organisms. Some mortality of crayfish and minnows was observed, but no brook trout mortality occurred.   Chlorpyrifos-methyl has not been developed for forestry use in Canada.

Azamethiphos.   Azamethiphos applied to a forest block at 0.07 kg/ha twice over a six day period had no noticeable effect on breeding songbird populations and little impact on aquatic organisms aside from inducing large increases in the drift of one family of caddisfly larvae (34).   Azamethiphos has not been developed for forestry use in Canada.

Carbamate insecticides

Aminocarb.   Next to fenitrothion, aminocarb has been the insecticide used most extensively in forestry in Canada over the past decade.   Application rates of up to 0.175 kg/ha have been found to have little or no impact on forest songbird populations or small mammal breeding activity, but do cause considerable knockdown of terrestrial arthropods, particularly at higher application rates (35, 36).   Short-lived but fairly extensive honeybee mortality has been documented when aminocarb has been applied while active foraging was underway, but the overall colony vigor was not seriously effected (37).   Aminocarb does not appear to cause bumble bee mortality at operational application rates, but does affect solitary bees (18).

Aminocarb has very little impact on aquatic organisms at application rates up to 0.175 kg/ha aside from occasionally inducing very modest increases in the drift of aquatic invertebrates (10, 38).   Although extensive operational spraying with aminocarb has not been accompanied by any reports of fish mortality, laboratory studies have shown nonyl phenol, a solvent present in some commercial aminocarb formulations, substantially increases the toxicity of aminocarb to fish (38).   Recent introduction of commercial aminocarb formulations without nonyl phenol for forestry use in Canada has greatly increased the margin of safety towards fish.

Carbaryl.   Carbaryl has been field tested in Canada at a rate of 0.28 kg/ha applied twice.   This rate is considerably lower than application rates widely utilized for forest insect control programs in the United States.   At this low application rate no significant adverse effects were found on forest songbirds, wild pollinators, or fruit set in a forest wildflower (39). Non-target arthropod knockdown was light. This is in contrast to heavy impacts on wild pollinators and fruit set reported in areas treated with carbaryl at 0.84-2.24 kg/ha in the United States (31, 40). Effects on stream invertebrates at 0.28 kg/ha were also much less severe than those associated with high application rates. Some increased aquatic invertebrate drift accompanied each carbaryl application at 0.28 kg/ha, but did not result in any overall decrease in any group of aquatic insect or major shifts in the diets of native fish (39). Substantial and prolonged depression of aquatic insect populations has been documented following carbaryl applications of 0.84 kg/ha (41).

Synthetic pyrethroid insecticides

Permethrin. Terrestrial impact studies on single and double applications of 17.5 g permethrin/ha to forest ecosystems have revealed little or no adverse effects on forest songbirds, small mammals, honeybee colonies, or ground insects, but short-lived and sometimes heavy knockdown of arboreal and flying invertebrates have been documented (42-44). Extensive aquatic impact studies have, in contrast, shown permethrin to have considerable impact on aquatic organisms. Permethrin applications to forest streams at rates of between 8.8 and 70 g/ha all induced dramatic increases in the drift of stream invertebrates, accompanied by benthos depletions persisting beyond the year of treatment at the highest application rate (45, 46). Recovery of benthos populations, in terms of numbers of organisms at the order level, occurred within two months with single applications of 8.8 or 17.5 g/ha (46). Benthos population recovery took about four months following a single application of 35 g/ha or double applications of 17.5 g/ha, while benthos remained suppressed for up to sixteen months in a stream treated with 70 g/ha (45-47). Benthos depletions at application rates of 35 and 70 g/ha resulted in large shifts in the diets of native brook trout populations from aquatic insects to terrestrial arthropods for most of the year of treatment, while fish diets in streams treated at 17.5 g/ha or less deviated from normal for much shorter periods (46,47).

Caged and native fish studies did not reveal apparent direct effects on fish at applications of 70 g/ha or less, but a 140 g/ha application to a small lake caused limited fish mortality in addition to severely depressing zooplankton and bottom fauna populations (48). Fish population studies in an Atlantic salmon nursery stream treated with two applications of 17.5 g/ha suggest that some brook trout and juvenile Atlantic salmon emigrated from the treated areas for several months in response to the depleted food resource (49). Growth of salmon parr remaining in the treated area slowed down for several months. Later in the season fish populations in the treated area recovered and growth rates recovered and growth rates increased to exceed growth rates at untreated control sites.

In light of its demonstrated high hazard towards aquatic ecosystems, permethrin will not be developed for widescale use in forestry situations in Canada, but may be utilized in selected situations such as plantation pest control where introduction of the insecticide into productive waters can be avoided.

Studies such as those summarized have helped to provide information on the relative safety or hazard of various insecticides to different components of forest ecosystems. Wise selection and use of insecticides by forest managers taking this type of information into account can allow protection of both forestry and other environmental qualities in areas threatened by attack from forest pests.

Acknowledgments

Many present and former staff and student assistants of the Environmental Impact Sections of the Forest Pest Management Institute and the Chemical Control Research Institute contributed in large measure to the studies referred to in this article. The stenographic and editorial assistance of Jean McAlpine and Karen Griffiths is acknowledged with appreciation.

Literature Cited

1. Kendeigh, S.C. Ecol. Monographs 1944, 14, 1–106.
2. Kendeigh, S.C. "Bird population studies in the coniferous forest biome during a spruce budworm outbreak"; Biological Bulletin No. 1, Ontario Department of Lands and Forests: Maple, Ont., 1947; pp. 1–100.
3. Symons, P.E.K. Residue Reviews 1977, 38, 1–36.
4. Roberts, J.R.; Greenhalgh, R.; Marshall, W.K., Eds. "Proceedings of a symposium on fenitrothion"; Publication No. 16073, National Research Council Canada: Ottawa, Ont., 1977.
5. Kingsbury, P.D.; McLeod, B.B. "Fenitrothion and forest avifauna – Studies on the effects of high dosage applications"; Report FPM-X-43, Forest Pest Management Institute: Sault Ste. Marie, Ont., 1981.
6. Buckner, C.H.; Sarrazin, R.; McLeod, B.B. in "Proceedings of a symposium on fenitrothion"; Roberts, J.R.; Greenhalgh, R.; Marshall, W.K., Eds.; National Research Council Canada: Ottawa, Ont., 1977; pp. 377–390.
7. Buckner, C.H. "The biological side effects of fenitrothion in forest ecosystems"; Report CC-X-67, Chemical Control Research Institute: Ottawa, Ont., 1974.
8. Pearce, P.A.; Busby, D.G. in "Environmental surveillance in New Brunswick, 1978-79"; Varty, I.W., Ed.; University of New Brunswick: Fredericton, N.B., 1980; pp. 24–28.

9. Busby, D.G.; Pearce, P.A.; Garrity, N.R. Bull. Environm. Contam. Toxicol. 1981, 26, 401-6.

10. Kingsbury, P.D. "Aquatic impact studies by FPMI in Quebec spruce budworm spray block 305 in 1977"; Report FPM-X-12, Forest Pest Management Institute: Sault Ste. Marie, Ont., 1978.

11. Holmes, S.B. "Aquatic impact studies of a spruce budworm control program in the lower St. Lawrence region of Quebec in 1978"; Report FPM-X-26, Forest Pest Management Institute: Sault Ste. Marie, Ont., 1979.

12. Kingsbury, P.D. "Fenitrothion in a lake ecosystem"; Report CC-X-127, Chemical Control Research Institute: Ottawa, Ont., 1977.

13. Kingsbury, P.D. "A study of the distribution, persistence and biological effects of fenitrothion applied to a small lake in an oil formulation"; Report FPM-X-13, Forest Pest Management Institute: Sault Ste. Marie, Ont., 1978.

14. Buckner, C.H.; Sarrazin, R. "Studies of the environmental impact of the 1974 spruce budworm control operation in Quebec"; Report CC-X-93, Chemical Control Research Institute: Ottawa, Ont., 1975.

15. Buckner, C.H; McLeod, B.B. "Ecological impact studies of experimental and operational spruce budworm control programs on selected non-target organisms in Quebec in 1976"; Report CC-X-137, Chemical Control Research Institute: Ottawa, Ont., 1977.

16. Plowright, R.C.; Pendrel, B.A.; McLaren, I.A. Can. Ent. 1978, 110, 1145-56.

17. Plowright, R.C.; Thomson, J.D.; Thaler, G.R. Can. Ent. 1980, 112, 765-9.

18. Plowright, R.C.; Rodd, F.H. Can. Ent. 1980, 112, 259-69.

19. Varty, I.W. in "Proceedings of a symposium on fenitrothion"; Roberts, J.R.; Greenhalgh, R.; Marshall, W.K., Eds.; National Research Council Canada: Ottawa, Ont., 1977; pp. 343-75.

20. Kingsbury, P.D. in "Aerial control of forest insects in Canada"; Prebble, M.L., Ed; Department of the Environment: Ottawa, Ont., 1975; pp. 180-92.

21. Grant, C.D. J. Fish. Res. Bd. Can. 1967, 24, 823-32.

22. Kingsbury, P.D. Proc. Ent. Soc. Ont. 1975, 106, 19-24.

23. Pearce, P.A. in "Aerial control of forest insects in Canada"; Prebble, M.L., Ed.; Department of the Environment: Ottawa, Ont., 1975; pp. 306-13.

24. Buckner, C.H.; McLeod, B.B.; Lidstone, R.G. "Environmental impact of spruce budworm control programs in New Brunswick in 1976"; Report CC-X-135, Chemical Control Research Institute: Ottawa, Ont., 1977.

25. McLeod, B.B.; Millikin, R.L. "Environmental impact assessment of experimental spruce budworm adulticide trials: Effects on forest avifauna"; Report FPM-X-54, Forest Pest Management Institute: Sault Ste. Marie, Ont., 1982.

26. Klaverkamp, J.F.; Hobden, B.R.; Harrison, S.E.   Proc. West.
     Pharmacol. Soc. 1975, 18, 358-61.
27. Rabeni, C.F.; Stanley, J.G.   Bull. Environ. Contam. Toxicol.
     1979, 23, 327-34.
28. Buckner, C.H.; McLeod, B.B.   "Impact of aerial applications
     of Orthene upon non-target organisms"; Report CC-X-104, Chem-
     ical Control Research Institute: Ottawa, Ont., 1975.
29. Shepherd, R.F., Ed.   "Operational field trials against the
     Douglas-fir tussock moth with chemical and biological insect-
     icides"; Report BC-X-201, Pacific Forest Research Centre:
     Victoria, B.C., 1980.
30. Richmond, M.L.; Henny, C.J.; Floyd, R.L.; Mannan, R.; Finch,
     D.M.; De Weese, L.R.   "Effects of Sevin-4-Oil, Dimilin and
     Orthene on forest birds in Northwestern Oregon"; Research
     Paper PSW-148, Pacific Southwest Forest and Range Exper-
     imental Station: Berkeley, Ca., 1979.
31. Shea, P.J. in "The Douglas-fir tussock moth: A synthesis";
     Technical Bulletin 1585, USDA Forest Service: Washington,
     D.C., 1978; pp. 122-9.
32. Holmes, S.B.; Millikin, R.L.   "A preliminary report on the
     effects of a split application of RELDAN on aquatic and ter-
     restrial ecosystems"; File Report 13, Forest Pest Management
     Institute: Sault Ste. Marie, Ont., 1981.
33. Kingsbury, P.D.; Holmes, S.B.   "A preliminary report on the
     impact on stream fauna of high dosage applications of
     RELDAN"; File Report 2, Forest Pest Management Institute:
     Sault Ste. Marie, Ont., 1980.
34. Kingsbury, P.D.; Holmes, S.B.; Millikin, R.L.   "Environmental
     effects of a double application of azamethiphos on selected
     terrestrial and aquatic organisms"; Report FPM-X-33, Forest
     Pest Management Institute: Sault Ste. Marie, Ont., 1980.
35. Buckner, C.H.; McLeod, B.B.   "Impact of experimental spruce
     budworm suppression trials upon forest dwelling birds in
     Newfoundland in 1977"; Report FPM-X-9, Forest Pest Management
     Institute: Sault Ste. Marie, Ont., 1977.
36. Kingsbury, P.D.; McLeod, B.B.; Millikin, R.L.   "The environ-
     mental impact of nonyl phenol and the MATACIL formulation.
     Part 2: Terrestrial ecosystems"; Report FPM-X-36, Forest
     Pest Management Institute: Sault Ste. Marie, Ont., 1981.
37. Buckner, C.H.; McLeod, B.B.; Kingsbury, P.D.   "Studies of the
     impact of the carbamate insecticide MATACIL on components of
     forest ecosystems"; Report CC-X-91, Chemical Control Research
     Institute: Ottawa, Ont., 1975.
38. Holmes, S.B.; Kingsbury, P.D.   "The environmental impact of
     nonyl phenol and the MATACIL formulation. Part 1: Aquatic
     ecosystems"; Report FPM-X-35, Forest Pest Management
     Institute: Sault Ste. Marie, Ont., 1980.

39. Holmes, S.B.; Millikin, R.L.; Kingsbury, P.D. "Environmental effects of a split application of SEVIN-2-OIL"; Report FPM-X-46, Forest Pest Management Institute: Sault Ste. Marie, Ont., 1981.

40. Miliczkey, E.K.; Osgood, E.A. "The effects of spraying with SEVIN-4-OIL on insect pollinators and pollination in a spruce-fir forest"; Tech. Bull. No. 90., Life Sciences and Ag. Exp. Sta.: Orono, Me., 1979.

41. Courtemanch, D.L.; Gibbs, K.E. Can. Ent. 1980, 112, 271-6.

42. Kingsbury, P.D.; McLeod, B.B. "Terrestrial impact studies in forest ecosystems treated with double applications of permethrin"; Report FPM-X-28, Forest Pest Management Institute: Sault Ste. Marie, Ont., 1979.

43. Kingsbury, P.D.; Kreutzweiser, D.P. "Environmental impact assessment of a semi-operational permethrin application"; Report FPM-X-30, Forest Pest Management Institute: Sault Ste. Marie, Ont., 1980.

44. Kreutzweiser, D.P. "The effects of permethrin on the invertebrate fauna of a Quebec forest"; Report FPM-X-50, Forest Pest Management Institute: Sault Ste. Marie, Ont., 1982.

45. Kingsbury, P.D.; Kreutzweiser, D.P. "Impact of double applications of permethrin on forest streams and ponds"; Report FPM-X-27, Forest Pest Management Institute: Sault Ste. Marie, Ont., 1979.

46. Kingsbury, P.D.; Kreutzweiser, D.P. "Dosage-effect studies on the impact of permethrin on trout streams"; Report FPM-X-31, Forest Pest Management Institute: Sault Ste. Marie, Ont., 1980.

47. Kreutzweiser, D.P.; Kingsbury, P.D. "Recovery of stream benthos and its utilization by resident fish following high dosage permethrin applications"; Report FPM-X-59, Forest Pest Management Institute: Sault Ste. Marie, Ont., 1982.

48. Kingsbury, P.D. "Studies on the impact of aerial applications of the synthetic pyrethroid NRDC-143 on aquatic ecosystems"; Report CC-X-127, Chemical Control Research Institute: Ottawa, Ont., 1976.

49. Kingsbury, P.D., Ed. "Permethrin in New Brunswick salmon nursery streams"; Report FPM-X-52, Forest Pest Management Institute: Sault Ste. Marie, Ont., 1983.

RECEIVED September 9, 1983

Mount St. Helens: The May 1980 Eruptions and Forest Rehabilitation

JACK K. WINJUM

Weyerhaeuser Company, Centralia, WA 98531

Forest rehabilitation in the blast zone of Mt. St. Helens resulting from the eruption of May 18, 1980, is proceeding rapidly, both by nature and by man. Of the 60,000 ha (150,000 ac) of forest land devastated, most of the western half (27,540 ha or 68,000 ac) is owned by Weyerhaeuser Company and is managed as part of its S.W. Washington tree farm. Studies of natural recovery of the forest ecosystem began in June 1980. Sample plots showed natural vegetation appearing within a few weeks. Plants with surviving root systems pushed new shoots up through the tephra deposition. Cover reached 50 percent by fall in many areas and one year later approached a normal 90+ percent. Monthly census observations indicate a near full reappearance of terrestrial animals and birds. Fish now occupy most of the rivers, streams and lakes of the area. Salvage of dead merchantable trees on about 9,300 ha (23,000 ac) was underway by fall 1980 and was completed by November 1982. Experimental tree planting began in the blast zone June 1980 with favorable results. In March 1981, 2,000 ha (5,000 ac) were operationally planted and by winter 1985 about 17,000 ha (43,000 ac) will be in plantations within the western blast zone.

Rehabilitation of forest lands devastated by the eruptions of Mount St. Helens in May 1980 is proceeding rapidly, both by nature and by man. This paper sketches rehabilitation in the western portion of the 60,000 ha (150,000 ac) blast zone which lies to the north of the volcano. Lands in the western blast zone are primarily owned by Weyerhaeuser Company and have been managed for commercial forest crops for many decades. Rehabilitation here includes natural vegetation, camp cleanup, road reconstruction,

0097-6156/84/0238-0377$06.00/0
© 1984 American Chemical Society

salvage logging, reforestation and associated research on all during the last 34 months.

Ground access into the area, both by rail and truck roads, was basically reestablished during the summer months of 1980. Eventually 1,020 km (638 mi) of roads, including several bridges, were repaired or newly built on Company lands. Three non-resident type logging camps near the western boundary of the blast zone were inundated by volcanic mudflows on May 18, 1980. The camps were cleaned up; one was abandoned and two were operable during the early rehabilitation effort. Salvage logging of commercial size dead trees both standing and down on about 9,300 ha (23,000 ac) began September 1980 and was completed in November 1982 as planned.

In June 1980, a team of Company scientists and operations foresters scoped the need for new technical information as a result of the eruptions. Key needs were:

Ash Properties
. Depth, chemical, physical
. Microclimatology
. Erosion/hydrology

Woods Operations
. Inventory of devastation
. Salvage wood properties
. Equipment modifications

Forest Rehabilitation
. Natural revegetation
. Grasses/N-fixers
. Forest regeneration
  - site preparation
    .after salvage logging
    .dead plantations
  - planting methods
  - seeding
  - species selection

Protection and Management
. Insects/disease
. Wild fire/controlled burning
. Animals and fish

Stand Development
. Growth
. Mortality
. Fertilization

We have undertaken research or development on nearly all these needs; several needs are covered in cooperative work with other organizations. Many results are already implemented.

Natural revegetation in the northwest blast zone, about 24 km (15 mi) from the volcano, began in early June 1980. It progressed surprisingly well through July and August especially on forest lands harvested from three to ten years previous. Plant species were predominantly those that grew new shoots up through the tephra cover (average depth 10 cm (2.5 in)) from surviving root systems. The most common species from among 31 observed in 1980 were: fireweed (Epilobium angustifolium L.); Canadian thistle (Circium arvense (L.) Scop.) and bracken fern (Pteridium aquilinum (L.) Kuhn.). In many such locations plant cover approached 50 percent by fall 1980 compared to a normal of about 90 percent. By fall 1982, nearly all lands in this area had natural revegetation at normal cover levels. Moving toward Mount St. Helens, revegetation still is proportionately less until at the base of the volcano abundant plant recovery no doubt will take many decades.

Tree planting tests in the blast zone began in June 1980 with the outplanting of a few hundred barerooted seedlings of Douglas-fir (Pseudotsuga menzeisii (Mirb.) Franco) and noble fir (Abies procera Rehder). By digging through the tephra cover and planting with roots into original soil, seedlings survived and grew well. Planting with roots totally in the tephra gave poor seedling performance primarily because of the absence of nitrogen, a key plant nutrient. Based upon this research result, operational tree planting on Weyerhaeuser lands in the blast zone began in February 1981. Approximately 2,000 ha (5,000 ac) were planted this first winter, 3,600 ha (9,000 ac) the second winter and another 4,500 ha (11,000 ac) are currently undergoing reforestation. The Company target is to reforest a total of 17,000 ha (43,000 ac) in the blast zone by spring 1985.

At monthly intervals since summer 1980, wildlife biologists have conducted systematic observations of animal recovery in the blast zone. As the renewed vegetative cover progressed, nearly all animals including upland species, fish and birds known to have existed on harvested lands in the area prior to the eruption have been detected. Most notable among the game species to rapidly recover were the Roosevelt elk (Cervus elaphus roosevelti) and black tailed deer (Odocoileus hemionus columbianus).

Provided new devastating volcanic events do not occur, almost complete recovery of the commercial forest lands near Mount St. Helens should be possible within the 1980 decade. Congressional legislation calls for 44,550 ha (110,000 ac) of lands near Mount St. Helens with unique features as a result of the 1980 volcanism to be preserved in a National Volcanic Monument for long-term scientific research, recreation and tourism.

RECEIVED September 9, 1983

Use, Ecotoxicology, and Risk Assessment of Herbicides in the Forest

LOGAN A. NORRIS[1]

U.S. Department of Agriculture, Forest Service, Pacific Northwest Forest and Range Experiment Station, Corvallis, OR 97331

Present risk assessment strategies are oriented to single organisms, and they do not evaluate risks at the ecosystem level. An ecotoxicological risk assessment requires information from studies of environmental chemistry (for evaluating exposure to specific organisms), toxicology (for determining the direct toxic effects of exposure to specific organisms), and ecology (for integrating the consequences of both direct and indirect effects of herbicides and projecting them to the ecosystem level). The National Research Council, Committee to Review Methods for Ecotoxicology, proposed a system for assessing ecotoxicological effects for use in administering the Toxic Substance Control Act. Most aspects of this system are already in use in forestry, but integration among disciplines and a mechanism for making risk assessments at the ecosystem level are lacking.

The predominant use of herbicides in forestry is for weed and brush control, both for establishment of young tree seedlings and for their later release from competing species. Other uses include vegetation control on rights-of-way, timber stand improvement through the removal of defective or non-commercial trees or through thinning in overstocked stands, range improvement for grazing of domestic animals, improvement of animal habitat, control of poisonous and noxious weeds, and maintenance of fire breaks.

Decisions about the use of herbicides in forests customarily take into account social and political considerations. In addition, they **must** include technically sound assessments of risk (1). Traditional risk assessments are basically assessments of single organisms, however, not of an ecosystem (2).

[1]Current address: Forest Science Department, Oregon State University, Corvallis, OR 97331

Ecotoxicology is a relatively new term used to describe the field of study that integrates the behavior of chemicals in the environment, traditional toxicity testing, and the response of communities of organisms. For perhaps the first time, it integrates the efforts of environmental chemists, toxicologists, biologists, and ecologists and may enable assessments of risk to an ecosystem to be made. Ecotoxicology is not a new field of study, but until recently it had relatively few practitioners and lacked an easily identifiable title. It gained some prominence when the National Research Council, Environmental Studies Board, appointed the Committee to Review Methods for Ecotoxicology in 1979 (3-4).

Although the committee specifically addressed the Toxic Substance Control Act (TSCA), the recommendations of the committee can lead to better risk assessments for forest herbicides as well. In many respects it may be possible to perform ecotoxicological risk assessments much sooner for herbicides and forestry than for the many chemicals and environments covered by TSCA. The reason is that the pesticide registration process already requires much of the basic chemical and biological data needed for single-organism assessments, and forestry research already has in place many of the studies needed for estimating the integrated response of ecosystems.

The purpose of this paper is to (1) clarify the distinction between traditional risk assessments involving single species and assessments that integrate effects among species, including both direct and indirect effects; (2) show the kinds of information needed for ecosystem assessments at the forest watershed level; and (3) review the recommendations of the National Research Council Committee in terms of the type of information needed and its availability for herbicides and forestry.

Herbicide Risk Assessment at the Ecosystem Level in Forestry

Assessments of environmental impacts from herbicides are usually done at the single-species level. These assessments use toxicological data from laboratory bioassay tests and estimates of exposure from laboratory or field studies of environmental chemistry. Few tests have assessed the impacts of herbicides on organisms in the field and few, if any, at the ecosystem level. There are two main reasons why there have been so few field or ecosystem tests: They are exceedingly difficult and costly, and the current philosophies of risk assessment have evolved from classical toxicology and the federal regulatory framework that covers pharmaceuticals, food additives, and pesticides.

Techniques for evaluating impacts of herbicides at the ecosystem level are needed because traditional methods of risk assessment emphasize <u>direct</u> <u>effects</u> of chemicals on selected species. <u>Indirect</u> <u>effects</u> have been largely ignored, and they may be of equal or greater importance in maintaining the structure and function of an ecosystem and the well-being of its inhabitants.

<u>Direct Effects, Indirect Effects, and Types of Toxicity</u>
<u>Testing.</u> Direct effects.--Direct effects of herbicides on organisms are those that result from the direct contact of a specific organism with an herbicide. Direct effects can be studied and evaluated in terms of currently accepted dose-response theory. The characteristics of exposure (magnitude, frequency, and duration) are one of the two essential ingredients of risk assessment. Toxicity, an intrinsic property of the chemical, is the other. The nature of the response of an organism depends on the basic properties and characteristics of the chemical and organism, and the characteristics of the exposure the organism receives.

Testing for direct effects.--The theories applicable to direct chemical effects on one organism are applicable to all organisms in an ecosystem because the direct interaction between the organism and the chemical is a one-on-one process. The difficulty is that ecosystems have many kinds of organisms, most of which are not likely to be involved in traditional programs of toxicological testing. Through careful selection of representative test species, however, it is possible to estimate direct toxic effects on many organisms through classical dose-response experimentation on traditional test species.

I do not mean that more accurate estimates of toxicity to squirrels or ptarmigans could not be obtained by including these species in testing, but the expected <u>gain</u> in accuracy over testing with rats and chickens is probably not worth the added expense. Furthermore, the number of species in the forest is large, and it is impossible to test them all. Therefore, the use of representative species in traditional testing is a reasonably accurate and efficient means of estimating the inherent toxicity characteristics of a specific herbicide. Because this system is not foolproof, it is important that researchers and herbicide users be alert for unusual effects of herbicides on non-target species.

There are some aspects of toxicity testing that should be improved. Toxicological testing has traditionally evaluated only a few responses of organisms, like survival or pathological responses. Recently there has been more study of other parameters, such as growth and reproductive success; however, these tests all focus on the well-being of the individual, not on communities of organisms and their interactions. The consequences that accrue to an ecosystem from changes in the numbers or activities of all the directly affected organisms should also be assessed.

Blanck and Gustafsson (5) said that "ecological and
pollutant realism" are necessary in testing toxic effects.
Ecological realism is attained when the test conditions reflect
important characteristics of the natural environment. To a
major degree, both of these characteristics are lacking in
single-species testing. Tests of single species cannot delineate
the complexity of the structure and function of the ecosystem;
therefore, they lack ecological realism. For example, although
there are numerous studies that include the effects of a
chemical on the survival or growth of individuals of various
fish species, measurements of behavorial or interspecific
effects are uncommon. Alteration of predator-prey interactions,
for instance, can markedly alter survivability (of either
species) in a way not predicted by traditional testing
procedures (6).

Pollutant realism is achieved when the test system includes
sufficient diversity of components and the physical and chemical
properties so that the pollutant behaves in the test system as
it would in nature. Pollutant realism is lacking because, in
most test protocols, the pollutant does not interact with any
part of the environment, except the organism. A lack of
pollutant realism in traditional tests may result in
overestimates of risk. As an example, substantial information
is now available about the toxicity of TCDD to numerous species
when they are exposed via injection, incubation, diet, or dermal
application. At Times Beach, Missouri, the TCDD is in the soil,
and because it has apparently been there for some time, it is
probably tightly bound to the soil. Little is published about
the toxicity of TCDD bound to soil, for any means of exposure.
Intuitively, I suspect the TCDD is less toxic when bound to soil
than in the forms commonly used in toxicity testing. Thus, the
risks of TCDD-induced toxicity to humans at Times Beach may be
much smaller than would be suggested by the results of
traditional testing which lacks this aspect of pollutant realism.

As another example, traditional testing with aquatic species
relies on constant levels of exposure (for example, 10 mg/liter
for 24, 48, or 96 hours). In the forest, exposure levels of
herbicides in streams will never be constant over time.
Virtually all the research on herbicides in forest streams shows
that the residue levels reach a maximum shortly after
application and then decline rapidly. Although the
instantaneous maximum concentration may be 0.037 mg/liter, the
concentration 1 hour later may be 0.010 mg/liter, 0.002 mg/liter
at 24 hours, and below the detectable level after 48 hours. The
problem is to evaluate this type of dynamic exposure in terms of
the type of information that is available from traditional
testing (2). The approach often taken is to assume that the
maximum concentration defined in field monitoring was present
for a full 48 or 96 hours, and to estimate toxic effects based
on 48- or 96-hour toxicity tests. The consequence in almost

every case is an overestimate of risk as shown for some aquatic invertebrates and methoxychlor (7-8).

Overestimates of risk may lead to the imposition of unnecessarily restrictive policies or procedures. Although this conservative attitude is attractive in many respects, it is important to determine what is going to be gained in terms of protection of the species involved (another form of benefits), and what is going to be lost in terms of resource production (another form of risk).

Does this mean traditional testing of the direct effects of toxicity is no longer valuable? Certainly not, but it does need to be expanded and modified to include aspects of ecological and pollutant realism. Single-species-testing will continue to be the predominant form of testing because it can yield a great deal of information, quickly, at minimum cost. Ecological realism cannot and need not be part of every test. Specific tests can be designed to provide ecologically relevant information within the framework of traditional dose-response relationships. Examples are dose-response tests of predator-prey interactions, and intraspecific and interspecific tests of competition for food, space, and other requirements. Tests can also be designed to be pollutant relevant within the framework of traditional dose-response relationships. Examples are dose response testing where the concentration of chemical is varied over time (and some alternative expressions of exposure developed--perhaps the integral of concentration over time), exposure via weathered substrates (containing known levels of chemical), and exposure in dynamic rather than static systems.

It is not realistic to expect that all relevant combinations of chemicals and organisms can be included in the tests which are designed to attain ecological and pollutant realism described above. What is needed is a research effort, not a regulatory effort. By this, I mean the tests I have described should not be made part of the pesticide registration process. Research is needed to develop more fully the concepts embodied in these tests and to test the concepts to determine their scope of inference. This will provide a better basis for evaluating the potential for direct effects of herbicides in the forest, both for management and regulatory purposes.

Indirect effects.—Indirect effects are those that do not require a direct interaction between the herbicide and an organism. As an example, herbicides, because they directly influence plant cover, result in modification of animal habitat (food, cover, microclimate) which, in turn, influences carrying capacity for specific wildlife species. As a result of the interrelations within food chains, direct effects on relatively minor species can be transferred indirectly to organisms at higher trophic levels. Other examples of indirect effects are those that result from the alteration of vegetation density and species composition. For instance, severe and prolonged

deforestation can substantially alter the nutrient cycling
relationships for an entire forest watershed (9).

Indirect effects can be substantially more far-reaching (in
an ecosystem perspective) than direct chemical effects. Most
herbicides used in the forest are not likely to directly affect
many organisms in any ecosystem because few herbicides used in
forestry are so inherently toxic or so widely distributed that
the avoidance or detoxification mechanisms of all organisms
would be overwhelmed. On the other hand, severe deleterious
direct effects on only a few key organisms or ecosystem
processes can have far-reaching (indirect) effects for many
other components of the ecosystem.

A key point is that all indirect effects are the result of a
direct effect on some aspect of the system. This is extremely
important in planning methods for assessing indirect effects.
Because the direct effect can be evaluated by use of established
dose response theory and by tests, many of the indirect effects
can be evaluated by use of the existing ecosystem data bases and
current studies of ecosystem processes without a large amount of
specific testing (10).

Testing for indirect effects.--In studies of indirect
effects, it may be possible to examine the processes involved
and to manipulate them by a variety of techniques, some of which
may not involve the chemical in question at all. For instance,
if a non-chemical technique produces the same effects on primary
productivity as the herbicide does, it is useful for studying
the effects of reduced primary production on higher trophic
levels.

Testing for Effects of Herbicides at the Watershed Level

Many chemicals are regulated by the Federal Insecticide,
Fungicide, and Rodenticide Act (FIFRA), and their properties are
as diverse as the properties of ecosystems. In forestry,
however, relatively few herbicides are used very much. In
fiscal year 1981, for instance, the USDA Forest Service used
more than 25 different herbicides in the National Forests, but
2,4-D and picloram alone and in combination accounted for 70% of
the total amount of herbicide applied. Atrazine, glyphosate,
dalapon, simazine, fosamine, and hexazinone accounted for an
additional 18% (2).

The properties or characteristics of chemicals that
influence their behavior in the environment and can be used to
focus attention to those most likely to cause changes in
ecosystems at the watershed level of resolution (4) these are:
compounds that contain heavy metals; and compounds with low
water solubility and high fat solubility, high equilibrium vapor
pressure, high degree of stability, or a high degree of mobility
in soil. With the possibile exception of mobility in soil for
one or two compounds, none of the herbicides in the top 88% of

the amount used in National Forests in fiscal year 1981 have
these characteristics.

Forest watersheds are made up of diverse and complex subsets
of interacting systems. There are some major processes,
however, that involve or affect all or most of the subsets and
that can be studied or measured as indicators of change in
ecosystems at the watershed level. These processes include
carbon fixation by primary producers, transfers of energy,
nutrient cycling, and the decomposition of various kinds of
organic substrates. They are often measured in ecosystem
studies at the watershed level (11). To determine if changes
are occurring in ecosystem processes or watershed responses, it
is necessary to have systems for accumulating long-term baseline
data, including measures of the variation of systems over time.
The use of paired watersheds (control and treated) is
necessary. Unfortunately, there are few forest watersheds that
can be used in assessments of this kind.

The number of such watersheds is vanishingly small compared
to the matrix of herbicides (even groups of herbicides) and
environments pertinent to the use of herbicides in the forest.
For this reason and because watershed level studies are
extremely expensive and take a long time, they should be part of
a research program and not part of the pesticide registration
process. Research needs to be done to establish the
relationships between small-scale, process studies (such as
carbon or nitrogen fixation) and the watershed response studies
of water, nutrient, and sediment yield (12-13). By testing the
direct effects of herbicides on these processes, and coupling
them with the indirect effects as measured by or inferred from
studies of other types of changes (often from ecosystem response
studies that do not involve herbicides at all), reasonable
estimates of the effects of herbicide use at the watershed level
can be made.

A Proposed System and a Procedure for Assessing Ecotoxicological Effects

In most cases I have abstracted the essential points of the
Committee's recommendations for assessing ecotoxicological
effects (3), and then added (in parentheses) my comments and
evaluation of the relevance to herbicides and forestry.

Types of Tests. The Committee identified the following types of
tests as needed in a system for assessing ecotoxicological
effects:

1. Single-species-tests (single-species-testing, both
    traditional tests and tests modified to include
    ecosystem and pollutant realism are needed).

2. Population tests (population tests proposed by the
    Committee include construction of actuarial life tables

and survivorship curves and changes in population gene
pools, migratory behavior patterns, and food
preferences. This approach is still in the research
stage, and more research will be needed before suitable
test procedures can be developed. It should continue
to be important more as a research tool than as part of
the pesticide registration process for herbicides in
forestry).

3. Multi-species tests (these should include many types of
   interactions, such as competition, symbiosis,
   parasitism, host-plant relationships, and predator-prey
   interactions. As with the population tests, the
   multi-species tests may have greater value as a
   research tool than as an across-the-board regulatory
   tool for herbicides in forestry).

4. Ecosystem tests. These are needed at several levels;
   for example, laboratory microcosms, greenhouse studies,
   field enclosures, and field tests in natural
   ecosystems. (These represent three levels of the same
   type of testing, but they have different emphases. The
   microcosms are most easily managed, and they can be
   replicated and can test a wide range of experimental
   variables. Field enclosures have a higher degree of
   ecological and pollutant realism, and opportunities for
   replication exist, but they require more intensive
   study and fewer experiments like this can be conducted;
   thus, few variables can be examined. Field tests in
   natural ecosystems are the most realistic but the most
   difficult to control and conduct; there would likely be
   few of these.)

5. Models. Both empirical and simulation models are
   needed. (Models can help bridge the gap between
   experimental conditions and the real world and between
   actual observations and predictions. Obviously, models
   can be no better than the data used to construct them,
   and much of these data will come from the tests
   described above. The tremendous advantage of models
   comes as increased experience and better data bases
   permit their refinement to the degree that they can be
   used in place of, or to guide some of the more complex
   testing described above. Well-validated models can be
   a powerful research and regulatory tool.)

A System for Assessment. Improvement and expansion of specific
tests as discussed are important, but equally so is a system or
procedure for making ecotoxicological assessments from the
information from these tests. The Committee proposed both a
system for evaluating effects and a procedure for
implementation. Evaluating environmental effects of herbicides
in the forest requires two subsystems, a multi-level integrated

test system and a system of baseline and experimental ecosystems
for monitoring and study.

The integrated test system approach is proposed as an
alternative to the more traditional hierarchical testing
approach (14), although many of the elements in the hierarchical
approach remain. The difference is that in the hierarchical
approach, individual tests tend to stand alone with little
overlap. The Committee recognized that no one type of test can
produce the diversity of information needed and some overlap
among tests is good. Therefore, integration of results and an
analysis of combined results were proposed as a more effective
scheme. These would ultimately require fewer, not more, costly
and difficult field tests. The integrated system needs to
produce data on:

1. The characteristics of the chemical and its behavior in
    the environment. (This is traditional environmental
    chemistry (15-16) and, for herbicides in forestry,
    requires little change.)

2. The physiological responses of species related to the
    presence of the chemical. (This is traditional
    single-species testing (14) but with some additional
    tests to improve ecological and pollutant realism.)

3. Changes in species interaction.

4. Changes in the functional processes of the ecosystem
    (like mineralization; and nutrient, soil, water, and
    energy fluxes).

Baseline ecosystems are undisturbed systems used for
monitoring and studying the structure and function of the
ecosystem. Experimental ecosystems, paired with undisturbed
baseline ecosystems, are used to determine the specific effects
of herbicides on ecosystem dynamics. Mathematical models to
facilitate understanding of the interactions among system
components and the effect of the use of herbicides in the forest
on these components should be developed from this system of
study.

Implementation. Implementation of this assessment strategy
sounds formidable when viewed from the perspectives of TSCA, but
for herbicides in forestry, much of the work is already
underway. The Committee identified the following steps in
implementation, and I have commented (in parentheses) on the
status of each step:

1. Select baseline ecosystems. (Much of this is already
    done via Ecological Reserves established by the "Man
    and the Biosphere Program" and the system of
    experimental forests maintained by the USDA Forest
    Service.)

2. Characterize each baseline ecosystem. (Much of this is
    already done or is being done under research efforts
    funded by various groups, such as the National Science
    Foundation and USDA Forest Service.)

3.   Establish experimental ecosystems. (Much work remains
      to be done. Monitoring and experimental systems need
      to be established in connection with each baseline
      ecosystem. The concept is that the monitoring and
      experimental systems could be disturbed and studied,
      and the findings related to the characteristics of the
      baseline ecosystem. The monitoring and experimental
      systems may vary in size from petri dish microcosms to
      full-scale field sites, although there are likely to be
      few of the latter.)
4.   Develop models of the dynamics of the baseline
      ecosystems. (Much of this is already underway via the
      research programs identified in 2. Models of pesticide
      behavior have been developed, but they are based
      primarily on agricultural uses. They need to be
      modified and validated for herbicides in the forest.)

Assessment. The material presented thus far explains the basis
and structure of an assessment system and the steps needed to
implement it (have it ready to use).
      The following steps (proposed by the Committee) show how the
information for assessment of ecotoxicological risks is
developed once a system is in place:
1.   Characterize the physical-chemical properties of the
      chemical and how it is used to determine which
      ecosystems may be the direct recipient of the
      chemical. (This information is already available as
      part of the FIFRA registration.)
2.   The key species and processes of the ecosystem in
      question, as identified in the baseline ecosystem, are
      used in single-species and microcosm tests to determine
      the potential points of chemical entry and impact.
      (The single species test procedures are already well
      developed and are used in the FIFRA registration
      process. They need some modification, however, to
      achieve ecological and pollutant realism, and they need
      to be expanded to include some types of organisms not
      included in testing strategies at present. The
      microcosm tests are not part of the registration
      process and are intended to test for effects on the
      interactions of key species or the processes of key
      ecosystems.)
3.   With the information from these tests, the models are
      used to predict both direct and indirect responses of
      the ecosystem.
4.   The model outputs are then checked experimentally by
      manipulating the experimental baseline system to
      simulate the impact of the chemical. (The
      opportunities for this type of testing are limited

because of the scarcity of baseline forest ecosystems. The need for this step for herbicides and the forest may not be great because of the relatively small impact of herbicides in the forest ecosystem compared with some other types of perturbations such as logging, burning, landslides, and debris torrents. Experimental manipulation may be called for if the models indicate that some extraordinary response may occur, such as elimination of nitrogen-fixing organisms or the loss of an organism essential in the processing of stream detritus. Otherwise, use of the models to identify points for study during pilot scale field testing for efficacy may be sufficient.)

5. The final step is to test for anticipated effects of the chemical using a multi-species integrated approach. (Because the list is in steps, it may appear that this integrated testing is done last, but in fact it is done concurrently with steps 3 and 4. Much of the basis for the integrated testing is already in place in FIFRA.)

The information from these five steps can be used to make accurate assessments of ecotoxicological risk, but it will require a different mix and emphasis of disciplines than are presently involved. Assessments of risk for herbicides in forestry have usually been done by those with traditional training in toxicology and environmental chemistry. Unfortunately, neither of these disciplines have developed an "ecosystem" perspective. They tend to focus narrowly. Those trained in ecology (and its associated specialties) must be added to this process to achieve the integration of thinking and study necessary for risk assessments that focus beyond individual organisms. Fortunately, in forestry many ecologists and ecosystem specialists are already at work in research, although their attention has not yet included herbicides to any great degree. With some refocusing of their efforts (or with additional efforts), it will be relatively easy to integrate the efforts of toxicologists, environmental chemists, and ecologists for accomplishing ecotoxicological risk assessments for herbicides in forestry.

Conclusions

It may appear to be a nearly overwhelming task to conduct ecotoxicological risk assessments for herbicides in forestry. But much of the basic ecological work is already being done and more sophisticated toxicological test protocols are being developed to improve the validity of test results by achieving a higher degree of ecological and pollutant realism. What is most seriously lacking at this point is integration of the information developed by environmental chemists and toxicologists with information developed by biologists and ecologists. In addition, ecologists need to include herbicides as a method of perturbation in their ecosystem studies (at some normal level of use, not to create ecological extremes as was done in the Hubbard Brook studies [9]). ' The ecotoxicology testing strategies proposed by the Committee may be most important used in connection with the Toxic Substances Control Act, but they can also be used to help improve the quality and accuracy of the risk assessment process for herbicides in forestry.

When priorities are developed, the need for implementing a formal strategy for ecotoxicological assessments of herbicides in forestry may not be as pressing as it is for other chemicals in other areas because: (1) In forestry, there are relatively few chemicals that receive sufficiently wide use that they need detailed attention; (2) less than 1% of the forest land is treated with pesticide of any kind in any one year (less is treated with herbicide); (3) large, contiguous forest areas are not treated with herbicides (typically treated areas are widely scattered and range from less than 2 ha to 200 ha in size); and (4) areas that are treated are usually treated only once, twice, or perhaps three times early in the 30- to 50-year growth cycle in the Southeastern United States, or the 70- to 120-year growth cycle in the Western United States.

Literature Cited

1. "The Biologic and Economic Assessment of 2,4,5-T," Technical Bulletin 1671; U.S. Department of Agriculture, Washington, D.C., 445 p.
2. Norris, L. A.; Lorz, H. W.; Gregory, S. V. "Influence of Forest and Rangeland Management on Anadromous Fish Habitat in Western North America," General Technical Report PNW-149; USDA Forest Service, Pacific Northwest Forest and Range Experiment Station, Portland, Oregon, 1983; 95 p.
3. "Testing for the Effects of Chemicals on Ecosystems," National Research Council, National Academy Press: Washington, D.C., 1981; 103 p.
4. "Working Papers Prepared as Background for Testing Effects of Chemicals on Ecosystems," National Research Council, National Academy Press: Washington, D.C., 1981; 257 p.
5. Blanck, H. G. D.; Gustafsson, K. "An Annotated Literature Survey of Methods for Determination of Effects and Fate of Pollutants in Aquatic Environments," National Swedish Environmental Protection Board: Uppsala, 1978.
6. Fisher, N. S.; Carpenter, E. J.; Remsen, C. C.; Wurster, C. F. Microbiol. Ecol. 1974, 1, 39.
7. Eisele, P. J. Ph.D. Thesis, University of Michigan, Ann Arbor, 1974.

8. Eisele, P. J.; Hartung, R. <u>Trans. Amer. Fish. Soc.</u> 1976, <u>105</u>, 628.
9. Bormann, F. H.; Likens, G. E. "Pattern and Process in a Forested Ecosystem." Springer-Verlag: New York, 1979; 253 p.
10. Pimentel, D.; Edwards, C. A. <u>Bioscience</u> 1982, <u>32</u>, 595.
11. Franklin, J. F.; Dempster, L. J.; Waring, R. J. "Research on Coniferous Forest Ecosystems." USDA Forest Service, Pacific Northwest Forest and Range Experiment Station; Portland, Oreg. 1972; 323 p.
12. Hall, C. A. S.; Day, J. W., Jr. "Ecosystem Modeling in Theory and Practice - An Introduction with Case Histories," John Wiley & Sons: New York, 1977; 684 p.
13. Innis, G. S. "Grassland Simulation Model," Springer-Verlag: New York, 1978; 298 p.
14. Hushon, J. M.; Clerman, R. J.; Wagner, B. O. <u>Environ. Sci. Technol.</u> 1979, <u>13</u>, 1201.
15. Haque, R.; Freed, V. H. "Environmental Dynamics of Pesticides," Plenum Press: New York, 1975; 387 p.
16. Howard, P. H.; Saxena, J.; Sikka, H. <u>Environ. Sci. Technol.</u> 1978, <u>12</u>, 398.

RECEIVED September 9, 1983

INDEXES

Author Index

Subject Index

397

Production by Paula Bérard
Indexing by Florence Edwards
Jacket design by Anne G. Bigler

Elements typeset by Hot Type Ltd., Washington, DC
Printed and bound by Maple Press Co., York, PA